NEW YORK FIELD CODES SERIES

VOLUME V

NEW YORK FIELD CODES SERIES

Volume I. The Code of Civil Procedure of the State of New-York (1850)

Volume II. The Code of Criminal Procedure of the State of New York (1850)

Volume III. The Civil Code of the State of New York (1865)

Volume IV. The Penal Code of the State of New York (1865)

Volume V. The Political Code of the State of New York (1860)

NEW YORK FIELD CODES SERIES

VOLUME V

STATE OF NEW YORK.

THE

POLITICAL CODE

OF THE

STATE OF NEW YORK.

REPORTED COMPLETE

BY THE

COMMISSIONERS OF THE CODE.

TO BE SUBMITTED TO THE LEGISLATURE ON THE 10TH DAY OF APRIL, 1860, PURSUANT TO CHAPTER 266 OF THE STATUTES OF 1857.

ALBANY, OCTOBER 10th, 1859.

General Introduction to the Series
by Michael Weber

THE LAWBOOK EXCHANGE, LTD.
Clark, New Jersey

New York Field Codes Series
ISBN 978-1-886363-40-3

Vol. I. The Code of Civil Procedure of the State of New-York
ISBN 978-1-886363-34-2

Vol. II. The Code of Criminal Procedure of the State of New York
ISBN 978-1-886363-35-9

Vol. III. The Civil Code of the State of New York
ISBN 978-1-886363-38-0

Vol. IV. The Penal Code of the State of New York
ISBN 978-1-886363-36-6

Vol. V. The Political Code of the State of New York
ISBN 978-1-886363-37-3

Lawbook Exchange edition 2011

The quality of this reprint is equivalent to the quality of the original work.

THE LAWBOOK EXCHANGE, LTD.
33 Terminal Avenue
Clark, New Jersey 07066-1321

Please see our website for a selection of our other publications and fine facsimile reprints of classic works of legal history:
www.lawbookexchange.com

Library of Congress Cataloging-in-Publication Data

New York (State). Commissioners of the Code.
The political code of the State of New-York / reported complete by the Commissioners of the Code ; to be submitted to the Legislature on the 10th day of April, 1860, pursuant to chapter 266 of the Statutes of 1857, Albany, October 10th, 1859.
p. cm. (New York Field codes, 1850-1865)
Originally published: Albany : Weed, Parsons & Co., 1860.
ISBN 1-886363-37-4 (acid-free paper)
1. Constitutions—New York (State) I. Title. II. Series.
KFN5680 1846.A6N48 1997
342.747'02—dc21 97-49219
CIP

Printed in the United States of America on acid-free paper

GENERAL INTRODUCTION
TO THE SERIES

These five volumes (of which this is Volume V) contain the complete texts of the law codes drafted for New York State by David Dudley Field, and his colleagues during the years 1847 to 1865. They include Field's two procedural codes—Civil Procedure and Criminal Procedure—and three substantive codes—Political, Penal, and Civil. The two procedural codes were drafted first, pursuant to Article VI, Section 24, of the 1846 New York State Constitution, which stated:

> The Legislature at its first session after the adoption of the Constitution, shall provide for the appointment of three commissioners, whose duty it shall be to revise, reform, simplify, and abridge the rules and practice, pleadings, forms, and proceedings of the courts of record of this State, and to report thereon to the Legislature, subject to their adoption and modification from time to time.[1]

A separate provision of the Constitution called for commissioners "to reduce into a written and systematic code the whole body of the law of this state, or so much and such parts thereof as to the said commissioners shall seem practicable and expedient." This provision eventually resulted in the substantive political, penal, and civil codes.[2]

Field was perhaps the leading American proponent of codification. He served with both groups of commissioners.

---

[1] Quoted in Mildred V. Coe and Lewis W. Morse, "Chronology of the Development of the David Dudley Field Code," *Cornell Law Quarterly* 27 (1942): 238.

[2] Alison Reppy, "The Field Codification Concept," in *David Dudley Field: Centenary Essays Celebrating One Hundred Years of Legal Reform,* ed. Alison Reppy (New York: New York University School of Law, 1949), 37. Reppy's chapter is very useful for untangling the convoluted history of the commissions, the writing of the codes, and the fates of the codes in the New York legislature.

More than any other individual, Field was responsible for the drafting of all the codes. (He has been called "an inexhaustible one man codifying machine."[3])

New York, however, enacted only three: the Code of Civil Procedure—which is often referred to simply as "the Field Code"—and, after many years, the Code of Criminal Procedure and the Penal Code. But the significance of Field's work extended far beyond New York State. As one legal scholar has observed, Field's efforts changed how lawyers and judges do their work and led to "new ways of understanding the law itself."[4]

The Codification Movement

Field's codes were part of a wider codification movement in the United States in the first half of the nineteenth century.[5] In the 1830s, for example, a few years before Field's work began in New York, U.S. Supreme Court Justice Joseph Story was active in attempting to codify the Massachusetts law. The codification movement was an attempt to clarify the law and remove obsolete rules so that the law could be intelligible to ordinary citizens. Its proponents considered the existing body of law, based as it was on English common law, "inaccessible and uncertain . . . unnecessarily mysterious, complex, and overly technical."[6] Field remarked:

> The common law of New York, like the common law of England, from which it is in great part derived, consists of a vast number of rules of property and of conduct, which have been applied by the judicial tribunals, and which had their origin either in legislative enactments, now forgotten, or in

---

[3] Robert W. Gordon, review of *The American Codification Movement: A Study of Antebellum Legal Reform,* by Charles C. Cook, *Vanderbilt Law Review* 36 (1983): 435.

[4] William P. LaPiana, "Just the Facts: The Field Code and the Case Method," *New York Law School Law Review* 36 (1991): 304.

[5] See Charles C. Cook, *The American Codification Movement: A Study of Antebellum Legal Reform* (Westport, Conn.: Greenwood, 1981).

[6] Ibid., 5.

> traditions from ancient times, or in the consciences of the judges, as the cases came before them.[7]

Proponents of codification took to heart the critical observation of the great English reformer Jeremy Bentham that common law judges made law "as a man makes laws for his dog. When your dog does anything you want to break him of, you wait till he does it, and then you beat him for it."[8] They wanted more system, more precision, and more simplicity in the law. Many were impressed by France's Civil Code, established by Napoleon in 1804, which Edward Livingston had applied to Louisiana in the 1820s.

For some American codifiers, flushed by post-Revolutionary War patriotism, the great weight of the English common law was seen as an alien, un-American presence. A few wanted to go so far as to abolish the common law entirely. Most of the reformers, however, including Field, were not so radical. Their goal was to reduce the common law power of judges and give state legislators the chance to shape the law by reducing to statutory form those parts of the common law that could be plainly stated in a concise book of statutes.

Field's Range of Influence

David Dudley Field (1805–1894) was born in Haddam, Connecticut, into a family of high achievers.[9] Both his father, a minister, and mother were the children of Revolutionary War officers. Among his siblings were Stephen Johnson Field (1816–1899), who was appointed by President Lincoln to the United

---

[7] Introduction to *The Civil Code of the State of New York* (1865), in vol. III of this series, xiv.

[8] Quoted in Lawrence M. Friedman, *American Law* (New York: Norton, 1984), 92.

[9] Useful biographical sources are Helen K. Hoy, "David Dudley Field," in *Great American Lawyers,* ed. William Draper Lewis, vol. 5 (Philadelphia: Winston, 1908; reprint, South Hackensack, N.J.: Rothman, 1971); and the biography written by Field's younger brother, Henry M. Field, *The Life of David Dudley Field* (New York: Scribner's, 1898).

States Supreme Court in 1863, and Cyrus West Field, who laid the first transatlantic cable in 1866. While Field had extra ordinary intelligence, ability, and diligence, he was also competitive, cantankerous, and stubborn. He outlived three wives. (His childhood nurse called him "a most determined fellow."[10]) Not everyone felt affection for him, but very few questioned his legal skill. A colleague, subsequently dean of New York University's Law School, said, "For at least a third of a century, David Dudley Field was the most commanding figure at the American bar."[11]

After attending Williams College, Field studied law in Albany and New York City and was admitted to the New York Bar in 1828. He was active in politics as a Democrat but broke with the party over the Mexican War and slavery and in the 1850s became one of the founders of the Republican Party. Field played an important role in securing Abraham Lincoln's nomination as the Republican candidate for president in 1860. After the Civil War, however, he returned to the Democratic fold and was a close associate of Samuel J. Tilden.

Field was active as a lawyer for 60 years and participated in many notable cases heard by the Supreme Court, including *Ex parte Milligan* (1866), *Cummings* v. *Missouri* (1867), *Ex parte McArdle* (1868), and *United States* v. *Cruikshank* (1876). He provoked considerable controversy in the late 1860s and 1870s by serving as counsel to Jay Gould and James Fisk during the scandal involving the Erie Railroad and by defending New York's notorious William Marcy "Boss" Tweed.

The Origin of the Codes

Field valued precision and clarity. He greatly admired the sciences and mathematics, saying of the latter, "Its superiority over every other department of learning . . . is to be ascribed, I fancy, to the precision of its language."[12] No doubt this penchant

---

[10] Quoted in Stephen N. Subrin, "David Dudley Field and the Field Code: A Historical Analysis of an Earlier Procedural Vision," *Law and History Review* 6 (Fall 1988): 314.
[11] Austin Abbot, quoted in Field, *Life,* vii.
[12] Subrin, "David Dudley Field and the Field Code," 315.

contributed to Field's interest in the movement for codification of the law. He began working for codification in the late 1830s and was instrumental in having the provisions mandating commissions to reform the law of the state written into the 1846 New York Constitution.

Field's goal was to put all of New York's law into written form and to combine in one set of procedures the whole of actions in both law and equity. He wanted to reform the procedural law so that a legal dispute could be started with pleadings that clearly related what happened and settled in one court in one action. In his 1847 essay "What Shall Be Done with the Practice of the Courts?" Field wrote:

> What I propose, then, in respect to cases of legal cognizance, is this: that the present forms of action be abolished, and in their stead a complaint and answer required, each setting forth the real claim and defense of the parties. Such pleadings would be precisely similar to those proposed for equity cases, and we should thus have a uniform course of pleading for all cases, legal and equitable.
>
> . . .
>
> Let the plaintiff set forth his cause of action in his complaint briefly, in ordinary language, and without repetition; and let the defendant make his answer in the same way. Let each party verify his allegation by making oath that he believes it to be true. The complaint will then acquaint the defendant with the real charge, while the answer will inform the plaintiff of the real defense. The disputed facts will be sifted from the undisputed, and the parties will go to trial knowing what they have to answer. The plaintiff will state his case as he believes it, and as he expects to prove it. The defendant, for his part, will set forth what he believes and expects to establish . . . He will not be perplexed with questions of double pleading, nor shackled by ancient technical rules.[13]

---

[13] Quoted in Kermit L. Hall, William M. Wiecek, and Paul Finkelman, eds., *American Legal History: Cases and Materials,* 2nd ed. (New York: Oxford University Press, 1996), 323.

In September 1847 Field became one of the three commissioners—the other two were Arphaxad Loomis and David Graham—appointed by the New York legislature to reform legal procedures as mandated by the Constitution.[14] He replaced Nicholas Hill, who resigned because he was appalled that his colleagues were contemplating changes "so purely experimental, so sudden and general, and so perilous."[15] Field dominated the commission's work, which proceeded swiftly. The commission presented a draft of a Code of Civil Procedure to the legislature on February 29, 1848. The draft was enacted into law on April 12 of that year and has become known as the "Field Code." Subsequently the commission presented additional reports, proposing amendments to the code, some of which the legislature enacted. On December 31, 1849, the commission completed its work by presenting two complete codes: Civil Procedure and Criminal Procedure. Published in 1850, these codes are reprinted as volumes I and II of the present series. Years later, on July 1, 1881, an amended version of the Code of Criminal Procedure was enacted.[16]

Meanwhile, a separate commission also created in 1847 and charged with codifying the substantive law had made little progress, and it was abolished in 1850. But after intense effort Field in 1857 persuaded the legislature to set up a new commission empowered to fulfill the Constitution's mandate "to reduce into a written and systematic code the whole body of the law of the state of New York." Field, William Curtis Noyes, and Alexander W. Bradford were selected as the commissioners.[17] Over the next eight years they labored on three codes: a Political Code, embracing "the laws respecting the government of the state, its civil polity, the functions of its public officers, and the political rights and duties of its citizens"; a Civil Code, covering "the laws of personal rights and relations of property, and of obligations"; and a Penal Code, defining "all the crimes for which persons can be punished and the punishment for the

---

[14] Coe and Morse, "Chronology," 238.

[15] Lawrence M. Friedman, *A History of American Law,* 2nd ed. (New York: Simon & Schuster, 1986), 391.

[16] Reppy, "The Field Codification Concept," 33–8.

[17] Ibid., 38.

crime."[18] Field himself personally prepared the civil code. The entire scheme roughly paralleled the France's Code Napoleon. The Political Code was submitted to the legislature and published in 1860, the final version of the Penal Code was submitted in 1864 and published in 1865, and the final version of the Civil Code was submitted and published in 1865.[19] We reprint them in volumes III-V of the present series.

Field remained devoted to the cause of codification for the rest of his life. His interest even extended to the codification to international law, and in the 1870s he prepared a draft outline for a code of international law. He traveled to both Europe and Asia and was gratified to see the influence his New York codification work was having in Great Britain as well as in India and other British colonies.

When Field died in 1894 at the age of 89, a member of the New York Bar paid him this tribute:

> The magnitude of the results of his labors can scarcely be overestimated. . . . That he exerted a greater influence in modifying and simplifying the judicial systems of the United States and England than any other man of his time will hardly be denied. The world over, wherever the prevailing jurisprudence has had its origin in the English common law, the form and manner of conducting litigations and transacting the business of the courts are due to the influence of David Dudley Field.[20]

The Reception and Significance of the Field Codes

As we have seen, the New York legislature quickly passed Field's Code of Civil Procedure. The legislature later amended the code several times, however, and considerably diluted its concision and weakened the force of Field's reforms.

The other codes encountered much more difficulty in New York. Only two were enacted and both not until 1881: the Code of Criminal Procedure, which had been submitted initially in late

---

[18] Coe and Morse, "Chronology," 244–5.

[19] Ibid., 245.

[20] Quoted in Hoy, "David Dudley Field," 128.

1849, and the Penal Code of 1865. The New York Assembly passed the Civil Code four times, and the entire legislature did so twice—only to have it vetoed each time by the governor.[21] The Civil Code, which the commissioners claimed made important changes in "the rights of married women, the adoption of children, and the assimilation of the laws of real and personal by politicians. James C. Carter, a prominent property,"[22] sparked particularly intense debate. Opposition within the legal profession was intense, and the New York City Bar Association in 1883 unanimously passed a resolution against it.[23]

Opposition to the Civil Code—and to the codification movement in general—centered around two general points. The first was that no code, however skillfully prepared, could encompass all the wealth of experience embodied in the common law. The second was that codification would take control of the law away from the courts, where it belonged, and give it to legislatures run by politicians. James C. Carter. A prominent New York lawyer and a leading opponent of codification—he termed Field's work "grossly defective"[24]—wrote in essays in the 1880s:

> The question is [whether the] growth, development and improvement of the law [should] remain under the guidance of men selected by the people on account of their special qualifications for the work [or] be transferred to a numerous legislative body, disqualified by the nature of their duties for the discharge of this supreme function . . . [Courts apply] "a social standard of justice[,] . . . the product of the combined operation of the thought, the morality, the intellectual and moral culture of the time."[25]

These arguments carried the day in New York.

---

[21] Reppy, "The Field Codification Concept," 46.

[22] *Civil Code,* vol. III of this series, xxxi.

[23] Morton J. Horwitz, *The Transformation of American Law: 1870-1960* (Cambridge: Harvard University Press, 1977), 118.

[24] Quoted in Hoy, "David Dudley Field," 165.

[25] Quoted in Friedman, *A History of American Law,* 404.

But outside New York, especially in the newer western states and territories that did not have an inherited body of law, Field's codes enjoyed considerably more success. The Code of Civil Procedure—the "Field Code"—was adopted in Missouri as early as 1849. California, newly admitted to the Union, followed in 1851 with the help of Field's brother Stephen, who had been elected to the California legislature in 1850 after moving from New York the previous year. By 1862 ten more states and territories had adopted the Code of Civil Procedure, and by 1900 another 12 had done so.[26] In addition several states adopted a procedural criminal code and substantive penal, political, and civil codes based on Field's work. Indeed California enacted adaptations of all five of Field's codes. Portions of these codes are still in effect today.[27]

Ironically Field's attempts through codification to limit the role in America of English-derived common law had consequences for legal reform in Great Britain itself. The authors and proponents of the English Judicature Acts of 1873 and 1875, many of whom knew Field personally, were influenced by his work. Field's codes inspired lawmakers in the British colonies of India, Singapore, and Hong Kong as well.[28]

Field's codes, then, had great impact both in the United States and internationally and clearly are worthy of study today. Scholars agree, however, that Field's outstanding achievement remains the New York Code of Civil Procedure, the "Field Code." That code and the 1938 Federal Rules of Civil Procedure, which it influenced, remain the two most fundamental sets of

---

[26] The states and territories that adopted the Code of Civil Procedure by 1862 were, in addition to Missouri, California, Iowa, Indiana, Kansas, Minnesota, Nebraska, Nevada, Ohio, and Washington. By 1900 they had been joined by Arizona, Colorado, Idaho, Montana, New Mexico, North Carolina, North and South Dakota, Oklahoma, South Carolina, Utah, and Wyoming. Ibid., 394.

[27] See E. Allan Farnsworth, *An Introduction to the Legal System of the United States,* 2nd ed. (New York: Oceana, 1983); Friedman, *A History of American Law,* 405; and Horwitz, *The Transformation of American Law,* 117–8.

[28] Reppy, "The Field Codification Concept," 48.

rules in American civil procedure."[29] Section 554 of the Code of Civil Procedure contained the following revolutionary declaration:

> The distinction between actions at law and suits in equity, and for the forms of all such actions and suits heretofore existing, are abolished; and, there shall be in this state, hereafter, but one form of action, for the enforcement or protection of private rights and the redress or prevention of private wrongs, which shall be denominated a civil action.[30]

As Field intended, the code simplified the pleadings of plaintiff and defendant, limiting the former to a concise factual complaint, demurrer, and reply and the latter to a concise factual answer and demurrer. It adopted the rules of equity for the application of relief.[31] In the words of the great legal scholar Roscoe Pound:

> No treatises on the theory of legislation and no polemical tracts on law reform have led to such far-reaching concrete results. It [the Code of Civil Procedure] stands toward procedure in the world of the common law where Beccaria's treatise on Crimes and Punishments stood toward the nineteenth-century criminal law. It showed the way.[32]

Michael Weber

---

[29] Roscoe Pound, "David Dudley Field: An Appraisal," in *David Dudley Field: Centenary Essays Celebrating One Hundred Years of Legal Reform,* ed. Alison Reppy (New York: New York University School of Law, 1949), 11; Suprin, "David Dudley Field and the Field Code," 312.

[30] See page 225 of volume I of this series.

[31] Reppy, "The Field Codification Concept," 49–51.

[32] Roscoe Pound, "David Dudley Field: An Appraisal," 8.

STATE OF NEW YORK.

THE

POLITICAL CODE

OF THE

STATE OF NEW YORK.

REPORTED COMPLETE

BY THE

COMMISSIONERS OF THE CODE.

TO BE SUBMITTED TO THE LEGISLATURE ON THE 10TH DAY OF APRIL, 1860, PURSUANT TO CHAPTER 266 OF THE STATUTES OF 1857.

ALBANY, OCTOBER 10th, 1859.

ALBANY:
WEED, PARSONS & COMPANY, PRINTERS.
1860.

CONTENTS.

PRELIMINARY PROVISIONS.

PART I.

PART II.

BOUNDARIES AND DIVISIONS OF THE STATE.

PART III.

TITLE I.

PUBLIC OFFICERS.

CHAPTER I.

CLASSIFICATION.

CHAPTER II.

LEGISLATIVE OFFICERS.

ARTICLE I.

NUMBER, DESIGNATION AND MODE OF ELECTION.

ARTICLE II.

GENERAL PROVISIONS RELATING TO LEGISLATIVE OFFICERS.

ARTICLE III.

TAKING TESTIMONY IN LEGISLATIVE PROCEEDINGS.

ARTICLE IV.

ENACTMENT OF STATUTES.

ARTICLE V.

PROMULGATION OF STATUTES.

ARTICLE VI.

OPERATION OF STATUTES.

CHAPTER III.

EXECUTIVE OFFICERS.

ARTICLE I.

CLASSIFICATION, NUMBER AND DESIGNATION OF EXECUTIVE OFFICERS.

ARTICLE II.

MODE OF ELECTION OR APPOINTMENT, AND TERM OF OFFICE.

ARTICLE III.

GENERAL PROVISIONS RESPECTING THE GOVERNOR.

ARTICLE IV.

GENERAL PROVISIONS RESPECTING THE SECRETARY OF STATE.

ARTICLE V.

GENERAL PROVISIONS RESPECTING THE COMPTROLLER.

ARTICLE VI.

GENERAL PROVISIONS RESPECTING THE TREASURER.

ARTICLE VII.

GENERAL PROVISIONS RESPECTING THE STATE ENGINEER AND SURVEYOR.

ARTICLE VIII.

GENERAL PROVISIONS RESPECTING THE BANK SUPERINTENDENT.

ARTICLE IX.

GENERAL PROVISIONS RESPECTING THE INSURANCE SUPERINTENDENT.

ARTICLE X.

THE POWERS AND DUTIES OF OTHER EXECUTIVE OFFICERS.

ARTICLE XI.

PROVISIONS RELATING TO THE DUTIES AND POWERS OF TWO OR MORE EXECUTIVE OFFICERS.

CHAPTER IV.

JUDICIAL OFFICERS.

ARTICLE I.

NUMBER AND DESIGNATION.

ARTICLE II.

MODE OF ELECTION OF JUDICIAL OFFICERS.

CHAPTER V.

MINISTERIAL AND OTHER OFFICERS CONNECTED WITH THE COURTS.

ARTICLE I.

NUMBER AND DESIGNATION.

ARTICLE II.

MODE OF ELECTION AND APPOINTMENT.

CHAPTER VI.

GENERAL PROVISIONS RELATING TO DIFFERENT CLASSES OF OFFICERS.

ARTICLE I.

DISQUALIFICATIONS.

ARTICLE II.

RESTRICTIONS UPON THE RESIDENCE OF OFFICERS AND THE EXERCISE OF THEIR POWERS.

ARTICLE III.

APPOINTMENT, AND COMMENCEMENT AND DURATION OF TERMS.

ARTICLE IV.

NOMINATIONS AND COMMISSIONS OF OFFICERS.

ARTICLE V.

THE OATH OF OFFICE AND OFFICIAL BOND, AND DUTY.

ARTICLE VI.

RESIGNATIONS, REMOVALS, VACANCIES, AND THE MODE OF SUPPLYING THEM.

ARTICLE VII.

PROCEEDINGS TO COMPEL THE DELIVERY OF BOOKS AND PAPERS BY OFFICERS TO THEIR SUCCESSORS.

TITLE II.

GENERAL RIGHTS OF THE STATE.

CHAPTER I.

RIGHTS OVER PERSONS.

CHAPTER II.

RIGHTS OVER PROPERTY.

TITLE III.

PUBLIC WAYS.

CHAPTER I.

PUBLIC WATERS.

ARTICLE I.

GENERAL PROVISIONS RESPECTING PUBLIC WATERS AND OBSTRUCTIONS THEREIN.

ARTICLE II.

NAVIGATION.

ARTICLE III.

FLOATING LUMBER.

ARTICLE IV.

WRECKS.

ARTICLE V.

SANDY HOOK PILOTS.

ARTICLE VI.

HELLGATE PILOTS.

ARTICLE VII.

NEW YORK PORT-WARDENS.

ARTICLE VIII.

NEW YORK HARBOR-MASERS.

ARTICLE IX.

SPECIAL REGULATIONS FOR THE PORT OF NEW YORK.

ARTICLE X.

ALBANY HARBOR-MASTERS.

CHAPTER II.

HIGHWAYS.

ARTICLE I.

ENUMERATION OF HIGHWAYS.

ARTICLE II.

RULES AND RESTRICTIONS RESPECTING THE USE OF HIGHWAYS.

ARTICLE III.

POWERS AND DUTIES OF HIGHWAY OFFICERS.

ARTICLE IV.

HIGHWAY TAXES.

ARTICLE V.

PERFORMANCE OF HIGHWAY LABOR, AND COMMUTATION.

ARTICLE VI.

LAYING OUT, ALTERING AND DISCONTINUING ROADS.

ARTICLE VII.

ERECTION AND MAINTENANCE OF BRIDGES.

ARTICLE VIII.

OBSTRUCTIONS AND INJURIES TO HIGHWAYS.

CHAPTER III.

RAILWAYS.

ARTICLE I.

GENERAL POWERS AND DUTIES OF RAILWAY COMPANIES.

ARTICLE II.

CONSTRUCTION OF RAILWAYS.

ARTICLE III.

RAILWAY TRAFFIC.

CHAPTER IV.

CANALS.

CHAPTER V.

TURNPIKES AND PLANKROADS.

ARTICLE I.

CONSTRUCTION OF TURNPIKES AND PLANKROADS.

ARTICLE II.

USE OF TURNPIKES AND PLANKROADS.

ARTICLE III.

INSPECTION AND REPAIRS.

CHAPTER VI.

TOLL BRIDGES.

CHAPTER VII.

FERRIES.

CHAPTER VIII.

MISCELLANEOUS PROVISIONS RELATING TO SEVERAL OF THE PUBLIC WAYS.

TITLE IV.

GENERAL POLICE OF THE STATE.

CHAPTER I.

WEIGHTS AND MEASURES.

CHAPTER II.

TIME.

CHAPTER III.

MONEY.

CHAPTER IV.

AUCTIONS.

ARTICLE I.

AUCTION DUTIES.

ARTICLE II.

AUCTIONEERS.

ARTICLE III.

REGULATIONS RESPECTING SALES.

ARTICLE IV.

ACCOUNTING.

ARTICLE V.

FRAUDS AND PENALTIES.

CHAPTER V.

PEDDLING.

CHAPTER VI.

DRUGS.

CHAPTER VII.

FIRES.

CHAPTER VIII.

FISHING AND HUNTING.

CHAPTER IX.

RACING.

CHAPTER X.

PRIZE AND GAME FIGHTING, AND GAMING.

CHAPTER XI.

LICENSES.

CHAPTER XII.

INNS.

CHAPTER XIII.

UNCLAIMED PROPERTY.

CHAPTER XIV.

REGISTRY OF BIRTHS, MARRIAGES AND DEATHS.

CHAPTER XV.

SEPULTURE.

CHAPTER XVI.

DISSECTION.

CHAPTER XVII.

OBSERVANCE OF SUNDAY.

CHAPTER XVIII.

WILLFUL MISCHIEF.

PART IV.

GENERAL LAWS FOR THE GOVERNMENT OF COUNTIES, CITIES, TOWNS AND VILLAGES.

TITLE I.

GENERAL PROVISIONS.

TITLE II.

THE GOVERNMENT OF COUNTIES.

CHAPTER I.

COUNTIES AS BODIES CORPORATE.

CHAPTER II.

COUNTY OFFICERS.

ARTICLE I.

THE BOARD OF SUPERVISORS.

ARTICLE II.

THE COUNTY TREASURER.

ARTICLE III.

THE COUNTY CLERK.

ARTICLE IV.

THE SHERIFF.

ARTICLE V.

THE SURROGATE.

CHAPTER III.

COUNTY CHARGES.

CHAPTER V.

DIVISIONS OR ALTERATION OF BOUNDS OF COUNTIES.

TITLE III.

THE GOVERNMENT OF CITIES.

CHAPTER I.

CITIES AS BODIES CORPORATE.

CHAPTER II.

CITY OFFICERS.

CHAPTER III.

ACTIONS AGAINST CITIES.

TITLE IV.

GOVERNMENT OF TOWNS.

CHAPTER I.

THE TOWN AS A CORPORATE BODY.

CHAPTER II.

TOWN MEETINGS.

ARTICLE I.

ANNUAL AND SPECIAL TOWN MEETINGS.

ARTICLE II.

THE CONDUCT OF TOWN MEETINGS.

ARTICLE III.

ELECTION OF TOWN OFFICERS.

CHAPTER III.

TOWN OFFICERS.

ARTICLE I.

QUALIFICATIONS, TERMS OF OFFICE AND COMPENSATION.

ARTICLE VI.

THE BOARD OF AUDITORS.

ARTICLE VII.

PROVISIONS RELATING TO SEVERAL TOWN OFFICERS.

CHAPTER IV.

STRAYS.

CHAPTER V.

LEGAL PROCEEDINGS BY AND AGAINST TOWNS.

CHAPTER VI.

TOWN CHARGES.

CHAPTER VII.

DIVISION OR ALTERATION OF BOUNDS OR TOWNS.

TITLE V.

THE GOVERNMENT OF VILLAGES.

CHAPTER I.

INCORPORATION OF VILLAGES.

CHAPTER II.

VILLAGE OFFICERS.

ARTICLE I.

ELECTION AND QUALIFICATION OF OFFICERS.

ARTICLE II.

THE BOARD OF TRUSTEES.

ARTICLE III.

OTHER OFFICERS.

CHAPTER III.

TAXES.

CHAPTER IV.

SIDEWALKS.

CHAPTER V.

CEMETERIES.

CHAPTER VI.

FIRE COMPANIES.

CHAPTER VII.

POUNDS.

GENERAL PROVISIONS.

CONSTITUTION OF THE UNITED STATES.

WE, the people of the United States, in order to form a more perfect union, establish justice, ensure domestic tranquillity, provide for the common defence, promote the general welfare, and secure the blessings of liberty to ourselves and our posterity, do ordain and establish this constitution for the United States of America.

ARTICLE I.

SECTION 1.

Legislative powers.

1. All legislative powers herein granted shall be vested in a congress of the United States, which shall consist of a senate and house of representatives.

SECTION 2.

House of representatives; its members; by whom chosen.

1. The house of representatives shall be composed of members chosen every second year by the people of the several states; and the electors in each state shall have the qualifications requisite for electors of the most numerous branch of the state legislature.

Qualifications of representatives.

2. No person shall be a representative who shall not have attained to the age of twenty-five years, and been seven years a citizen of the United States, and who shall not, when elected, be an inhabitant of that state in which he shall be chosen.

Representatives and taxes to be apportioned according to numbers.

Actual enumeration every ten years.

3. Representatives and direct taxes shall be apportioned among the several states which may be included within this union, according to their respective numbers, which shall be determined by adding to the whole number of free persons, including those bound to service for a term of years, and excluding Indians not taxed, three-fifths of all other persons. The actual enumeration shall be made within three years after the first meeting of the congress

of the United States, and within every subsequent term of ten years, in such manner as they shall by law direct. The number of representatives shall not exceed one for every thirty thousand, but each state shall have at least one representative; and until such enumeration shall be made, the state of New-Hampshire shall be entitled to choose three; Massachusetts eight; Rhode Island and Providence Plantations one; Connecticut five; New-York six; New-Jersey four; Pennsylvania eight; Delaware one; Maryland six; Virginia ten; North-Carolina five; South-Carolina five; and Georgia three.

Limitation of the ratio of representation, &c.

First apportionment of representatives.

Vacancies, how filled.

4. When vacancies happen in the representation from any state, the executive authority thereof shall issue writs of election to fill such vacancies.

Powers of the house.

5. The house of representatives shall choose their speaker and other officers, and shall have the sole power of impeachment.

SECTION 3.

Senators, how chosen

1. The senate of the United States shall be composed of two senators from each state, chosen by the legislature thereof, for six years; and each senator shall have one vote.

The senate divided into three classes.

When vacated and filled.

Vacancies.

2. Immediately after they shall be assembled in consequence of the first election, they shall be divided, as equally as may be, into three classes. The seats of the senators of the first class shall be vacated at the expiration of the second year, of the second class at the expiration of the fourth year, and of the third class at the expiration of the sixth year, so that one-third may be chosen every second year; and if vacancies happen by resignation or otherwise, during the recess of the legislature of any state, the executive thereof may make temporary appointments until the next meeting of the legislature, which shall then fill such vacancies.

Qualifications of senators.

3. No person shall be a senator who shall not have attained to the age of thirty years, and been nine years a citizen of the United States, and who shall not, when elected, be an inhabitant of that state for which he shall be chosen.

President of the senate.

4. The vice-president of the United States shall be president of the Senate, but shall have no vote, unless they be equally divided.

Ib. and other officers.

5. The senate shall choose their other officers and also a president *pro tempore*, in the absence of the vice-president, or when he shall exercise the office of president of the United States.

The sole power to try impeachments, in the senate, &c.

6. The senate shall have the sole power to try all impeachments. When sitting for that purpose, they shall be on oath or affirmation. When the president of the United

States is tried, the chief justice shall preside; and no person shall be convicted without the concurrence of two-thirds of the members present.

7. Judgment in cases of impeachment shall not extend further than to removal from office, and disqualification to hold and enjoy any office of honor, trust or profit under the United States; but the party convicted shall nevertheless be liable and subject to indictment, trial, judgment and punishment, according to law. Extent of judgment in case of impeachment.

Section 4.

1. The times, places and manner of holding elections for senators and representatives, shall be prescribed in each state by the legislature thereof; but the congress may, at any time, by law, make or alter such regulations, except as to the places of choosing senators. Elections for senators and representatives, how regulated.

2. The congress shall assemble at least once in every year, and such meeting shall be on the first Monday in December, unless they shall by law appoint a different day. Meetings of congress.

Section 5.

1. Each house shall be the judge of the elections, returns and qualifications, of its own members, and a majority of each shall constitute a quorum to do business; but a smaller number may adjourn from day to day, and may be authorized to compel the attendance of absent members in such manner and under such penalties as each house may provide. Each house judge of the election of its own members. Quorum.

2. Each house may determine the rules of its proceedings, punish its members for disorderly behavior, and with the concurrence of two-thirds, expel a member. To determine its own rules, &c.

3. Each house shall keep a journal of its proceedings, and from time to time publish the same, excepting such parts as may in their judgment require secrecy; and the yeas and nays of the members of either house on any question shall, at the desire of one-fifth of those present, be entered on the journal. To keep and publish journals, &c.

4. Neither house, during the session of congress, shall, without the consent of the other, adjourn for more than three days, nor to any other place than that in which the two houses shall be sitting. Adjournment.

Section 6.

1. The senators and representatives shall receive a compensation for their services, to be ascertained by law, and paid out of the treasury of the United States. They shall in all cases, except treason, felony and breach of the peace, be privileged from arrest during their attendance at the Senators and representatives to be paid, &c. Privileges.

session of their respective houses, and in going to or returning from the same; and for any speech or debate in either house, they shall not be questioned in any other place.

Disability to hold offices.

2. No senator or representative shall, during the time for which he was elected, be appointed to any civil office under the authority of the United States, which shall have been created, or the emoluments whereof shall have been increased during such time; and no person holding any office under the United States, shall be a member of either house during his continuance in office.

SECTION 7.

Revenue bills.

1. All bills for raising revenue shall originate in the house of representatives; but the senate may propose or concur with amendments as on other bills.

The forms of proceeding on bills.

2. Every bill which shall have passed the house of representatives and the senate, shall, before it become a law, be presented to the president of the United States; if he approve he shall sign it; but if not, he shall return it, with his objections, to that house in which it shall have originated; who shall enter the objections at large on their journal, and proceed to reconsider it. If, after such reconsideration, two-thirds of that house shall agree to pass the bill, it shall be sent, together with the objections, to the other house, by which it shall likewise be reconsidered, and if approved by two-thirds of that house, it shall become a law. But in all cases, the votes of both houses shall be determined by yeas and nays, and the names of the persons voting for and against the bill, shall be entered on the journal of each house respectively. If any bill shall not be returned by the president within ten days (Sundays excepted) after it shall have been presented to him, the same shall be a law in like manner as if he had signed it, unless the congress by their adjournment prevent its return, in which case it shall not be a law.

The forms of proceeding on joint resolutions, except for adjournment.

3. Every order, resolution or vote, to which the concurrence of the senate and house of representatives may be necessary, (except on a question of adjournment,) shall be presented to the president of the United States; and before the same shall take effect, shall be approved by him, or being disapproved by him, shall be repassed by two-thirds of the senate and house of representatives, according to the rules and limitations prescribed in the case of a bill.

SECTION 8.

Congress have power to lay taxes, &c.

The congress shall have power;

1. To lay and collect taxes, duties, imposts and excises; to pay the debts and provide for the common defense and

general welfare of the United States; but all duties, imposts and excises shall be uniform throughout the United States:

2. To borrow money on the credit of the United States:

3. To regulate commerce with foreign nations, and among the several states, and with the Indian tribes:

4. To establish an uniform rule of naturalization, and uniform laws on the subject of bankruptcies throughout the United States:

5. To coin money, regulate the value thereof, and of foreign coin, and fix the standard of weights and measures:

6. To provide for the punishment of counterfeiting the securities and current coin of the United States:

7. To establish post-offices and post-roads:

8. To promote the progress of science and useful arts, by securing for limited times, to authors and inventors the exclusive right to their respective writings and discoveries:

9. To constitute tribunals inferior to the supreme court: to define and punish piracies and felonies committed on the high seas, and offenses against the law of nations:

10. To declare war, grant letters of marque and reprisal, and make rules concerning captures on land and water:

11. To raise and support armies; but no appropriation of money to that use, shall be for a longer term than two years:

12. To provide and maintain a navy:

13. To make rules for the government and regulation of the land and naval forces:

14. To provide for calling forth the militia to execute the laws of the union, suppress insurrections and repel invasions:

15. To provide for organizing, arming and disciplining the militia, and for governing such part of them as may be employed in the service of the United States, reserving to the states respectively the appointment of the officers, and the authority of training the militia according to the dicipline prescribed by congress:

16. To exercise exclusive legislation, in all cases whatsoever, over such district (not exceeding ten miles square) as may, by cession of particular states, and the acceptance of congress, become the seat of government of the United States, and to exercise like authority over all places purchased, by the consent of the legislature of the state in which the same shall be, for the erection of forts, magazines, arsenals, dock-yards and other needful buildings: and,

17. To make all laws which shall be necessary and proper for carrying into execution the foregoing powers, and all other powers vested by this constitution in the government of the United States, or in any department or officer thereof.

Section 9.

Importation of certain persons not to be prohibited until 1808.

1. The migration or importation of such persons as any of the states now existing shall think proper to admit, shall not be prohibited by the congress prior to the year one thousand eight hundred and eight, but a tax or duty may be imposed on such importation, not exceeding ten dollars for each person.

Writ of habeas corpus.

2. The privilege of the writ of *habeas corpus* shall not be suspended, unless when, in cases of rebellion or invasion, the public safety may require it.

Bills of attainder, &c. Direct taxes.

3. No bill of attainder, or *ex post facto* law, shall be passed.

4. No capitation or other direct tax shall be laid, unless in proportion to the census or enumeration herein before directed to be taken.

No export duty nor preference of one state to another, &c.

5. No tax or duty shall be laid on articles exported from any state. No preference shall be given by any regulation of commerce or revenue to the ports of one state over those of another; nor shall vessels bound to or from one state be obliged to enter, clear or pay duties in another.

Money to be expended by legal appropriation only.

6. No money shall be drawn from the treasury, but in consequence of appropriations made by law; and a regular statement and account of the receipts and expenditures of all public money shall be published from time to time.

Titles of nobility, &c.

7. No title of nobility shall be granted by the United States, and no person holding any office of profit or trust under them, shall, without the consent of the congress, accept of any present, emolument, office or title of any kind whatever, from any king, prince or foreign state.

Section 10.

Powers forbidden to the states individually.

1. No state shall enter into any treaty, alliance or confederation; grant letters of marque and reprisal; coin money; emit bills of credit; make any thing but gold and silver coin a tender in payment of debts; pass any bill of attainder, *ex post facto* law, or law impairing the obligation of contracts; or grant any title of nobility.

Powers which the states can exercise only under the sanction of congress.

2. No state shall, without the consent of the congress, lay any imposts or duties on imports or exports, except what may be absolutely necessary for executing its inspection laws; and the net produce of all duties and imposts, laid by any state on imports or exports, shall be for the use of the treasury of the United States, and all such laws shall be subject to the revision and control of the congress. No state shall, without the consent of congress, lay any duty of tonnage, keep troops or ships of war in time of peace, enter into any agreement or compact with another state, or with a foreign power, or engage in war, unless actually invaded or in such imminent danger as will not admit of delay.

ARTICLE II.

SECTION 1.

1. The executive power shall be vested in a president of the United States of America. He shall hold his office during the term of four years, and, together with the vice-president, chosen for the same term, be elected as follows: Executive power vested in a president, &c.

2. Each state shall appoint, in such manner as the legislature thereof may direct, a number of electors, equal to the whole number of senators and representatives to which the state may be entitled in the congress; but no senator or representative, or person holding an office of trust or profit under the United States, shall be appointed an elector. Electors of president and vice-president, &c.

[3. The electors shall meet in their respective states, and vote by ballot for two persons, of whom one at least shall not be an inhabitant of the same state with themselves. And they shall make a list of all the persons voted for, and of the number of votes for each; which list they shall sign and certify, and transmit sealed to the seat of the government of the United States, directed to the president of the senate. The president of the senate shall, in the presence of the senate and house of representatives, open all the certificates, and the votes shall then be counted. The person having the greatest number of votes shall be the president, if such number be a majority of the whole number of electors appointed; and if there be more than one who have such majority, and have an equal number of votes, then the house of representatives shall immediately choose, by ballot, one of them for president; and if no person have a majority, then from the five highest on the list the said house shall, in like manner, choose the president. But in choosing the president, the votes shall be taken by states, the representation from each state having one vote; a quorum for this purpose shall consist of a member or members from two-thirds of the states, and a majority of all the states shall be necessary to a choice. In every case, after the choice of the president, the person having the greatest number of votes of the electors, shall be the vice-president. But if there should remain two or more who have equal votes, the senate shall choose from them, by ballot, the vice-president.[1]] Meeting of the electors of president, &c. Their proceedings. [1 Annulled. See amendments, art. 12.]

4. The congress may determine the time of choosing the electors, and the day on which they shall give their votes; which day shall be the same throughout the United States. Time of choosing electors.

5. No person, except a natural born citizen, or a citizen of the United States at the time of the adoption of this constitution, shall be eligible to the office of president; neither shall any person be eligible to that office, who shall Qualifications of the president

not have attained to the age of thirty-five years, and been fourteen years a resident within the United States.

In case of vacancy in the office of president, the vice-president to act, &c.

6. In case of the removal of the president from office, or of his death, resignation, or inability to discharge the powers and duties of the said office, the same shall devolve on the vice-president, and the congress may, by law, provide for the case of removal, death, resignation or inability both of the president and vice-president, declaring what officer shall then act as president and, such officer shall act accordingly, until the disability be removed, or a president shall be elected.

Compensation of the president

7. The president shall, at stated times, receive for his services a compensation, which shall neither be increased nor diminished during the period for which he shall have been elected, and he shall not receive within that period any other emolument from the United States, or any of them.

The president to take an oath.

8. Before he enter on the execution of his office, he shall take the following oath or affirmation:

> "I do solemnly swear [or affirm] that I will faithfully execute the office of president of the United States, and will, to the best of my ability, preserve, protect and defend the constitution of the United States."

SECTION 2.

Powers of the president.

1. The president shall be commander-in-chief of the army and navy of the United States, and of the militia of the several states, when called into the actual service of the United States; he may require the opinion, in writing, of the principal officer in each of the executive departments, upon any subject relating to the duties of their respective offices; and he shall have power to grant reprieves and pardons for offenses against the United States, except in cases of impeachment.

Ib.

2. He shall have power, by and with the advice and consent of the senate, to make treaties, *provided* two-thirds of the senators present concur; and he shall nominate, and by and with the advice and consent of the senate, shall appoint ambassadors, other public ministers, and consuls, judges of the supreme court, and all other officers of the United States, whose appointments are not herein otherwise provided for, and which shall be established by law. But the congress may, by law, vest the appointment of such inferior officers as they think proper, in the president alone, in the courts of law or in the heads of departments.

3. The president shall have power to fill up all vacancies that may happen during the recess of the senate, by the judges in every state shall be bound thereby, anything

granting commissions which shall expire at the end of their next session.

SECTION 3.

1. He shall, from time to time, give to the congress information of the state of the union, and recommend to their consideration such measures as he shall judge necessary and expedient; he may, on extraordinary occasions, convene both houses, or either of them, and in case of disagreement between them, with respect to the time of adjournment, he may adjourn them to such time as he shall think proper; he shall receive ambassadors and other public ministers; he shall take care that the laws be faithfully executed; and shall commission all the officers of the United States. Other duties and powers.

SECTION 4.

1. The president, vice-president and all civil officers of the United States, shall be removed from office on impeachment for, and conviction of, treason, bribery or other high crimes and misdemeanors. Officers liable to impeachment.

ARTICLE III.

SECTION 1.

1. The judicial power of the United States shall be vested in one supreme court, and in such inferior courts as the congress may, from time to time ordain and establish. Judicial power The judges, both of the supreme and inferior courts, shall hold their offices during good behavior; and shall, at stated times, receive for their services a compensation which shall not be diminished during their continuance in office. Judges to hold their offices during good behavior, &c.

SECTION 2.

1. The judicial power shall extend to all cases in law and equity, arising under this constitution, the laws of the United States, and treaties made, or which shall be made, under their authority; to all cases affecting ambassadors, other public ministers and consuls; to all cases of admiralty and maritime jurisdiction; to controversies to which the United States shall be a party; to controversies between two or more states, between a state and citizens of another state, between citizens of different states, between citizens of the same state claiming lands under grants of different states, and between a state, or the citizens thereof, and foreign states, citizens or subjects. Extent of the judicial power. (Modified. See amendment No. 11.)

2

Original and appellate jurisdiction of the supreme court.

2. In all cases affecting ambassadors, other public ministers and consuls, and those in which a state shall be party, the supreme court shall have original jurisdiction. In all other cases before mentioned, the supreme court shall have appellate jurisdiction, both as to law and fact, with such exceptions and under such regulations as the congress shall make.

Tr al of crimes to be by jury, &c.

3. The trial of all crimes, except in cases of impeachment, shall be by jury, and such trial shall be held in the state where the said crimes shall have been committed; but when not committed within any state, the trial shall be at such place or places as the congress may by law have directed.

SECTION 3.

Definition of treason.

1. Treason against the United States shall consist only in levying war against them, or adhering to their enemies, giving them aid and comfort. No person shall be convicted of treason unless on the testimony of two witnesses to the same overt act, or on confession in open court.

Congress to declare its punishment.

2. The congress shall have power to declare the punishment of treason; but no attainder of treason shall work corruption of blood, or forfeiture, except during the life of the person attainted.

ARTICLE IV.

SECTION 1.

Credit in one state to the public acts, &c. of another.

1. Full faith and credit shall be given in each state to the public acts, records and judicial proceedings of every other state. And the congress may, by general laws, prescribe the manner in which such acts, records and proceedings shall be proved, and the effect thereof.

SECTION 2.

Reciprocity of citizens.

1. The citizens of each state shall be entitled to all privileges and immunities of citizens in the several states.

Criminals flying from one state to another, to be delivered upon demand.

2. A person charged in any state with treason, felony or other crime, who shall flee from justice, and be found in another state, shall, on demand of the executive authority of the state from which he fled, be delivered up, to be removed to the state having jurisdiction of the crime.

Runaways to be delivered up

3. No person held to service or labor in one state under the laws thereof, escaping into another, shall, in consequence of any law or regulation therein, be discharged from such service or labor; but shall be delivered up on claim of the party to whom such service or labor may be due.

SECTION 3.

1. New states may be admitted by the congress into this union; but no new state shall be formed or erected within the jurisdiction of any other state, nor any state be formed by the junction of two or more states, or parts of states, without the consent of the legislatures of the states concerned, as well as of the congress. New states may be admitted into the union, &c.

2. The congress shall have power to dispose of and make all needful rules and regulations respecting the territory or other property belonging to the United States; and nothing in this constitution shall be so construed as to prejudice any claims of the United States, or of any particular state. Congress to have power over territory &c.

SECTION 4.

1. The United States shall guaranty to every state in this union a republican form of government, and shall protect each of them against invasion; and on application of the legislature, or of the executive, (when the legislature can not be convened,) against domestic violence. Republican form of government guaranteed to each state, &c.

ARTICLE V.

1. The congress, whenever two-thirds of both houses shall deem it necessary, shall propose amendments to this constitution; or, on the application of the legislatures of two-thirds of the several states, shall call a convention for proposing amendments, which in either case, shall be valid to all intents and purposes, as part of this constitution, when ratified by the legislatures of three-fourths of the several states, or by conventions in three-fourths thereof, as the one or the other mode of ratification may be proposed by the congress; provided, that no amendment which may be made prior to the year one thousand eight hundred and eight shall in any manner affect the first and fourth clauses in the ninth section of the first article: and that no state, without its consent, shall be deprived of its equal suffrage in the senate. Mode of amending this constitution.

ARTICLE VI.

1. All debts contracted and engagements entered into, before the adoption of this constitution, shall be as valid against the United States under this constitution, as under the confederation. Assumption of former debts.

2. This constitution, and the laws of the United States which shall be made in pursuance thereof; and all treaties made, or which shall be made, under the authority of the United States, shall be the supreme law of the land; and This constitution, &c., the supreme law; the state judges bound thereby.

the judges in every state shall be bound thereby; anything in the constitution or laws of any state to the contrary notwithstanding.

Certain officers to take oath to support constitution.

3. The senators and representatives before mentioned, and the members of the several state legislatures, and all executive and judicial officers, both of the United States and of the several states, shall be bound by oath or affirmation to support this constitution; but no religious test shall ever be required as a qualification to any office or public trust under the United States.

No religious test.

ARTICLE VII.

Ratification.

1. The ratification of the conventions of nine states shall be sufficient for the establishment of this constitution between the states so ratifying the same.

Done in convention, by the unanimous consent of the states present, the seventeenth day of September, in the year of our Lord one thousand seven hundred and eighty-seven, and of the independence of the United States of America, the twelfth. In witness whereof, we have hereunto subscribed our names.

GEORGE WASHINGTON,

President, and deputy from Virginia.

NEW HAMPSHIRE.
John Langdon,
Nicholas Gilman.

MASSACHUSETTS.
Nathaniel Gorham,
Rufus King.

CONNECTICUT.
William Samuel Johnson,
Roger Sherman.

NEW YORK.
Alexander Hamilton.

NEW JERSEY.
William Livingston,
David Brearly,
William Patterson,
Jonathan Dayton.

PENNSYLVANIA.
Benjamin Franklin,
Thomas Mifflin,
Robert Morris,
George Clymer,
Thomas Fitzsimons,
Jared Ingersoll,
James Wilson,
Gouverneur Morris.

DELAWARE.
George Read,
Gunning Bedford, jun.,
John Dickinson,
Richard Bassett,
Jacob Broom.

MARYLAND.
James M'Henry,
Daniel of St. Tho. Jenifer,
Daniel Carroll.

VIRGINIA.
John Blair,
James Madison, jun.

NORTH CAROLINA.
William Blount,
Richard Dobbs Spaight,
Hugh Williamson.

SOUTH CAROLINA.
John Rutledge,
Charles Cotesworth Pinckney.
Charles Pinckney,
Pierce Butler.

GEORGIA.
William Few,
Abraham Baldwin.

Attest, WILLIAM JACKSON, *Secretary.*

[The following extract from the journals of congress, shows the adoption of the constitution, and the time when it took effect.]

IN CONGRESS,

SATURDAY, SEPTEMBER 13, 1788.

On the question to agree to the following proposition, it was resolved in the affirmative by the unanimous votes of nine states, viz., of New Hampshire, Massachusetts, Connecticut, New York, New Jersey, Pennsylvania, Virginia, South Carolina, and Georgia.

Whereas the convention assembled in Philadelphia, pursuant to the resolution of congress of the 21st February, 1787, did, on the 17th of September in the same year, report to the United States in congress assembled, a constitution for the people of the United States; whereupon congress, on the 28th of the same September, did resolve unanimously, "that the said report, with the resolutions and letter accompanying the same, be transmitted to the several legislatures, in order to be submitted to a convention of delegates chosen in each state by the people thereof, in conformity to the resolves of the convention made and provided in that case:" and whereas the constitution so reported by the convention, and by congress transmitted to the several legislatures, has been ratified in the manner therein declared to be sufficient for the establishment of the same, and such ratifications duly authenticated have been received by congress, and are filed in the office of the secretary; therefore,

The constitution declared to be ratified.

Resolved, That the first Wednesday in January next be the day for appointing electors in the several states, which before the said day shall have ratified the said constitution; that the first Wednesday in February next be the day for the electors to assemble in their respective states, and vote for a president; and that the first Wednesday in March next be the time, and the present seat of congress the place, for commencing proceedings under the said constitution.

Federal government to go into operation on the 4th of March 1789.

AMENDMENTS TO THE CONSTITUTION OF THE UNITED STATES.

[The following amendments were proposed at the first session of the first congress of the United States, which was begun and held in the city of New York, on the 4th of March, 1789, and were adopted by the requisite number of states. 1 vol., Laws U. S., p. 72.]

[The following preamble and resolution preceded the original proposition of the amendments, and as they have been supposed by a high equity judge, (8th Wendell's Reports, p. 100,) to have an important bearing on the construction of those amendments, they are here inserted. They will be found in the journals of the first session of the first congress.

CONGRESS OF THE UNITED STATES.

Begun and held at the city of New York on Wednesday the 4th of March, 1789.

The conventions of a number of states having, at the time of their adopting the constitution, expressed a desire, in order to prevent misconstruction or abuse of its powers, that further declaratory and restrictive clauses should be added; and as extending the ground of public confidence in the government, will best insure the beneficent ends of its institution,

Resolved, By the senate and house of representatives of the United States of America in congress assembled, two-thirds of both houses concurring, that the following articles be proposed to the legislatures of the several states, as amendments to the constitution of the United States; all or any of which articles, when ratified by three-fourths of the said legislatures, to be valid to all intents and purposes, as part of the said constitution, namely:]

ARTICLE 1.

Restrictions on the powers of congress.

Congress shall make no law respecting an establishment of religion, or prohibiting the free exercise thereof; or abridging the freedom of speech, or of the press; or the right of the people peaceably to assemble, and to petition the government for a redress of grievances.

ARTICLE 2.

Right of the people to keep arms, &c.

A well regulated militia being necessary to the security of a free state, the right of the people to keep and bear arms shall not be infringed.

ARTICLE 3.

Quartering of soldiers, &c.

No soldier shall, in time of peace, be quartered in any house without the consent of the owner, nor in time of war but in a manner to be prescribed by law.

ARTICLE 4.

The right of the people to be secure in their persons, houses, papers and effects, against unreasonable searches and seizures, shall not be violated; and no warrants shall issue, but upon probable cause, supported by oath or affirmation, and particularly describing the place to be searched, and the persons or things to be seized. Search warrants, &c.

ARTICLE 5.

No person shall be held to answer for a capital or otherwise infamous crime, unless on a presentment or indictment of a grand jury, except in cases arising in the land or naval forces, or in the militia, when in actual service, in time of war or public danger; nor shall any person be subject for the same offense to be twice put in jeopardy of life or limb; nor shall be compelled, in any criminal case, to be a witness against himself, nor be deprived of life, liberty or property, without due process of law; nor shall private property be taken for public use without just compensation. Proceedings against persons charged with crimes. Their rights.

ARTICLE 6.

In all criminal prosecutions, the accused shall enjoy the right to a speedy and public trial, by an impartial jury of the state and district wherein the crime shall have been committed, which district shall have been previously ascertained by law, and to be informed of the nature and cause of the accusation; to be confronted with the witnesses against him; to have compulsory process for obtaining witnesses in his favor; and to have the assistance of counsel for his defense. Further rights.

ARTICLE 7.

In suits at common law, where the value in controversy shall exceed twenty dollars, the right of trial by jury shall be preserved; and no fact tried by a jury shall be otherwise reëxamined in any court of the United States, than according to the rules of the common law. Right of trial by jury.

ARTICLE 8.

Excessive bail shall not be required, nor excessive fines imposed, nor cruel and unusual punishments inflicted. Excessive bail, &c.

ARTICLE 9.

The enumeration in the constitution of certain rights, shall not be construed to deny or disparage others retained by the people. Construction of constitution.

ARTICLE 10.

Powers reserved to the states.

The powers not delegated to the United States by the constitution, nor prohibited by it to the states, are reserved to the states respectively, or to the people.

[The following amendment was proposed at the second session of the third congress. It is printed in the Laws of the United States, 1st vol., p. 73, as article 11.]

ARTICLE 11.

Restriction of judicial powers.

The judicial power of the United States shall not be construed to extend to any suit in law or equity, commenced or prosecuted against one of the United States by citizens of another state, or by citizens or subjects of any foreign state.

[The three following sections were proposed as amendments at the first session of the eighth congress.

They are printed in the Laws of the United States as article 12.]

ARTICLE 12.

Mode of electing the president and vice-president of the United States.

1. The electors shall meet in their respective states, and vote by ballot for president and vice-president, one of whom, at least, shall not be an inhabitant of the same state with themselves; they shall name in their ballots the person voted for as president, and in distinct ballots the person voted for as vice-president; and they shall make distinct lists of all persons voted for as president, and of all persons voted for as vice-president, and of the number of votes for each, which lists they shall sign and certify, and transmit sealed to the seat of the government of the United States, directed to the president of the senate; the president of the senate shall, in the presence of the senate and house of representatives, open all the certificates, and the votes shall then be counted: the person having the greatest number of votes for president, shall be the president, if such number be a majority of the whole number of electors appointed; and if no person have such majority, then from the persons having the highest numbers, not exceeding three, on the list of those voted for as president, the house of representatives shall choose immediately, by

President.

ballot, the president. But in choosing the president, the votes shall be taken by states, the representation from each state having one vote; a quorum for this purpose shall consist of a member or members from two-thirds of the states, and a majority of all the states shall be necessary to a choice. And if the house of representatives shall not choose a president whenever the right of choice shall devolve upon them, before the fourth day of March next following, then the vice-president shall act as president, as in the case of the death or other constitutional disability of the president.

2. The person having the greatest number of votes as vice-president, shall be the vice-president, if such number be a majority of the whole number of electors appointed; and if no person have a majority, then from the two highest numbers on the list, the senate shall choose the vice-president: a quorum for the purpose shall consist of two-thirds of the whole number of senators, and a majority of the whole number shall be necessary to a choice. Vice-president.

3. But no person constitutionally ineligible to the office of president shall be eligible to that of vice-president of the United States. Vice-president.

[In the edition of the Laws of the U. S., before referred to, there is an amendment printed as article 13, prohibiting citizens from accepting titles of nobility or honor, or presents, offices, &c., from foreign nations. But, by a message of the president of the United States of the 4th of February, 1818, in answer to a resolution of the house of representatives, it appears that this amendment had been ratified only by 12 states, and therefore had not been adopted. See vol. iv. of the printed papers of the 1st session of the 15th Congress, No. 76.]

CONSTITUTION OF THE STATE OF NEW YORK.

[ADOPTED NOVEMBER 3, 1846.]

We the people of the State of New York, grateful to Almighty God for our freedom, in order to secure its blessings, do establish this constitution.

ARTICLE I.

Section 1. No member of this state shall be disfranchised, or deprived of any of the rights or privileges secured to any citizen thereof, unless by the law of the land or the judgment of his peers.

Section 2. The trial by jury, in all cases in which it has been heretofore used, shall remain inviolate forever. But a jury trial may be waived by the parties in all civil cases, in the manner to be prescribed by law. Trial by jury.

Section 3. The free exercise and enjoyment of religious profession and worship, without discrimination or prefer- Religious liberty.

ence, shall forever be allowed in this state to all mankind; and no person shall be rendered incompetent to be a witness on account of his opinions on matters of religious belief; but the liberty of conscience hereby secured shall not be so construed as to excuse acts of licentiousness, or justify practices inconsistent with the peace or safety of this state.

Writ of habeas corpus.

SECTION 4. The privilege of the writ of *habeas corpus* shall not be suspended, unless when, in cases of rebellion or invasion, the public safety may require its suspension.

Bail, fines.

SECTION 5. Excessive bail shall not be required, nor excessive fines imposed, nor shall cruel and unnatural punishments be inflicted, nor shall witnesses be unreasonably detained.

Grand jury.

SECTION 6. No person shall be held to answer for a capital or otherwise infamous crime, (except in cases of impeachment, and in cases of militia, when in actual service; and the land and naval forces in time of war, or which this state may keep with the consent of congress in time of peace; and in cases of petit larceny, under the regulation of the legislature,) unless on presentment or indictment of a grand jury; and in any trial in any court whatever, the party accused shall be allowed to appear and defend in person and with counsel as in civil actions. No person shall be subject to be twice put in jeopardy for the same offense; nor shall he be compelled, in any criminal case, to be a witness against himself; nor be deprived of life, liberty or property without due process of law; nor shall private property be taken for public use without just compensation.

Private property.

SECTION 7. When private property shall be taken for any public use, the compensation to be made therefor, when such compensation is not made by the state, shall be ascertained by a jury, or by not less than three commissioners appointed by a court of record, as shall be prescribed by law. Private roads may be opened in a manner to be prescribed by law; but in every case the necessity of the road, and the amount of all damages to be sustained by the opening thereof, shall be first determined by a jury of freeholders, and such amount, together with the expenses of the proceeding, shall be paid by the person to be benefited.

Private roads.

Freedom of speech and of the press.

SECTION 8. Every citizen may freely speak, write and publish his sentiments on all subjects, being responsible for the abuse of that right; and no law shall be passed to restrain or abridge the liberty of speech or of the press. In all criminal prosecutions or indictments for libels, the truth may be given in evidence to the jury; and if it shall appear to the jury that the matter charged as libelous is true, and was published with good motives and for justifiable ends, the party shall be acquitted; and the jury shall have the right to determine the law and the fact.

SECTION 9. The assent of two-thirds of the members elected to each branch of the legislature shall be requisite to every bill appropriating the public moneys or property for local or private purposes. Two-third bills.

SECTION 10. No law shall be passed abridging the right of the people peaceably to assemble and petition the government, or any department thereof; nor shall any divorce be granted, otherwise than by due judicial proceedings; nor shall any lottery hereafter be authorized or any sale of lottery tickets allowed within this state. Right of petition. Divorces. Lotteries.

SECTION 11. The people of this state, in their right of sovereignty, are deemed to possess the original and ultimate property in and to all lands within the jurisdiction of the state; and all lands, the title to which shall fail from a defect of heirs, shall revert or escheat to the people. Right of property in lands. Escheats.

SECTION 12. All feudal tenures of every description, with all their incidents, are declared to be abolished, saving however, all rents and services certain, which at any time heretofore have been lawfully created or reserved. Feudal tenures abolished.

SECTION 13. All lands within this state are declared to be allodial, so that, subject only to the liability to escheat, the entire and absolute property is vested in the owners according to the nature of their respective estates. Allodial tenure

SECTION 14. No lease or grant of agricultural land, for a longer period than twelve years, hereafter made, in which shall be reserved any rent or service of any kind, shall be valid. Certain leases invalid.

SECTION 15. All fines, quarter sales or other like restraints upon alienation, reserved in any grant of land hereafter to be made, shall be void. Fines and quarter sales abolished.

SECTION 16. No purchase or contract for the sale of lands in this state, made since the fourteenth day of October, one thousand seven hundred seventy-five, or which may hereafter be made, of or with the Indians, shall be valid, unless made under the authority and with the consent of the legislature. Sale of lands.

SECTION 17. Such parts of the common law, and of the acts of the legislature of the colony of New York, as together did form the law of the said colony, on the nineteenth day of April, one thousand seven hundred and seventy-five, and the resolutions of the congress of the said colony, and of the convention of the State of New York, in force on the twentieth day of April, one thousand seven hundred and seventy-seven, which have not since expired or been repealed or altered, and such acts of the legislature of this state as are now in force, shall be and continue the Old colony laws and acts of the legislature.

law of this state, subject to such alterations as the legislature shall make concerning the same. But all such parts of the common law, and such of the said acts or parts thereof as are repugnant to this constitution, are hereby abrogated; and the legislature, at its first session after the adoption of this constitution, shall appoint three commissioners, whose duty it shall be to reduce into a written and systematic code the whole body of the law of this state, or so much and such parts thereof as to the said commissioners shall seem practicable and expedient. And the said commissioners shall specify such alterations and amendments therein as they shall deem proper; and they shall at all times make reports of their proceedings to the legislature, when called upon to do so; and the legislature shall pass laws regulating the tenure of office, the filling of vacancies therein, and the compensation of said commissioners; and shall also provide for the publication of the said code, prior to its being presented to the legislature for adoption.

Common law. Commissioners to be appointed. Their duties.

Grants of land since 1775.

SECTION 18. All grants of land within this state, made by the king of Great Britain, or persons acting under his authority, after the fourteenth day of October, one thousand seven hundred and seventy-five, shall be null and void; but nothing contained in this constitution shall affect any grants of land within this state, made by the authority of the said king, or his predecessors, or shall annul any charters to bodies politic and corporate, by him or them made, before that day; or shall affect any such grants or charters since made by this state, or by persons acting under its authority, or shall impair the obligation of any debts contracted by the state or individuals, or bodies corporate, or any other rights of property, or any suits, actions, rights of action, or other proceedings in courts of justice.

Prior grants.

ARTICLE II.

Qualification of voters.

SECTION 1. Every male citizen of the age of twenty-one years, who shall have been a citizen for ten days, and an inhabitant of this state one year next preceding any election, and for the last four months a resident of the county where he may offer his vote, shall be entitled to vote at such election, in the election district of which he shall at the time be a resident, and not elsewhere, for all officers that now are or hereafter may be elective by the people; but such citizen shall have been for thirty days next preceding the election, a resident of the district from which the officer is to be chosen for whom he offers his vote. But no man of color, unless he shall have been for three years a citizen of this state, and for one year next preceding any election shall have been seized and possessed of a freehold estate

Freehold required for man of color.

of the value of two hundred and fifty dollars, over and above all debts and incumbrances charged thereon, and shall have been actually rated and paid a tax thereon, shall be entitled to vote at such election. And no person of color shall be subject to direct taxation unless he shall be seized and possessed of such real estate as aforesaid.

SECTION 2. Laws may be passed excluding from the right of suffrage all persons who have been or may be convicted of bribery, of larceny, or of any infamous crime; and for depriving every person who shall make, or become directly or indirectly interested in any bet or wager depending upon the result of any election, from the right to vote at such election. **Persons excluded from right of suffrage.**

SECTION 3. For the purpose of voting, no person shall be deemed to have gained or lost a residence, by reason of his presence or absence, while employed in the service of the United States; nor while engaged in the navigation of the waters of this state, or of the United States, or of the high seas; nor while a student of any seminary of learning; nor while kept at any alms-house, or other asylum, at public expense; nor while confined in any public prison. **Certain employments not to affect residence of voters**

SECTION 4. Laws shall be made for ascertaining by proper proofs the citizens who shall be entitled to the right of suffrage hereby established. **Laws to be passed.**

SECTION 5. All elections by the citizens shall be by ballot, except for such town officers as may by law be directed to be otherwise chosen. **Election to be by ballot.**

ARTICLE III.

SECTION 1. The legislative power of this state shall be vested in a senate and assembly. **Legislative power.**

SECTION 2. The senate shall consist of thirty-two members, and the senators shall be chosen for two years. The assembly shall consist of one hundred and twenty-eight members, who shall be annually elected. **Senate, number of. Assembly, number of.**

SECTION 3. The state shall be divided into thirty-two districts, to be called senate districts, each of which shall choose one senator. The districts shall be numbered from one to thirty-two inclusive. **State divided into 32 senate districts.**

District number one (1) shall consist of the counties of Suffolk, Richmond and Queens. **Number 1.**

District number two (2) shall consist of the county of Kings. **Number 2.**

District number three (3) number four (4) number five (5) and number six (6) shall consist of the city and county of New York; and the board of supervisors of said city and county shall, on or before the first day of May, one **Numbers 3, 4, 5 and 6.**

Board of supervisors of the city of New York to divide the county into four senate districts. thousand eight hundred and forty-seven, divide the said city and county into the number of senate districts to which it is entitled, as near as may be of an equal number of inhabitants, excluding aliens and persons of color not taxed, and consisting of convenient and contiguous territory; and no assembly district shall be divided in the formation of a senate district. Certificate, &c., to be filed. The board of supervisors, when they shall have completed such division, shall cause certificates thereof, stating the number and boundaries of each district, and the population thereof, to be filed in the office of the secretary of state, and of the clerk of the said city and county.

Number 7. District number seven (7) shall consist of the counties of Westchester, Putnam and Rockland.

Number 8. District number eight (8) shall consist of the counties of Dutchess and Columbia.

Number 9. District number nine (9) shall consist of the counties of Orange and Sullivan.

Number 10. District number ten (10) shall consist of the counties of Ulster and Greene.

Number 11. District number eleven (11) shall consist of the counties of Albany and Schenectady.

Number 12. District number twelve (12) shall consist of the county of Rensselaer.

Number 13. District number thirteen (13) shall consist of the counties of Washington and Saratoga.

Number 14 District number fourteen (14) shall consist of the counties of Warren, Essex and Clinton.

Number 15. District number fifteen (15) shall consist of the counties of St. Lawrence and Franklin.

Number 16. District number sixteen (16) shall consist of the counties of Herkimer, Hamilton, Fulton and Montgomery.

Number 17. District number seventeen (17) shall consist of the counties of Schoharie and Delaware.

Number 18. District number eighteen (18) shall consist of the counties of Otsego and Chenango.

Number 19. District number nineteen (19) shall consist of the county of Oneida.

Number 20. District number twenty (20) shall consist of the counties of Madison and Oswego.

Number 21. District number twenty-one (21) shall consist of the counties of Jefferson and Lewis.

Number 22. District number twenty-two (22) shall consist of the county of Onondaga.

Number 23. District number twenty-three (23) shall consist of the counties of Cortland, Broome and Tioga.

Number 24. District number twenty-four (24) shall consist of the counties of Cayuga and Wayne.

District number twenty-five (25) shall consist of the counties of Tompkins, Seneca and Yates. Number 25.

District number twenty-six (26) shall consist of the counties of Steuben and Chemung. Number 26.

District number twenty-seven (27) shall consist of the county of Monroe. Number 27.

District number twenty-eight (28) shall consist of the counties of Orleans, Genesee and Niagara. Number 28.

District number twenty-nine (29) shall consist of the counties of Ontario and Livingston. Number 29.

District number thirty (30) shall consist of the counties of Allegany and Wyoming. Number 30.

District number thirty-one (31) shall consist of the county of Erie. Number 31.

District number thirty-two (32) shall consist of the counties of Chautauque and Cattaraugus. Number 32.

Census to be taken in 1855, and every ten years.

SECTION 4. An enumeration of the inhabitants of the state shall be taken, under the direction of the legislature, in the year one thousand eight hundred and fifty-five, and at the end of every ten years thereafter; and the said districts shall be so altered by the legislature, at the first session after the return of every enumeration, that each senate district shall contain, as nearly as may be, an equal number of inhabitants, excluding aliens, and persons of color not taxed; and shall remain unaltered until the return of another enumeration, and shall at all times consist of contiguous territory; and no county shall be divided in the formation of a senate district, except such county shall be equitably entitled to two or more senators.

Senate districts how altered.

Members of assembly, how apportioned and chosen.

SECTION 5. The members of assembly shall be apportioned among the several counties of this state, by the legislature, as nearly as may be, according to the number of their respective inhabitants, excluding aliens, and persons of color not taxed, and shall be chosen by single districts.

Boards of supervisors in certain counties to divide the same into assembly districts.

The severel boards of supervisors, in such counties of this state as are now entitled to more than one member of assembly, shall assemble on the first Tuesday of January next, and divide their respective counties into assembly districts equal to the number of members of assembly to which such counties are now severally entitled by law, and shall cause to be filed, in the offices of the secretary of state and the clerks of their respective counties, a description of such assembly districts, specifying the number of each district and the population thereof, according to the last preceding state enumeration, as near as can be ascertained. Each assembly district shall contain, as nearly as may be, an equal number of inhabitants, excluding aliens, and persons

Description of assembly districts to be filed.

Content of assembly districts.

of color not taxed, and shall consist of convenient and contiguous territory; but no town shall be divided in the formation of assembly districts.

Legislature to reapportion members of assembly.

The legislature, at its first session after the return of every enumeration, shall reapportion the members of assembly among the several counties of this state, in manner aforesaid, and the boards of supervisors in such counties as may be entitled, under such reapportionment, to more than one member, shall assemble at such time as the legislature making such reapportionment shall prescribe, and divide such counties into assembly districts, in the manner herein directed; and the apportionment and districts, so to be made, shall remain unaltered until another enumeration shall be taken under the provisions of the preceding section.

Each county entitled to one member.

Every county heretofore established and separately organized, except the county of Hamilton, shall always be entitled to one member of the assembly; and no new county shall be hereafter erected, unless its population shall entitle it to a member.

Hamilton county.

The county of Hamilton shall elect with the county of Fulton, until the population of the county of Hamilton shall, according to the ratio, be entitled to a member.

Pay of members.

SECTION 6. The members of the legislature shall receive for their services a sum not exceeding three dollars a day, from the commencement of the session; but such pay shall not exceed in the aggregate three hundred dollars for per diem allowance, except in proceedings for impeachment. The limitation as to the aggregate compensation shall not take effect until after the year one thousand eight hundred and forty-eight. When convened in extra session by the governor, they shall receive three dollars per day. They shall also receive the sum of one dollar for every ten miles they shall travel in going to and returning from their place of meeting, on the most usual route. The speaker of the assembly shall, in virtue of his office, receive an additional compensation, equal to one-third of his per diem allowance as a member.

Additional compensation to speaker.

No member to receive an appointment.

SECTION 7. No member of the legislature shall receive any civil appointment within this state, or to the senate of the United States, from the governor, the governor and senate, or from the legislature, during the term for which he shall have been elected; and all such appointments, and all votes given for any such member, for any such office or appointment, shall be void.

Persons disqualified from being members.

SECTION 8. No person being a member of congress, or holding any judicial or military office under the United States, shall hold a seat in the legislature. And if any person shall, after his election as a member of the legislature, be elected to congress, or appointed to any office, civil or military, under the government of the United States, his acceptance thereof shall vacate his seat.

SECTION 9. The elections of senators and members of assembly, pursuant to the provisions of this constitution, shall be held on the Tuesday succeeding the first Monday of November, unless otherwise directed by the legislature. Time of election fixed.

SECTION 10. A majority of each house shall constitute a quorum to do business. Each house shall determine the rules of its own proceedings, and be the judge of the elections, returns and qualifications of its own members, shall choose its own officers; and the senate shall choose a temporary president, when the lieutenant-governor shall not attend as president, or shall act as governor. Powers of each house.

SECTION 11. Each house shall keep a journal of its proceedings, and publish the same, except such parts as may require secrecy. The doors of each house shall be kept open, except when the public welfare shall require secrecy. Neither house shall, without the consent of the other, adjourn for more than two days. Journals to be kept.

SECTION 12. For any speech or debate in either house of the legislature, the members shall not be questioned in any other place. No member to be questioned, &c.

SECTION 13. Any bill may originate in either house of the legislature, and all bills passed by one house may be amended by the other. Bills may originate in either house.

SECTION 14. The enacting clause of all bills shall be, "The people of the State of New York, represented in senate and assembly, do enact as follows," and no law shall be enacted except by bill. Enacting clause of bills.

SECTION 15. No bill shall be passed unless by the assent of a majority of all the members elected to each branch of the legislature, and the question upon the final passage shall be taken immediately upon its last reading, and the yeas and nays entered on the journal. Assent of a majority of all the members required, &c.

SECTION 16. No private or local bill which may be passed by the legislature shall embrace more than one subject, and that shall be expressed in the title. Restriction as to private and local bills.

SECTION 17. The legislature may confer upon the boards of supervisors, of the several counties of the state, such further powers of local legislation and administration as they shall from time to time prescribe. Local legislation conferred on boards of supervisors.

ARTICLE IV.

SECTION 1. The executive power shall be vested in a governor, who shall hold his office for two years: a lieu- Executive power, how vested.

tenant-governor shall be chosen at the same time, and for the same term.

Requisite qualifications of governor.

SECTION 2. No person except a citizen of the United States, shall be eligible to the office of governor; nor shall any person be eligible to that office who shall not have attained the age of thirty years, and who shall not have been five years next preceding his election a resident within this state.

Time and manner of electing governor and lieutenant-governor.

SECTION 3. The governor and lieutenant-governor shall be elected at the times and places of choosing members of the assembly. The persons respectively having the highest number of votes for governor and lieutenant-governor shall be elected; but in case two or more shall have an equal and the highest number of votes for governor, or for lieutenant-governor, the two houses of the legislature, at its next annual session, shall, forthwith, by joint ballot, choose one of the said persons so having an equal and the highest number of votes for governor or lieutenant-governor.

Duties and power of governor.

SECTION 4. The governor shall be commander-in-chief of the military and naval forces of the state. He shall have power to convene the legislature (or the senate only) on extraordinary occasions. He shall communicate by message to the legislature, at every session, the condition of the state, and recommend such matters to them as he shall judge expedient. He shall transact all necessary business with the officers of the government, civil and military. He shall expedite all such measures as may be resolved upon by the legislature, and shall take care that the laws are faithfully executed. He shall, at stated times, receive for his services a compensation to be established by law, which shall neither be increased nor diminished after his election and during his continuance in office.

His compensation.

Pardoning power vested in the governor

SECTION 5. The governor shall have the power to grant reprieves, commutations and pardons after conviction, for all offenses except treason and cases of impeachment, upon such conditions, and with such restrictions and limitations, as he may think proper, subject to such regulation as may be provided by law relative to the manner of applying for pardons. Upon conviction for treason, he shall have power to suspend the execution of the sentence until the case shall be reported to the legislature at its next meeting, when the legislature shall either pardon, or commute the sentence, direct the execution of the sentence or grant a further reprieve. He shall annually communicate to the legislature each case of reprieve, commutation or pardon granted; stating the name of the convict, the crime of which he was convicted, the sentence and its date, and the date of the commutation, pardon or reprieve.

SECTION 6. In case of the impeachment of the governor, or his removal from office, death, inability to discharge the powers and duties of the said office, resignation or absence from the state, the powers and duties of the office shall devolve upon the lieutenant-governor for the residue of the term, or until the disability shall cease. But when the governor shall, with the consent of the legislature, be out of the state in time of war, at the head of a military force thereof, he shall continue commander-in-chief of all the military force of the state. Powers of governor to devolve on lieutenant-governor.

SECTION 7. The lieutenant-governor shall possess the same qualifications of eligibility for office as the governor. He shall be president of the senate, but shall have only a casting vote therein. If, during a vacancy of the office of governor, the lieutenant-governor shall be impeached, displaced, resign, die, or become incapable of performing the duties of his office, or be absent from the state, the president of the senate shall act as governor until the vacancy be filled or the disability shall cease. Requisite qualifications of lieutenant-governor. To be president of the Senate, and to act as governor in certain cases.

SECTION 8. The lieutenant-governor shall, while acting as such, receive a compensation which shall be fixed by law, and which shall not be increased or diminished during his continuance in office. Compensation of lieutenant-governor in certain cases.

SECTION 9. Every bill, which shall have passed the senate and assembly, shall, before it becomes a law, be presented to the governor; if he approve, he shall sign it; but if not he shall return it, with his objections, to that house in which it shall have originated, who shall enter the objections at large on their journal, and proceed to reconsider it. If after such reconsideration two-thirds of the members present shall agree to pass the bill, it shall be sent, together with the objections, to the other house, by which it shall likewise be reconsidered; and if approved by two-thirds of all the members present, it shall become a law, notwithstanding the objections of the governor. But in all such cases the votes of both houses shall be determined by yeas and nays, and the names of the members voting for and against the bill shall be entered on the journal of each house respectively. If any bill shall not be returned by the governor within ten days (Sundays excepted) after it shall have been presented to him, the same shall be a law, in like manner as if he had signed it, unless the legislature shall, by their adjournment, prevent its return; in which case it shall not be a law. Bills to be presented to the governor for signature. If returned by him with objections, how disposed of. Bills to be returned within ten days.

ARTICLE V.

SECTION 1. The secretary of state, comptroller, treasurer and attorney-general, shall be chosen at a general election, State officers how elected and terms of office and shall hold their offices for two years. Each of the officers in this article named (except the speaker of the assembly), shall at stated times, during his continuance in office, receive for his services a compensation, which shall not be increased or diminished during the term for which he shall have been elected; nor shall he receive, to his use, any fees or perquisites of office, or other compensation.

State engineer and surveyor, how chosen and terms of office.

SECTION 2. A state engineer and surveyor shall be chosen at a general election, and shall hold his office two years; but no person shall be elected to said office who is not a practical engineer.

Canal commissioners, how chosen and terms of office.

SECTION 3. Three canal commissioners shall be chosen at the general election which shall be held next after the adoption of this constitution, one of whom shall hold his office for one year, one for two years, and one for three years. The commissioners of the canal fund shall meet at the capitol on the first Monday of January next after such election, and determine by lot which of said commissioners shall hold his office for one year, which for two, and which for three years; and there shall be elected annually thereafter one canal commissioner, who shall hold his office for three years.

Inspectors of state prisons, how elected and terms of office.

SECTION 4. Three inspectors of state prisons shall be elected at the general election which shall be held next after the adoption of this constitution, one of whom shall hold his office for one year, one for two years, and one for three years. The governor, secretary of state, and comptroller shall meet at the capitol on the first Monday of January next succeeding such election, and determine by lot which of said inspectors shall hold his office for one year, which for two, and which for three years; and there shall be elected annually thereafter one inspector of state prisons, who shall hold his office for three years; said inspectors shall have the charge and superintendence of the state prisons, and shall appoint all the officers therein. All vacancies in the office of such inspector shall be filled by the governor, till the next election.

Commissioners of the land office.

SECTION 5. The lieutenant-governor, speaker of the assembly, secretary of state, comptroller, treasurer, attorney-general, and state engineer and surveyor, shall be the commissioners of the land office.

Commissioners of the canal fund.

The lieutenant-governor, secretary of state, comptroller, treasurer and attorney-general, shall be the commissioners of the canal fund.

Canal board.

The canal board shall consist of the commissioners of the canal fund, the state engineer and surveyor, and the canal commissioners.

SECTION 6. The powers and duties of the respective boards, and of the several officers in this article mentioned, shall be such as now are or hereafter may be prescribed by law. Powers and duties of the boards and officers named in this article.

SECTION 7. The treasurer may be suspended from office by the governor during the recess of the legislature, and until thirty days after the commencement of the next session of the legislature, whenever it shall appear to him that such treasurer has, in any particular, violated his duty. The governor shall appoint a competent person to discharge the duties of the office, during such suspension of the treasurer. Treasurer may be suspended by governor.

SECTION 8. All offices for the weighing, gauging, measuring, culling or inspecting any merchandise, produce, manufacture or commodity whatever, are hereby abolished, and no such office shall hereafter be created by law; but nothing in this section contained shall abrogate any office created for the purpose of protecting the public health or the interests of the state in its property, revenue, tolls or purchases, or of supplying the people with correct standards of weights and measures, or shall prevent the creation of any office for such purposes hereafter. Certain officers abolished.

ARTICLE VI.

SECTION 1. The assembly shall have the power of impeachment, by the vote of the majority of all the members elected. Assembly to impeach. The court for the trial of impeachments shall be composed of the president of the senate, the senators, or a major part of them, and the judges of the court of appeals, or a major part of them. Court of impeachment. On the trial of an impeachment against the governor, the lieutenant-governor shall not act as a member of the court. No judicial officer shall exercise his office after he shall have been impeached, until he shall have been acquitted. Before the trial of an impeachment, the members of the court shall take an oath or affirmation truly and impartially to try the impeachment, according to evidence; and no person shall be convicted, without the concurrence of two-thirds of the members present. Judgment in cases of impeachment shall not extend further than to removal from office, or removal from office and disqualification to hold and enjoy any office of honor, trust or profit under this state; but the party impeached shall be liable to indictment, and punishment according to law.

SECTION 2. There shall be a court of appeals, composed of eight judges, of whom four shall be elected by the electors of the state for eight years, and four selected from the Court of appeals.

class of justices of the supreme court having the shortest time to serve. Provision shall be made by law, for designating one of the number elected as chief judge, and for selecting such justices of the supreme court, from time to time, and for so classifying those elected, that one shall be elected every second year.

Supreme court.

SECTION 3. There shall be a supreme court, having general jurisdiction in law and equity.

State to be divided into districts.

SECTION 4. The state shall be divided into eight judicial districts, of which the city of New York shall be one; the others to be bounded by county lines and to be compact and equal in population as nearly as may be. There shall be four justices of the supreme court in each district; and as many more in the district composed of the city of New York as may from time to time be authorized by law, but not to exceed in the whole such number, in proportion to its population as shall be in conformity with the number of such judges in the residue of the state, in proportion to its population. They shall be classified so that one of the justices of each district shall go out of office at the end of every two years. After the expiration of their terms, under such classification, the term of their office shall be eight years.

Number of justices of supreme court in each.

Justices of supreme court to be classified.

Jurisdiction, &c., may be altered.

SECTION 5. The legislature shall have the same powers to alter and regulate the jurisdiction and proceedings, in law and equity as they have heretofore possessed.

Presiding judge to be designated.

SECTION 6. Provision may be made by law for designating, from time to time, one or more of the said justices, who is not a judge of the court of appeals, to preside at the general terms of the said court to be held in the several districts. Any three or more of the said justices, of whom one of the said justices so designated shall always be one, may hold such general terms. And any one or more of the justices may hold special terms and circuit courts, and any one of them may preside in courts of oyer and terminer in any county.

Who may hold general and special terms, and circuit courts, &c.

Compensation to judicial officers.

SECTION 7. The judges of the court of appeals and justices of the supreme court shall severally receive at stated times, for their services, a compensation to be established by law, which shall not be increased or diminished during their continuance in office.

Judges of court of appeals, &c., to hold no other office.

SECTION 8. They shall not hold any other office or public trust. All votes for either of them for any elective office, (except that of justice of the supreme court or judge of the court of appeals,) given by the legislature or the people, shall be void. They shall not exercise any power of appointment to public office. Any male citizen of the

Counselors and attorneys.

age of twenty-one years, of good moral character, and who possesses the requisite qualifications of learning and ability, shall be entitled to admission to practice in all the courts of this state.

SECTION 9. The classification of the justices of the supreme court; the times and place of holding the terms of the court of appeals, and of the general and special terms of the supreme court within the several districts, and the circuit courts and courts of oyer and terminer within the several counties, shall be provided for by law. Classification of justices, and terms of court to be provided for by law.

SECTION 10. The testimony in equity cases shall be taken in like manner as in cases at law. Testimony in equity cases.

SECTION 11. Justices of the supreme court and judges of the court of appeals may be removed by concurrent resolution of both houses of the legislature, if two-thirds of all the members elected to the assembly and a majority of all the members elected to the senate, concur therein. All judicial officers, except those mentioned in this section, and except justices of the peace, and judges and justices of inferior courts not of record, may be removed by the senate on the recommendation of the governor; but no removal shall be made by virtue of this section, unless the cause thereof be entered on the journals, nor unless the party complained of shall have been served with a copy of the complaint against him, and shall have had an opportunity of being heard in his defense. On the question of removal, the ayes and noes shall be entered on the journals. Removal of certain judicial officers.

SECTION 12. The judges of the court of appeals shall be elected by the electors of the state, and the justices of the supreme court by the electors of the several judicial districts, at such times as may be prescribed by law. Manner of electing judges of court of appeals and justices of supreme court.

SECTION 13. In case the office of any judge of the court of appeals, or justice of the supreme court, shall become vacant before the expiration of the regular term for which he was elected, the vacancy may be filled by appointment by the governor, until it shall be supplied at the next general election of judges, when it shall be filled by election for the residue of the unexpired term. Power of governor to fill certain vacancies.

SECTION 14. There shall be elected in each of the counties of this state, except the city and county of New York, one county judge, who shall hold his office for four years. He shall hold the county court, and perform the duties of the office of surrogate. The county court shall have such jurisdiction in cases arising in justices' courts, and in special cases, as the legislature may prescribe; but shall have no original civil jurisdiction, except in such special cases. Judges of county courts, how chosen and term of office.

The county judge, with two justices of the peace to be designated according to law, may hold courts of sessions, Power county judge.

with such criminal jurisdiction as the legislature shall prescribe, and perform such other duties as may be required by law.

His salary.

The county judge shall receive an annual salary, to be fixed by the board of supervisors, which shall be neither increased nor diminished during his continuance in office. The justices of the peace, for services in courts of sessions, shall be paid a per diem allowance out of the county treasury.

When two may be elected.

In counties having a population exceeding forty thousand, the legislature may provide for the election of a separate officer to perform the duties of the office of surrogate.

Equity jurisdiction.

The legislature may confer equity jurisdiction, in special cases, upon the county judge.

Inferior local courts.

Inferior local courts, of civil and criminal jurisdiction, may be established by the legislature in cities; and such courts, except for the cities of New York and Buffalo, shall have an uniform organization and jurisdiction in such cities.

Two local judicial officers may be elected in each county.

SECTION 15. The legislature may, on application of the board of supervisors, provide for the election of local officers, not to exceed two in any county, to discharge the duties of county judge and of surrogate, in cases of their inability or of a vacancy, and to exercise such other powers in special cases as may be provided by law.

Judicial districts to be reorganized.

SECTION 16. The legislature may reorganize the judicial districts, at the first session after the return of every enumeration under this constitution, in the manner provided for in the fourth section of this article, and at no other time; and they may, at such session, increase or diminish the number of districts, but such increase or diminution shall not be more than one district at any one time. Each district shall have four justices of the supreme court; but no diminution of the districts shall have the effect to remove a judge from office.

Justices of the peace how elected.

SECTION 17. The electors of the several towns shall, at their annual town meeting, and in such manner as the legislature may direct, elect justices of the peace, whose term of office shall be four years. In case of an election to fill a vacancy occurring before the expiration of a full term, they shall hold for the residue of the unexpired term. Their number and classification may be regulated by law. Justices of the peace and judges or justices of inferior courts, not of record, and their clerks, may be removed, after due notice and an opportunity of their being heard in their defense, by such county, city or state courts as may be prescribed by law, for causes to be assigned in the order of removal.

SECTION 18. All judicial officers of cities and villages, and all such judicial officers as may be created therein by law, shall be elected at such times and in such manner as the legislature may direct. Certain judicial officers in cities and villages how elected.

SECTION 19. Clerks of the several counties of this state shall be clerks of the supreme court, with such powers and duties as shall be prescribed by law. A clerk of the court of appeals, to be *ex-officio* clerk of the supreme court, and to keep his office at the seat of government, shall be chosen by the electors of the state; he shall hold his office for three years, and his compensation shall be fixed by law and paid out of the public treasury. County clerks to be clerks of supreme court. Clerk for the court of appeals, how chosen and term of office.

SECTION 20. No judicial officer, except justices of the peace, shall receive to his own use any fees or perquisites of office. No judicial officer except, &c., to receive fees.

SECTION 21. The legislature may authorize the judgments, decrees and decisions of any local inferior court of record of original civil jurisdiction, established in a city, to be removed for review directly into the court of appeals. Certain judgments and decrees may be removed to court of appeals.

SECTION 22. The legislature shall provide for the speedy publication of all statute laws, and of such judicial decisions as it may deem expedient. And all laws and judicial decisions shall be free for publication by any person. Publication of laws.

SECTION 23. Tribunals of conciliation may be established, with such powers and duties as may be prescribed by law; but such tribunals shall have no power to render judgment to be obligatory upon the parties, except they voluntarily submit their matters in difference, and agree to abide the judgment, or assent thereto in the presence of such tribunal, in such cases as shall be prescribed by law. Tribunals of conciliation.

SECTION 24. The legislature, at its first session after the adoption of this constitution, shall provide for the appointment of three commissioners, whose duty it shall be to revise, reform, simplify and abridge the rules and practice, pleadings, forms and proceedings of the courts of record of this state, and to report thereon to the legislature, subject to their adoption and modification from time to time. Commissioners to revise, &c., the rules, &c., of courts of record.

SECTION 25. The legislature at its first session after the adoption of this constitution, shall provide for the organization of the court of appeals, and for transferring to it the business pending in the court for the correction of errors, and for the allowance of writs of error, and appeals to the court of appeals, from the judgments and decrees of the present court of chancery and supreme court, and of the courts that may be organized under this constitution. Organization of court of appeals.

ARTICLE VII.

Canal debt.

SECTION 1. After paying the expenses of collection, superintendence and ordinary repairs, there shall be appropriated and set apart in each fiscal year, out of the revenues of the state canals, commencing on the first day of June, one thousand eight hundred and forty-six, the sum of one million and three hundred thousand dollars, until the first day of June, one thousand eight hundred and fifty-five, and from that time the sum of one million and seven hundred thousand dollars in each fiscal year, as a sinking fund, to pay the interest and redeem the principal of that part of the state debt called the canal debt as it existed at the time first aforesaid, and including three hundred thousand dollars then to be borrowed, until the same shall be wholly paid; and the principal and income of the said sinking fund shall be sacredly applied to that purpose.

Sinking fund, $1,300,000.

$1,700,000.

General Fund, debt.

SECTION 2. After complying with the provisions of the first section of this article, there shall be appropriated and set apart out of the surplus revenues of the state canals, in each fiscal year, commencing on the first day of June, one thousand eight hundred and forty-six, the sum of three hundred and fifty thousand dollars, until the time when a sufficient sum shall have been appropriated and set apart, under the said first section, to pay the interest and extinguish the entire principal of the canal debt; and after that period, then the sum of one million and five hundred thousand dollars in each fiscal year, as a sinking fund, to pay the interest and redeem the principal of that part of the state debt called the general fund debt, including the debt for loans of the state credit to railroad companies which have failed to pay the interest thereon, and also the contingent debt on state stocks loaned to incorporated companies which have hitherto paid the interest thereon, whenever and as far as any part thereof may become a charge on the treasury or general fund, until the same shall be wholly paid; and the principal and income of the said last mentioned sinking fund shall be sacredly applied to the purpose aforesaid; and if the payment of any part of the moneys to the said sinking fund shall at any time be deferred, by reason of the priority recognized in the first section of this article, the sum so deferred, with quarterly interest thereon, at the then current rate, shall be paid to the last mentioned sinking fund, as soon as it can be done consistently with the just rights of the creditors holding said canal debt.

Sinking fund, $350,000.

$1,500,000.

$200,000 of the surplus Canal revenues annually appropriated to General Fund, and

[SECTION 3. After paying the said expenses of superintendence and repairs of the canals, and the sums appropriated by the first and second sections of this article, there shall be paid out of the surplus revenues of the canals, to the treasury of the state, on or before the thirtieth day of September, in each year, for the use and benefit of the general fund, such sum, not exceeding two hundred thousand dollars, as may be required to defray the necessary expenses of the state; and the remainder of the revenues of the said canals shall, in each fiscal year, be applied, in such manner as the legislature shall direct, to the completion of the Erie canal enlargement, and the Genesee Valley and Black River canals, until the canals shall be completed.

the remainder to specified public works.

Annulled.

If at any time after the period of eight years from the adoption of this constitution, the revenues of the state, unappropriated by this article, shall not be sufficient to defray the necessary expenses of the government, without continuing or laying a direct tax, the legislature may, at its discretion, supply the deficiency, in whole or in part, from the surplus revenues of the canals, after complying with the provisions of the first two sections of this article, for paying the interest and extinguishing the principal of the canal and general fund debt; but the sum thus appropriated from the surplus revenues of the canals shall not exceed annually three hundred and fifty thousand dollars, including the sum of two hundred thousand dollars provided for by this section for the expenses of the government, until the general fund debt shall be extinguished, or until the Erie canal enlargement and Genesee Valley and Black River canals shall be completed, and after that debt shall be paid, or the said canals shall be completed, then the sum of six hundred and seventy-two thousand five hundred dollars, or so much thereof as shall be necessary, may be annually appropriated to defray the expenses of the government.]

Certain deficiencies in the revenues of the State not exceeding $350,000, annually to be supplied from the revenues of the Canals.

SECTION 4. The claims of the state against any incorporated company to pay the interest and redeem the principal of the stock of the state loaned or advanced to such company, shall be fairly enforced, and not released or compromised; and the moneys arising from such claims shall be set apart and applied as part of the sinking fund provided in the second section of this article. But the time limited for the fulfillment of any condition of any release or compromise, heretofore made or provided for, may be extended by law.

Loans to incorporated companies not to be released or compromised.

SECTION 5. If the sinking funds, or either of them, provided in this article, shall prove insufficient to enable the state, on the credit of such fund, to procure the means to satisfy the claims of the creditors of the state as they become payable, the legislature shall, by equitable taxes,

Legislature shall by equitable taxes increase the rev-

enues of the sinking funds in certain cases so increase the revenues of the said funds as to make them, respectively, sufficient perfectly to preserve the public faith. Every contribution or advance to the canals, or their debt, from any source, other than their direct revenues, shall, with quarterly interest, at the rates then current, be repaid into the treasury, for the use of the state, out of the canal revenues, as soon as it can be done consistently with the just rights of the creditors holding the said canal debt.

State canals not to be sold or leased.

SECTION 6. The legislature shall not sell, lease, or otherwise dispose of any of the canals of the state; but they shall remain the property of the state and under its management forever.

Salt Springs.

SECTION 7. The legislature shall never sell or dispose of the salt springs belonging to this state. The lands contiguous thereto, and which may be necessary and convenient for the use of the salt springs, may be sold by authority of law and under the direction of the commissioners of the land office, for the purpose of investing the moneys arising therefrom in other lands alike convenient; but by such sale and purchase the aggregate quantity of these lands shall not be diminished.

Appropriation bills.

SECTION 8. No moneys shall ever be paid out of the treasury of this state, or any of its funds, or any of the funds under its management, except in pursuance of an appropriation by law; nor unless such payment be made within two years next after the passage of such an appropriation act; and every such law, making a new appropriation, or continuing or reviving an appropriation, shall distinctly specify the sum appropriated, and the object to which it is to be applied; and it shall not be sufficient for such law to refer to any other law to fix such sum.

State credit not to be loaned.

SECTION 9. The credit of the state shall not, in any manner, be given or loaned to, or in aid of any individual association or corporation.

Power to contract debts limited.

SECTION 10. The state may, to meet casual deficits or failures in revenues, or for expenses not provided for, contract debts but such debts, direct and contingent, singly or in the aggregate, shall not at any time exceed one million of dollars; and the moneys arising from the loans creating such debts, shall be applied to the purpose for which they were obtained, or to repay the debt so contracted, and to no other purpose whatever.

Debts to repel invasion, &c., may be contracted.

SECTION 11. In addition to the above limited power to contract debts, the state may contract debts to repel invasion, suppress insurrection, or defend the state in war; but the money arising from the contracting of such debts shall be applied to the purpose for which it was raised, or to repay such debts, and to no other purpose whatever.

SECTION 12. Except the debts specified in the tenth and eleventh sections of this article, no debt shall be hereafter contracted by or on behalf of this State, unless such debt shall be authorized by a law, for some single work or object, to be distinctly specified therein; and such law shall impose and provide for the collection of a direct annual tax to pay, and sufficient to pay the interest on such debt as it falls due, and also to pay and discharge the principal of such debt within eighteen years from the time of the contracting thereof. Limitation of the legislative power in the creation of debts.

No such law shall take effect until it shall, at a general election, have been submitted to the people, and have received a majority of all the votes cast for and against it at such election.

On the final passage of such bill in either house of the legislature, the question shall be taken by ayes and noes, to be duly entered on the journals thereof, and shall be: "Shall this bill pass, and ought the same to receive the sanction of the people?"

The legislature may at any time, after the approval of such law by the people, if no debt shall have been contracted in pursuance thereof, repeal the same; and may at any time, by law, forbid the contracting of any further debt or liability, under such law; but the tax imposed by such act, in proportion to the debt and liability which may have been contracted, in pursuance of such law, shall remain in force and be irrepealable, and be annually collected, until the proceeds thereof shall have made the provision hereinbefore specified to pay and discharge the interest and principal of such debt and liability.

The money arising from any loan or stock creating such debt or liability shall be applied to the work or object specified in the act authorizing such debt or liability, or for the repayment of such debt or liability and for no other purposes whatever.

No such law shall be submitted to be voted on, within three months after its passage, or at any general election, when any other law, or any bill, or any amendment to the constitution shall be submitted to be voted for or against.

SECTION 13. Every law which imposes, continues or revives a tax, shall distinctly state the tax and the object to which it is to be applied; and it shall not be sufficient to refer to any other law to fix such tax or object. Manner of passing bills, imposing a tax.

SECTION 14. On the final passage, in either house of the legislature, of every act which imposes, continues or revives a tax, or creates a debt or charge, or makes, continues or revives any appropriation of public or trust money, or property, or releases, discharges or commutes any claim or demand of the state, the question shall be taken by ayes and noes, which shall be duly entered on the journals, and three-fifths of all the members elected to either house, shall, in all such cases, be necessary to constitute a quorum therein.

ARTICLE VIII.

Corporations how created.

SECTION 1. Corporations may be formed under general laws; but shall not be created by special act, except for municipal purposes, and in cases where, in the judgment of the legislature, the object of the corporation cannot be attained under general laws. All general laws and special acts, passed pursuant to this section, may be altered from time to time or repealed.

Debts of corporations.

SECTION 2. Dues from corporations shall be secured by such individual liability of the corporators and other means as may be prescribed by law.

Corporations defined.

SECTION 3. The term corporations, as used in this article, shall be construed to include all associations and joint stock companies having any of the powers or privileges of corporations not possessed by individuals or partnerships. And all corporations shall have the right to sue and shall be subject to be sued in all courts, in like cases as natural persons.

Charters for banking purposes.

SECTION 4. The legislature shall have no power to pass any act granting any special charter for banking purposes; but corporations or associations may be formed for such purposes under general laws.

Specie payments.

SECTION 5. The legislature shall have no power to pass any law sanctioning in any manner, directly or indirectly, the suspension of specie payments, by any person, association or corporation issuing bank notes of any description.

Registry of bills or notes.

SECTION 6. The legislature shall provide by law for the registry of all bills or notes, issued or put in circulation as money, and shall require ample security for the redemption of the same in specie.

Individual responsibility of stockholders.

SECTION 7. The stockholders in every corporation and joint stock association for banking purposes, issuing bank notes or any kind of paper credits to circulate as money, after the first day of January, one thousand eight hundred and fifty, shall be individually responsible, to the amount of their respective share or shares of stock in any such corporation or association, for all its debts and liabilities of every kind, contracted after the said first day of January, one thousand eight hundred and fifty.

Insolvency of banks, preference.

SECTION 8. In case of the insolvency of any bank or banking association, the billholders thereof shall be entitled to preference, in payment, over all other creditors of such bank or association.

Organization of cities and villages.

SECTION 9. It shall be the duty of the legislature to provide for the organization of cities and incorporated villages, and to restrict their power of taxation, assessment, borrowing money, contracting debts and loaning their credit, so as to prevent abuses in assessments, and in contracting debt by such municipal corporations.

ARTICLE IX.

Common School, Literature and United States Deposit Funds.

SECTION 1. The capital of the common school fund, the capital of the literature fund and the capital of the United States deposit fund, shall be respectively preserved inviolate. The revenue of the said common school fund shall be applied to the support of common schools, the revenue of the said literature fund shall be applied to the support of academies, and the sum of twenty-five thousand dollars of the revenues of the United States deposit fund shall each year be appropriated to and made part of the capital of the said common school fund.

ARTICLE X.

Sheriffs, clerks of counties, register and clerk of N. Y., coroners and district attorneys.

SECTION 1. Sheriffs, clerks of counties, including the register and clerk of the city and county of New York, coroners and district attorneys, shall be chosen by the electors of the respective counties, once in every three years and as often as vacancies shall happen. Sheriffs shall hold no other office, and be ineligible for the next three years after the termination of their offices. They may be required by law to renew their security from time to time; and in default of giving such new security, their offices shall be deemed vacant. But the county shall never be made responsible for the acts of the sheriff.

Governor may remove.

The governor may remove any officer, in this section mentioned, within the term for which he shall have been elected, giving to such officer a copy of the charges against him, and an opportunity of being heard in his defense.

Officers how chosen or appointed.

SECTION 2. All county officers whose election or appointment is not provided for by this constitution, shall be elected by the electors of the respective counties, or appointed by the boards of supervisors, or other county authorities, as the legislature shall direct. All city, town and village officers whose election or appointment is not provided for by this constitution, shall be elected by the electors of such cities, towns and villages, or of some division thereof, or appointed by such authorities thereof as the legislature shall designate for that purpose. All other officers whose election or appointment is not provided for by this constitution, and all officers whose offices may hereafter be created by law, shall be elected by the people, or appointed as the legislature may direct.

Duration of office. SECTION 3. When the duration of any office is not provided by this constitution, it may be declared by law, and if not so declared, such office shall be held during the pleasure of the authority making the appointment.

Time of election. SECTION 4. The time of electing all officers named in this article shall be prescribed by law.

Vacancies in office, how filled. SECTION 5. The legislature shall provide for filling vacancies in office, and in case of elective officers, no person appointed to fill a vacancy shall hold his office by virtue of such appointment longer than the commencement of the political year next succeeding the first annual election after the happening of the vacancy.

Political year. SECTION 6. The political year and legislative term shall begin on the first day of January; and the legislature shall, every year assemble on the first Tuesday in January, unless a different day shall be appointed by law.

Removal from office. SECTION 7. Provision shall be made by law for the removal for misconduct or malversation in office of all officers (except judicial) whose powers and duties are not local or legislative and who shall be elected at general elections, and also for supplying vacancies created by such removal.

When office deemed vacant. SECTION 8. The legislature may declare the cases in which any office shall be deemed vacant, when no provision is made for that purpose in this constitution.

ARTICLE XI.

Militia. SECTION 1. The militia of this state shall, at all times hereafter be armed and disciplined, and in readiness for service; but all such inhabitants of this state, of any religious denomination whatever, as from scruples of conscience may be averse to bearing arms, shall be excused therefrom, upon such conditions as shall be prescribed by law.

Manner of choosing or appointing militia officers. SECTION 2. Militia officers shall be chosen, or appointed, as follows: captains, subalterns and non-commissioned officers shall be chosen by the written votes of the members of their respective companies. Field officers of regiments and separate battalions, by the written votes of the commissioned officers of the respective regiments and separate battalions; brigadier-generals and brigade inspectors, by the field officers of their respective brigades; major-generals, brigadier-generals and commanding officers of regiments or separate battalions shall appoint the staff officers to their respective divisions, brigades, regiments or separate battalions.

SECTION 3. The governor shall nominate, and with the consent of the senate appoint, all major-generals, and the commissary-general. The adjutant-general and other chiefs of staff departments, and the aids-de-camp of the commander-in-chief, shall be appointed by the governor, and their commissions shall expire with the time for which the governor shall have been elected. The commissary-general shall hold his office for two years. He shall give security for the faithful execution of the duties of his office, in such manner and amount as shall be prescribed by law. Officers to be appointed by governor and senate. Commissary-general.

SECTION 4. The legislature shall by law direct the time and manner of electing militia officers, and of certifying their elections to the governor. Election of militia officers.

SECTION 5. The commissioned officers of the militia shall be commissioned by the governor; and no commissioned officer shall be removed from office, unless by the senate on the recommendation of the governor, stating the grounds on which such removal is recommended, or by the decision of a court-martial, pursuant to law. The present officers of the militia shall hold their commissions subject to removal, as before provided. Officers how commissioned.

SECTION 6. In case the mode of election and appointment of militia officers hereby directed shall not be found conducive to the improvement of the militia, the legislature may abolish the same and provide by law for their appointment and removal, if two-thirds of the members present in each house shall concur therein. Election of militia officers may be abolished.

ARTICLE XII.

SECTION 1. Members of the legislature, and all officers, executive and judicial, except such inferior officers as may be by law exempted, shall, before they enter on the duties of their respective offices, take and subscribe the following oath or affirmation: Oath of office prescribed.

"I do solemnly swear (or affirm, as the case may be) that I will support the constitution of the United States, and the constitution of the State of New York; and that I will faithfully discharge the duties of the office of according to the best of my ability."

And no other oath, declaration or test shall be required as a qualification for any office or public trust.

ARTICLE XIII.

SECTION 1. Any amendment or amendments to this constitution may be proposed in the senate and assembly; and Amendments.

if the same shall be agreed to by a majority of the members elected to each of the two houses, such proposed amendment or amendments shall be entered on their journals with the yeas and nays taken thereon, and referred to the legislature to be chosen at the next general election of senators, and shall be published for three months previous to the time of making such choice; and if in the legislature so next chosen, as aforesaid, such proposed amendment or amendments shall be agreed to by a majority of all the members elected to each house, then it shall be the duty of the legislature to submit such proposed amendment or amendments to the people, in such manner and at such time as the legislature shall prescribe; and if the people shall approve and ratify such amendment or amendments, by a majority of the electors qualified to vote for members of the legislature voting thereon, such amendment or amendments shall become part of the constitution.

Future conventions how called.

SECTION 2. At the general election to be held in the year eighteen hundred and sixty-six, and in each twentieth year thereafter, and also at such time as the legislature may by law provide, the question, "Shall there be a convention to revise the constitution, and amend the same?" shall be decided by the electors qualified to vote for members of the legislature; and in case a majority of the electors so qualified, voting at such election, shall decide in favor of a convention for such purpose, the legislature at its next session shall provide by law for the election of delegates to such convention.

ARTICLE XIV.

Election.

SECTION 1. The first election of senators and members of assembly, pursuant to the provisions of this constitution, shall be held on the Tuesday succeeding the first Monday of November, one thousand eight hundred and forty-seven.

Term of office of senators and members of assembly.

The senators and members of assembly who may be in office on the first day of January, one thousand eight hundred and forty-seven, shall hold their offices until and including the thirty-first day of December following, and no longer.

First election of Governor and Lieutenant-Governor, when.

SECTION 2. The first election of governor and lieutenant-governor, under this constitution, shall be held on the Tuesday succeeding the first Monday of November, one thousand eight hundred and forty-eight; and the governor and lieutenant-governor, in office when this constitution shall take effect, shall hold their respective offices until and including the thirty-first day of December of that year.

SECTION 3. The secretary of state, comptroller, treasurer, attorney-general, district attorneys, surveyor-general, canal commissioners and inspectors of state prisons, in office when this constitution shall take effect, shall hold their respective offices until and including the thirty-first day of December, one thousand eight hundred and forty-seven, and no longer. State officers and others to remain in office, till 31st Dec., 1847.

SECTION 4. The first election of judges and clerk of the court of appeals, justices of the supreme court, and county judges, shall take place at such time between the first Tuesday of April and the second Tuesday of June, one thousand eight hundred and forty-seven, as may be prescribed by law. The said courts shall respectively enter upon their duties, on the first Monday of July next thereafter; but the term of office of said judges, clerk and justices, as declared by this constitution, shall be deemed to commence on the first day of January, one thousand eight hundred and forty-eight. First election of judicial officers, when.

SECTION 5. On the first Monday of July one thousand eight hundred and forty-seven, jurisdiction of all suits and proceedings then pending in the present supreme court and court of chancery, and all suits and proceedings originally commenced and then pending in any court of common pleas, (except in the city and county of New York,) shall become vested in the supreme court hereby established. Proceedings pending in courts of common pleas, and in suits originally commenced in justices' courts, shall be transferred to the county courts provided for in this constitution, in such manner and form and under such regulations as shall be provided by law. The courts of oyer and terminer hereby established shall, in their respective counties, have jurisdiction on and after the day last mentioned, of all indictments and proceedings then pending in the present courts of oyer and terminer, and also of all indictments and proceedings then pending in the present courts of general sessions of the peace; except in the city of New York, and except in cases of which the courts of sessions hereby established may lawfully take cognizance; and of such indictments and proceedings as the courts of sessions hereby established shall have jurisdiction on and after the day last mentioned. Jurisdiction of suits.

SECTION 6. The chancellor and the present supreme court shall, respectively, have power to hear and determine any of such suits and proceedings ready on the first Monday of July, one thousand eight hundred and forty-seven, for hearing or decision, and shall, for their services therein, be entitled to their present rates of compensation, until the first day of July, one thousand eight hundred and forty- Chancellor and supreme court.

eight, or until all such suits and proceedings shall be sooner heard and determined. Masters in chancery may continue to exercise the functions of their office in the court of chancery, so long as the chancellor shall continue to exercise the functions of his office under the provisions of this constitution.

Masters in chancery.

And the supreme court hereby established shall also have power to hear and determine such of said suits and proceedings as may be prescribed by law.

Vacancy in office of chancellor, or justice of present supreme court, how filled.

SECTION 7. In case any vacancy shall occur in the office of chancellor or justice of the present supreme court, previously to the first day of July, one thousand eight hundred and forty-eight, the governor may nominate, and by and with the advice and consent of the senate appoint, a proper person to fill such vacancy. Any judge of the court of appeals or justice of the supreme court, elected under this constitution, may receive and hold such appointment.

Offices abolished.

SECTION 8. The offices of chancellor, justice of the existing supreme court, circuit judge, vice-chancellor, assistant vice-chancellor, judge of the existing county courts of each county, supreme court commissioner, master in chancery, examiner in chancery, and surrogate, (except as herein otherwise provided,) are abolished from and after the first Monday of July, one thousand eight hundred and forty-seven, (1847.)

Chancellor and Justices eligible

SECTION 9. The chancellor, the justices of the present supreme court and the circuit judges, are hereby declared to be severally eligible to any office at the first election under this constitution.

Officers to hold until expiration of term.

SECTION 10. Sheriffs, clerks of counties, (including the register and clerk of the city and county of New York,) and justices of the peace and coroners, in office when this constitution shall take effect, shall hold their respective offices until the expiration of the term for which they were respectively elected.

Judicial officers may receive fees until &c.

SECTION 11. Judicial officers in office when this constitution shall take effect, may continue to receive such fees and perquisites of office as are now authorized by law, until the first day of July, one thousand eight hundred and forty-seven, notwithstanding the provisions of the twentieth section of the sixth article of this constitution.

Local courts to remain until, &c.

SECTION 12. All local courts established in any city or village, including the superior court, common pleas, sessions and surrogates' courts of the city and county of New York, shall remain, until otherwise directed by the legislature, with their present powers and jurisdictions; and the judges of such courts and any clerks thereof in office on the first day of January, one thousand eight hundred and forty-seven, shall continue in office until the expiration of their terms of office, or until the legislature shall otherwise direct.

SECTION 13. This constitution shall be in force from and including the first day of January, one thousand eight hundred and forty-seven, except as is herein otherwise provided. Constitution goes into operation.

DONE in convention, at the capitol, in the city of Albany, the ninth day of October, in the year one thousand eight hundred and forty-six, and of the independence of the United States of America the seventy-first.

In witness whereof, we have hereunto subscribed our names.

JOHN TRACY, *President*,

and Delegate from the county of Chenango.

JAMES F. STARBUCK,
H. W. STRONG,
FR. SEGER,
} *Secretaries.*

[The following delegates composed the convention which formed the foregoing constitution.]

ALBANY.
Horace K. Willard,
Benjamin Stanton,
Ira Harris,,
Peter Shaver.

ALLEGANY.
William G. Angel,
Calvin T. Chamberlain.

BROOME.
John Hyde.

CATTARAUGUS.
George A. S. Crooker,
Alonzo Hawley.

CAYUGA.
Daniel John Shaw,
Peter Yawger,
Elisha W. Sheldon.

CHAUTAUQUE.
George W. Patterson,
Richard P. Marvin

CHEMUNG.
William Maxwell.

CHENANGO.
John Tracy,
Elisha B. Smith.

CLINTON.
Lemuel Stetson.

COLUMBIA.
Ambrose L. Jordan,
George C. Clyde.

CORTLAND.
John Miller.

DELAWARE.
David S. Waterbury,
Isaac Burr.

DUTCHESS.
Peter K. Dubois,
Charles H. Ruggles,
James Tallmadge.

ERIE.
Absalom Bull,
Amos Wright,
Aaron Salisbury,
Horatio J. Stow.

ESSEX.
George A. Simmons.

FRANKLIN.
Joseph R. Flanders.

FULTON.
John L. Hutchinson.

GENESEE.
Samuel Richmond,
Moses Taggart.

GREENE.
James Powers,
Robert Dorlon.

HERKIMER.
Michael Hoffman,
Arphaxed Loomis.

JEFFERSON.
Elihu McNiel,
Alpheus S. Greene,
Azel W. Danforth.

KINGS.
Conrad Swackhamer,
Tunis G. Bergen,
Henry C. Murphy.

LEWIS.
Russell Parish.

LIVINGSTON.
William H. Spencer,
Allen Ayrault.

MADISON.
Federal Dana,
Benjamin F. Bruce.

MONROE.
Enoch Strong,
Harry Backus,
Frederick F. Backus.

MONTGOMERY.
John Bowdish,
John Nellis.

NEW YORK.
Wm. S. Conely,
Solomon Townsend,
George S. Mann,
Henry Nicoll,
John H. Kennedy,
Charles O'Conor,
Alexander F. Vache,
Samuel J. Tilden,
Benjamin F. Cornell,
John L. Stephens,
David R. F. Jones,
Lorenzo B. Shepard,
John H. Hunt,
Campbell P. White,
Robert H. Morris,
Stephen Allen.

NIAGARA.
John W. McNitt,
Hiram Gardner.

ONEIDA.
Charles P. Kirkland,
Hervey Brayton,
Julius Candee,
Edward Huntington.

ONONDAGA.
Elijah Rhodes,
Cyrus H. Kingsley,
David Munro,
William Taylor.

ONTARIO.
Robert C. Nicholas,
Alvah Worden.

ORANGE.
John W. Brown,
Lewis Cuddeback,
George W. Tuthill.

ORLEANS.
William Penniman.

OSWEGO.
Sereno Clark,
Orris Hart.

OTSEGO.
Levi S. Chatfield,
David B. St. John,
Samuel Nelson.

PUTNAM.
Gouverneur Kemble.

QUEENS.
John L. Riker.

RENSSELAER.
Perry Warren,
Abram Witbeck,
William H. Van Schoonhoven.

RICHMOND.
John T. Harrison.

ROCKLAND.
John J. Wood.

SARATOGA.
James M. Cook,
John K. Porter.

SCHENECTADY.
Daniel D. Campbell.

SCHOHARIE.
John Gebhard, Jr.,
William C. Bouck.

SENECA.
Ansel Bascom.

ST. LAWRENCE.
Bishop Perkins,
John Leslie Russell,
Jonah Sanford.

STEUBEN.
William Kernan,
Robert Campbell, Jr.,
Benjamin S. Brundage.

SUFFOLK.
Abel Huntington,
Churchill C. Cambreling.

SULLIVAN.
William B. Wright.

TIOGA.
John J. Taylor.

TOMPKINS.
Thomas B. Sears,
John Youngs

ULSTER.
James C. Forsyth,
George G. Graham.

WARREN.
William Hotchkiss.

WASHINGTON.
Edward Dodd,
Albert L. Baker.

WAYNE.
Horatio N. Taft,
Ornon Archer.

WESTCHESTER.
Aaron Ward,
John Hunter.

WYOMING.
Andrew W. Young.

YATES.
Elijah Spencer.

[The following amendment to the constitution was proposed by the legislature in 1853, agreed to by a majority of the members elected to each of the two houses for that year, referred to the legislature to be chosen at the next general election of senators (the legislature of 1854), published for three months previous to making such choice, agreed to by a majority of the members elected to each house of the legislature (the legislature of 1854), submitted to the people, and approved and ratified at an election held on the third Wednesday of February, 1854.]

[Substitute for section three, of article seven, the following:]

After paying the said expenses of collection, superintendence and repairs of the canals, and the sums appropriated by the first and second sections of this article, there shall be appropriated and set apart in each fiscal year, out of the surplus revenues of the canals, as a sinking fund, a sum sufficient to pay the interest as it falls due, and extinguish the principal within eighteen years, of any loan made under this section; and if the said sinking fund shall not be sufficient to redeem any part of the principal at the stipulated times of payment, or to pay any part of the interest of such loan, as stipulated, the means to satisfy any such deficiency shall be procured on the credit of the said sinking fund. After complying with the foregoing provisions, there shall be paid annually out of said revenues, into the treasury of the state, two hundred thousand dollars, to defray the necessary expenses of government. The remainder shall, in each fiscal year, be applied to meet appropriations for the enlargement and completion of the canals mentioned in this section, until the said canals shall be completed. In each fiscal year thereafter the remainder shall be disposed of in such a manner as the legislature may direct, but shall at no time be anticipated or pledged for more than one year in advance. The legislature shall annually, during the next four years, appropriate to the enlargement of the Erie, the Oswego, the Cayuga and Seneca canals, and to the completion of the Black River and Genesee Valley canals, and for the enlargement of the locks on the Champlain canal, whenever from dilapidation or decay it shall be necessary to rebuild them, a sum not

Sinking fund to pay interest and extinguish principal in 18 years.

$200,000 payable annually out of revenues into treasury.

exceeding two millions two hundred and fifty thousand dollars. The remainder of the revenues of the canals, for the current fiscal year in which such appropriation is made, shall be applied to meet such appropriation; and if the same shall be deemed insufficient, the legislature shall at the same session provide for the deficiency by loan.

Legislature to borrow $1,500,000.

The legislature shall also borrow one million and five hundred thousand dollars to refund to the holders of the canal revenue certificates, issued under the provisions of chapter four hundred and eighty-five of the Laws of the year one thousand eight hundred and fifty-one, the amount received into the treasury thereon. But no interest to accrue after July first, one thousand eight hundred and fifty-five, shall be paid on such certificates. The provisions of section twelve of this article, requiring every law for borrowing money to be submitted to the people, shall not apply to loans authorized by this section. No part of the revenues of the canals, or of the funds borrowed under this section, shall be paid or applied upon or in consequence of any alleged contract made under chapter four hundred and eighty-five of the Laws of the year one thousand eight hundred and fifty-one, except to pay for work done or materials furnished prior to the first day of June, one thousand eight hundred and fifty-two. The rates of toll on persons or property transported on the canals shall not be reduced below those for the year one thousand eight hundred and fifty-two, except by the canal board, with the concurrence of the legislature. All contracts for work or materials on any canal shall be made with the person who shall offer to do or provide the same at the lowest price, with adequate security for their performance.

Provisions of § 12 not to apply to loans authorized by this section.

THE

POLITICAL CODE

OF THE

STATE OF NEW YORK.

AN ACT

TO ESTABLISH A POLITICAL CODE.

The People of the State of New York, represented in Senate and Assembly, do enact as follows:

PRELIMINARY PROVISIONS.

SECTION 1. Title of Code.
2. Division of Code.
3. Sovereignty of state.
4. Who are the people.
5. Who are citizens.
6. Residence and domicil.
7. Domicil, how determined.
8. All persons within the state subject to its jurisdiction.
9. Allegiance.
10. Renouncing allegiance.
11. Persons not citizens.
12. General rights.
13. Eligibility to office.
14. Rights and duties of persons not electors.
15. Of citizens of other states.
16. Of aliens.
17. Transient aliens and citizens of other states, when not liable to tax.
18. Trade with belligerent state.
19. Other rights not affected by state of war.

Title of Code. SECTION 1. This act shall be known as the POLITICAL CODE OF THE STATE OF NEW YORK.

Division of Code. § 2. This Code is divided into four parts:

The FIRST declares what persons compose the people of the state, and the political rights and duties of all persons subject to its jurisdiction;

The SECOND defines the territory of the state and its civil divisions;

The THIRD relates to the general government of the state, the functions of its public officers, its public ways, its general police and civil polity;

The FOURTH relates to the local government of counties, cities, towns and villages.

PART I.

§ 3. The sovereignty of the state resides in the people thereof; and all writs and processes are issued in their name. Sovereignty of state.

§ 4. The people, as a political body, consist: Who are the people.

1. Of citizens who are electors:

2. Of citizens not electors.

§ 5. The citizens of the state are: Who are citizens.

1. All persons born in this state and domiciled within it, except the children of transient aliens and of alien public ministers and consuls;

2. All persons born out of this state who are citizens of the United States and domiciled within this state.

§ 6. Residence may be permanent or temporary. Domicil is the place of permanent residence; the home. There may be a domicil in one place and a residence for a particular purpose in another. For the purpose of jurisdiction a cor- Residence and domicil poration has a residence wherever it has an office or agency for the transaction of business.

Domicil, how determined.

§ 7. Every person has, in law, a domicil. In determining the domicil, the following rules are to be observed:

1. It is the place where one remains, when not called elsewhere for labor or other special or temporary purpose, and to which he returns in seasons of repose.

2. There can be only one domicil;

3. A domicil cannot be lost till another is gained;

4. The domicil of the father during his life, and, after his death, the domicil of the mother, while she remains unmarried, is the domicil of the unmarried minor child;

5. The domicil of the husband is the domicil of the wife;

6. The domicil of an unmarried minor who has a parent living cannot be changed by either his own act or that of his guardian;

7. The domicil can be changed only by the union of act and intent.

All persons within the state subject to its jurisdiction

§ 8. Every natural person while within this state is subject to its jurisdiction and entitled to its protection. Every corporation which has a residence in this state may be sued in the courts of this state, and is subject to the laws of this state in respect to all transactions within the state.

§ 9. Allegiance is the obligation of fidelity and obedience which every citizen owes to the state. Allegiance.

§ 10. Allegiance may be renounced by a formal act of renunciation and a change of domicil. Renouncing allegiance.

§ 11. Persons in the state, not its citizens, are either: Persons not citizens.

1. Citizens of other states, or

2. Aliens.

§ 12. Besides the political rights and duties prescribed by the Constitution of the United States and the Constitution of this State, every person within this state has the following legal rights, among others: General rights.

1. Exemption from all authority over his person or property but such as is derived from the people of this state through their grant to the United States, by the Constitution of the United States or through their own constitution and laws;

2. The right to do any act not forbidden by law.

§ 13. Every elector is eligible to the office for which he is an elector, except where otherwise Eligibility to office.

specially provided; and no person is eligible who is not such an elector.

Rights and duties of persons not electors.

§ 14. An elector has no rights or duties beyond those of a citizen not an elector, except the right and duty of holding and electing to office.

Of citizens of other states.

§ 15. A citizen of the United States, who is not a citizen of this state, has the same rights and duties as a citizen of this state not an elector, except as provided by section 14.

Of aliens.

§ 16. An alien has the same rights and duties as a citizen of the United States who is not a citizen of this state, except that he cannot hold real property in this state without having, in due form of law, declared his intention of becoming a citizen.

Transient aliens and citizens of other states when not liable to tax

§ 17. A transient alien, or a citizen of the United States who is not a citizen of this state, is not liable to taxation in this state, for personal property lying without the state.

Trade with belligerent state.

§ 18. During a war between the United States and any other government or country, all trade and intercourse between persons in this state and the subjects or citizens of that government or country is illegal, except under special license from the government of the United States.

§ 19. The rights and duties of persons in this state are not affected by a state of war between the United States and any other government or country, or between any foreign governments or countries, otherwise than as provided in the last section, except that they cannot trade with either of the belligerents in articles contraband of war, or enter places regularly blockaded.

Other rights not affected by state of war.

PART II.

BOUNDARIES AND DIVISIONS OF THE STATE.

§ 20. The sovereignty and jurisdiction of this state extend to all places within its bounds, which are hereby declared to be as follows: Beginning at Lyon's point in the mouth of a stream called Byram river, where it falls into Long Island Sound, and running thence up along that stream to a rock at the ancient road or wading place in that stream, which rock bears north twelve degrees and forty-five minutes east, five hundred and fifty rods from Lyon's point; then north twenty-three degrees and forty-five minutes west, two thousand two hundred and ninety-two rods; then east-northeast thirteen

Territory of the state.

miles and sixty-four rods, which lines were established in the year 1725, by Francis Harrison, Cadwallader Colden and Isaac Hicks, commissioners on the part of the then province of New York, and Jonathan Law, Samuel Eells, Roger Wolcott, John Copp and Edmund Lewis, commissioners on the part of the then colony of Connecticut, and were run as the magnetic needle then pointed; then along an east-northeast continuation of the last mentioned course, one mile three-quarters of a mile and twenty-one rods, to a monument erected in the year 1731, by Cadwallader Colden, Gilbert Willett, Vincent Matthews and Jacobus Bruyn, junior, commissioners on the part of the province of New York, and Samuel Eells, Roger Wolcott and Edmund Lewis, commissioners on the part of the colony of Connecticut; which monument is at the southeast corner of a tract known and distinguished as the oblong or equivalent lands; then north twenty-four degrees and thirty minutes west, until intersected by a line run by the last mentioned commissioners on a course south twelve degrees and thirty minutes west, from a monument erected by them in the south bounds of Massachusetts; which monument stands in a valley in the Taghkanick mountains, one hundred and twenty rods eastward from a heap of stones in those bounds, on the top or ridge of the most westerly of those mountains; then north twelve degrees and thirty minutes east, from a monument erected by the last mentioned commissioners at the place of intersection, and standing on the north side of a hill southeasterly from the easternmost end of the long pond, along that line to the aforesaid monument erected on the south bounds of Massachusetts, being the northeast corner of the oblong; then north eighty-nine degrees eight minutes forty-one seconds west, along the north bounds of the oblong forty chains to a monument, being a marble post marked on the south and west sides N. Y, and east side M. S., and north side 1853. Thence north twelve degrees fifty-seven minutes and sixteen seconds west, two hundred and seven chains forty-nine links to the New York line and a marble post marked on the east side M. S., on the west side N. Y., and on the south side 1853; then north fifteen degrees twelve minutes and nine seconds east along the line established in the year 1787, by Thomas Hutchins, John Ewing and David Rittenhouse, commissioners appointed by the United States, in congress assembled, forty-seven miles seventy-three chains and eighty one links, to a red or black oak tree marked by them, which line was run by them as the magnetic needle pointed in that year; then north eighty-two degrees and twenty minutes as the magnetic needle pointed in the year 1814, fifty chains to a monument erected for the southwest corner of the State of Vermont, by Smith

Thompson, Simeon De Witt and George Tibbitts, commissioners on the part of this state, and Joseph Beeman, junior, Henry Olin and Joel Pratt, second commissioners on the part of the State of Vermont, which monument stands on the brow of a high hill descending to the west; then northerly in a straight line to a point which is distant ten chains, on a course south thirty-five degrees west, from the most westerly corner of a lot of land distinguished in the records of the town of Pownal, in the State of Vermont, as the fifth division of the right of Gamaliel Wallace, and which, in the year 1814, was owned and occupied by Abraham Vosburgh; then north thirty-five degrees east to that corner, and along the westerly bounds of that lot thirty chains to a place on the westerly bank of Hosick river, where a hemlock tree heretofore stood, noticed in those records as the most northerly corner of the lot; then north one degree and twenty minutes west, six chains to a monument erected by the said commissioners, standing on the westerly side of Hosick river, on the north side of the highway leading out of Hosick into Pownal, and near the northwesterly corner of the bridge crossing that river; then north twenty-seven degrees and twenty minutes east, thirty chains through the bed of that river to a large roundish rock on its northeasterly bank; then north twenty-five degrees west, sixteen chains and seventy links; then north nine degrees west, eighteen chains and sixty links to a white oak tree at the southwest corner of the land occupied in 1814 by Thomas Wilsey; then north eleven degrees east, seventy-seven chains to the north side of a highway where it is met by a fence dividing the possession of said Thomas Wilsey, junior, and Emery Hunt; then north forty-six degrees east, six chains; then south sixty-six degrees east, twenty-six chains and twenty-five links; then north nine degrees east, twenty-seven chains and fifty links to a blue slate stone anciently set up for the southwest corner of Bennington; then north seven degrees and thirty minutes east, forty-six miles, forty-three chains and fifty links to a bunch of hornbeam saplings on the south bank of Poultney river, the northernmost of which was marked by the last mentioned commissioners, and from which a large butternut tree bears north seventy degrees west, thirty links, a large hard maple tree south two chains and eighty-six links, and a white ash tree on the north side of the river, north seventy-seven degrees east; which several lines from the monument erected for the southwest corner of the State of Vermont, were established by the last mentioned commissioners, and were run by them as the magnetic needle pointed in the year 1814; then down the Poultney river through its deepest channel to East bay; then through the middle of the deepest channel of East bay and its waters to where the same communicate with Lake Champlain; then through the middle of the deepest channel of Lake Champlain to the eastward of the islands called the Four Brothers, and the westward of the islands called the Grand isle and Long isle, or the Two Heroes, and to the westward of the Isle La Mott to the line in the forty-fifth degree of north latitude, established by treaty for the boundary line between the United States and the British dominions; then west along that line to the River St. Lawrence; then along the line established by the commissioners appointed under the sixth article of the treaty of Ghent, into and up the River St Lawrence to the waters of Lake Ontario; then along the same line, through the waters of that lake and of the Niagara river to the waters of Lake Erie; then westerly through the same, and along the said line until intersected by a meridian line drawn through the most westerly bent or inclination of Lake Ontario; then south along such meridian line to a monument in the beginning of the forty-third degree of north latitude, erected in the year 1787 by Abraham Hardenburgh and William W. Morris, commissioners on the part of this state, and Andrew Ellicott and Andrew Porter, commissioners on the part of the State of Pennsylvania, for the purpose of marking the termination of the line of jurisdiction between this state and the State of Pennsylvania; then east along the line established and marked by the last mentioned commissioners to the ninetieth milestone in the same parallel of latitude, erected in the year 1786 by James Clinton and Simeon De Witt, commissioners on the part of this state, and Andrew Ellicott, commissioner on the part of Pennsylvania, which ninetieth milestone stands on the western side of the south branch of the Tioga river; then east along the line established and marked by the last mentioned commissioners, to a stone erected in the year 1774 on a small island in the Delaware river, by Samuel Holland and David Rittenhouse, commissioners on the part of the colonies of New York and Pennsylvania, for the purpose of marking the beginning of the forty-third degree of north latitude; then down along the Delaware river to a point opposite to the fork or branch formed by the junction of the stream called Mahackamask with the Delaware river, in the latitude of forty-one degrees twenty-one minutes thirty-seven seconds north; then in a straight line to the termination, on the east bank of the Delaware river, of a line run in the year 1774, by William Wickham and Samuel Gale, commissioners on the part of the then colony of New York, and John Stevens and Walter Rutherford, commissioners on the part of the then colony of New Jersey; then along that line to a rock on the west side of the Hudson river, in the latitude of forty-one degrees north marked by those commissioners; thence in continuation of that line in the same direction, to a point in the middle of the river, opposite that rock; thence along the middle of the river, of the bay of New York, of the waters between Staten island and New Jersey, and of Raritan bay to the main sea, and then to the place of beginning, including Staten island, and the islands of meadow on the west side thereof, Shooter's island, Long island, the Isle of Wight, now called Gardiner's island, Fisher's island, Shelter island, Plumb island, Robins island, Ram island, the Gull islands, and all the waters of the bay of New York within the bounds above described, and including also Bedlow's and Ellis' islands, and all the islands in the bay of New York, whether within the bounds above described or not; subject, however, to the provisions of a certain agreement between this state and the State of New Jersey, dated on the 16th day of September, 1833, which are as follows:

Article First. The boundary line between the two States of New York and New Jersey, from a point in the middle of Hudson river opposite the point on the west shore thereof, in the forty-first degree of north latitude, as heretofore ascertained and marked, to the main sea, shall be the middle of the said river, of the bay of New York, of the waters between Staten island and New Jersey, and of Raritan bay to the main sea, except as hereinafter otherwise particularly mentioned.

ARTICLE SECOND. The State of New York shall retain its present jurisdiction of and over Bedlow's and Ellis' islands, and shall also retain exclusive jurisdiction of and over the other islands lying in the waters above mentioned, and now under the jurisdiction of that state.

ARTICLE THIRD. The State of New York shall have and enjoy exclusive jurisdiction of and over all the waters of the bay of New York, and of and over all waters of Hudson river lying west of Manhattan island, and to the south of the mouth of Spuytenduyvel creek, and of and over the lands covered by the said waters to the low-water mark on the westerly or New Jersey side thereof; subject to the following rights of property and of jurisdiction of the State of New Jersey, that is to say:

1. The State of New Jersey shall have the exclusive right of property in and to the land under water lying west of the middle of the bay of New York, and west of the middle of that part of the Hudson river which lies between Manhattan island and New Jersey.

2. The State of New Jersey shall have exclusive jurisdiction of and over the wharves, docks and improvements made, and to be made, on the shore of the said state, and of and over all vessels aground on said shore, or fastened to any such wharf or dock; except that the said vessels shall be subject to the quarantine or health laws, and laws in relation to passengers, of the State of New York, which now exist, or which may hereafter be passed.

3. The State of New Jersey shall have the exclusive right of regulating the fisheries on the westerly side of the middle of the said waters, provided that the navigation be not obstructed or hindered.

Article Fourth. The State of New York shall have exclusive jurisdiction of and over the waters of the Kill van Kull, between Staten island and New Jersey, to the westernmost end of Shooter's island, in respect to such quarantine laws, and laws relating to passengers, as now exist, or may hereafter be passed under the authority of that state, and for executing the same; and the said state has also exclusive jurisdiction for the like purposes, of and over the waters of the sound, from the westernmost end of Shooter's island to Woodbridge creek, as to all vessels bound to any port in the said State of New York.

ARTICLE FIFTH. The State of New Jersey shall have and enjoy exclusive jurisdiction of and over all the waters of the sound between Staten island and New Jersey, lying south of Woodbridge creek, and of and over all the waters of Raritan bay lying westward of a line drawn from the light-house at Prince's bay to the mouth of Mattavan creek, subject to the following rights of property and jurisdiction of the State of New York:

1. The State of New York shall have exclusive right of property in and to the land under water, lying between the middle of the said waters and Staten island.

2. The State of New York shall have the exclusive jurisdiction of and over the wharves, docks and improvements made, and to be made, on the shore of Staten island; and of and over all vessels aground on said shore, or fastened to any such wharf or dock; except that the said vessel shall be subject to the quarantine or health laws, and laws in relation to passengers, of the State of New Jersey, which now exist, or which may hereafter be passed.

3. The State of New York shall have the exclusive right of regulating the fisheries between the shore of Staten island and the middle of the said waters, provided that the navigation of the said waters be not obstructed or hindered.

Article Sixth. Criminal process issued under the authority of the State of New Jersey, against any person accused of an offense committed within that state; or committed on board of any vessel being under the exclusive jurisdiction of that state as aforesaid; or committed against the regulations made, or to be made by that state in relation to the fisheries mentioned in the third article; and also civil process issued under the authority of the State of New Jersey against any person domiciled in that state, or against property taken out of that state to evade the laws thereof; may be served upon any of the said waters within the exclusive jurisdiction of the State of New York, unless such person or property shall be on board a vessel aground upon or fastened to the shore of the State of New York, or fastened to a wharf adjoining thereto; or unless such person shall be under arrest, or such property shall be under seizure by virtue of process or authority of the State of New York.

Article Seventh. Criminal process issued under the authority of the State of New York, against any person accused of an offense committed within that state; or committed on board of any vessel being under the exclusive jurisdiction of that state as aforesaid; or committed against the regulations made or to be made by that state in relation to the fisheries mentioned in the fifth article; and also civil process issued under the authority of the State of New York, against any person domiciled in that state, or against property taken out of that state to evade the laws thereof; may be served upon any of the said waters within the exclusive jurisdiction of the State of New Jersey, unless such person or property shall be on board a vessel aground upon or fastened to the shore of the State of New Jersey, or fastened to a wharf adjoining thereto; or unless such persons shall be under arrest, or such property shall be under seizure, by virtue of process or authority of the State of New Jersey.

§ 21. In respect to places within the foregoing boundaries, ceded by the state to the United States, the jurisdiction of this state is concurrent with that of the United States, according to the terms of cession in each case respectively.

The places heretofore ceded are as follows:[1]

A tract of land at Montook point, in the county of Suffolk, known by the name of Turtle hill;

A tract of ten acres at Eaton's neck, in the town of Huntington, in the county of Suffolk;

Three certain islands in the harbor of New York, viz.: Bedlow's island and Ellis or Oyster

[1] See note to § 22.

island, bounded on all sides by the waters of the Hudson river, and Governor's island, bounded on all sides by the waters of the East river and Hudson river;

Great Gull island and Little Gull island, situated in the county of Suffolk, and bounded on all sides by the waters of the East river;

A tract of five acres at Sands or Natch point, on Long island, situated in the town of North Hempstead, and county of Queens;

A tract at Bluff point on Staten island;

Two tracts of land and water in the city of New York;

A tract of land covered with the waters of the East river, at the Wallabout bay, and adjoining the navy yard of the United States;

A tract of half an acre in the town of Buffalo, in the county of Erie;

A tract of land in the town of Greenbush, in the manor of Rensselaerwyck, county of Rensselaer;

Thirty acres of land covered with water, situate in the town of New Utrecht, in the county of Kings;

A tract of land at the village of Rome, in the county of Oneida; and another tract of land in the town of Watervliet, in the county of Albany;

Lots at Rouse's Point, in the county of Clinton;

A tract of five acres on the head of Galoo island, in Lake Ontario;

A small island near Rouse's Point, in Lake Champlain;

A tract of six acres at the mouth of the Oswego river, in the county of Oswego;

A tract of three acres and one hundred and fifteen rods at the mouth of Genesee river;

A tract in the town of Sodus, in the county of Wayne;

A tract of land at Oldfield point, on Long Island sound, in the county of Suffolk;

A tract of land at Throg's neck, in the county of Westchester;

Two tracts of land in the town of New Utrecht, in the county of Kings;

A tract of land and beach in the town of Islip, in the county of Suffolk;

A tract of land in the town of Haverstraw, in the county of Rockland;

A tract of land in the town of Cornwall, in the county of Orange;

A tract of land in the town of Lyme, in the county of Jefferson;

A tract of land containing three acres on the south side of the west end of Plumb island, in the county of Suffolk;

A tract of land, situated at Prince's bay, in the town of Westfield, and county of Richmond; only so long as the said tract shall be used and occupied as a site for a light-house;

A tract of land, not exceeding one acre, on the southeastern point of Staten island, for the purpose of erecting a light-house;

A tract of land in the town of Watervliet, in the county of Albany, for the purpose of erecting and maintaining thereon arsenals, magazines, dock-yards, and other necessary buildings;

A tract of land in the town of Rye, in the county of Westchester, and on Captain's island, for the purpose of erecting and maintaining thereon a light-house and other necessary buildings;

Horse island, in the town of Hounsfield, in the county of Jefferson, for the purpose of erecting and maintaining thereon a light-house;

A tract of land, not exceeding five acres, on the western extremity of North Brothers' Island, in Long Island sound, in the county of Queens, for the purpose of erecting a light-house on the same;

A tract of land covered with water, in the town of

Esopus, in the county of Ulster, for the purpose of erecting a light-house or beacon-light on the same;

A tract of land in the town of Watervliet, in the county of Albany, for the purpose of erecting and maintaining thereon arsenals, magazines and other necessary buildings;

Tracts of land in the city of Brooklyn, in the county of Kings, for the purpose of erecting and maintaining a navy hospital and other necessary buildings;

A tract of land on Staten island, for the purpose of constructing and maintaining proper defenses for the protection of the harbor of New York;

A tract of land in the town of Esopus, in the county of Ulster, for the purpose of erecting and maintaining a light-house on the same;

A tract of land, near the mouth of the Oswego river, in the county of Oswego, for the purpose of reëstablishing the military post, of rebuilding the forts, redoubts and barracks, and of improving the parade ground;

A tract of land in the south village of Black Rock, between Lake street and Broadway, and the easterly line of the Buffalo and Black Rock railroad, for the purpose of erecting and establishing a fort, battery, barracks, parade ground or military post, and to lands covered by fort Niagara and such others adjacent thereto as shall be necessary for the accommodation of that post;

A point of land in the south village of Black Rock, for military purposes;

Blocks Nos. 167, 168 and 186, in the south village of Black Rock, for the purpose of erecting barracks and defensive works;

Certain lands in the south village of Black Rock in the county of Erie;

Lots of ground in or near the city of Buffalo, at or near the mouth of Genesee river, for the site of fortifications or defensive works;

A tract of land in the village of Sackett's Harbor, in the county of Jefferson, for military purposes;

Islands in the river St. Lawrence, for beacon-lights and other necessary government purposes;

An island in Long Island sound, called North Dumplin or Hammock, for the purpose of erecting a light-house thereon;

A point near Tarrytown point, for the purpose of erecting a beacon-light thereon;

A tract of land in the southerly margin of Big Buffalo creek, in the county of Erie, for the purpurpose of erecting and maintaining piers and a light-house;

A tract of land in the city of Buffalo and town of Black Rock, in the county of Erie, for the erection and maintaining of a sea wall thereon;

A tract of land on Gardiner's island, in the town of East Hampton, in the county of Suffolk, for the erection and maintaining thereon a light-house and other necessary buildings;

Lands in the city of Brooklyn, in the county of Kings, to be used and occupied as a navy yard and navy hospital;

A tract of land on Staten island, in the rear of Elm Tree beacon, for a beacon or range light;

Point du Roche, on the west side of Lake Champlain, for a light-house;

South point of the island east of Barren island, in the North river, for a beacon;

The north point of the island opposite and east of Coeymans bar, in the North river, for a beacon;

The point of the island at the mouth of Schodack channel, in the North river, for a beacon;

The extreme eastern point of the north fork of Long island, for a beacon;

A tract of land on or near Carlton head, in the St. Lawrence river, for a light-house;

One acre of land in the city of Buffalo, in the

county of Erie, for a court-house, custom-house, post-office, and other necessary buildings;

A tract of land in the city of Oswego, in the county of Oswego, for the erection of a custom-house, warehouse, post-office and court-rooms;

A tract of land in the city of Buffalo, in the county of Erie, for the erection of a beacon;

The south end of Cow or Campbell's island, in the Hudson river, for a beacon-light;

Little island, in the Hudson river, for a beacon-light;

Priming Hook point, east side of the Hudson river, for a beacon-light;

The point between Athens and Catskill, on the east side of Hudson river, for a beacon-light;

Little island, in the Hudson river, opposite New Baltimore;

A point near "Great West Bay," Suffolk county, Long island, for a first-class light-house;

A point in Lloyd's harbor, Suffolk county, Long island, for a beacon-light;

Horton's point, Suffolk county, Long island, for a light-house;

Race point, Fisher's island, Suffolk county, Long island, for a light-house;

Windmill point, Lake Champlain, for a light-house;

A tract of land in "Isle au Motte," Lake Champlain, for a beacon-light;

A tract of land near Whitehall, Lake Champlain, for nine beacon-lights;

A tract of land at Pryman's hook, in the county of Columbia;

A tract of land on the south point of the island known as Calvers plat, in the county of Columbia, for a light-house;

A tract of land near Mull's plat, in the county of Rensselaer, for a light-house or beacon-light;

A tract of land on the north point of Poplar island, in the town of Schodack, in the county of Rensselaer, for a light-house or beacon-light;

A tract of land in the town of Plattsburgh, for the erection of a custom-house, warehouse, post-office or court-room;

A tract of land at Crown Point, Lake Champlain, for a light-house;

A tract of land in the village of West Troy, and county of Albany, for arsenal purposes;

The consent of the State of New York has been given to the purchase, by the United States, of the following places:

Six lots of land in the city of Brooklyn, in the county of Kings, for revenue purposes;

A tract of land in the city of New York, for the

purposes of an assay office, revenue offices, and post-office;

A tract of land in the village of Ogdensburgh, in the county of St. Lawrence, for the purposes of a custom-house and post-office, with court-rooms;

A tract of land on Long island, in the county of Queens, for the erection of forts, magazines, dock-yards, wharves, and other necessary structures;

A tract of land in the city of New York, for the erection of a post-office;

All which are more particularly described in the acts of cession or consent, respectively.

Counties of the state.

§ 22. The state is divided into sixty counties, the boundaries whereof remain as now declared by statute. They are named Suffolk, Queens, Kings, Richmond, New York, Westchester, Putnam, Dutchess, Rockland, Orange, Ulster, Sullivan, Delaware, Greene, Columbia, Albany, Rensselaer, Schoharie, Schenectady, Saratoga, Montgomery, Hamilton, Washington, Warren, Essex, Clinton, Franklin, St. Lawrence, Herkimer, Oneida, Madison, Oswego, Lewis, Jefferson, Otsego, Chenango, Broome, Cortland, Tompkins, Tioga, Steuben, Onondaga, Cayuga, Seneca, Ontario, Yates, Wayne, Livingston, Monroe, Genesee, Orleans, Niagara, Erie, Allegany, Cattaraugus, Chautauqua, Chemung, Fulton, Wyoming and Schuyler,

It will be observed that we have not attempted a revision of the boundaries of places ceded to the United States, or of the counties, towns, cities and villages of the state. These are matters somewhat local and subject to change, and have therefore been left to rest in the existing provisions of law. In this respect we have followed the example of the Massachusetts revisers.

§ 23. The state is divided into eight judicial districts, arranged as follows: Judicial districts of the state.

The first judicial district consists of the city and county of New York.

The second judicial district consists of the counties of Richmond, Suffolk, Queens, Kings, Westchester, Orange, Rockland, Putnam and Dutchess.

The third judicial district consists of the counties of Columbia, Sullivan, Ulster, Greene, Albany, Schoharie and Rensselaer.

The fourth judicial district consists of the counties of Warren, Saratoga, Washington, Essex, Franklin, St. Lawrence, Clinton, Montgomery, Hamilton, Fulton and Schenectady.

The fifth judicial district consists of the counties of Onondaga, Oneida, Oswego, Herkimer, Jefferson and Lewis.

The sixth judicial district consists of the counties of Otsego, Delaware, Madison, Chenango, Broome, Tioga, Chemung, Tompkins, Cortland and Schuyler

The seventh judicial district consists of the counties of Livingston, Wayne, Seneca, Yates, Ontario, Steuben, Monroe and Cayuga.

The eighth judicial district consists of the counties of Erie, Chautauqua, Cattaraugus, Orleans, Niagara, Genesee, Allegany and Wyoming.

Senatorial districts of the state.

§ 24. The state is divided into thirty-two senate districts, arranged as follows:

The first senate district consists of the counties of Suffolk, Queens and Richmond.

The second senate district consists of the first, second, third, fourth, fifth, seventh, eleventh, thirteenth, and nineteenth wards of the city of Brooklyn, in the county of Kings.

The third senate district consists of the sixth, eighth, ninth, tenth, twelfth, fourteenth, fifteenth, sixteenth, seventeenth and eighteenth wards of the city of Brooklyn, and the county towns of the county of Kings.

The fourth senate district consists of the first, second, third, fourth, fifth, sixth, seventh, eighth and fourteenth wards of the city of New York.

The fifth senate district consists of the tenth, eleventh, thirteenth and seventeenth wards of the city of New York.

The sixth senate district consists of the ninth

fifteenth, sixteenth and eighteenth wards of the city of New York.

The seventh senate district consists of the twelfth, nineteenth, twentieth, twenty-first and twenty-second wards of the city of New York.

The eighth senate district consists of the counties of Westchester, Putnam and Rockland.

The ninth senate district consists of the counties of Orange and Sullivan.

The tenth senate district consists of the counties of Ulster and Greene.

The eleventh senate district consists of the counties of Dutchess and Columbia.

The twelfth senate district consists of the counties of Rensselaer and Washington.

The thirteenth senate district consists of the county of Albany.

The fourteenth senate district consists of the counties of Delaware, Schoharie and Schenectady.

The fifteenth senate district consists of the counties of Montgomery, Fulton, Saratoga and Hamilton.

The sixteenth senate district consists of the counties of Warren, Essex and Clinton.

The seventeenth senate district consists of the counties of St. Lawrence and Franklin.

The eighteenth senate district consists of the counties of Jefferson and Lewis.

The nineteenth senate district consists of the county of Oneida.

The twentieth senate district consists of the counties of Herkimer and Otsego.

The twenty-first senate district consists of the county of Oswego.

The twenty-second senate district consists of the county of Onondaga.

The twenty-third senate district consists of the counties of Madison, Chenango and Cortland.

The twenty-fourth senate district consists of the counties of Tompkins, Tioga and Broome.

The twenty-fifth senate district consists of the counties of Wayne and Cayuga.

The twenty-sixth senate district consists of the counties of Ontario, Yates and Seneca.

The twenty-seventh senate district consists of counties of Chemung, Schuyler and Steuben.

The twenty-eighth senate district consists of the county of Munroe.

The twenty-ninth senate district consists of the counties of Niagara, Orleans and Genesee.

The thirtieth senate district consists of the counties of Wyoming, Livingston and Allegany.

The thirty-first senate district consists of the county of Erie.

The thirty-second senate district consists of the counties of Chautauqua and Cattaraugus.

§ 25. The state is divided into assembly districts, the boundaries whereof are fixed in each county by the board of supervisors thereof, from time to time, as prescribed in the Constitution. Assembly districts of the state.

§ 26. The state is divided into thirty-three congressional districts arranged as follows: Congressional districts of the state.

The first congressional district consists of the counties of Suffolk, Queens, Richmond and Kings, excepting the city of Brooklyn.

The second congressional district consists of that portion of the city of Brooklyn in the county of Kings which composed the city of Brooklyn previous to the year 1854.

The third congressional district consists of the first, second, third, fifth and eighth wards in the city and county of New York.

The fourth congressional district consists of the fourth, sixth, tenth and fourteenth wards in the city and county of New York.

The fifth congressional district consists of the seventh and thirteenth wards in the city and county of New York, and that part of the city of Brooklyn in the county of Kings which composed the city of Williamsburgh previous to the year 1854.

The sixth congressional district consists of the eleventh, fifteenth and seventeenth wards in the city and county of New York.

The seventh congressional district consists of the ninth, sixteenth and twentieth wards in the city and county of New York.

The eighth congressional district consists of the twelfth, eighteenth and nineteenth wards in the city and county of New York.

The ninth congressional district consists of the counties of Westchester, Rockland and Putnam.

The tenth congressional district consists of the counties of Orange and Sullivan.

The eleventh congressional district consists of the counties of Ulster and Greene.

The twelfth congressional district consists of the counties of Dutchess and Columbia.

The thirteenth congressional district consists of the county of Rensselaer.

The fourteenth congressional district consists of the county of Albany.

The fifteenth congressional district consists of the counties of Washington, Saratoga, Warren and Hamilton.

The sixteenth congressional district consists of the counties of Essex, Clinton and Franklin.

The seventeenth congressional district consists of the counties of St. Lawrence and Herkimer.

The eighteenth congressional district consists of the counties of Fulton, Montgomery, Schenectady and Schoharie

The nineteenth congressional district consists of the counties of Otsego and Delaware.

The twentieth congressional district consists of the county of Oneida.

The twenty-first congressional district consists of the counties of Cortland, Broome and Chenango.

The twenty-second congressional district consists of the counties of Oswego and Madison.

The twenty-third congressional district consists of the counties of Jefferson and Lewis.

The twenty-fourth congressional district consists of the county of Onondaga.

The twenty-fifth congressional district consists of the counties of Cayuga and Wayne.

The twenty-sixth congressional district consists of the counties of Ontario, Seneca and Yates.

The twenty-seventh congressional district consists of the counties of Tompkins, Chemung and Tioga.

The twenty-eighth congressional district consists of the counties of Steuben and Livingston.

The twenty-ninth congressional district consists of the county of Monroe.

The thirtieth congressional district consists of the counties of Genesee, Wyoming and Allegany.

The thirty-first congressional district consists of the counties of Orleans and Niagara.

The thirty-second congressional district consists of the county of Erie.

The thirty-third congressional district consists of the counties of Chautauqua and Cattaraugus.

Towns of the state.

§ 27. The counties, with the exception of the county of New York, are divided into towns as follows, the boundaries whereof remain as now declared by statute, or by the supervisors pursuant to statute:

In the county of Suffolk are Brookhaven, East

Hampton, Huntington, Islip, Riverhead, Shelter Island, Smithtown, Southampton and Southold.

In the county of Queens are Flushing, Hempstead, Jamaica, Newtown, North Hempstead and Oyster Bay.

In the county of Kings are Flatbush, Flatlands, Gravesend and New Utrecht.

In the county of Richmond are Castleton, Northfield, Southfield and Westfield.

In the county of Westchester are Bedford, Cortlandt, Eastchester, Greenburgh, Harrison, Mamaroneck, Mount Pleasant, New Rochelle, Newcastle, Northcastle, North Salem, Pelham, Poundridge, Rye, Scarsdale, Somers, Lewisboro', Westchester, Ossinsing, West Farms, Morrisania, White Plains, Yonkers and Yorktown.

In the county of Putnam are Carmel, Kent, Patterson, Philipstown, Putnam Valley and Southeast.

In the county of Dutchess are Amenia, Beckman, Clinton, Dover, Fishkill, La Grange, Hyde Park, Milan, Northeast, Pawling, Pine Plains, Pleasant Valley, Poughkeepsie, Redhook, Rhine beck, Stanford, Union Vale, Washington and East Fishkill.

In the county of Rockland are Clarkstown, Ramapo, Haverstraw and Orangetown.

In the county of Orange are Blooming Grove, Mount Hope, Cornwall, Crawford, Deerpark, Goshen, Minisink, Greenville, Montgomery, Monroe, Newburgh, New Windsor, Wallkill, Warwick, Hamptonburgh, Chester and Wawayanda.

In the county of Ulster are Esopus, Hurley, Kingston, Marbletown, Marlborough, New Paltz, Olive, Plattekill, Rochester, Saugerties, Shandaken, Shawangunk, Gardiner, Wawarsing, Woodstock, Rosendale, Lloyd, Denning and Hardenbergh.

In the county of Sullivan are Bethel, Cochecton, Fallsburgh, Liberty, Lumberland, Tusten, Highland, Mamakating, Nevisink, Rockland, Thompson, Forestburgh, Collikoon, and Fremont.

In the county of Delaware are Andes, Bovina, Colchester, Davenport, Delhi, Franklin, Hamden, Hancock, Harpersfield, Kortright, Masonville, Meredith, Middletown, Roxbury, Sidney, Stamford, Tompkins and Walton.

In the county of Greene are Athens, Cairo, Catskill, Coxsackie, Durham, Hunter, Greenville, Lexington, Halcott, New Baltimore, Windham, Prattsville, Ashland and Jewett.

In the county of Columbia are Ancram, Austerlitz, Canaan, Chatham, Claverack, Clermont, Copake, Germantown, Ghent, Hinsdale, Kinderhook, New Lebanon, Livingston, Stuyvesant, Taghkanick, Gallatin, Stockport and Greenport.

In the county of Albany are Bern, Bethlehem, Coeymans, Guilderland, Knox, Rensselaerville, Watervliet, Westerlo and New Scotland.

In the county of Rensselaer are Berlin, Brunswick, Grafton, Greenbush, North Greenbush, East Greenbush, Hosick, Lansingburgh, Nassau, Petersburgh, Pittstown, Sand Lake, Schaghticoke, Schodack, Stephentown and Poestenkill.

In the county of Schoharie are Blenheim, Broome, Carlisle, Cobleskill, Fulton, Jefferson, Middleburgh, Schoharie, Sharon, Summit, Conesville, Seward, Esperance, Wright, Gilboa and Richmondville.

In the county of Schenectady are Duanesburgh, Glenville, Niskayuna, Princetown and Rotterdam.

In the county of Saratoga are Ballston, Charlton, Clifton Park, Corinth, Day, Edinburgh, Galway, Greenfield, Hadley, Halfmoon, Malta, Milton, Moreau, Northumberland, Providence, Saratoga, Saratoga Springs, Stillwater, Waterford and Wilton.

In the county of Montgomery are Amsterdam, Canajoharie, Charleston, Florida, Glen, Minden, Palatine, Rook, Mohawk and St. Johnsville.

In the county of Fulton are Broadalbin, Ephratah, Johnstown, Mayfield, Northampton, Oppenheim, Stratford, Bleecker, Perth and Caroga.

In the county of Hamilton are Hope, Lake Pleasant, Wells, Morehouse, Arietta, Long Lake, Gilman and Indian Lake.

In the county of Washington are Argyle, Cambridge, Dresden, Easton, Fort Ann, Fort Edward, Granville, Greenwich, Hampton, Hartford, Hebron, Jackson, Kingsbury, Putnam, Salem, White Creek and Whitehall.

In the county of Warren are Thurman, Stony Creek, Bolton, Caldwell, Chester, Hague, Johnsburgh, Luzerne, Queensbury, Warrenburgh and Holicon.

In the county of Essex are Chesterfield, Crown Point, Essex, Elizabethtown, Jay, Keene, North Elba, Lewis, Minerva, Moriah, Newcomb, Schroon, Ticonderoga, Westport, Willsborough, Wilmington, St. Armand and North Hudson.

In the county of Clinton are Beekmantown, Dannemora, Champlain, Chazy, Altona, Mooers, Peru, Plattsburgh, Saranac, Ellenburgh, Au Sable, Black Brook, Clinton and Schuyler Falls.

In the county of Franklin are Bangor, Brandon, Chateaugay, Constable, Dickinson, Duane, Fort

Covington, Malone, Moira, Westville, Bellmont, Bombay, Franklin, Harrietstown and Burke.

In the county of St. Lawrence are Brasher, Canton, De Kalb, De Puyster, Edwards, Fowler, Gouverneur, Hammond, Hopkinton, Lawrence, Lisbon, Louisville, Madrid, Massena, Morristown, Norfolk, Oswegatchie, Parishville, Pierrepont, Potsdam, Rossie, Russell, Stockholm, Hermon, Pitcairn, Macomb, Colton and Fine.

In the county of Herkimer are Columbia, Danube, Fairfield, Frankfort, German Flatts, Herkimer, Litchfield, Manheim, Newport, Norway, Russia, Salisbury, Schuyler, Starks, Warren, Winfield, Little Falls, Wilmurt and Ohio.

In the county of Oneida are Annsville, Augusta, Boonsville, Bridgewater, Camden, Deerfield, Florence, Floyd, Lee, Paris, Remsen, Rome, Sangerfield, Steuben, Trenton, Vernon, Verona, Vienna, Western, Westmoreland, Whitestown, Kirkland, New Hartford, Marshall, Marcy and Ava.

In the county of Madison are Brookfield, Cazenovia, De Ruyter, Eaton, Fenner, Georgetown, Hamilton, Lebanon, Lenox, Madison, Nelson, Smithfield, Sullivan and Stockbridge.

In the county of Oswego are Albion, Boylston, Constantia, Granby, Hannibal, Hastings, Mexico, New Haven, Orwell, Parish, Redfield, Richland,

Sandy Creek, Scriba, Volney, Williamstown, Amboy, Palermo, Schroeppel and West Monroe.

In the county of Lewis are Greig, Denmark, Lowville, Harrisburgh, Leyden, Martinsburgh, Pinckney, Turin, Watson, West Turin, Diana, Croghan, Osceola, New Bremen, Montague, High Market and Lewis.

In the county of Jefferson are Adams, Alexandria, Antwerp, Brownville, Champion, Ellisburgh, Henderson, Hounsfield, Le Ray, Lorraine, Lyme, Orleans, Pamelia, Philadelphia, Rodman, Rutland, Watertown, Wilna, Clayton, Theresa, Worth and Cape Vincent.

In the county of Otsego are Burlington, Butternuts, Cherry Valley, Roseboom, Decatur, Edmeston, Exeter, Hartwick, Laurens, Maryland, Middlefield, Milford, New Lisbon, Otego, Oneonta, Otsego, Pittsfield, Plainfield, Richfield, Springfield, Unadilla, Westford, Worcester and Morris.

In the county of Chenango are Bainbridge, Afton, Columbus, Coventry, Guilford, German, Greene, Lincklaen, Macdonough, New Berlin, Norwich, Otselic, Oxford, Pharsalia, Pitcher, Plymouth, Preston, Sherburne, Smithville, Smyrna and North Norwich.

In the county of Broome are Chenango, Binghamton, Port Crane, Colesville, Conklin, Lisle,

Sanford, Union, Vestal, Windsor, Triangle, Barker, Nanticoke and Maine.

In the county of Cortland are Cincinnatus, Freetown, Marathon, Homer, Preble, Scott, Solon, Taylor, Truxton, Virgil, Willet, Cortlandville, La Peer, Harford and Cuyler.

In the county of Tompkins are Caroline, Danby, Dryden, Enfield, Ithaca, Groton, Hector, Lansing, Newfield and Ulysses.

In the county of Tioga are Barton, Berkshire, Candor, Newark, Nichols, Owego, Spencer, Tioga and Richford.

In the county of Chemung are Big Flats, Catlin, Chemung, Baldwin, Elmira, Horseheads, Erin, Van Etten, Southport and Veteran.

In the county of Steuben are Addison, Bath, Cameron, Canisteo, Cohocton, Dansville, Erwin, Greenwood, Hornby, Hornellsville, Howard, Jasper, Corning, Prattsburgh, Pulteney, Troupsburgh, Urbana, Wayne, Wheeler, Woodhull, Rathbone, Bradford, Campbell, Lindley, Caton, Avoca, Hartsville, Thurston, West Union, Wayland and Fremont.

In the county of Schuyler are Orange, Tyrone, Reading, Catharine, Dix, Cayuga and Hector.

In the county of Onondaga are Camillus, Cicero,

Clay, Fabius, La Fayette, Lysander, Manlius, Marcellus, Onondaga, Otisco, Pompey, Salina, Spafford, Tully, Elbridge, Van Buren, Skaneateles, De Witt and Geddes.

In the county of Cayuga are Aurelius, Brutus, Cato, Conquest, Fleming, Genoa, Ira, Ledyard, Locke, Mentz, Owasco, Sennett, Scipio, Sempronius, Springport, Stirling, Venice, Victory, Summer Hill, Moravia, Niles, Montezuma and Throop.

In the county of Seneca are Covert, Fayette, Junius, Lodi, Ovid, Romulus, Tyre, Waterloo, Seneca Falls and Varick.

In the county of Ontario are East Bloomfield, West Bloomfield, Bristol, Canandaigua, Farmington, Gorham, Hopewell, Manchester, Naples, Phelps, Richmond, Seneca, Victor, Canadice and South Bristol.

In the county of Yates are Barrington, Benton, Italy, Jerusalem, Middlesex, Milo, Torrey, Starkey and Potter.

In the county of Wayne are Arcadia, Butler, Galen, Lyons, Macedon, Marion, Ontario, Palmyra, Huron, Rose, Savannah, Sodus, Williamson, Wolcott and Walworth.

In the county of Livingston are Avon, Caledonia, Conesus, Genesco, Groveland, Leicester Lima, Livonia, Mount Morris, Sparta, West

Sparta, North Dansville, Nunda, Portage, Springwater, York and Ossian.

In the county of Monroe are Brighton, Chili, Clarkson, Union, Gates, Greece, Henrietta, Mendon, Ogden, Parma, Penfield, Perrington, Pittsford, Riga, Rush, Sweden, Wheatland, Irondequoit and Webster.

In the county of Genesee are Alabama, Alexander, Batavia, Bethany, Bergen, Byron, Elba, Le Roy, Pembroke, Stafford, Darien, Pavilion and Oakfield.

In the county of Wyoming are Attica, Bennington, Castile, China, Covington, Gainesville, Middlebury, Orangeville, Perry, Sheldon, Warsaw, Wethersfield, Java, Eagle, Pike and Genesee Falls.

In the county of Orleans are Barre, Carlton, Clarendon, Gaines, Murray, Ridgeway, Shelby, Yates and Kendall.

In the county of Niagara are Cambria, Hartland, Lewiston, Lockport, New Fane, Niagara, Pendleton, Porter, Royalton, Somerset, Wilson and Wheatfield.

In the county of Erie are Alden, Amherst, Aurora, Boston, Clarence, Concord, Collins, North Collins, Colden, Eden, Newstead, Evans, Hamburgh, Holland, Sardinia, Wales, Marilla, Lancaster, Elma, Tonawanda, Grand Island, Black Rock, Chicktawauga, Brandt, Ellicot and West Seneca.

In the county of Allegany are Allen, Alfred, Almond, Andover, Angelica, Belfast, Bolivar, Burns, Caneadea, Centerville, Cuba, Friendship, Grove, New Hudson, Hume, Independence, Rushford, Scio, Willing, Wellsville, Birdsall, Amity, Ward, Genesee, West Almond, Clarksville, Wirt, Granger and Alma.

In the county of Cattaraugus are Ashford, Connewango, Ellicottville, Farmersville, Franklinville, Freedom, Great Valley, Hinsdale, Little Valley, Bucktooth, Machias, Napoli, Olean, Otto, East Otto, Perrysburgh, Randolph, Yorkshire, Lyndon, New Albion, Mansfield, Allegany, Leon, Persia, Dayton, Humphrey, Coldspring, Portville, Carrollton, Ischua and South Valley.

In the county of Chautauqua are Busti, Carrol, Kiantone, Chautauqua, Clymer, Ellery, Ellicott, Ellington, Gerry, Hanover, Harmony, Mina, Pomfret, Portland, Ripley, Sheridan, Stockton, Villenova, Westfield, Charlotte, French Creek, Arkwright, Cherry Creek, Poland and Sherman.

Cities of the state.

§ 28. There are in the state the following cities, the boundaries and divisions whereof remain as now declared by statute:

New York; county of New York.

Albany; in the county of Albany.

Hudson; in the county of Columbia.

Schenectady; in the county of Schenectady.

Troy; in the county of Rensselaer.

Utica; in the county of Oneida.

Buffalo; in the county of Erie.

Brooklyn; in the county of Kings.

Rochester; in the county of Monroe.

Syracuse; in the county of Onondaga.

Auburn; in the county of Cayuga.

Oswego; in the county of Oswego.

Poughkeepsie; in the county of Dutchess.

§ 29. There are in the state the following villages established and bounded by special statutes: Villages of the state.

In the county of Albany, West Troy.

In the county of Allegany, Angelica.

In the county of Broome, Binghamton.

In the county of Cattaraugus, Ellicottville and Olean.

In the county of Cayuga, Aurora, Moravia, Port Byron and Weedsport.

In the county of Chautauqua, Dunkirk, Fredonia, Jamestown, Mayville and Westfield.

In the county of Chemung, Elmira and Horseheads.

In the county of Chenango, Bainbridge, Greene,

New Berlin, Norwich, Oxford, Sherburne and Smyrna.

In the county of Clinton, Clintonville and Plattsburgh.

In the county of Columbia, Kinderhook.

In the county of Cortland, Homer.

In the county of Delaware, Delhi and Deposit.

In the county of Dutchess, Pleasant Valley and Rhinebeck.

In the county of Erie, Auroraville, Black Rock, Ebenezer and Springville.

In the county of Fulton, Johnstown and Rawsonville.

In the county of Genesee, Alexander, Batavia and Le Roy.

In the county of Greene, Athens and Catskill.

In the county of Herkimer, Herkimer, Little Falls, Mohawk and Newport.

In the county of Jefferson, Brownville, Carthage, Sackett's Harbor and Watertown.

In the county of Livingston, Dansville, Geneseo and Mount Morris.

In the county of Madison, Canastota, Cazenovia, Chittenango, Clarkville, De Ruyter, Hamilton, Madison, Morrisville and Sullivan.

In the county of Monroe, Brockport, Honeoye Falls, Mendon and Pittsford.

In the county of Montgomery, Amsterdam, Canajoharie and Fort Plain.

In the county of Niagara, Lewiston and Lockport.

In the county of Oneida, Bridgewater, Camden, Clinton, Oneida Castle, Remsen, Rome, Trenton, Vernon and Whitesborough.

In the county of Onondaga, Fayetteville, Geddes, Jordan, Liverpool, Manlius and Skaneateles.

In the county of Ontario, Canandaigua, Clifton Springs and Geneva.

In the county of Orange, Goshen, Montgomery, Newburgh and Walden.

In the county of Orleans, Albion, Gaines, Knowersville and Medina.

In the county of Oswego, Cleveland, Constantia, Fulton and Pulaski.

In the county of Otsego, Cherry Valley, Cooperstown, Laurens and Unadilla.

In the county of Putnam, Coldspring.

In the county of Queens, Astoria, Flushing and Jamaica.

In the county of Rensselaer, Castleton, Greenbush, Hoosick Falls, Lansingburgh and Nassau.

In the county of Richmond, Tompkinsville.

In the county of St. Lawrence, Canton, Ogdensburgh, Potsdam and Waddington.

In the county of Saratoga, Ballston Spa, Galway, Saratoga Springs, Schuylerville, Stillwater and Waterford.

In the county of Schoharie, Esperance.

In the county of Schuyler, Havana and Watkins.

In the county of Seneca, Seneca Falls and Waterloo.

In the county of Steuben, Bath.

In the county of Suffolk, Greenport and Sag Harbor.

In the county of Sullivan, Bloomingburgh and Monticello.

In the county of Tioga, Owego.

In the county of Tompkins, Ithaca.

In the county of Ulster, Kingston and Rondout.

In the county of Warren, Glens Falls.

In the county of Washington, Argyle, Fort Ann, Salem, Sandy Hill, Union Village and Whitehall.

In the county of Wayne, Clyde, Lyons, Newark and Palmyra.

In the county of Westchester, Peekskill, Portchester, Sing Sing and Yonkers.

In the county of Wyoming, Attica, Perry and Warsaw.

In the county of Yates, Penn Yan.

Other villages have been established under the general law for the incorporation of villages, passed the 7th day of December, 1848 ; the names of which with their boundaries are recorded in the offices of the clerks of their respective counties.

In the New York Civil List (1859, p. 33, note) it is stated that the village of Bridgewater, in Oneida county, is not now considered a corporation.

PART III.

TITLE I.

PUBLIC OFFICERS.

CHAPTER I.

CLASSIFICATION.

§ 30. The public officers of the state are classified as:

1. Legislative;
2. Executive;
3. Judicial;
4. Ministerial officers and officers of the courts;

But this classification shall not be construed as defining the legal powers of either class.

1 R. S., 304, § 1.

CHAPTER II.

LEGISLATIVE OFFICERS

ARTICLE I.

NUMBER, DESIGNATION AND MODE OF ELECTION.

Number and designation.

§ 31. The Legislative officers are:

Thirty-two senators;

One hundred and twenty-eight members of assembly;

A speaker of the assembly, from its own body;

For each house, a clerk, a sergeant-at-arms, a doorkeeper and so many other subordinate officers as each house respectively may deem necessary.

1 R. S., 304, § 1.

§ 32. The time and manner of election and term of office of the senators are prescribed by the Constitution. Each senate district chooses one senator. Mode of election of senators.

1 R. S., 308, §§ 1, 2.

§ 33. The time and manner of election and term of office of the members of Assembly are prescribed by the Constitution. The number of members to be chosen in the several counties is as follows: Mode of election of members of assembly.

In the county of Albany, four.
In the county of Allegany, two.
In the county of Broome, one.
In the county of Cattaraugus, two.
In the county of Cayuga, two.
In the county of Chautauqua, two.
In the county of Chemung, one.
In the county of Chenango, two.
In the county of Clinton, one.
In the county of Columbia, two.
In the county of Cortland, one.
In the county of Delaware, two.
In the county of Dutchess, two.
In the county of Erie, four.
In the county of Essex, one.
In the county of Franklin, one.
In the counties of Fulton and Hamilton, one.
In the county of Genesee, one.
In the county of Greene, one.

In the county of Herkimer, two,

In the county of Jefferson, three.

In the county of Kings, seven.

In the county of Lewis, one.

In the county of Livingston, two.

In the county of Madison, two.

In the county of Monroe, three.

In the county of Montgomery, one.

In the city and county of New York, seventeen.

In the county of Niagara, two.

In the county of Oneida, four.

In the county of Onondaga, three.

In the county of Ontario, two.

In the county of Orange, two.

In the county of Orleans, one.

In the county of Oswego, three.

In the county of Otsego, two.

In the county of Putnam, one.

In the county of Queens, two.

In the county of Rensselaer, three.

In the county of Richmond, one.

In the county of Rockland, one.

In the county of St. Lawrence, three.

In the county of Saratoga, two.

In the county of Schenectady, one.

In the county of Schoharie, one.

In the county of Schuyler, one.

In the county of Seneca, one.

In the county of Steuben, three.
In the county of Suffolk, two.
In the county of Sullivan, one.
In the county of Tioga, one.
In the county of Tompkins, one.
In the county of Ulster, three.
In the county of Warren, one.
In the county of Washington, two.
In the county of Wayne, two.
In the county of Westchester, three.
In the county of Wyoming, one.
In the county of Yates, one.

1 R. S., 308, § 2, amended; Laws of 1857, ch. 337, § 1.

§ 34. The remaining legislative officers are chosen by each house as prescribed by the Constitution. When the lieutenant-governor acts as governor, or is absent from the senate, it must choose a temporary president from its own body, to serve during his disability or absence. In case it devolves upon such temporary president to act as governor, the senate must choose from its own body another person to preside. Election or appointment of other legislative officers.

1 R. S., 309, §§ 6, 7

ARTICLE II.

GENERAL PROVISIONS RELATING TO LEGISLATIVE OFFICERS.

Legislative officers' privilege from arrest.

§ 35. Every member and every officer of either house is privileged from arrest in civil actions, while attending upon its sessions, and every member is thus privileged for fourteen days previous and subsequent to each session, and while absent, during the session, with leave of the house. But this privilege does not exempt him from arrest in an action for a forfeiture, misdemeanor, or breach of trust in any office or public employment.

Power of legislature to punish for offenses.

§ 36. Each house may punish, by imprisonment, as for a contempt, the following offenses, and no others:

1. The arrest of any of its members or officers in violation of the last section, in which case it may also discharge the person arrested;

2. Disorderly conduct in the immediate view and presence of the house, tending to interrupt its proceedings, or impair the respect due to its authority;

3. The publication of a false and malicious report of its proceedings, or of the conduct of a member, in his legislative capacity;

4. The giving or offering of a bribe to a member,

or attempting by menace, or other corrupt means, directly or indirectly, to influence a member in giving or withholding his vote, or in not attending the house of which he is a member;

5. Neglect to attend or to be examined as a witness, when duly required to give testimony in legislative proceedings.

But no imprisonment by either house shall extend beyond the same session of the legislature.

§ 37. The compensation of the several officers of the two houses shall be the following, beyond which no allowance or other compensation shall be paid to any of them for any service whatever, viz.: Compensation of clerks &c.

To the clerk of each house, twelve hundred dollars per annum, payable on the adjournment of the legislature, and fifty dollars for attending the opening of the next legislature;

To each of the assistant clerks, not exceeding three in the senate, and four in the assembly, six hundred dollars;

To the sergeant-at-arms and door-keeper of each house, and to the librarian of the assembly, and to one assistant to each of them, the same compensation and mileage as to a member of the legislature;

To each of the messengers of either house, not

exceeding three for the senate and ten for the assembly, one dollar for each day's actual attendance in the performance of his duties.

Certificate of amount of compensation of legislative officers.

§ 38. The compensation of the members of the legislature, and of the officers of the two houses, shall be paid upon the certificate of the presiding officer of the house to which the member or officer belongs; and if the compensation depend upon the number of days' attendance, or if mileage be allowed, the certificate shall state the estimated distance of the place of meeting from the residence of the member or officer, and the number of days' attendance, including the time after his arrival at the place of meeting, or on his way thither, during which he is prevented by illness from attending.

Supplies.

§ 39. The clerk of each house shall furnish its members, officers and reporters with stationery, writing materials, and newspapers, not exceeding in the aggregate amount thirty dollars for each person. These may be furnished by the clerk, by his giving to the persons entitled thereto written orders on the publishers or venders of the newspapers designated by such person, or upon any stationer or bookseller designated by such person, for the articles to be supplied; such orders returned to the clerk, accompanied by the certificate of the person in whose favor it was drawn, that he had received such articles, shall be a sufficient voucher to the clerk, and from him to the comptroller, of the delivery thereof. The clerk shall also, under the direction and subject to the approval of the comptroller, purchase such furniture as may be necessary for the house of which he is clerk, including the Legislative Manual, pay the postage of the letters, papers and documents sent or received by members, and the expenses of transmitting the journals and documents of the two houses to members and officers.

Laws of 1859, ch. 1.

§ 40. The clerk of each house shall, at the end of each month during the sessions, account to the comptroller for all moneys received up to that time; and, within ten days of the close of the session, shall file with the comptroller an abstract, in such form and containing such particulars as the comptroller shall direct, of all newspapers ordered by him for the members, and of all other expenditures by him, with the vouchers therefor; and shall give him satisfactory evidence that the expenditures were reasonable. Clerks to account to comptroller.

§ 41. All payments made pursuant to this article shall be made out of the general fund, and there shall be no appropriation for a contingent fund for the legislature or for either house. Neither house shall, without the consent of the other, order to be printed more than four thousand Limitation on certain expenses.

copies of any paper; or the purchase of any books, the aggregate amount of which shall exceed one hundred dollars; or appoint any committee of its own members or others at the public expense, except in case of contested elections; or incur any expense whatever, except as provided in this article, and except the reasonable expense of witnesses and commissioners to take testimony when required, as provided in this Code.

Clerk's bond.

§ 42. The clerk of each house, before entering upon his office, shall execute a bond to the people, with such security as the comptroller shall approve, conditioned for the faithful performance of all the duties of his office, and accounting for all moneys that may come to his hands by virtue thereof.

Clerk's duties.

§ 43. The clerk of each house shall keep a true record of all its proceedings, and take charge of and keep on file all documents of that house, and those presented to it, and prepare indexes to the journals and documents, and deliver to the secretary of state, duly certified, an engrossed copy of all acts and joint resolutions which originated in the house of which he is clerk. But either house may authorize title-deeds or other original documents, belonging to any person, to be delivered to him.

ARTICLE III.

TAKING TESTIMONY IN LEGISLATIVE PROCEEDINGS.

§ 44. Every legislative committee, whether it be a committee of either house or a joint committee of the two houses, may take the testimony of any witness voluntarily appearing before it for examination; and when authorized to send for persons or papers, may issue subpœnas to compel the attendance of witnesses in this state, or commissions to examine witnesses who are out of this state, or unable to attend the committee, or excused from attendance; such subpœnas and commissions to be in the form used by the courts, and to be served and executed in like manner; but the testimony shall be private unless otherwise ordered by the legislature or the house appointing the committee.

Power of committees to subpœna and examine witnesses.

§ 45. Upon the application of any person desirous to obtain testimony respecting the election of any member of either house, for the purpose of contesting an election, or resisting a contest thereof, any county judge, or mayor, or recorder of any city, shall issue a subpœna directed to the witnesses named by the applicant, requiring their attendance before him, at a specified time and

Proceedings in contest of elections.

place, to be examined respecting such election; and he shall also, at the same time, deliver to the applicant a notice to the opposite party, stating the name and purpose of the applicant and the time and place fixed for the examination, and the names of the witnesses to be examined.

Services of process; returning of testimony.

§ 46. The subpœna and notice shall be served in the manner required for subpœnas and notices in civil actions; the witnesses shall be entitled to the like fees; the examination shall be conducted in the like manner as the examination of witnesses conditionally in civil actions; and the testimony, together with the subpœna notice, and proof of service, shall be certified by the officer, and inclosed under seal to the clerk of the house to which the election pertains.

ARTICLE IV.

ENACTMENT OF STATUTES.

Notice of application for statutes.

§ 47. All persons intending to apply to the legislature:

1. To divide or alter the bounds of a county, city or village, or to erect a new county, or to incorporate a new city or village;

2. To remove a court-house;

3. To impose a tax for making or improving a road, or for any other local purpose in any county, whereby any of the inhabitants of such county may be subjected to taxation;

4. To authorize the construction of a dam on any public water;

5. To create a corporation, or to amend the charter of a corporation;

6. To release lands escheated to the state;

Shall give public notice of their intention to make such application, specifying the nature and object thereof, by advertisement, published at least once a week for six weeks immediately before the application, in the state paper and in a newspaper printed in each county where the object of the application is to be carried into effect; or, in the cases mentioned in the fifth and six subdivisions, in the county where the corporation is, or is to be, established, or where the lands lie. If the application be for an act of incorporation, the notice must specify the amount of capital required; and if for an amendment of a charter, it must state specifically the amendment desired. If the application be within the first subdivision of this section, before the legislature act upon it, the applicants shall lay before them an accurate survey and map of the territory described, verified by the oath of the surveyor making the same; and in case any law is passed upon the application, the survey and map shall be filed in the office of the surveyor-general.

1 R. S., 371, §§ 1 to 7. Ib., 402, § 3. Ib., 291, §§ 1 to 3.

Certificates of the enactment.

§ 48. When the governor approves a bill he shall indorse thereon a certificate of his approval and deliver it to the secretary of state. When a bill is passed by either house, by the votes of two-thirds of all the members present, notwithstanding the objections of the governor, the presiding officer shall indorse thereon a certificate of such passage; and when so passed by both houses, the presiding officer of the house last passing it, shall deliver it so indorsed to the secretary of state.

1 R. S., 372, § 4, last clause; 373, § 6, and last clause of § 7.

Certificate of mode of passage.

§ 49. No bill shall be deemed to have been passed by the votes of two-thirds of all the members present, nor to have been passed when three-fifths of all the members elected to each house were present, unless so certified by the presiding officer of each house.

1 R. S., 375, § 25; Laws of 1847, 276, § 1.

This provision we have modified by extending it to the case of bills to the passage of which a two-third vote of all the members present is required. That it should be made applicable to that case appears from 1 R. S., 374, § 16.

Secretary of state's indorsement.

§ 50. The secretary of state shall receive every bill passed, and indorse upon it his certificate of the day, month and year when it became a law, and deposit the same, so indorsed, in his office; and such certificate shall be conclusive evidence of the facts therein declared.

1 R. S., 373, §§ 10, 11.

ARTICLE V.

PROMULGATION OF STATUTES.

§ 51. The secretary of state, within thirty days after each session of the legislature, must cause to be printed by the printer of the statutes, and published, all the laws and joint resolutions passed at such session; and each volume shall contain his certificate that it was printed under his direction. In the printing he shall omit the certificate required by section 50 to be indorsed upon the original bills; but he shall insert immediately after the title of each law the word "passed," adding the day, month and year. If the bill was duly certified as passed by the votes of two-thirds of the members present in each house, he shall further add "by a two-third vote." If it was duly certified as passed when three-fifths of all the members

Secretary of state to cause statutes to be published.

elected to each house were present, he shall add "three-fifths being present."

1 R. S., 373, §§ 13, 14, 15; 375, § 25, last clause.

Evidence of mode of passage.

§ 52. The addition, "*by a two-third vote*" or "*three-fifths being present*," in the printed volume, is presumptive evidence that the bill was duly certified to have been so passed, and the absence of such addition is presumptive evidence that it was not so certified.

1 R. S., 374, § 16; 375, § 26.

List of officers to be published.

§ 53. There shall be prefixed to the statutes published in each year the names and residence of the governor, the lieutenant-governor, senators and members of assembly, and presiding officers of both houses, in office at the time of the passage of such statutes.

1 R. S., 375, § 30.

Distribution of statutes.

§ 54. The statutes so published are to be distributed by the secretary of state, in the mode directed in article IV of chapter III of this title, entitled "*General provisions respecting the secretary of state.*"

Statutes to be transmitted to each county.

§ 55. The secretary of state shall transmit, in the order in which they are passed, to each county treasurer in the state, copies of all general statutes and of such local statutes as relate to the affairs of such county; and each treasurer shall cause the same to be published in the papers designated, as provided in the next section, the expense of which, not exceeding twenty cents for each folio, will be a county charge.

1 R. S., 374, §§ 20, 21, 23.

§ 56. The board of supervisors of each county shall, at their annual meeting, designate two papers to publish these statutes in their county, as follows: Each member of the board shall designate, by ballot, one newspaper printed in the county, and the paper having the highest number of ballots and that having the next highest, shall be the two papers designated. In case there be but one paper printed in the county, the publication shall be in that paper. Designation of county paper.

1 R. S., 374, § 22.

§ 57. The publication of all statutes thus published must be completed within four months after the final adjournment of the legislature in each year; and the whole of every statute which, in the ordinary type of the paper in which it is published, would not occupy more than two columns, must be published in one issue thereof, and when it exceeds that space it must be published as rapidly as it may be, by occupying that space in each successive issue. Time of publication.

1 R. S, 375, § 29.

§ 58. The secretary of state shall also publish, as soon after the adjournment of the legislature as possible, all the general statutes, in a cheap General statutes in pamphlet form.

pamphlet form, and send them to the county clerks and supervisors for distribution, in the proportion of one for each hundred persons in the county.

This provision, in its application to all general statutes, is new.

ARTICLE VI.

OPERATION OF STATUTES.

When statutes take effect.

§ 59. Every statute, unless a different time is prescribed therein, takes effect on the twentieth day after its final passage.

1 R. S., 373, § 12.

Effect of amendment.

§ 60. Where a section or part of a statute is amended, it is not to be considered as having been repealed and re-enacted in the amended form; but the portions which are not altered are to be considered as having been the law, from the time when they were enacted, and the new provisions are to be considered as having been enacted at the time of the amendment.

Court of Appeals, 1857, Ely *v.* Holton, 15 N. Y. R. (1 E. P. Smith's), 595.

Construction of statutes.

§ 61. The rules for the construction of statutes are contained in the Code of Civil Procedure.

§ 62. Any statute may be repealed at any time, except when it is otherwise provided therein. Parties acting under any statute shall be deemed to have acted in contemplation of this power of repeal. Repeal of statutes.

CHAPTER III.

EXECUTIVE OFFICERS.

ARTICLE I.

CLASSIFICATION, NUMBER AND DESIGNATION OF EXECUTIVE OFFICERS.

§ 63. Executive officers are either: Classification.

1. Civil, or

2. Military.

Civil executive officers are:

1. General, for the whole state;

2. Special, for special duties in different parts of the state;

3. Local, for a particular part of the state.

Military officers.

§ 64. Military officers are designated and regulated by the militia laws.

Number and designation.

§ 65. The number and designation of the civil executive officers are as follows:

A governor;

A private secretary for the governor;

A lieutenant-governor;

A secretary of state;

A comptroller;

A treasurer;

An attorney-general;

A state engineer and surveyor;[1]

A bank superintendent;[2]

An insurance superintendent;[3]

A state superintendent of public instruction;[4]

A deputy for each of the eight last mentioned officers;[5]

A state superintendent of weights and measures;[6]

An inspector of gas meters;[7]

Twenty-two regents of the university;

Three canal commissioners;[8]

An auditor of the canal department;[8]

[1] 1 R. S., 304.

[2] Ib., 1168.

[3] Laws of 1859, p. 882.

[4] Laws of 1854, ch. 97.

[5] 1 R. S., 387, § 27; 391, § 21; 396, § 6; Laws of 1854, ch. 288; 1 R. S. 1169; Laws of 1859, p. 882.

[6] 1 R. S., 306.

[7] Laws of 1859, ch. 311.

[8] 1 R. S., 425, § 12.

Three canal appraisers;[1]

Three state assessors, who with the commissioners of the land office constitute the board of equalization;[2]

Two loan commissioners in each county for loaning certain moneys of the United States, who may be designated as the loan commissioners for the county for which they are appointed;[3]

Three inspectors of state prisons;[1]

A superintendent of the Onondaga Salt Springs;

An agent for the Onondaga Indians;[4]

A superintendent of the Brothertown Indians;

A commissioner for the St. Regis Indians;[5]

A receiver of the profits of the state pier at Sag Harbor;[1]

So many directors of incorporated banks as the state is authorized by acts of incorporation to appoint;[1]

A county treasurer for each county except that of New York;[6]

A health officer, a resident physician, and a health commissioner, for the city and county of New York,[7] and for the cities of Albany and Hudson;

[1] R. S., 306.
[2] Laws of 1859, ch. 312.
[3] R. S., 564, §§ 4, 7.
[4] Ib.. 307.
[5] 1 R. S., 306, 686.
[6] Laws of 1858, ch. 368.
[7] Ib., 304; 326, § 24.

A health officer for each county except that of New York;[1]

Three commissioners of excise in each county who constitute a board, designated as the board of commissioners of excise of such county;[2]

Fifteen wreck-masters in the county of Suffolk; twelve in the county of Queens; three in the county of Kings; two in the county of Richmond, and two in the county of Westchester;[3]

A county sealer of weights and measures of each county;[4]

A town sealer of weights and measures of each town;

Three inspectors of plank and turnpike roads in each county in which there is any such road;[5]

Eleven harbor-masters for the port of New York,[6] and one for the port of Albany;[7]

Nine port-wardens who constitute a board, designated as the port-wardens of the port of New York, and two special wardens for that port;[8]

Five commissioners of police for the metropolitan police district, who together with the mayors of

[1] 1 R. S., 307.
[2] Laws of 1857, ch. 628.
[3] 2 R. S., 104, § 28.
[4] 1 R. S., 306.
[5] 1 R. S., 1104, § 98.
[6] Ib., 304.
[7] Ib., 1062, § 10.
[8] Laws of 1857, ch. 405.

the cities of Brooklyn and New York, constitute the board of police for that district;[1]

Five pilot commissioners in the city of New York who constitute a board, designated as the board of commissioners of pilots.[2]

One, two, or three inspectors of damaged goods, whenever their appointment is necessary in each of the cities of Albany, Troy and Hudson, and in each other county, except that of New York, Kings and Richmond;[3]

Such other officers as are chosen to fill offices created by or under the authority of the general laws for the government of counties, cities, towns and villages, or of the charters or special laws respecting the same; or of the Health Laws, the School Laws, the Militia Laws, the Election Laws, the Poor Laws and the Fiscal Laws.

[1] Laws of 1857, ch. 569.
[2] Laws of 1853, ch. 497.
[3] From 1 R. S., 1070, § 14.

ARTICLE II.

MODE OF ELECTION OR APPOINTMENT, AND TERM OF OFFICE.

Certain executive officers elected.

§ 66. The mode of election of the governor, the lieutenant-governor, the secretary of state, the comptroller, the treasurer, the attorney-general, the state engineer and surveyor, the canal commissioners and the inspectors of state prisons, is prescribed by the Constitution.

Const., art V, XIV.

County treasurer.

§ 67. The county treasurer in each county is elected at a general election, enters upon the duties of his office on the first day of January next after his election, and holds his office for three years.

1 R. S., 326, § 17.

1 R. S., 326, § 17. In the county of Kings, by § 19, Ib., and in the county of Monroe, by Laws of 1859, ch. 26, the county treasurer enters upon his office at a different time; but the rule, it is supposed, ought to be uniform.

State Superintendent of public instruction.

§ 68. The state superintendent of public instruction is chosen by joint ballot of the senate and assembly, on the first Tuesday in April, in the year 1860, and in every third year thereafter.

School Laws, 1 R. S., Laws of 1854, ch, 97.

§ 69. The governor, the lieutenant-governor, the secretary of state and the state superintendent of public instruction are regents of the university by right of office. The other regents are chosen by the joint ballot of the senate and assembly, and may be removed by joint resolution. Regents of the university.

1 R. S., 863, § 4; Laws of 1854, ch. 97.

§ 70. The state superintendent of weights and measures is appointed by the governor, lieutenant-governor and secretary of state, or any two of them, at a meeting called for that purpose by the secretary of state. State superintendent of weights and measures.

2 R. S., 4, §§ 16, 18.

§ 71. The following executive officers are appointed by the governor with the consent of the senate:. Officers appointed by the governor with consent of the senate.

The bank superintendent;[1] the insurance superintendent;[2] the canal appraisers;[3] the state assessors;[4] the inspector of gas meters;[5] the loan commissioners for the several counties; the superintendent of the Onondaga salt springs; the harbor-masters for the ports of New York and Albany;[6] the port-wardens and special wardens of the port of New York; the five commissioners of police for the metropolitan police district; the health officer; the resident physician, and the health commissioner for the city and county of New York; the agent for the

[1] 1 R. S., 1168, § 262.
[2] Laws of 1859, ch. 366.
[3] 1 R. S., 325, § 12.
[4] Laws of 1859, ch. 312.
[5] Ib., ch. 311.
[6] 1 R. S., 1062, § 10.

Onondaga tribe of Indians; the superintendent of the Brothertown Indians; and bank directors.[1] During the recess of the senate, the governor may appoint, subject to its subsequent consent.

Their terms of office.

§ 72. The officers enumerated in the last section hold their respective offices for two years, except the inspector of gas meters, who holds his office for five years, the bank superintendent, the insurance superintendent, the canal appraisers, the state assessors and the commissioners of the metropolitan police district, and the port-wardens and special wardens of the port of New York, who hold their respective offices for three years; the superintendent of Onondaga salt springs and bank directors, who hold their offices for one year, and the port-warden of Albany, who holds his office during the governor's pleasure.

1 R. S., 325; Ib., 1168, 262; Laws of 1857, ch. 569: 1 R. S., 1062, § 10: Laws of 1859, chs. 311, 312, 366.
2 Laws of 1857, ch. 538.

State assessors.

§ 73. One of the state assessors is appointed in each year, and their terms of office commence on the first day of April.

Laws of 1859, ch. 312.

Qualifications and term of office of police commissioners.

§ 74. Two of the commissioners of the metropolitan police district are appointed from the city of New York, in the year 1862, and every third year thereafter. One is appointed from the same city, one from the county of Kings, and one from

[1] 1 R. S., 325.

the county of Richmond or Westchester, in the year 1861, and every third year thereafter.

Laws of 1857, ch. 569, § 2.

§ 75. One of the wardens of the port of New York must be a resident of Brooklyn. Three of them must be nautical men. The terms of office of those now in office are fixed by designation pursuant to special statute.[1] No person but a licensed physician shall be appointed to the office of resident physician, health commissioner or health officer of the city of New York.[2] Port-wardens and officers of health of New York.

§ 76. The following executive officers are appointed by the governor alone: Officers appointed by the governor.

Wreck masters; health officers of the cities of Albany and Hudson; the peacemakers of the Brothertown Indians; the receiver of the profits of the state pier at Sag Harbor; the private secretary of the governor.

1 R. S., 326; § 24; Ib., 310, § 6.

§ 77. The officers enumerated in the last section hold their respective offices for two years, except the governor's private secretary, who holds his office during the governor's pleasure. Their terms of office.

1 R. S., 326, § 24; Ib., 310, § 6.

§ 78. The inspectors of damaged goods, whenever their appointment is necessary, are appointed in the cities of Albany, Troy and Hudson, by the Inspectors of damaged goods.

[1] Laws of 1857, ch. 405. [2] 1 R. S., 326, § 22.

mayor or recorder of those cities respectively; and in every other county, except that of New York, Kings and Richmond, by the county judge.

1 R. S., 1070, § 14.

Commissioners of excise.

§ 79. One of the commissioners of excise in each county is appointed on the second Tuesday of May, in the year 1860 and each alternate year thereafter, by the county judge and the two justices of the sessions, or a majority of them, of which the county judge is to be one, at the place where the county courts are required to be held. In case of a vacancy in the office of county judge the appointment is made by the justices of the sessions. In the city and county of New York the appointment is made by the chief justice of the superior court, the first judge of the common pleas, and the recorder, or any two them. Their terms of office commence of the first of January next after the appointment; and all hereafter appointed hold their offices for six years. The terms of those first appointed expire according to a determination made by lot, pursuant to a special statute.

Laws of 1857, ch. 628, § 1.

Inspectors of plank and turnpike roads.

§ 80. The inspectors of plank and turnpike roads are appointed by the boards of supervisors of their respective counties. Those only are to be appointed who are not interested in any such roads in the county.

1 R. S., 1104, § 98.

Sealers of

§ 81. County sealers of weights and measures are

appointed by the boards of supervisors of their county. Town sealers of weights and measures are appointed by the supervisor and the justices of the peace of the town. Weights and measures.

1 R. S., 325, §§ 15, 16.

§ 82. The commissioner for the St. Regis tribe of Indians is appointed by the board of supervisors of the county of Franklin. The mode of his election, his term of office, and his functions, are prescribed by the "*Act for the protection and civilization of the St. Regis Indians*," passed April 19, 1858. Commissioner of the St. Regis Indians.

Laws of 1858, ch. 368, p. 634.

ARTICLE III.

GENERAL PROVISIONS RESPECTING THE GOVERNOR.

SECTION 83. Powers and duties of the governor.
84. Exchanging statutes with other states.
85. Recovery of kidnapped or enslaved citizens.
86. Expenses.
87. Apprehension of criminals.
88. Governor's records.
89. Person acting as governor.

§ 83. In addition to those prescribed by the constitution, the governor has the powers and duties prescribed in this and the following sections: Powers and duties of governor.

1. He is to supervise the official conduct of all executive and ministerial officers;

2. He is to see that all offices are filled, and the duties thereof performed, or in default thereof apply such remedy as the law allows, and if the

remedy is imperfect, acquaint the legislature there with at its next session;

3. He is to make the appointments and supply the vacancies mentioned in this Code;

4. He is the sole official organ of communication between the government of this state and the government of any other state, or of the United States;

5. He has the custody of the great and privy seals of the state, descriptions whereof are deposited in the office of the secretary of state. The privy seal shall be used for military commissions, and all such documents as have issued under the great seal since the sixteenth day of March, seventeen hundred and seventy-eight, shall continue to be issued under the great seal, except copies of records and papers, certified by the secretary of state under his seal of office;

6. Whenever any suit or legal proceeding is pending against this state, or which may affect the title of this state to any property, or which may result in any claim against the state, he may direct the attorney-general to appear on behalf of the state, and may employ such additional counsel as he may judge expedient;

7. He may employ for the executive duties such clerks, not exceeding three, and such messengers, not exceeding two, as he may deem expedient, at a

salary not exceeding six hundred dollars for each person, and may dismiss them at pleasure;

8. He shall have such other powers and perform such other duties as are devolved upon him by this Code, or any other law of this state.

See 1 R. S., 381, §§ 4, 12, 15; Ib., 84, § 3.

§ 84. The governor shall transmit, free of expense, to the executive of each state in the Union, three copies of the statutes of each year and of the reports of the court of appeals as soon as published, and request a similar transmission to be made to him of the statutes and reports of the highest courts of the several states; and when the statutes of a state are received, he shall deposit one copy thereof in the state library, one in the senate chamber, and one in the assembly chamber; if but one copy be received, it shall be deposited in the state library. Exchanging statutes with other states.

1 R. S., 382, §§ 16, 17, 19.

§ 85. Whenever the governor receives information satisfactory to him, that any inhabitant of this state has been kidnapped and taken from this state into any other state or territory of the United States, for the purpose of being there held in slavery, or is wrongfully imprisoned or held in slavery in any such state or territory, on the allegation or pretense that he is a slave, or by color of any usage or rule of law prevailing in such state or territory is deemed to be a slave, or not entitled of Recovery of kidnapped or enslaved citizens.

right to the personal liberty belonging to a citizen, it is the duty of the governor to take such measures as he may deem necessary to procure his liberty and return. And for this purpose he may employ such agent or agents as he may judge expedient, who shall proceed to collect the proper proof to establish the right of such person to freedom, and, under direction of the governor shall take such other measures and proceedings as may be necessary.

1 R. S., 382, §§ 21, 22.

Expenses. § 86. The accounts for all services and expenses incurred in carrying into effect the preceding two sections, shall be audited by the comptroller, and paid by the treasurer, on his warrant, out of any monies in the treasury not otherwise appropriated.

Ib., § 23.

Apprehension of criminals. § 87. The duty of the governor respecting fugitives from justice is prescribed by title IV of part VI of the Code of Criminal Procedure, entitled "*Of proceedings against fugitives from justice.*"

Governor's records. § 88. The governor shall cause to be kept the following records:

1. A register of all applications for pardon or for commutation of any sentence, with a list of the official signatures and recommendations in favor of each application;

2. A separate register of the judges' reports to him of the testimony in capital cases, and of any action he may take thereon;

3. A separate register of all other applications made to him for any official action;

4. An account of all his official expenses and disbursements, including the incidental expenses of his department, and of all rewards offered by him for the apprehension of criminals.

These records and the originals of all applications, petitions, recommendations and reports therein mentioned, shall be preserved in the office of the governor; but whenever an application for appointment to office is refused by him, he may in his discretion return the papers relating to the application.

Laws of 1858, ch. 64, §§ 1, 2, 3.

§ 89. Every provision in the constitution and statutes, in relation to the powers and duties of the governor, and in relation to acts and duties to be performed by others towards him, extends to the persons performing, for the time being, the duties of governor Person acting as governor.

1 R. S., 382, § 20.

ARTICLE IV.

GENERAL PROVISIONS RESPECTING THE SECRETARY OF STATE.

Custody of records.

§ 90. The secretary of state is charged with the custody of all statutes and joint resolutions of the legislature, all documents which pass under the great seal, and of all the books, records, deeds, parchments, maps and papers now deposited in his office, or which may hereafter be there deposited, pursuant to law, and he shall from time to time make all necessary provisions for their arrangement and preservation.

1 R. S., 384, § 1.

General duties of the secretary of state.

§ 91. It is the duty of the secretary of state:

1. To attend at every session of the legislature, for the purpose of receiving bills which shall have become laws, and to perform such other duties as may then be devolved upon him by resolution of the two houses or either of them;

2. To attend the governor whenever required by him, for the purpose of receiving documents which have passed the great seal;

3. To receive and keep all conveyances and mortgages belonging to the state;

4. To receive and record, in proper books, the depositions made or furnished him, as required by law, by resident aliens desirous to take and hold real property.

5. To distribute annually the statutes, the legislative journals and documents, and the reports of the court of appeals as required by section 93;

6. To distribute the acts of congress received at his office, in the same manner as the statutes of this state;

7. To transmit to the clerk of every county and town hereafter erected, a complete set, if possible, of the revised and subsequent statutes, and to the clerk of every new county, a complete set of the reports of the court of appeals; and whenever any volume of the statutes or reports furnished to any county or town is destroyed by fire, to replace it, if possible.

8. To purchase under the direction of the governor such of the statutes and reports, which he is required to distribute, as are not provided for him in some other manner;

9. To transmit annually, in the month of May, to each county clerk, a certified list of licensed pedlars, and a copy of the reports received by him for the preceding year, from the agents of the state prisons.

1 R. S., 384, 385, 386.

§ 92. The original statutes and joint resolutions passed at each session, the secretary of state shall immediately thereafter cause to be bound in volumes of convenient size. He shall also compare with this original a copy of the printed statutes: Preservation of original statutes and corrected copy.

and having noted therein, at the end of each statute or resolution, any error in the printed copy, deposit the same with the original volume in his office. Each such volume shall be lettered on the back with its title and the date of the session. He shall also cause indexes to the statutes to be prepared as soon as practicable after such session of the legislature, and deliver them to the printer of the statutes.

1 R. S., 384, §§ 6, 7.

Distribution of statutes, journals and documents.

§ 93. Immediately after the bills, statutes, journals and documents of any session are bound, in the manner provided for in article IX of this chapter, the secretary of state shall distribute the same as follows;

1. To the clerk of the senate, for the use of the senate, four copies of the bills; and to the clerk of the assembly, for the use of the assembly, eight copies;

2. To the clerk of the senate, for the use of the senate, sixteen copies of the statutes, journals and documents; and to the clerk of the assembly, for the use of the assembly, eighteen copies;

3. To the governor for the use of the executive chamber, to the lieutenant-governor, to each member of the legislature, to each of the clerks of the two houses, to each judge of the court of appeals, to each justice of the supreme court; and to the following for their respective offices: the secretary

of state, the comptroller, the treasurer, the state engineer and surveyor, the attorney-general, the bank and insurance superintendents, the state superintendent of public instruction, the state superintendent of weights and measures, the auditor of the canal department, to each county clerk, to the canal commissioners for their office, the inspectors of state prisons for their office, and to the librarian of the state library, for the use of the library, each one copy of the statutes, journals and documents;[1]

4. To each of the incorporated colleges of the state one copy of the statutes and documents;[2]

5. To the athenæums of the cities of Philadelphia, Boston, New York and Albany, and to the Historical Society of the city of New York, one copy each of the statutes and journals;[3]

6. And, with the advice of the trustees of the state library, to such literary and scientific institutions and societies, not exceeding twenty in number, as in their judgment will preserve the same, and make them most accessible and useful to the public, one copy of the statutes, journals and documents;[4]

7. To each of the following officers, namely: town clerks, for the use of their respective towns; district attorneys, to be delivered to their succes-

[1] R. S., 385, § 8, except subdivisions 4, 5.

[2] Ib., 385, § 10.

[3] 1 R. S., 385, § 9.

[4] Ib., 385, § 12.

sors in office, and supervisors' clerks for the use of the board of supervisors, one copy of the statutes;[1]

8. To the secretary of state of the United States, four copies of the statutes.[2]

All which are to be transmitted at the expense of the state; the statutes, journals and documents, for the use of each county, and for the members of the legislature and other officers therein, to be trans mitted in boxes, to the clerk of each county, and the rest in such manner as the secretary may think best: the statutes to be transmitted within sixty days after the adjournment of the legislature.[3] He shall also put up, in boxes, the laws directed to be sent by the governor to the several states in the Union, and shall transmit the same at the expense of the state in such manner as the governor shall direct.[4] And he shall also offer for sale at an advance not exceeding ten per cent on the original cost, such number of copies as the senate and assembly may by joint resolution direct.[5]

[1] R. S., 385, § 7.
[2] Ib., 385, § 9.
[3] Ib., 402, § 2.
[4] Ib., 386, §§ 19, 20.
[5] Ib., 405, § 15.

Census. § 94. In the year 1865, and every tenth year thereafter, the secretary of state shall cause to be made a census of the state. He shall appoint for this purpose one or more marshals in each town or ward, and furnish each marshal with a certificate of his appointment, designating the district for which he is appointed. If any marshal neglects to perform his duties, the secretary of state shall remove him and appoint another. He shall in each such year prepare the necessary blank returns for the purpose of collecting the information hereinafter required, and provide copies of the provisions of this article relating to the census, and shall, on or before the first day of May in such year, furnish to the clerk of each county twice as many of such returns and of the provisions of the statute as there are election districts in his county, who in turn must forward to the clerks of the towns, and to the clerks of the common councils of the cities within the county, a sufficient number to supply each marshal of such town or city with two sets of blank returns and one copy of the provisions of the statute.

1 R. S., 5th ed., 373, §§ 1 to 5, 14.

§ 95. It is the duty of each marshal to proceed on the first Monday in June in such year to enumerate the inhabitants of his district, and to obtain the statistical information required, by actual inquiry at every dwelling-house, or of the head of every family residing therein, and by such other means as are in his power; and to enter the enumeration and other information in the blank returns. Every person whose usual place of abode on such first day of June is in any family, shall be returned as of such family, and every *Duty of marshals.*

person, casually absent, as belonging to the place in which he usually resides. Each marshal must prepare duplicate copies of his return, and subscribe and verify under oath a certificate upon each copy that his return is true and accurate to the best of his knowledge and belief, and stating the number of pages of which it consists; the necessary oath shall be administered by any officer authorized so to do, and without any charge therefor. The marshal must, on or before the first day of July in the same year, transmit both copies to the county clerk. If any marshal neglects to do so for five days after the first of July, the clerk of the county shall go or send to obtain the returns; and the expense of so doing shall be deducted from the compensation of the marshal.

1 R. S., 5th ed., 373, §§ 6 to 11.

Duty of county clerks.

§ 96. Immediately upon receiving the returns, each county clerk shall, by express, transmit one copy of each, carefully packed in boxes, to the secretary of state; the other copies he shall cause to be arranged by towns and wards, and bound and preserved as records of his office.

Ib., §§ 11, 17.

Secretary's report of result.

§ 97. The secretary of state shall report to the legislature a general account of the result, specifying it for the several towns, wards, cities and counties, with a full recapitulation of the whole.

Ib., § 12.

§ 98. Any person being the head of a family or member thereof, above the age of twenty-one years, who refuses to give the information required by a marshal, relative to any particular required by the returns concerning such family or person, or willfully gives false information concerning the same, is liable to a penalty of fifty dollars, to be recovered by the supervisor of the town, and paid over to the town superintendent for the benefit of the common schools; except that in the city of New York it is to be recovered by the mayor, aldermen and commonalty, and paid over to the board of education for the benefit of the common schools of the city. Penalty for refusing to give information.

1 R. S., 5th ed., 373, § 15.

§ 99. The marshal's compensation is two dollars for each day actually and necessarily employed in his duties as such. Their compensation and that of the county clerks, for their services in respect to the census, are to be audited by the supervisors of their respective counties; except in the city and county of New York, where it shall be audited by the common council and assessed as part of the contingent expenses. Compensation of marshals and county clerks.

Ib., §§ 13, 19.

§ 100. The secretary of state shall also appoint suitable persons to take an enumeration of the Census of Indians.

Indians upon the several reservations in the state, and to ascertain the number of acres of land cultivated by them and such other information as the secretary prescribes. Their compensation, not exceeding two dollars per day, certified by him, and all other expenses incurred by him in executing the provisions of the six preceding sections, shall be paid by the treasurer upon the warrant of the comptroller.

1 R. S., 5th ed., 373, § 16.

ARTICLE V.

GENERAL PROVISIONS RESPECTING THE COMPTROLLER.

General duties of the comptroller.

§ 101. It is the duty of the comptroller:

1. To superintend the fiscal concerns of the state;

2. To report to the legislature, annually, a complete statement of the funds of the state, of its

revenues and of the public expenditures during the preceding fiscal year, and, as far as practicable, an account of the same down to the termination of the current calendar year; together with a detailed estimate of the expenditures to be defrayed from the treasury for the ensuing fiscal year, specifying therein each object of expenditure, and distinguishing between such as are provided for by permanent or temporary appropriations and such as must be provided for by a new statute, and suggesting the means from which such expenditures are to be defrayed;

3. To suggest plans for the improvement and management of the public revenue;

4. To keep and state all accounts in which the state is interested;

5. To examine and settle the accounts of all persons indebted to the state, and to certify the amount or balance to the treasurer;

6. To direct and superintend the collection of all monies due to the state

7. To examine and liquidate the claims of all persons against the state, in cases where there is sufficient provision of law for the payment thereof; and where there is no sufficient provision, to examine the claim and report the facts, with his opinion thereon, to the legislature;

8. To require all persons who have received any monies belonging to the state, and have not accounted therefor, to settle their accounts;

9. To draw warrants on the treasurer for the payment of all monies directed by law to be paid out of the treasury; but no warrant shall be drawn unless authorized by law, and every warrant shall refer to the law under which it is drawn;[1]

10. To keep in his office all leases, mortgages, bonds and other securities for money given to the people of the state, unless otherwise specially directed;[2]

11. To deposit the certificates for stock of any kind, owned by the people of this state, for safe keeping in such banks as he may select;[3]

12. To vote, either in person or by proxy, in behalf of the state, at all elections of directors of banks or other corporations or joint stock companies at which this state is entitled to vote;[4]

13. To procure from the books of the banks in which the treasurer makes his deposits, monthly statements of the monies received and paid on account of the treasurer;[5]

14. To countersign and enter all checks drawn by the treasurer, and all receipts for money paid

[1] 1 R. S., 388, § 1; 408, §§ 21, 22; 390, § 12.

[2] Ib., 391, § 19.

[3] 1 R. S., 391, § 20.

[4] Ib., 391, § 16.

[5] Ib., 389, § 8.

to the treasurer; and no such receipts shall be evidence of payment, unless so countersigned;[1]

15. To keep an account between the state and the treasurer, and therein charge the treasurer with the balance in the treasury when he came into office, and with all monies received by him, and credit him with all warrants drawn on and paid by him;[2]

16. To examine carefully on the first Tuesday of every month, or oftener if he deems it necessary, the accounts of the debts and credits in the bank books kept by the treasurer, and if he discovers any irregularity or deficiency therein, unless the same be rectified or explained to his satisfaction, to report the same forthwith, in writing, to the governor;[3]

17. To require, from time to time, all persons who have received moneys or securities, or have had the disposition or management of any property of the state, of which an account is kept in his office, to render statements thereof to him; and all such persons shall render such statement at such time and in such form as he shall require.[4]

§ 102. He has power to require any person presenting an account for settlement to be sworn Oath to account.

[1] 1 R. S., 389, § 6.

[2] Ib., 390, § 9.

[3] 1 R. S., 390, § 2.

[4] Ib., 389, § 2.

before him, and to answer orally as to any facts relating to its correctness.

1 R. S., 389, § 5.

Repayment of monies paid under mistake.

§ 103. Whenever he is satisfied that moneys have been paid into the treasury through mistake, he may draw his warrant therefor on the treasurer, in favor of the person who made such payment; but this provision shall not extend to payments on account of taxes, nor to payments on bonds and mortgages.

1 R. S., 391, § 18.

Releasing lands from liens

§ 104. He may, with the consent of the attorney-general, if they are satisfied that the interests of the state will not be prejudiced, release any portion of real property, subject to a judgment in favor of the people of this state, from the lien created by such judgment; and he may also acknowledge satisfaction of a judgment in favor of the people, when it is satisfied by payment.

1 R. S., 406, §§ 6, 9.

Disposition of certain surplus monies.

§ 105. Whenever any real property mortgaged to the people of this state, or bought in for the benefit of the state, or for which a certificate shall have been given to a former purchaser, is sold by the attorney-general on a foreclosure by notice, or under a judgment, or is resold by the state engineer and surveyor, for a greater sum than the amount due to the state, with costs and expenses, the surplus moneys received into the treasury, after a conveyance has been executed to the purchaser, shall be paid to the person legally entitled to such real property at the time of the foreclosure or of the forfeiture of the original contract; but the comptroller shall not draw his warrant for surplus money, unless upon satisfactory proof by affidavit or otherwise, of the legal right of such person.

1 R. S., 407, § 10.

§ 106. Whenever any real property purchased by the attorney-general in behalf of the state on the foreclosure of mortgage, is resold by the commissioners of the land office for a greater sum than the amount bid by the attorney-general on such purchase, the comptroller shall give credit to the mortgagor, on his bond, for the amount at which the same were resold, after deducting therefrom the costs and expenses of such sale; and if the same be resold for an amount greater than the amount due to the people of this state from the mortgagor, or if the mortgagor shall have paid into the treasury the balance due on his mortgage, after the purchase by the attorney-general; and if on the resale thereof by the commissioners of the land office, there is any excess above the amount due to this state, and the costs and expenses of such foreclosure, purchase and sale, the comptroller shall refund such excess to the mortgagor, his assignee or other person entitled thereto; and if there be interfering claims to such surplus monies

Disposition of certain surplus monies.

the comptroller shall refer such claims to the attorney-general, whose decision, as to the rights of the respective claimants, shall be conclusive in respect to any claim against the state.

1 R. S., 407, §§ 11, 12.

Comptroller to purchase fuel &c.

§ 107. Fuel and stationery for the senate and assembly, and the requisite stationery for recording their official proceedings, fuel and stationery for the several state offices except those of the bank superintendent and the insurance superintendent, and fuel to be used in the capitol, so far as a probable estimate thereof for a year or less period can be made, shall be purchased on sealed proposals to be received on public notice. The comptroller shall employ the proper agents to execute this section; shall fix, and, by his warrant on the treasury, pay their compensation, and the expense of the purchases. He shall from time to time make regulations in respect to giving such notice and accepting proposals, and requiring security for performance, and in respect to preserving the fuel and stationery, distributing them to the proper offices and departments for use, and accounting for the use thereof; which regulations, and the purchases and distributions made, he shall report to the legislature at their annual session. The cost of the fuel and stationery distributed to the canal department shall be refunded to the treasury by the commissioners of the canal fund.

1 R. S., 391, § 26.

§ 108. Whenever the comptroller deems it expedient he may issue a notice, in the name of the people, to any person who has received monies belonging to the state, for which he has not accounted, and in case of his death, to his legal representatives, requiring that within a limited period, not less than sixty nor more than ninety days from its date, all the accounts and vouchers for the expenditure of such monies shall be rendered to the comptroller; which notice shall be served by the sheriff of the county where the person to whom it is directed resides, by delivering a copy to him, or by leaving a copy at his usual place of residence, at least forty days before the expiration of the time limited therein; and the sheriff's certificate of service, specifying the time and manner, shall be evidence thereof. Comptroller to issue notice to any person who has not accounted.

1 R. S., 329, §§ 27 to 30.

§ 109. If the person served fail to render such accounts and vouchers within the time limited, the comptroller shall state an account against him charging interest at the rate of 7 per cent per annum from the time the notice was served; a copy of which account shall be delivered to the attorney-general for prosecution; and the defendant, unless sued as the representative of the original party, shall pay the costs of the action in any event thereof. Prosecution of claim.

1 R. S., 393, §§ 31, 33.

Comptroller to settle accounts if rendered.

§ 110. Whenever accounts and vouchers are rendered pursuant to such notice, or without notice, the comptroller shall proceed immediately to examine them, and if they are regular and sufficient shall settle the account, but if any necessary voucher is wanting, or, in his opinion, insufficient, he shall give notice to the person tendering the account and require him to supply the defect within a limited period, of not less than sixty nor more than ninety days; and at the expiration of the time limited, the comptroller shall settle the account upon the vouchers and proofs which have been delivered to him. A copy of the account so settled, he shall transmit to the person who rendered the account, and if a balance is certified to be due to the state, and the same is not paid to the treasurer, within ninety days thereafter, the comptroller shall deliver a copy of the account to the attorney-general for prosecution; and if on the trial of the action the defendant give any evidence other than such as was produced to the comptroller, he shall pay the costs of the action in any event thereof.

1 R. S., 393, §§ 34 to 36.

Comptroller's account is evidence in behalf of the state.

§ 111. Copies of the accounts mentioned in the two last sections, certified by the comptroller, shall be presumptive evidence that the balance therein stated is due to the state, and from the person against whom is the account.

1 R. S., 393, § 35.

§ 112. Where any number of persons have received monies for which they are accountable to the state, the comptroller may, in his discretion, settle the account of any one or more of them separately; and in such case no person, in any action brought for any balance certified to be due from him, shall take the objection that any other person was concerned with him in the receipt or expenditure of the monies. Separate accounting with joint debtors.

1 R. S., 393, §§ 37, 38.

§ 113. Nothing contained in the preceding five sections shall be construed to impair any legal remedy for the recovery of any debt due to the people of the state. Other remedies not impaired.

Ib., 393, § 39.

§ 114. The comptroller shall transmit annually, by mail or otherwise, to each person who has given bonds as auctioneer, a copy of the statutes regulating auctions, as they are passed from time to time; and he shall also annually present to the legislature the returns made by the auctioneers. Auction Laws.

Ib., 390, § 12.

§ 115. He may from time to time cause to be published, in one or more of the newspapers printed in the state, such statutes or parts of statutes relating to the payment of moneys due the state, or the duties of its public officers, as he deems necessary; and the expenses of the publica- Publication of certain statutes: expenses.

tion, and also all the reasonable expenses of the comptroller, when necessarily absent on official business, shall be paid out of the treasury.

1 R. S., 391, §§ 17, 22.

Powers of deputy comptroller.

§ 116. The deputy comptroller may perform any of the duties of his principal, except the drawing of warrants on the treasury, the auditing of public accounts, and the duties of the comptroller as commissioner of the land office, commissioner of the canal fund and state canvasser. But during an absence of such principal from the state, or a vacancy in the office, he shall perform all the duties attached by law to the office of his principal.

1 R. S., 21; 408, § 18.

ARTICLE VI.

GENERAL PROVISIONS RESPECTING THE TREASURER.

General duties of the treasurer.

§ 117. It is the duty of the treasurer:

1. To receive all monies which shall, from time to time, be paid into the treasury of this

state,[1] and to deposit the same, except such as belong to the canal fund, within three days after receiving them, to the account of the treasurer, in such bank or banks in the city of Albany as in the opinion of the comptroller and treasurer shall be safe, and pay the highest rate of interest to the state therefor ;[2]

2. To keep a bank book, in which shall be entered his account of deposits in bank, and moneys drawn therefrom, and to exhibit the same to the comptroller, for his inspection, on the first Tuesday in every month, and oftener, if required ;[3]

3. To pay all warrants legally drawn on the treasury by the comptroller or by the auditor of the canal department; and no moneys shall be paid out of the treasury, except on the warrant of the comptroller or auditor ;[4]

4. To report to the legislature, at its annual session, the exact balance in the treasury to the credit of the state, with a summary of the receipts and payments of the treasury during the preceding fiscal year, and as far as practicable an account of the same down to the termination of the current calendar year,[5] which report shall also present the total amount of transfers and assign-

[1] 1 R. S., 395, § 1.
[2] Ib., 396, § 8.
[3] Ib., 396, § 14.
[4] 1 R. S., 395, § 5; 425, § 14, &c.; People v. Schoonmaker, 3 Kern., 283.
[5] 1 R. S., 396, § 7; 408, §§ 21, 22.

ments of securities made by the bank superintendent, and countersigned by the treasurer;[1]

5. To do such acts in respect to the banking and insurance departments, as are prescribed by the provisions respecting *Banking* and *Insurance* contained in the CIVIL CODE.[2]

[1] Laws of 1857, ch. 103, § 3. [2] Laws of 1857, ch. 103.

Deposits in the Manhattan Bank

§ 118. All monies directed by law to be deposited in the Manhattan Bank in the city of New York, to the credit of the treasurer, shall there remain, subject to be drawn as the same may be required, or to be transferred by the comptroller to banks designated pursuant to subdivision one of the preceding section, whenever he deems that the interests of the state will be promoted thereby.

1 R. S., 396, §§ 9, 10.

Duty of banks keeping deposits of the treasurer.

§ 119. Each of the banks having state deposits shall every month transmit to the comptroller a statement of the monies which have been received and paid by them on account of the treasury.

1 R. S., 396, § 12.

Mode of drawing funds.

§ 120. The treasurer shall not draw, nor shall such banks pay any monies on account of the treasury, except by checks subscribed by him as treasurer and countersigned by the comptroller.

1 R. S., 396, § 13.

Treasurer to give bond.

§ 121. The treasurer shall, within ten days after he receives notice of his election, and before he enters upon the execution of his office, give a bond to the people in the sum of $50,000, with not less than four sufficient sureties to be approved by the president of the senate and speaker of the house of assembly, conditioned that he will faithfully execute the duties of his office; which bond shall be deposited in the office of the secretary of state, and shall be deemed to extend to the faithful execution of the office of treasurer by the person elected thereto, until a new appointment of treasurer be made and a new bond given thereunder.

1 R. S., 395, §§ 2, 3.

§ 122. After the new appointment is made, and such new bond given, upon the filing in the office of the secretary of state, of a certificate from the commissioners who shall have examined and settled the accounts of the treasurer of the preceding year, certifying that such accounts are regularly stated and balanced, and that the balance, if any there be, in moneys, securities and other effects, is actually in the treasury, or deposited as by law directed, the bond given by such treasurer and his sureties shall be discharged and delivered up to be canceled. Discharging the bond.

1 R. S., 395, § 4.

§ 123. The deputy treasurer may perform any of the duties of the treasurer, except the signing of checks, and the duties of the treasurer as commis- Powers of deputy treasurer.

sioner of the land office, commissioner of the canal fund, and state canvasser. The treasurer is responsible for the conduct of his deputy.

1 R. S., 396, § 6.

Commissioners to audit treasurer's accounts at close of fiscal year.

§ 124. The accounts of the treasury shall be annually closed on the 30th of September, and examined during the months of October, November and December by commissioners appointed by and pursuant to "An act to provide for the examination annually of the accounts of the treasurer and canal department, and the securities of the banking department," passed April 15, 1857. The commissioners shall, during the same time, examine into the condition of the bank, insurance and canal departments.

1 R. S., 306, § 15; Laws of 1857, ch. 592. We have added the insurance department to those mentioned by the statute.

Course of the examination.

§ 125. The commissioners shall examine the accounts and vouchers relating to all monies received into and paid out of the treasury during the preceding fiscal year, and shall certify and report to the legislature at its next session the amount of monies received into and the amount of monies paid out of the treasury during such year by virtue of warrants drawn on the treasury by the comptroller or by the auditor, the amount of monies received by the treasurer when he entered his office, and the balance in the treasury at the close of the fiscal year. They shall also compare the warrants drawn by the comptroller or auditor on the treasury during such fiscal year with the several laws under which the same purport to have been drawn, and shall in like manner certify and report whether the comptroller or auditor had power to draw such warrants; and if any are found which in the opinion of the commissioners he had no power to draw, they shall be specified, with the reasons for the opinion. The majority of the committee may perform all its duties.

1 R. S., 397, §§ 16, 17, 19, 20; Laws of 1857, ch. 592.

§ 126. Whenever the treasurer dies or resigns during his term, or is succeeded at the expiration of his term by another, these commissioners shall examine his accounts. They shall be governed, in their examination, certificate and report, by the provisions of the preceding section.

Commissioners to audit treasurer's accounts when he leaves office.

1 R. S., 397, §§ 21, 22.

ARTICLE VII.

GENERAL PROVISIONS RESPECTING THE STATE ENGINEER AND SURVEYOR.

From 1 R. S., 400, 401; Ib., 1232, § 30, subdiv. 103, 104.

General duties of the state engineer and surveyor.

§ 127. In addition to the duties in respect to the canals, prescribed by law, it is the duty of the state engineer and surveyor:

1. To superintend the surveys and sales of lands belonging to the people of this state, in the mode required by law, and according to the directions of the commissioners of the land office, where such directions shall have been given;

2. To retain in his office a map of this state, and from time to time to delineate thereon the boundaries of all towns or counties erected or altered by the legislature;

3; To collect and preserve all maps, plans, drawings, levels and surveys made for the use of the state;

4. To preserve together in his office, and open to the inspection of the citizens of the state at all reasonable hours, all maps, drawings and other documents furnished to his office in pursuance of the provisions of title III of this Code, entitled "*Public ways.*"

5. To make an annual report to the legislature, containing the reports received from railway companies, and presenting the information contained in them, in a tabular form, preserving under the various heads of expenses of each company the distinction between the cost of freight traffic and of passenger traffic.

1 R. S., 1232, § 30, subdv. 103, 104.

§ 128. Whenever the boundaries of a town appear, to be so described, in any act erecting or altering it, that he cannot delineate them on the map of the state without a survey specially made for that purpose, he shall direct the supervisor of the town to cause the survey to be made, and to transmit it to his office. New surveys of towns.

§ 129. If the supervisor neglects to do so, the state engineer and surveyor shall give notice thereof to the attorney-general, to the end that he may prosecute such delinquent supervisor for the penalty imposed by law; which penalty, when recovered, shall be paid to the state engineer and surveyor, and be by him applied to the making of a map of the town. Supervisor who fails to make survey to be prosecuted.

§ 130. Whenever a dispute arises between the officers of two or more towns respecting the town lines, on the same being represented to the state engineer and surveyor, he shall hear the allegations and proofs of the parties, and, if necessary, shall direct a survey to be made, and shall determine such dispute. The determination shall be filed in the office of the secretary of state, and shall be conclusive upon the subject, until the legislature by statute otherwise direct. Dispute as to town lines.

§ 131. The deputy state engineer and surveyor may perform any of the duties of his principal, except as commissioner, trustee, or member of any board. Power of deputy.

2 Laws of 1857, ch. 633, § 3.

ARTICLE VIII.

GENERAL PROVISIONS RESPECTING THE BANK SUPERINTENDENT.

Annual report.

§ 132. It is the duty of the bank superintendent to report annually to the legislature:

1. A summary of the state of every incorporated bank, banking association and individual banker, from whom reports have been received during the preceding year, at the several dates to which such reports refer, with an abstract of the whole amount of banking capital returned by them, of the whole amount of their debts and liabilities, specifying particularly the amount of circulating notes outstanding, and the total amount of means and resources, with the amount of specie held by them at the times of their several returns, and such other information, in relation to them, as in his judgment may be useful;

2. A statement of the banking associations and bankers whose business has been closed during the year, with the amount of their circulation redeemed, and the rate of such redemption per cent, and the amount outstanding;

3. A statement of the condition of every savings bank and institution for savings from which reports have been received for the preceding year;

4. Any amendment to the laws relative to

banking and savings banks, by which in his opinion the system may be improved, and the security of billholders and depositors may be increased;

5. The names and compensation of the clerks employed by him, and the whole amount of the expenses of the department during the year, and the amount, if any, for which the treasury is in advance.

The expense of the report shall be charged among the general expenses of the department.

1 R. S., 1171, § 272; Laws of 1857, ch. 136, § 2, and last clause of § 5.

§ 133. The bank superintendent shall not, either directly or indirectly, be interested in any bank, or banking association, or in the business of any individual banker. He shall give to the people of the state a bond in the penalty of fifty thousand dollars, with two sureties, to be approved by the comptroller and treasurer, conditioned for the faithful discharge of the duties of his office. He shall employ from time to time the necessary clerks to discharge the duties he shall assign to them, one of whom he shall appoint as his deputy. He shall furnish the necessary furniture, stationery, fuel, light and other proper conveniences for the transaction of the business of his department; the expense of which shall be paid, on his certificate and the warrant of the comptroller, in the first instance, out of the treasury, and collected from the Qualifications; deputy; expenses.

banks as prescribed in the provisions relating to *Banking* contained in the CIVIL CODE.

1 R. S., 1168, § 263; Laws of 1857, ch. 103, §§ 1, 5; 1 R. S., 1170, § 267.

ARTICLE IX.

GENERAL PROVISIONS RESPECTING THE INSURANCE SUPERINTENDENT.

SECTION 134. Annual report.
135. Qualifications; deputy; expenses.

Annual report. § 134. It is the duty of the insurance superintendent to report annually to the legislature:

1. Tabular statements, presenting the information received from insurance companies, pursuant to the requirements of the CIVIL CODE;[1]

2. The names and compensation of the clerks employed by him, and the whole amount of the expenses of the department during the year.

The expense of printing the report shall be charged among the general expenses of the department.[2]

[1] Laws of 1854, ch. 469, § 4. [2] Laws of 1859, ch. 366.

Qualifications; deputy; expenses. § 135. The insurance superintendent shall not, either directly or indirectly, be interested in any insurance company. He shall give to the people of the state a bond in the penalty of ten thousand dollars, with two sureties, to be approved by the comptroller, conditioned for the faithful discharge of the duties of his office. He shall employ from time to time the necessary clerks to discharge the duties he shall assign to them, one of whom he shall appoint as his deputy. He shall furnish the necessary furniture, stationery, fuel, lights and other proper conveniences for the transaction of the business of his department; the expense of which, with the monthly salaries of his clerks, shall be paid, on his certificate and the warrant of the comptroller, in the first instance, out of the treasury, and collected from the banks as prescribed in the provisions relating to *Insurance* contained in the CIVIL CODE.

Laws of 1859, ch. 366.

ARTICLE X.

THE POWERS AND DUTIES OF OTHER EXECUTIVE OFFICERS.

§ 136. The powers and duties of the attorney-general are prescribed by chapter I of title IV of part I of the CODE OF CIVIL PROCEDURE, entitled "*The Attorney-General;*"

Those of the state superintendent of public instruction, and of the regents of the university, by the "*School Laws;*"

Those of the state assessors, by the "*Fiscal Laws;*"

Those of the state superintendent of weights and measures, by chapter I of title IV of part III of this Code;

Those of the inspectors of gas meters, by the CIVIL CODE;

Those of the commissioners of excise, by chapter XI of title IV of part III of this Code;

Those of the commissioners of pilots of the port-wardens of the port of New York, and of the harbor masters, by chapter I of title III of part III of this Code;

Those of the commissioners of police of the metropolitan police district, by a statute entitled "*An act to establish a Metropolitan Police District, and to provide for the government thereof*," passed 15th April, 1857.

ARTICLE XI.

PROVISIONS RELATING TO THE DUTIES AND POWERS OF TWO OR MORE EXECUTIVE OFFICERS.

SECTION 137. Seals.
138. Annual reports.
139. Offices of the secretary of state, the comptroller, the treasurer, the attorney-general, the state engineer and surveyor, and the bank superintendent.
140. Certain officers to attend legislature.
141. Certain officers to file accounts of their fees.
142. Purchase to be for cash; form of vouchers.
143. Certain officers have power to administer oaths.
144. Extinguishment of claims.
145. Sales for quit-rents, if invalid.
146. Source of moneys for refunding.
147. Contract for public printing.
148. Contract for public binding.
149. Contract for printing the statutes.
150. Guaranty to be annexed to bids.
151. Legislative printing.
152. Certain copies to be full bound.
153. The state paper.
154. Proprietors to give bond.
155. Charges for advertising.

§ 137. Except where otherwise specially provided by law, the seals of office of the various executive officers shall be such as they respectively shall have devised, and of which they shall have caused a description and impression, with a certificate of the governor's approval, to be filed in the office of the secretary of state. The privy seal of this state shall be the seal for military commissions and all such matters as have issued under the great seal since March 16, 1778, except copies of papers and records certified under the seal of office of the secretary of state, shall continue to be issued under the great seal, and shall be made out and recorded in the secretary of state's office. Seals.

1 R. S., 4 ed., 387, § 26.

This provision, in its general application, is new. See Laws of 1859, ch. 366, § 4.

§ 138. Every officer required by law to submit an annual report to the legislature must complete such report, for the preceding fiscal year ending on the thirtieth day of September, on or before the tenth day of December succeeding, and deliver it on or before that day to the printer employed pursuant to this article. Annual reports.

Laws of 1859, ch. 437.

§ 139. The offices of the secretary of state, comptroller, treasurer, attorney-general, state engineer Offices of the secretary of state, the comptroller, the treasurer, the attorney-general, the state engineer and surveyor, and the bank and insurance superintendents.

and surveyor, bank superintendent and insurance superintendent shall be kept in the new state hall, in the city of Albany.

1 R. S., 408, § 19; Ib., 1170, § 267; Laws of 1859, ch. 366, § 6.

§ 140. It is the duty of the secretary of state, the comptroller, the treasurer, the attorney-general, and the state engineer and surveyor, to attend the legislature during its session, and to report upon all matters referred to them respectively by the legislature or by either house.

1 R. S., 407, § 14.

Certain officers to account of their fees.

§ 141. The secretary of state, the comptroller, and the state engineer and surveyor shall, on the first days of January, April, July and October, in each year, file with the treasurer an account in writing of all fees received by them respectively during the preceding quarter, and pay the amount thereof into the treasury.

Ib., § 15.

Purchases to be for cash; form of vouchers.

§ 142. All purchases for the use of any department, office or work of the government, shall be for cash and not on time. Each voucher, whether for a purchase or for a service, or other charge, shall be filled up at the time it is taken; and in all cases where the payment is not made directly by the governor or treasurer, proof in some apt form shall be furnished, on oath, that it was so filled up at the time it was taken, and that the money therein mentioned to have been paid was in fact paid in cash, or by draft on some specified bank. The auditor, in all cases where monies are paid from the canal fund, loans or revenues, and the comptroller, in all cases where payments are made from any other fund or revenue, shall, from time to time, prescribe forms and regulations to secure the faithful observance of this section, and may in all cases, if they shall deem it necessary, require proof on oath of the payment of the money.

1 R. S., 408, § 20; Laws of 1855, ch. 535.

§ 143. Whenever the governor, the secretary of state, the comptroller, the treasurer, the attorney-general, the state engineer and surveyor, the auditor of the canal department, the state assessors, the bank superintendent, and the insurance superintendent, or any of them, shall legally require proof, by affidavit, in any matter pertaining to his office, the officer requiring the proof may administer the necessary oath. Certain officers have power to administer oaths.

1 R. S., 405, § 1. We have added to the officers enumerated in that section the names of the auditor of the canal department, the bank superintendent, and the insurance superintendent.

§ 144. The comptroller, the attorney-general, and the state engineer and surveyor, or any two of them, with the consent of the governor, may, from time to time, extinguish any legal claim on Extinguishment of claims.

real property sold under the authority of this state, or granted, for a valuable consideration, under its authority. The money required for the purpose shall be paid out of the treasury; but in no case shall the aggregate of all sums paid for the extinguishment of such claims exceed the principal money, with interest at six per cent per annum, for which the real property was sold.

1 R. S., 406, § 2.

Sales for quit-rents if invalid.

§ 145. Whenever it appears to the comptroller, the attorney-general, and the state engineer and surveyor, or any two of them, that any sale of real property for arrears of quit-rents has been improperly made, or that such sale cannot, for any reason, be made effective, it is the duty of the officers so acting, or any two of them, to subscribe a certificate of the fact, and of the reasons why, in their judgment, such sale was improper, or why it cannot be made effectual, and file the same in the office of the comptroller; and thereupon the comptroller may cancel such sale on his books, and refund to the purchaser, his heirs or assigns, the amount of the consideration money paid, with interest at the rate of six per cent per annum from the time of such payment, not exceeding six years in the whole.

Ib., 406, §§ 3, 4.

Source of monies for refunding.

§ 146. Whenever such repayment is made, and whenever monies are refunded by the comptroller, for payments erroneously made into the treasury, on account of quit-rents, one-half shall be paid out of the common school fund and the other half out of the literature fund.

1 R. S., 406, § 5.

§ 147. The printing for the senate and assembly, and for all of the state officers, shall be done under contract as follows: The comptroller and secretary of state shall give at least twenty days' notice, in two newspapers published in each senate district in the state, that they will, on or before a specified day, receive sealed bids for such printing for two years, to be performed in the same style of execution, as to type and paper, as that theretofore furnished, and that they will receive separate bids for the printing to be done for the senate, assembly and state offices, or any portion of the printing to be done for the state offices. At the expiration of the time specified, they shall open the bids and enter into contract, to continue in force two years, with the person making the lowest bid, he giving a bond to the people of the state, to the satisfaction of the comptroller and secretary of state, for the faithful performance of the contract. But they need not accept any bid unless they deem it advantageous to the state. Contract for public printing.

1 R. S., 402, and last clause of § 13.

§ 148. At the same time and in the like manner they shall advertise for bids for the binding of the Contract for public binding.

journals and documents and enter into contract therefor, for the same time and upon the like conditions.

1 R. S., 404, § 13.

Contract for printing the statutes.

§ 149. They shall annually, in the like manner, advertise for bids for the printing of the statutes, and enter into contract therefor, for one year, and upon the like conditions.

1. R. S., 402, § 2.

By this and the preceding section the contracting is reduced, by modification in unimportant particulars, to a uniform system; except that the contract for printing the statutes are made annually; the others biennially.

Guaranty to be annexed to bids.

§ 150. To every bid made under one of the last three sections, there shall be annexed a guaranty that the bidder will, if accepted, enter into a contract according to the terms thereof, and give the security required by law, within the time specified; and to every such guaranty a certificate shall be annexed of the secretary of state, comptroller, attorney-general, treasurer or county judge of the county where the guarantor resides, that the guarantor is a man of property and able to make good his guaranty.

1 R. S., 403, § 5; 405, § 15.

Legislative printing.

§ 151. The printers to the senate and assembly must each print:

1. During each session of the legislature three hundred and ninety-nine copies of the journals of

the house to which he is printer, as the same are from time to time delivered to him by the clerk; two copies whereof must be delivered by him in sheets, as they are printed, to each of the clerks for the use of their respective houses, and one copy to the secretary of state; the remaining copies, with indexes printed by him from manuscript furnished by the secretary of state, as soon as may be after the close of each session must be delivered to the secretary;[1]

1. For the use of the members of the legislature during its session, two hundred and fifty copies of every bill, the printing of which shall be ordered by the house to which he is printer; twelve copies thereof must be delivered in sheets, to the secretary of state at the close of the session; sixty copies as they are printed to the senate; one hundred and fifty-eight to the assembly, and twenty to the state officers;[2]

3. Six hundred and fifty copies of messages from the governor, reports of standing or select committees, and reports and communications made in pursuance of law or of a resolution of either house, whenever ordered by the house to which he is printer; eighty copies whereof must be delivered to the senate; one hundred and sixty-eight copies to the assembly, and twenty copies to the state

[1] 1 R. S., 403, § 8. [2] Ib., 404, § 9.

officers, as they are printed; the remaining copies, as soon as may be after the close of each session, must be delivered to the secretary of state. Of the annual report of the bank superintendent, two hundred and seventy copies,[1] and of that of the insurance superintendent, fifteen hundred copies,[2] must be printed for the use of their respective departments. It is the duty of the printer who is employed under any contract hereafter made, to print the annual reports referred to in section 138, to distribute the same on or before the first day of the meeting of the legislature;[3]

4. An extra number of copies of bills, messages and the other documents specified in the last subdivision, whenever ordered by the house to which he is printer, in pursuance of the rules of such house or the joint rules of the two houses; one-third whereof must be delivered to the senate and two-thirds to the assembly, unless otherwise directed by law or the resolution of the house ordering such extra number.[4]

[1] 1 R. S., § 10; Ib., 1171, § 272.
[2] Laws of 1859, ch. 366, § 3.
[3] Laws of 1859, ch. 437.
[4] 1 R. S., 504, § 11.

Certain copies to be full bound.

§ 152. There shall be bound annually, in full binding, four copies of the senate and assembly bills, and sixteen copies of the journals and documents of both houses, for the senate library; and eight copies of the bills, and eighteen copies of the journals and documents, for the assembly library;

and seven copies of the journals and documents of each house for the state officers, and the residue of the journals and documents shall be bound in boards.

1 R. S., 404, § 12.

§ 153. The state paper is such daily newspaper in the city of Albany as is designated by the secretary of state, the comptroller and the treasurer, by contract entered into between them and the proprietor thereof, for the publication of all notices required by law to be published in the state paper.[1] Such officers shall make a certificate of the fact that the paper has been designated by them, pursuant to law, as the state paper; which certificate shall be published as a standing notice, at the head of the department of legal notices, in the paper, and without charge to the state.[2] The state paper.

[1] Laws of 1854, ch. 197, § 1.

[2] The provision of the latter part of this section is presented as a reasonable means of giving notice to the public of the designation made. The former provisions respecting the publication of such a certificate were of a temporary nature.

§ 154. Within five days after the making of any such contract, the proprietors of the paper shall execute a bond to the people of the state, with good and sufficient sureties, to be approved by the comptroller, in the penalty of five thousand dollars, for the faithful performance of the contract. Proprietors to give bond.

Laws of 1854, ch. 197, § 2.

Charges for advertising.

§ 155. The proprietors may charge for publication of such notices, for advertising, for the first insertion, not exceeding thirty cents for every folio of one hundred words, and for each subsequent insertion, not exceeding twenty cents for every folio; but no charge shall be made for any notices required in proceedings before surrogates, where the surrogate certifies that the property of the deceased is less than five thousand dollars in value.

Laws of 1854, ch. 197, § 3.

But the act in relation to the publication of *legal* notices (Laws of 1859, ch. 252) authorizes the proprietor of any newspaper to charge "for publishing any notice, order, citation, summons, or other proceeding or advertisement required by law to be published," not more than seventy-five cents per folio for the first insertion, and not more than thirty cents for each subsequent insertion.

CHAPTER IV.

JUDICIAL OFFICERS.

ARTICLE I.

NUMBER AND DESIGNATION.

§ 156. The number and designation of judicial officers are as follows:

Eight judges of the court of appeals;[1]

Five justices of the supreme court in the first judicial district;[2]

And four in each of the remaining seven judicial districts;[3]

A county judge in each county, except that of New York;[4]

A local officer designated as special county judge, in each of the counties of Jefferson, Oneida, St. Lawrence, Oswego, Orange, Chautauqua, Cayuga, Tioga,[5] Chenango,[6] Sullivan,[7] Washington,[8] Essex[9] and Tompkins;[10]

A surrogate in the county of New York,[11] St. Lawrence,[12] and in each other county that has created or shall create, that office in the mode prescribed by law;[13]

A local officer, designated as special surrogate, in each of the following counties: Jefferson, Oneida, St. Lawrence, Oswego, Orange, Chautauqua, Cayuga, Tioga,[14] and Washington.[15].

[1] Const., art. VI, § 2.

[2] Laws of 1852, ch. 374.

[3] Const., art. VI, § 4.

[4] Ib., § 14.

[5] 1 R. S., 305 and 314, §§ 18, 19; 314, § 21; repealed, Laws 1858, 286.

[6] 1 R. S., 315, § 26.

[7] Laws of 1854, ch. 88.

[8] Laws of 1855, ch. 148.

[9] Laws of 1857, vol. 2, ch. 463. The statute relating to this officer, in Essex county, designated him as "*special county judge and surrogate.*" There is no reason for retaining this anomaly.

[10] Laws of 1858, ch. 279, 438.

[11] Const., art. XIV, § 12; 1 R. S., 316, § 33.

[12] 1 R. S., 313, § 17.

[13] Ib., §§ 12, 15.

[14] 1 R. S., 314, §§ 18, 19.

[15] Laws of 1855, ch. 145.

Where the county judge is also surrogate, he may be designated simply as surrogate when acting as such. Where the surrogate is a distinct officer, the county judge or other officer, when acting as surrogate, shall be designated by his official title, with the addition of the words, "and acting surrogate;"[16]

Four justices of the peace in each town, except where a different number is provided for by special statute;[17]

So many justices of the peace in cities and in villages, and so many police justices in cities and villages, as are prescribed by their charters, or by special statutes;[18]

Six justices of the superior court of the city of New York;[19]

Three judges of the court of common pleas for that city.[20]

[16] Laws of 1853, ch. 648, § 1.

[17] 1 R. S., 321, § 68. There are now eight in Brookhaven, Suffolk county (Laws of 1854, ch. 94); five in each of the following towns: Hector, Tompkins county. (Laws of 1851, ch. 40.) Hanover, Chautauqua county. (Laws of 1852, ch 7.) Pomfret, Chautauqua co. (Ib., ch. 16.) Harmony, Chautauqua county. (Laws of 1855, ch. 12.) Beekmantown, Clinton county. (Laws of 1852, ch. 157.) Canton, St. Lawrence county. (Ib., ch. 79.) Potsdam, St. Lawrence county. (Laws of 1853, ch. 3.) Ellisburgh, Jefferson county. (Laws of 1854, ch. 26.) Lenox, Madison county. (Ib., ch. 31.) Champlain, Clinton county. (Ib., ch. 25.) Schodack, Rensselaer county. (Laws of 1857, ch. 59.) Niagara, Niagara county. (Ib., ch. 130.) Fort Ann, Washington county. (Ib., ch. 665.) One, and not more than four, in the town of Shelter Island. (Laws of 1852. ch. 53, § 1.)

[18] 1 R. S., 305.

[19] Code of Procedure, § 40.

[20] 1 R. S., 316, § 36; 317, § 41.

Three justices of the superior court of the city of Buffalo;[21]

A recorder in each of the cities of New York, Albany, Hudson, Troy, Schenectady, Utica, Oswego, Poughkeepsie;[22]

A city judge in the city and county of New York;[22]

A city judge of the city court of Brooklyn;[22]

Three justices of the marine court of the city of New York;[23]

Three justices of the peace of the justices' court, and two police justices, in the city of Albany;

Three justices of the justices' court in the cities of Hudson and Troy respectively;

A justice and a police justice in each of the first seven judicial districts of the city of New York, and a police justice in the eighth.[24]

[21] Laws of 1851, ch. 96, p. 222, § 1.

[22] 1 R. S., 305.

[23] Laws of 1852, 647.

[24] 1 R. S., 305; Laws of 1854, ch. 65.

ARTICLE II.

MODE OF ELECTION OF JUDICIAL OFFICERS.

Elected judges in the court of appeals.

§ 157. Four of the judges of the court of appeals are elected by the electors of the state, and hold their offices for eight years. One of the four is to be elected at the general election in the year 1861, and every alternate year thereafter.

Const., art. VI, §§ 2, 12; 1 R. S., 311, § 3.

Judges of the court of appeals taken from the supreme court.

§ 158. The remaining four judges of the court of appeals are taken in each year, from among the justices of the supreme court, in the following manner:

During the year 1861, and every alternate year thereafter, the justice in the second, the fourth, sixth and eighth judicial districts respectively, who then has the shortest time to serve, is to act as a judge of the court of appeals. During the year 1860, and every alternate year thereafter, the justice in the first, the third, fifth and seventh judicial districts respectively, who then has the shortest time to serve, is to act as a judge of the court of appeals.

1 R. S., 311, § 5.

§ 159. The justices of the supreme court are elected by the electors of their several judicial districts, and hold their offices for eight years, One in each district is to be elected at the general election in the year 1861, and every alternate year thereafter. And in the first district a fifth justice is to be elected at the general election in the year 1860, and every eighth year thereafter. Justices of the supreme court, how elected.

1 R. S., 312, § 6; Laws of 1852, ch. 374.

§ 160. The mode of filling vacancies in the court of appeals and the supreme court is prescribed by the Constitution. Vacancies.

Const., art. VI, § 13.

§ 161. The county judges are elected by the electors of their respective counties. Hereafter they are to be elected at the general election in the year 1863, and every fourth year thereafter. County judges.

Ib., § 14.

Surrogate of New York.

§ 162. The surrogate in the city and county of New York is elected by the electors of that city and county, and holds his office for three years. The next is to be elected at the general election in the year 1860, and every third year thereafter.

1 R. S., 316, § 33.

Surrogates in other counties.

§ 163. Surrogates, in counties other than New York, are elected at the same time, in the same manner, and for the same term as county judges.

When office of surrogate may be created.

§ 164. Whenever, in any county (except that of New York) which has a population exceeding forty thousand, the office of county judge is vacant, or its term is about to expire, the board of supervisors therein may, by resolution at any meeting, determine whether the office of surrogate shall be held as a separate office in such county. They may at the same time alter the salary of the county judge and fix the salary of the surrogate, if there is to be one, to take effect at the expiration of the current term of office. The clerk of the board shall immediately deliver the resolution to the county clerk, who shall file the same, and within ten days thereafter transmit a certified copy to the secretary of state.

1 R. S., 313, §§ 12, 15, 16.

Special county judges and special surrogates.

§ 165 The special county judges and special surrogates are elected by the electors of their respective counties at the general election next preceding the expiration of the term of office of their predecessors respectively. The term of office of all hereafter elected shall commence on the first day of January succeeding their election, and continue three years. Their compensation is fixed by the supervisors of the respective counties; and all fees received by them shall be paid to the county treasurer of their respective counties, to be applied towards the payment of county charges.

1 R. S., 314, §§ 18, 20.

In Chenango, Washington and Tompkins counties the term is now four years, while in other counties it is three. There seems to be no reason for retaining this anomaly. We have accordingly followed the term prescribed for the majority of counties in which the office exists.

§ 166. The special county judge in the county of Essex shall keep his office in the village of Elizabethtown. **Special county judge in Essex.**

Laws of 1857, ch. 461.

§ 167. The mode of election and term of office of justices of the peace, is prescribed by title IV of part IV of this Code, entitled "*General laws for the government of towns.*" They may be removed by the county court after notice of charges and an opportunity of being heard in defense, as prescribed in the CODE OF CRIMINAL PROCEDURE. **Justices of the peace.**

1 R. S., 321, §§ 68, 69.

Election of New York superior court and common pleas judges.

§ 168. The justices of the superior court of the city of New York, and the judges of the court of common pleas thereof, are elected by the electors of that city and county; and the term of office of each is six years. Two of the justices of the superior court and one of the judges of the court of common pleas are to be elected at the general election in the year 1861, and every alternate year thereafter.

1 R. S., 317, §§ 37, 40.

Justices of the superior court of Buffalo.

§ 169. The justices of the superior court of the city of Buffalo are elected by the electors of that city at an election on the first Tuesday of June. One is to be elected in the year 1861; one in 1862, and one in 1863, and thereafter one in each year preceding the expiration of a term. The term of office of all hereafter elected is eight years, except when elected to fill a vacancy.

Laws of 1854, ch. 96.

Recorders in cities.

§ 170. The recorders of cities are elected by the electors of their respective cities, and each holds his office for four years, except when elected to fill a vacancy.

1 R, S., 316, § 31.

There seems to be no reason why the term of office of the recorder of the city of New York should be different from that of the recorders of other cities. It is now three years. 1 R. S., 316, § 33. The above provision makes the term of all uniform.

§ 171. The city judge of the city of New York and the city judge, police justices and justices of the peace of the city of Brooklyn. The term of office of the city judge of Brooklyn is six years, that of each of the others four years; except in the case of one elected to fill a vacancy.

City judges of New York and Brooklyn and the police justices and justices of the peace of Brooklyn.

1 R. S., 316; Laws of 1854, ch. 314. The present statute provides that the term of office of the city judge and justices of Brooklyn shall commence on the first of May. It is supposed that one uniform provision contained in section 199, ought to apply to all these offices.

§ 172. The justices of the marine court of the city of New York are elected by the electors of that city and county, and those hereafter elected hold their offices six years. One of the three is to be elected at the general election in the year 1861, and one in each alternate year thereafter.

Justices of the marine court of New York city.

Laws of 1852, ch. 389.

§ 173. Whenever the supervisors of the city of New York are satisfied that any justice of the marine court is guilty of gross misconduct or habitual neglect of duty, or is incapable of performing his share of the duties of the court, they may by vote of a majority, suspend him from office and terminate his compensation. They shall thereupon present a statement of the grounds of their action to the court of common pleas of the city and county of New York, and serve a copy thereof

Removal of justices of marine court.

upon the justice suspended. The court of common pleas shall, upon notice to the justice, proceed, without unnecessary delay, to hear the parties, and the testimony, and shall restore or remove the justice, as may be just.

Modified form 1 R. S., 319, § 57.

Justices of district courts and police justices in New York city.

§ 174. The justices of the district and police courts of the city of New York are elected by the electors of their respective districts at the charter election in the year 1863, and every sixth year thereafter, and each holds his office six years. No person is eligible to the office except a counselor-at-law.

Laws of 1857, ch. 793; 1851, p. 937; 1852, p. 51; id. ch. 324.

Justices of justices' courts, justices of the peace and police justices in cities.

§ 175. The mode of electing the justices of justices' courts in cities, justices of the peace in cities, and of police justices in cities, when not provided in this article, is provided by the several charters and by special statutes.

CHAPTER V.

MINISTERIAL AND OTHER OFFICES CONNECTED WITH THE COURTS.

ARTICLE I.

NUMBER AND DESIGNATION.

§ 176. The number and designation of ministerial and other officers connected with the courts is as follows:

A sheriff, a county clerk, a deputy for each county clerk, and if necessary a special deputy, a district attorney, and four coroners for the city and county of New York; and the same for each other county, except that in the county of Rensselaer the number of coroners is five, one of whom must reside in the village of Greenbush,[1] and in the county of Queens the number of coroners is six, who must be so chosen that one shall reside in each town in that county;[2]

A register for the city and county of New York, and for each of the counties of Kings and Westchester;

A clerk of the court of appeals, and a deputy clerk;[3]

A state reporter for the court of appeals;[4]

[1] 1 R. S., 305; Laws of 1852, ch. 289; 1857, ch. 715.

[2] 1859, ch. 127.

[3] Const., art. VI., § 19; 1 R. S., 328, § 10.

[4] 1 R. S., 304, § 1.

A clerk of the superior court of the city of New York, of the court of common pleas of the city and county of New York, and of the superior court of Buffalo; deputy clerks, and as many bailiffs as the courts respectively may authorize their clerks to appoint;[1]

So many assistants of the surrogate of the county of New York as he may deem necessary, not exceeding the limit which the board of supervisors prescribe;[2]

A clerk for the surrogate of Erie, when the board of supervisors recommend that one be appointed;[3]

One or more clerks for the surrogate of Kings;[4]

A clerk for the marine court of the city of New York;[5] three deputies;[6] and bailiffs necessary to attend that court;[7]

A clerk of each of the district and the police courts of that city, and a deputy clerk for such of the clerks of the district courts as appoint one;[8]

[1] The present provisions are substantially to the same effect (Laws of 1847, ch. 432, p. 560, § 3; 1852, ch. 44, p. 39, § 1; Code of Procedure, § 39; Laws of 1853, ch. 529, p. 992; Laws of 1854, ch. 198, p. 464, § 1,) except that the limit to the number of assistants to the clerk of the New York superior court is to be prescribed by the supervisors. This provision we have omitted.

[2] Laws of 1847, ch. 332, § 7.

[3] Laws of 1857, ch. 789.

[4] Laws of 1849, ch. 173.

[5] Laws of 1852, ch. 647.

[6] Laws of 1857, ch. 295.

[7] Laws of 1853, ch. 529, p. 992.

[8] Laws of 1857, § 71.

A clerk for the city court of Brooklyn, and a deputy clerk if he appoints such;[1]

A clerk for each of the justices' courts in cities;[2]

A crier of each court of record;

A clerk to take testimony in the county of Kings;[3]

A clerk of the court of oyer and terminer and sessions of the city and county of New York, and a deputy clerk of the same in case the clerk appoint such;[4]

A clerk in each of the cities of Hudson, Schenectady, Buffalo, Syracuse, Oswego, Auburn, Utica, Rochester, Brooklyn;[5]

A marshal for each of the cities of Schenectady, Troy, Oswego, Auburn, Utica, Poughkeepsie;[6]

So many attorneys and counselors as are from time to time admitted to practice;

An attorney of the Seneca nation of Indians;[6]

Three hundred commissioners of deeds, and not more than five hundred notaries public, for the city and county of New York.[7]

[1] 1 R. S., 305; Laws of 1849, 170, §§ 7, 8, as amended by Laws of 1850, 948, §§ 2, 3.
[2] 1 R. S., 305.
[3] Laws of 1856, ch. 166.
[4] 1 R. S., 305; Ib., 328, § 8.
[5] 1 R. S., 305; Laws of 1854, ch. 90.
[6] 1 R. S., 305, 307.
[7] 1 R. S., 305; 1853, ch. 340; 1854, ch. 92; 1858, 44; 1859, ch. 485.

Not more than twenty-five notaries public in the city of Troy;[1]

Eight commissioners of deeds in the city of Auburn;[2]

So many commissioners of deeds in each of the cities of the state, except the cities of New York and Auburn, and so many notaries public in each, except the cities of New York and Troy, as shall from time to time be determined, in the following manner:

The common councils of the several cities, except New York and Auburn, on or before the first day of January, 1861, and at the end of every two years thereafter, shall, by resolution, fix the number of commissioners of deeds, to be appointed for their respective cities;[3] and on or before the 1st day of January, 1860, and at the end of every two years thereafter, the common councils of the several cities, except New York and Troy, shall fix, in the same manner, the number of notaries public, to be appointed for their respective cities;[4]

A copy of each determination of the number of commissioners of deeds and of notaries public, under the corporate seal of the city, and attested by the mayor, shall be transmitted to the governor within twenty days after the same has been made;

[1] Laws of 1858, ch. 57. p. 91.
[2] Laws of 1859, 431, § 7.
[3] 1 R. S., 307, § 5.
[4] 1 R. S., 307, § 2.

and no appointment shall be made exceeding the limitation;[1]

So many notaries public in each of the counties of this state as the governor and senate may think proper to appoint,[2] not exceeding, however, five hundred for the city and county of New York;[3]

Fifteen commissioners of deeds for the county of Saratoga, six of whom must reside in the village of Saratoga Springs,[4] six in the village of Ballston Spa,[5] and three in the village of Waterford;[6] three for the county of Steuben, one of whom must reside in the village of Bath, one in Corning, and one in Hornellsville.[7]

Such other officers as may be chosen to fill any ministerial or other office connected with the courts, which is created by or under authority of the general laws for the government of counties, cities, towns and villages, or by special charters or statutes.

[1] 1 R. S., 307, §§ 3, 4.
[2] Id., 306.
[3] Laws of 1859, ch. 485.
[4] Laws of 1858, ch. 109, § 1.
[5] Laws of 1859, p. 36.
[6] Laws of 1859, p. 259.
[7] Laws of 1857, 404, ch. 632.

ARTICLE II.

MODE OF ELECTION AND APPOINTMENT.

Certain elective officers.

§ 177. Sheriffs, county clerks (including registers), coroners and district attorney, and the clerk of the court of appeals, are elected in the mode prescribed by the Constitution.

Const., art. X, § 1; art. VI, § 19.

Election in new counties.

§ 178. The sheriffs, clerks and coroners first chosen in a new county shall be elected at the general election next succeeding the erection of the county, unless otherwise provided by law.

1 R. S., 321, § 67.

Registers.

§ 179. The registers of the counties of Kings and Westchester are to be elected at the general election in the year 1860, and as often as necessary thereafter. The term of office is three years.

Laws of 1852, ch. 83; 1858, 293.

State reporter.

§ 180. The state reporter is appointed by the governor, lieutenant-governor and attorney-general, and holds his office three years from the date of his appointment; but may be removed by the joint vote of both branches of the legislature.

1 R. S., 314, § 701.

Clerks and criers.

§ 181. The clerk of the superior court of the city of New York,[1] of the court of common pleas for the city and county of New York,[2] the superior court of the city of Buffalo,[3] and of the city court of Brooklyn,[4] criers of courts of record,[5] and clerks and assistants of surrogates, are appointed by their respective courts.

[1] 1 R. S., 318, § 42.
[2] Ib., § 48, Laws of 1854, ch. 198, § 1.
[3] Laws of 1854, ch. 96.
[4] 1 R. S., 318, § 47.
[5] By the Laws of 1755, ch. 530 (amended by Laws of 1859, ch. 166), criers of courts of record in each county, except New York and Kings, are appointed by the county judge. We have thought it better to leave the appointment of those officers to the respective courts.

Clerk of New York marine court.

§ 182. The clerk of the marine court of the city of New York is appointed by the supervisors, on or before the 1st day of January, 1862, and every fourth year thereafter.

Laws of 1850, ch. 389, § 4.

Suspension or removal of marine court clerk.

§ 183. The justices of the marine court have power to suspend their clerk, for gross misconduct in office, neglect of duty or incapacity to perform the same, and may designate a person to act as clerk meanwhile. The justices shall immediately present a statement of the causes of this action to the court of common pleas of the city and county of New York, which shall proceed thereupon in the manner provided in section 173. If an order is made for the removal of the clerk, the marine court shall designate a person to act as clerk until the vacancy is filled.

Modified from 1 R. S., 319, § 56.

Deputy and assistant clerks. § 184. Deputy clerks are appointed by their respective principals.

Other officers. § 185. All officers of courts, whose appointment is not otherwise provided for, shall be appointed by their respective courts.

1 R. S., 321, § 64.

Notaries. § 186. Notaries public are appointed by the governor with the consent of the senate, and hold their offices for two years.

1 R S, 319, §§ 50, 51.

Commissioners of deeds. § 187. Commissioners of deeds in cities are appointed by the common councils, in villages by the trustees thereof; and all vacancies are to be filled for the unexpired term in the same manner; but no supervisor can be appointed a commissioner of deeds.

1 R. S., 321, §§ 65, 66; Laws of 1857, ch. 632; Laws of 1858, ch. 109.

Attorneys and counselors. § 188. The admission of attorneys and counselors is regulated by the CODE OF CIVIL PROCEDURE.

The attorney of the Seneca nation. § 189. The attorney of the Seneca nation of Indians is appointed by the governor with the consent of the senate. He holds his office for two years.

1 R. S., 326, §§ 20, 21.

CHAPTER VI.

GENERAL PROVISIONS RELATING TO DIFFERENT CLASSES OF OFFICERS.

ARTICLE I.

DISQUALIFICATIONS.

§ 190. No person is capable of holding a civil office, who, at the time of his election or appointment, is not of the age of twenty-one years, and a citizen of this state. Age and citizenship.

1 R. S., 327, § 1.

§ 191. No person elected to the common council of any city can, during the term for which he was elected, be appointed to any office of profit in the gift of such common council; but this prohibition does not extend to officers whose Members of common council disqualified.

appointment is, by the Constitution, vested in the common council of a city.

1 R. S., 327, § 2.

Other disqualifications. § 192. Provisions respecting disqualification for particular offices are contained in the Constitution and in the provisions of the Codes concerning the various offices.

ARTICLE II.

RESTRICTIONS UPON THE RESIDENCE OF OFFICERS AND THE EXERCISE OF THEIR POWERS.

Residence. § 193. The following officers must reside within the county, city or town for which they are respectively elected or appointed:

County judges and special county judges, surrogates and special surrogates, recorders of cities, justices of the district and police courts in the city of New York and their clerks, justices of the peace in towns and cities, sheriffs, county clerks, registers, coroners, district attorneys, marshals, the clerk of oyer and terminer and sessions in New York, commissioners of deeds and notaries public.

1 R. S., 308.

Power. § 194. Executive officers, elected or appointed for any district, county, city or town, are confined thereto in the exercise of their duties, except where otherwise provided by law. Restrictions upon the residence and powers of judicial officers, and ministerial officers connected with courts, are contained in the CODE OF CIVIL PROCEDURE.

1 R. S., 308, § 14.

§ 195. In all cases not otherwise provided for, each deputy shall possess the powers and perform the duties attached by law to the office of his principal, during a vacancy in such office, and during the absence or inability of his principal, not extending, however, to the duties or powers of any other office which may be devolved upon the principal by virtue of his chief office. Powers of deputy.

1 R. S., 327, § 7.

ARTICLE III.

APPOINTMENT, AND COMMENCEMENT AND DURATION OF TERM.

§ 196. Every officer, the mode of whose appointment is not prescribed by the Constitution or statutes shall be appointed by the governor, with the consent of the senate. Appointment when not otherwise provided for.

1 R. S., 327, § 4.

§ 197. All assistants, deputies and other subor- Subordinates.

dinate officers, whose appointment is not otherwise prescribed, shall be appointed by the officer or body to which they are respectively subordinate.

1 R. S., 327, § 5.

Number of subordinates.

§ 198. When the number of such subordinate officers is not fixed by law, it shall be limited at the discretion of the appointing power.

Ib., § 6.

Commencement of term.

§ 199. All officers elected by the people shall enter on their duties on the first day of January following their election, except that justices of the peace in towns, elected to fill vacancies, or in new towns, shall enter on their duties immediately.

1 R. S., 327, § 3; 322, § 72.

Term of office when not prescribed.

§ 200. Every office, of which the duration is not prescribed by the Constitution or statutes, shall be held during the pleasure of the appointing power.

1 R. S., 328, § 11.

Holding over until successor has qualified.

§ 201. Every officer, except a justice of the supreme court, shall continue to discharge the duties of his office, although his term has expired until his successor is duly qualified.

Ib., § 21.

ARTICLE IV.

NOMINATIONS AND COMMISSIONS OF OFFICERS.

§ 202. Nominations made by the governor to the senate must be in writing, designating the residence of the nominee and the district for which he is intended to be appointed. Nominations to be in writing.

1 R. S., 329, § 14.

§ 203. Whenever the senate concur in a nomination or recommendation of removal by the governor, the clerk must immediately deliver a copy of the resolution of concurrence, certified by the president and the clerk, to the secretary of state, and another copy, certified by the clerk, to the governor. Resolution of concurrence.

Ib., § 15.

§ 204. Whenever any officer whose nomination is vested in the governor is removed by the legislature, the clerk of the house in which the resolution originated must immediately deliver a certified copy thereof to the governor. Resolution of removal.

Ib., § 16.

Commissions, how made out.

§ 205. The commissions of all civil officers appointed by the governor and senate, or by the governor, must be signed by the governor, and attested by the secretary of state under the great seal, and recorded by the secretary.

1 R. S. 329, § 17.

Commissions and removals, how forwarded.

§ 206. When an appointment or removal is made by the governor, the secretary of state must send the commission or supersedeas by mail to the clerk of the county where the person appointed or removed resides; and whenever the governor so directs, must dispatch a messenger to the person or to the county clerk with the commission or supersedeas, and cause notice of the supersedeas to be published for two weeks successively in the state paper; which publication shall be deemed a sufficient notice within the provisions of this title.

Ib., §§ 18, 19.

Certificate of canvassers.

§ 207. The certificate of the board of canvassers, authorized to canvass the votes given for any elective office, is evidence of the result.

Ib., § 20.

Appointment of ministerial and other officers connected with courts.

§ 208. The appointment of officers mentioned in chapter V of this title, where not otherwise provided for, must be made by writing, filed in the office of the appointing power, or the office of its clerk, as the case may be.

§ 209. The commissions of all other officers, where no special provision is made by law, must be signed by the presiding officer of the body, or by the person making the appointment. Other commissions.

ARTICLE V.

THE OATH OF OFFICE AND OFFICIAL BOND, AND DUTY.

§ 210. Before any officer enters on the duties of his office he must take the following oath: "I do solemnly swear" (or "affirm") "that I will support the Constitution of the United States and the Constitution of the State of New York, and that I will faithfully discharge the duties of the office of   , according to the best of my ability." Oath.

1 R. S., 330, § 22.

§ 211. Members of the legislature may take the oath of office at any time during the term for which they were elected. Oath of members of legislature.

1 R. S., 331, § 35.

When to be taken. § 212. Whenever a different time is not prescribed by law, the oath of office must be taken, subscribed and filed in the proper office, within fifteen days after the officer has notice of his election or appointment, or before the expiration of fifteen days from the commencement of his term of office.

1 R. S., 330, § 23.

Before whom. § 213. Except where otherwise provided, the oath may be taken before any justice of the supreme court, the secretary of state, the attorney-general, the lieutenant-governor, the president of the senate for the time being, the speaker of the house of assembly, a county judge, the mayor or recorder of a city, the clerk of a county or city, or of any court of record.

Ib., § 24.

Before whom taken. § 214. The oath of justices of the peace and commissioners of deeds must be taken before the county clerk of the county.

Ib., § 25.

Where deposited. § 215. Every oath of office, duly certified by the officer before whom the same was taken, must be filed within the time required by law, as follows, except when otherwise specially directed:

1. The oath of the governor, lieutenant-governor, justices of the supreme court, comptroller, secretary of state, attorney-general, treasurer,

state engineer and surveyor, state assessors bank superintendent, insurance superintendent and superintendent of public instruction; of the members of the senate and assembly, and of the clerks, sergeants-at-arms and doorkeepers thereof; of the canal commissioners, and all other executive officers, whose authority is not limited to any particular district or county, in the office of the secretary of state.

2. The oath of attorneys and counselors must be taken before the court admitting them, and filed in the office of the clerk.

3. The oath of clerks of courts in their respective offices.

4. The oath of notaries public, superintendents of canal repairs, and collectors of canal tolls, and of all judicial and executive officers appointed or elected for any county or city, and of all officers whose duties are local, or whose residence in any particular district or county is prescribed by law, in the offices of the clerks of their respective counties.

1 R. S., 330, § 27.

§ 216. Deputies must, within fifteen days after their appointment, take and file an oath in the manner required of their principals. Oath of deputies.

1 R. S., 331, § 28.

Filing bonds.

§ 217. Every official bond must be filed in the proper office within the time above prescribed for filing the oath, unless otherwise expressly provided by statute.

1 R. S., 331, § 29.

Notice of neglect.

§ 218. If any officer who is required to file his oath or bond with the secretary of state or with a county clerk, neglects to do so within the time required, it is the duty of such secretary or clerk immediately to give notice thereof to the governor. And when a justice of the peace neglects to file his oath, the county clerk must also give notice to the supervisor of the town.

Ib., § 30.

Notice of neglect.

§ 219. Whenever any officer who is required to file his bond with the comptroller neglects to do so within the time required, the comptroller must immediately give notice thereof to the governor, in case the officer was commissioned by him, and if otherwise, to the person or body which appointed the officer.

Ib., § 31.

Effect of bond.

§ 220. Every official bond continues in force so long as the officer continues to discharge the duties of his office, and until his successor is duly qualified.

Ib., § 32.

Sureties, when exempt.

§ 221. But the sureties in such bond shall be exonerated from liability for acts or omissions of their principal, after he has duly renewed his official bond, pursuant to law.

1 R. S., 331, § 33.

§ 222. If any person execute any of the functions of an office without having taken and duly filed the required oath of office, or without having executed and duly filed the required bond, he shall forfeit the office, and is guilty of a misdemeanor. **Penalty for acting without oath or bond.**

Ib., § 34.

§ 223. It is the duty of every officer of the state to maintain and defend its sovereignty and jurisdiction. **Duty to maintain the sovereignty of the state.**

1 R. S., 5th ed., 84, § 2.

ARTICLE VI.

RESIGNATIONS, REMOVALS, VACANCIES, AND THE MODE OF SUPPLYING THEM.

Resignations, to whom made. § 224. Resignations must be in writing, and made as follows:

1. By the governor, lieutenant-governor, secretary of state, comptroller, treasurer, attorney-general and superintendent of public instruction, to the legislature;

2. By all officers appointed by the governor alone, or by him with the consent of the senate, to the governor;

3. By senators and members of assembly, to the presiding officers of their respective houses, who shall immediately transmit the same to the secretary of state.

4. By sheriffs, coroners, county clerks and registers, to the governor;

5. By justices of the peace, to the supervisor of the town;

6. By all other appointed officers, to the body or officer that appointed them;

7. In all cases not otherwise provided for, by filing the resignation in the office of the secretary of state.

1 R. S., 332, §§ 36, 37.

Governor's power of removal. § 225. All officers, other than judges of courts of record, appointed by the governor alone for a certain time, or to supply a vacancy, may be removed by him.

1 R. S., 333, § 42.

§ 226. The office of any collector or receiver of public monies, appointed by the legislature, by the governor, or by the governor and senate; except of those officers for whose removal provision is otherwise made, may be declared vacant by the governor, in case it appears to him, on the report of the comptroller, that such officer has, in any particular, willfully violated his duty. Governor's power of removal.

1 R. S., 333, § 43.

§ 227. The governor may also declare vacant the office of any officer required to execute an official bond, whenever a judgment is obtained against him on the bond. Breach of official bond.

Ib., § 44.

§ 228. The case in which the treasurer may be suspended, and the mode of removing judges of courts of record, is prescribed by the Constitution. Special county judges and special surrogates may be removed in the same mode. Suspension of treasurer and removal of judges.

Const., art. V, § 7; art. VI, § 11; 1 R. S., 314, § 18.

§ 229. All officers appointed by the governor, with the consent of the senate, may be suspended by the governor, and removed by the senate on the recommendation of the governor. Suspension by governor and senate's power of removal.

Modified from 1 R. S., 333, § 46; 567, § 15; Laws of 1859, ch. 311, § 2.

§ 230. The governor may remove any sheriff, commissioner of police of the metropolitan police Removal of certain other officers for cause.

district, coroner, district attorney, county clerk or register, first giving to such officer a copy of the charges against him, and an opportunity of being heard in his defense.

1 R. S., 333, § 49.

District attorney to inquire into charges.

§ 231. The governor may, in his discretion, direct the district attorney of the county to conduct an inquiry into the truth of the charges, who in that case shall give at least eight days' notice to the officer accused, of the time and place when he will proceed to the examination of witnesses before the county judge. The examination shall proceed with all reasonable dispatch; and may be adjourned from day to day; witnesses may be compelled by the judge to attend and testify; and the testimony shall be certified by the judge, and transmitted by the district attorney to the governor.

1 R. S., 334, §§ 50, 53.

Vacancies, how occurring.

§ 232. Any office becomes vacant on the happening of either of the following events before the expiration of the term:

1. The death of the incumbent;

2. His resignation;

3. His removal from office;

4. His ceasing to be an inhabitant of the state, or, if the office be local, of the district, county,

town or city for which he was chosen, or within which the duties of his office are required to be discharged;

5. His conviction of an infamous crime, or of any offense involving a violation of his oath of office;

6. His refusal or neglect to file his oath or bond within the time prescribed;

7. The decision of a competent tribunal, declaring void his election or appointment;[1]

8. Any one of the commissioners of police of the metropolitan police district who accepts any other place of public trust or emolument, or who receives any nomination for any elective public office, and does not, within ten days, publicly decline it, thereby vacates his office.[2]

[1] 1 R. S., 332, § 33. [2] Laws of 1857, ch. 569, § 2.

§ 233. Whenever any officer is convicted of an infamous crime, or of an offense involving a violation of his oath of office, and whenever any election or appointment is declared void by a competent tribunal, the court shall immediately give notice thereof to the governor, stating the cause of such conviction or decision. Notice of conviction.

1 R. S., 333, § 39.

§ 234. The governor shall immediately supply the vacancy if he has the power to do so, or give Duty of governor.

notice of the vacancy to the body or officer in whom the appointment is vested, or whose duty it is to order or give notice of an election to supply the vacancy.

1 R. S., 333, § 40.

Temporary appointments by the governor.

§ 235. The governor may supply vacancies, happening during the recess of the senate, in any office to which an appointment was made by the governor with the consent of the senate, by granting commissions, which shall expire at the end of twenty days from the commencement of the next meeting of the senate.

Ib., § 47.

Temporary appointments by the governor.

§ 236. Whenever a vacancy occurs, during the recess of the legislature, in the office of treasurer, or of any other officer appointed by the legislature, the governor shall appoint a person to execute the duties of the office, who shall hold his office until such vacancy is regularly supplied.

Ib., § 48.

Power of governor to fill vacancies.

§ 237. Whenever a vacancy occurs in the office of sheriff, county clerk or register, the governor shall appoint some fit person who was eligible to the office to execute the duties thereof, until it is supplied by an election, and the appointee shall execute the duties of the office until the first of January succeeding the general election next after the happening of the vacancy.

1 R. S., 334, §§ 54, 55, 57.

§ 238. When a vacancy exists, or a resignation has been sent in and accepted, to take effect at a future day, in the offices of secretary of state, comptroller, treasurer, attorney-general, state engineer and surveyor, state prison inspector, clerk of the court of appeals, or canal commissioner, or superintendent of public instruction, while the legislature is in session, the two houses thereof, by joint ballot, shall appoint a person to fill the vacancy; and any person appointed by the governor to any of these offices (except state prison inspector) may be removed from such office by joint resolution of both houses of the legislature, and upon such removal both houses shall forthwith, by joint ballot, appoint a person to the office made vacant thereby. Vanancies in certain offices.

1 R. S., 335, § 59.

§ 239. A vacancy in the office of canal commissioner, existing during a recess of the legislature, is to be filled by the governor, by appointment, to be filed in the office of the secretary of state; and the appointee holds his office until the first of January after the next general election, unless the unexpired term sooner expire. When the unexpired term extends beyond the first of January after the next general election succeeding the happening of the vacancy, there shall be chosen at such election a canal commissioner, to enter upon the duties of the office on the first of January after Vacancies in office of canal commissioner.

the election, and fill the same for the unexpired term.

1 R. S., 234, §§ 5 and 6.

Vacancy in office of commissioner of excise.

§ 240. A vacancy in the office of commissioner of excise is filled for the unexpired term by the officers who are authorized to appoint.

Laws of 1857. ch. 628, § 1.

Vacancy in office of police commissioner.

§ 241. The mode of filling vacancies in the office of police commissioner of the Metropolitan Police District, is prescribed by chapter 569 of the Laws of 1857, entitled "*An act to establish a Metropolitan Police District, and to provide for the government thereof,*" passed April 15, 1857.

Laws of 1857, ch. 569.

Vacancies in office of New York health commissioner.

§ 242. The board of health may supply any vacancy that may occur in the office of either of the health commissioners of the city of New York, whether arising from the temporary inability of the officer to discharge his duties or otherwise; but the person so appointed shall hold his office only until such inability be removed, or until an appointment.

Vacancies not otherwise provided for.

§ 243. In every case where no other provision is made by law for filling a vacancy in any office, the same shall be filled by appointment of the governor for the residue of the unexpired term. But if the office is elective, the appointment, in such case shall only run to the first of January succeeding the next general election after the happening of the vacancy; and if the unexpired term is one that continues beyond that time, it shall be filled at such election.

1 R. S., 335, § 59.

The provisions of 1 R. S., 316, §§ 33, 35, 326, § 18, vest in the supervisors the power of filling vacancies in the office of surrogate and recorder of New York, and in offices of county treasurers. The act of 1854 (Laws of 1854, ch. 96) directs a special election to fill a vacancy in the office of justice of the superior court of Buffalo. Those provisions we have omitted, leaving the cases to which they relate to be governed by this section.

§ 244. Any person chosen to fill a vacancy shall after taking his oath and executing the proper bonds, possess all the rights and powers, and be subject to all the liabilities, duties and obligations, of the officer whose vacancy he fills. **Officers chosen to fill vacancies.**

ARTICLE VII.

PROCEEDINGS TO COMPEL THE DELIVERY OF BOOKS AND PAPERS BY OFFICERS TO THEIR SUCCESSORS.

The provisions of this article are somewhat modified from 1 R. S., 335, §§ 60 to 66.

§ 245. Every public officer is entitled to the possession of all books and papers pertaining to **Possession of books and papers.**

his office, or in the custody of a former incumbent by virtue of his office. The willful concealment or withholding thereof, by any person, is a misdemeanor.

Proceedings to compel delivery.

§ 246. If any person, whether a former incumbent or another person, refuse or neglect to deliver to the actual incumbent any such books or papers, such actual incumbent may apply, by petition, to any court of record sitting in the county where the person so refusing or neglecting resides, or to any judge of the supreme court or county judge residing therein; and the court or officer applied to shall proceed, in a summary way, after notice to the adverse party, to hear the allegations and proof of the parties, and to order any such books or papers to be delivered to the petitioners.

Attachment and search warrant.

§ 247. The execution of the order, and the delivery of the books and papers, may be enforced by attachment, as for a witness, and also upon warrant, at the request of the petitioner, directed to the sheriff or constable of the county, commanding him to search, in the daytime, for such books and papers, and to take and deliver them to the petitioner

TITLE II.

GENERAL RIGHTS OF THE STATE.

CHAPTER I.

RIGHTS OVER PERSONS.

§ 248. The state has the following rights over persons within its limits, to be exercised in the cases and in the manner provided by law:

1. To punish for crime;

2. To imprison or confine, for the protection of the public peace or health or of individual life and safety;

3. To imprison or confine, for the purpose of enforcing civil remedies;

4. To establish custody and restraint for the persons of idiots, lunatics, drunkards and other persons of unsound mind;

5. To establish custody and restraint of paupers, for the purposes of their maintenance;

6. To establish custody and restraint of minors unprovided for by natural guardians, for the purposes of their education, reformation and maintenance;

7. To require services of persons, with or without compensation:

In military duty;

In jury duty;

As witnesses.

As town or village officers;

In highway labor;

In maintaining the public peace;

In enforcing the service of process;

In protecting life and property from fire, pestilence, wreck and flood;

And in such other cases as are provided by statute.

CHAPTER II.

RIGHTS OVER PROPERTY.

Original and ultimate title. § 249. The original and ultimate right to all property, real and personal, within the limits of this state, belongs to the people.

Escheat. § 250. All property, real and personal, within the limits of this state, which does not belong to any person, belongs to the people. Whenever the title to any property fails for want of heirs or next of kin it reverts to the people.

§ 251. All lands below common high water mark, where the tide flows, and all mines such as are enumerated in the two following sections, belong to the people. Lands under water and mines.

§ 252. The following mines, now or hereafter discovered, are the property of the people in their right of sovereignty: Enumeration of mines.

1. All mines of gold and silver;

2. All mines of other metals, upon lands owned by persons not being citizens of the United States;

3. All mines of other metals, upon lands owned by a citizen of the United States, the ore of which upon an average, contains less then two equal parts in value of copper, tin, iron and lead, or any of those metals.

The provisions of this and subsequent sections, relating to mines, are to the same effect as those of 1 R. S., 537; but it is submitted that they have become of doubtful expediency, and it were better that they should be repealed.

§ 253. All mines, and all minerals and fossils, now or hereafter discovered, upon any lands belonging to the people of this state, are the pro- Mines, minerals and fossils upon lands of the state.

perty of the people, subject to the provisions hereinafter made to encourage the discovery thereof.

1 R. S., 557, § 2.

What mines belong to the owners of the lands. § 254. All mines, of whatever description, other than mines of gold and silver, now or hereafter discovered, upon any lands owned by a citizen of the United States, the ore of which, upon an average, contains two equal third parts or more in value of copper, tin, iron and lead, or any of these metals, shall belong to the owner of such land.

Ib., § 3.

Discoverer, &c., when exempt. § 255. The discoverer and subsequent proprietor of any mine of gold or silver are exempt from paying to the state any part of the proceeds thereof, for the term of twenty-one years from the time of giving notice of such discovery in the manner hereinafter directed.

Ib., § 4.

Notice of discovery to secretary of state. § 256. No person discovering a mine of gold or silver within this state shall work the same until he gives written notice thereof to the secretary of state, describing particularly the nature and situation of the mine. Such notices shall be registered in a book to be kept by the secretary for that purpose.

Ib., § 5.

Privilege of discoverers. § 257. After the expiration of the term above specified, the discoverer of the mine, or his representatives, shall be preferred in any contract, for the working of such mine, made with the legislature or under its authority.

1 R. S., 555, § 6.

§ 258. Nothing contained in this title shall affect any grants heretofore made by the legislature to the discoverers of mines, nor be construed to give any person a right to break up or enter upon the lands of any other person, or of the people of this state, or to work any mine in such lands, unless the consent, in writing, of the owner thereof, or of the commissioners of the land office, when the lands belong to the people of this state, be previously obtained. Qualification.

§ 259. If any person, under pretense of any claim, inconsistent with the sovereignty and jurisdiction of the state, intrudes upon any of the waste or ungranted lands of the state, the district attorney of the county must immediately report the same to the governor, who shall thereupon, by a written order, direct the sheriff of the county to remove the intruder; and, if resistance to the execution of the order is made or threatened, the sheriff may call to his aid the power of the county, as in cases of resistance to the writs of the people. Intruders on public lands.

1 R. S., 5th ed, 84, §§ 4, 5.

§ 260. The state may acquire title to property by taxation and assessment in the modes authorized by statute. Acquisition by taxation and assessment.

By right of eminent domain.

§ 261. It may acquire, or authorize others to acquire, title to property, real or personal, for public use, by right of eminent domain, in the cases and in the mode authorized by statute.

TITLE III.

PUBLIC WAYS.

CHAPTER I.

PUBLIC WATERS.

ARTICLE I.

GENERAL PROVISIONS RESPECTING PUBLIC WATERS AND OBSTRUCTIONS THEREIN.

§ 262. Navigable waters, and all streams of sufficient capacity to transport the products of the country, are public ways for the purposes of navigation and of such transportation. What waters are public ways.

Brown v. Scofield, 8 Barb., 239; and see 20 Johns., 90; 3 Cai., 307; 10 Johns., 326; Clarke, 336; 3 Paige, 213.

§ 263. The following streams are declared public ways by special statutes: Certain streams.

Schroon river;[1]

Indian river;[2]

Saranac;[3]

Black river;[4]

Beaver river;[5]

West Canada Creek;[6]

Oswegatchie river;[7]

Grass river;[8]

Alden Meadow Brook;[9]

West branch of the St. Regis river;[10]

Salmon river;[11]

Ten Mile river;[12]

East branch of the Chazy river;[14]

Black river.[14]

[1] Laws of 1852, ch. 58, p. 56.
[2] Laws of 1853, ch. 113, p. 173.
[3] Ib., ch. 221, p, 416.
[4] Ib., ch. 452.
[5] Ib., ch. 643.
[6] Laws of 1854, ch. 200.
[7] Ib., ch. 205.
[8] Laws of 1854, ch. 210.
[9] Ib., ch. 215.
[10] Ib., 222.
[11] Ib., 395; 1855, 185; 1857, 133.
[12] Laws of 1857, 474.
[13] Ib., 704.
[14] Laws of 1858, 115.

§ 264. Whoever cuts or causes to be cut down any tree, so that it falls into any stream declared Penalty for felling trees into public waters.

by statute to be a public way, and does not remove it therefrom within twenty-four hours thereafter, is liable to a penalty of five dollars for every tree.

1 R. S., 1051, § 130.

Use of nets, &c., in the channel of the Hudson above New York city.

§ 265. No person shall use, in the channel of the River Hudson between the city of New York and the state dam at Fort Edward, any set-nets, weirs, hoop-nets or pikes, or place there any hedge, stake, post, pole, or other fixture, for any purpose whatever, under penalty of one hundred and fifty dollars.

2 R. S., 97, §§ 37, 38.

Use of nets, &c., in the Hudson, out of the channel.

§ 266. Hoop-nets, pikes or set-nets (if constructed with buoys not more than four feet in length and two feet in diameter) may be used for catching fish in the River Hudson, on and along the flats and shores of the river, and the necessary poles and other fixtures for the use of the same, may be set, so that the navigation of the river be not thereby obstructed or endangered. But none such shall be used in any place where, prior to the 11th day of April, one thousand eight hundred and fifteen, it was the practice to draw seines. Whoever uses any net or weir, or sets any pole, or other fixture in any part of that river, out of the channel and within those limits, other than those above permitted to be used, is liable to a penalty of twenty-five dollars for every offense, and is guilty of a misdemeanor.

1 R. S., 98, § 3; 97, § 40.

§ 267. Special provisions respecting obstructions in the harbor of New York are contained in article IX of this chapter. Obstructions in the port of New York.

ARTICLE II.

NAVIGATION.

§ 268. When steamers meet, each shall turn to the right, so as to pass without interference. Steamers meeting.

2 R. S., 92, § 1.

§ 269. When a passenger is to be landed from a steamer, by means of a small boat, he shall not be suffered to get into it until it is completely afloat and wholly disengaged from the steamer, except by the painter. Landing and receiving passengers by small boat.

2 R. S., § 2.

Lines used for landing, not to be drawn by machinery

§ 270. No line used for the purpose of landing or receiving passengers shall be attached in any way to the machinery of any steamer, nor shall the small boat used for such purpose be hauled in by means of such machinery. The master or person in charge of the steamer violating this provision is guilty of a misdemeanor.

2 R. S., 92, § 4; 93, § 13.

The engine to be stopped.

§ 271. During the landing and receiving of a passenger, and the going and returning of the small boat for the purpose, the engine shall be stopped, and shall not be put in motion except to give sufficient force to carry the small boat to the shore, or to keep the steamer in a proper direction and safe position.

3 R S., 92, §§ 3, 5.

Boat's oars and signals.

§ 272. In every such small boat there shall be kept a good and suitable pair of oars; and in the nighttime, a signal, by means of a horn or trumpet, shall be given to the steamer from the small boat, when, having landed or received its passengers, it is ready to leave the shore.

Ib., § 16.

Steamers overtaking.

§ 273. A steamer going in the same direction with another steamer ahead of it shall not approach or pass the other within the distance of twenty yards; and the steamer ahead shall not be so navigated as unnecessarily to bring it within twenty yards of the steamer following.

Ib., 92, § 7.

§ 274. When any steamer is running in the nighttime, her master shall cause her to carry two conspicuous lights, one exposed near her bows and the other near her stern, the last of which shall be at least twenty feet above her deck. Steamers to carry signals at night.

2 R. S., 92, § 8.

§ 275. Whenever any vessel is navigating any part of Lake Ontario or the Rivers Niagara and St. Lawrence, within the jurisdiction of this state, in the nighttime, her master shall cause a conspicuous light to be shown in her rigging at least twenty feet above her deck, and another light from the taffrail. Vessels in certain waters to show lights.

2 R. S., 94, § 22.

§ 276. Every master, or other person in charge, who violates any of the provisions of the preceding eight sections, incurs a penalty of two hundred and fifty dollars for each offense. Penalties.

2 R. S., 92, § 9.

§ 277. When any vessel is at anchor in the nighttime in the harbor of New York, at any point north of the village of Castleton on Staten island, and south of the south point of Blackwell's island, or in any part of the Hudson river, or on Lake Champlain, or in the harbors or ports on Lake Ontario and the Rivers Niagara and St. Lawrence, within the jurisdiction of this state, the master or other person at the time in charge of the vessel shall cause her peak to be lowered, and a Vessels at anchor to show lights.

conspicuous light shown in her rigging at least twenty feet above her deck, and another light from her taffrail, under penalty of fifty dollars for every neglect.

2 R. S., 93, §§ 14, 15, 21.

Rafts on the Hudson to show light.

§ 278. Every raft of timber floated on the River Hudson at night shall show two red lights, one at each end, and at least ten feet above the upper logs or plank of such raft, under penalty of fifty dollars for every neglect.

2 R. S., 94, § 19.

No recovery for collision in case of neglect.

§ 279. Neither the master or owner of any vessel, boat or raft can recover damages for injuries to the same or to himself by a collision growing out of non-compliance upon its part with the provisions of the preceding six sections.

2 R. S., 94, § 16.

Steamboats &c. to carry boats.

§ 280. Every vessel propelled by steam or fire, navigating any waters of this state, and carrying passengers, must be provided with boats as follows;

1. If of five hundred tons measurement, one first class life-boat, one row-boat twenty-five feet long by seven wide, capable of carrying fifty persons each, and at least one good row-boat besides;

2. If of two hundred and fifty tons measurement, and not five hundred, at least two ordinary row-boats;

3. If of less than two hundred and fifty tons burden, at least one small row or life boat.

All which boats must be attached in such manner that they can be launched at any time for immediate use.

From 2 R. S., 95, §§ 24, 25.

§ 281. The master and owners, and each of them, of any vessel not provided with boats, as required in the preceding section, are subject to a fine not exceeding two hundred and fifty dollars, recoverable by action in any court of record, to be paid to the treasurer of the county in which any of the defendants reside, for the use of the poor. Penalty.

§ 282. It is the duty of every master or other person in charge of a steamer navigating the River Hudson, and of every engineer and fireman thereof, to close the dampers in the pipes or chimneys of the steamer, or otherwise prevent the escape of sparks and coals, while passing along the eastern side of the river, opposite to or in front of the cities of Hudson and Poughkeepsie, and while lying at the docks there. A violation of this section is a misdemeanor, and every such person, and the owners of such steamer, are jointly and severally liable for all damages by fire occasioned by such violation. Dampers of steamer chimneys to be closed at Hudson and at Poughkeepsie.

2 R. S., 95, §§ 29 to 31.

§ 283. In passing through the East river, between the battery at the southern extremity of Regulation of course and speed on East river.

Manhattan island and Blackwell's island, steamers shall be navigated as nearly as possible along the middle of the river, and their speed shall not exceed at any time ten miles an hour,[1] and between the battery and Corlear's hook it shall not exceed eight miles an hour.[2] The master, pilot or engineer of any steamer violating this section is guilty of a misdemeanor, and they are also respectively liable to a penalty of two hundred and fifty dollars.[3]

[1] 2 R. S., 93, § 10.
[2] Laws of 1858, ch. 261, § 5.
[3] 2 R. S., 93, § 11.

Regulation of speed on the Hudson river.

§ 284. No steamer passing any public works of the United States or of this state, while in course of construction in the River Hudson or upon its banks, or while passing that part of the river opposite the docks, piers or wharves in the city of Albany, shall exceed a speed at the rate of six miles an hour, under penalty of one hundred dollars.

Ib., 96, § 35, and first clause of section 36.

Racing.

§ 285. If the master or other person in charge of a steamer navigating any of the waters of this state, and used for the conveyance of passengers, or if the engineer or other person in charge of the boiler or other apparatus for the generation of steam, does, for the purpose of increasing speed or excelling any other vessel in speed, suffer to be created an undue or an unsafe quantity of steam, he is guilty of a misdemeanor, and is liable to a penalty of five hundred dollars; fifty dollars of which shall go to the informer.

2 R. S., 94, § 32.

§ 286. The owners of every steamboat are responsible for the good conduct of the master or other person in charge employed by them, and they are jointly and severally liable for any penalty incurred by the master, engineer or other person in charge which cannot be collected from him by due course of law, as if they were his sureties. Owners liable for master's and engineer's penalties.

Ib., 93, § 12; 96, § 33.

§ 287. The punishment for willfully or negligently endangering life, is prescribed by the CRIMINAL CODE. Reference to Criminal Code.

2 Ib., 848.

§ 288. The penalties given by this and the preceding article may be recovered by the district attorney of any county bordering on the waters where the offense was committed, to whom notice of it is first given, and when recovered are to be for the use of the poor of such county, except when otherwise provided. The court may allow to the district attorney, out of the recovery, a sum not exceeding ten per cent of its amount, as an allowance in addition to his costs. Penalties.

Ib., 93, §§ 9, 14, 17, 32, 36.

ARTICLE III.

FLOATING LUMBER.

Definition. § 289. Lumber is used in this article to designate all timber, whether in logs, boards, planks or beams, and whether in rafts or otherwise, but does not include the sort of wood commonly called drift-wood.

2 R. S., 108, § 1; 110, § 21.

Owner may reclaim lumber. § 290. Whenever any lumber drifts upon any island in any of the waters of this state, or upon the bank of any such waters, the owner of the lumber may remove it, on paying, or tendering to the owner or occupant of the land, the amount of the damages which he has sustained by reason thereof, and which may accrue in its removal; and if the parties cannot agree as to the amount of such damages, either party may apply to any two of the fence viewers of the town or city, who, after hearing their proofs and allegations, shall determine the

the same at the expense of the owner of the lumber, and their decision shall be conclusive.

2 R. S., 108, §§ 1, 2.

§ 291. If the owner of such lumber does not within three months from the time when it was so drifted, take the same away, it is the duty of the owner or occupant of the land to deliver to the clerk of the city or town a notice, in writing, signed by him, describing the lumber, as near as may be, together with the quantity and mark or marks thereof, and the place where it is lodged, which notice the clerk shall file for the inspection of any person who requests it. Notice to town clerk.

Ib., §§ 4, 5.

§ 292. If no person within six months after the filing of such notice claims the lumber, the owner or occupant of the land shall give notice thereof in writing to the clerk, who shall cause the same to be sold by public auction, after giving at least twenty days' previous notice of such sale, by advertisement, posted in at least three of the public places of the city or town. Sale of unclaimed lumber.

Ib., § 7.

§ 293. The clerk is entitled to the same fees therefor as are allowed to officers making sales on executions out of justices' courts. The moneys arising from the sale shall be applied by the clerk: Application of proceeds.

1. To the payment of his fees;

2. To the payment of the damages sustained by the owner or occupant of the land by the drifting and in the removal of the lumber, if such damages are assessed by two of the fence viewers of the city or town, and a specification thereof, signed by them, is filed with such clerk, before the sale;

3. Any surplus to the treasurer of the county for the use of the poor.

1 R. S., 108, §§ 8, 9.

Lumber mark.

§ 294. Every person who puts any lumber into the waters of the River Hudson, or of its branches, to the northwest of Baker's falls, for rafting or floating down the river, or its branches, may select some mark, different from any previously recorded, and put the same in a conspicuous place upon each piece thereof, and enter the mark for record in the office of the clerk of the town of Queensberry. The clerk must record the same in a book kept for that purpose, and subject to the inspection of any person requiring it, and is entitled to a compensation of twenty-five cents for every such mark, to be paid by the person entering the same for record. A certified copy of such entry is presumptive evidence that the lumber having such mark is the property of the person by whom the mark was entered for record.

2 R. S., 109, §§ 12 to 14.

§ 295. If any person shall cut out, alter or deface any mark made upon any lumber, whether the same be recorded or not, or put a false mark upon any lumber floating in any of the waters of this state or lying on land; he shall, for every offense, forfeit to the owner of the lumber twenty-five dollars, and is guilty of a misdemeanor, and whoever converts to his own use, without the owner's consent, any such lumber floating or on land, shall, for every offense, forfeit to the owner treble damages. Defacing marks; converting lumber.

3 R. S., 109, §§ 10, 11.

§ 296. No person, not authorized as in the next section provided, shall stop, obstruct or bring to land on any island or shore of the River Hudson, north of the south limits of the city of Albany, any lumber floating in the river, without the consent of the owner of the lumber, under penalty of ten dollars for every offense, to be recovered by the owner or by the overseers of the poor of the city or town where the offense was committed, for the use of the poor thereof. Stopping lumber forbidden.

Ib., § 15.

§ 297. The common council of the city of Albany may, from time to time, appoint one or more persons, resident therein, to take into possession, for the benefit of the owner thereof, any lumber floating in the Hudson, opposite that city, whereof there is no person present Power of common council of Albany.

on behalf of the owner, to take charge. The persons so appointed shall proceed in the execution of their duties in such manner, and shall receive such compensation as the common council prescribe; but the compensation, in case of dispute, must be settled by any two fence viewers of the city.

2 R. S., 110, § 16.

Sale of lumber found at Albany.

§ 298. If the owner of the lumber does not take the same away, within three months after the time when it has been taken into possession by the persons so appointed, they must deliver to the clerk of the city of Albany a description thereof, in the manner prescribed in section 291; and in case no owner claims the same, within six months after filing the notice, the common council shall direct a sale thereof to be made by the clerk, who shall give the notice and be entitled to the compensation provided by sections 292 and 293.

Ib., § 17.

Application of proceeds.

§ 299. The proceeds shall be first applied to the payment of the charges of sale and the compensation of the persons by whom the lumber was taken into possession. The residue shall be paid to the chamberlain of the city, to be by him paid over to the owner, or his representatives or assigns, at any time within twelve months thereafter, on his producing to the common council satisfactory proof of ownership.

Ib., § 18.

§ 300. The rejection of any such claim by the common council is conclusive against the claimant, unless, within six months after it, he commences his action for such residue against the city of Albany. In case no claim is made or sustained to such monies they shall remain for the use of that city. Subsequent claim by the owner.

1 R. S., 110, §§ 19, 20.

ARTICLE IV.

WRECKS.

SECTION 301. Duties of wreck-masters, officers and citizens.
302. Officers, &c., entitled to salvage.
303. Penalties on officers.
304. Persons having wrecked property to deliver it to an officer.
305. Defacing marks and destroying invoices.
306. Owners of wrecked property may recover it.
307. Duties of sheriffs, coroners and wreck-masters.
308. Perishable property.
309. Order for surrender to claimant.
310. Claimant first to give bond.
311. Action on the bond.
312. Owner may sue, although claim rejected.
313. Salvage to be stated in writing.
314. Proceedings to fix disputed salvage.
315. If no claimant appears, property to be sold.
316. Notice of sales.
317. Notice of wrecked property.
318. Expense of notices.
319. Officers to present all offenses.

§ 301. It is the duty of the wreck-masters in each county to give all possible aid and assistance to all vessels stranded on its coasts, and to the persons on board the same, and to use their utmost endeavors to save and preserve such persons, vessels and their cargoes, and all goods and Duties of wreck-masters, officers and citizens.

merchandise which may be cast by the sea upon the land; and to this purpose they shall employ such and so many men as they may respectively think proper. It is the duty of all magistrates, constables and citizens to aid the wreck-masters when required.

2 R. S., 101, §§ 10, 11.

Officers, &c., entitled to salvage.

§ 302. All sheriffs, coroners and wreck-masters, and all persons employed by them, or aiding in the recovery and preservation of wrecked property, are entitled to a reasonable allowance as salvage for their services, and to all expenses incurred by them in the performance of such services, out of the property saved; and the officer having the custody of such property shall detain it until the same are paid; but the whole salvage claimed shall not exceed one-half of the value of the property or proceeds on which it is charged; and every agreement, order or adjustment allowing a greater salvage is void.

Ib., 102, §§ 12, 13.

Penalties on officers.

§ 303. Any officer who detains any wrecked property or the proceeds thereof, after the salvage and expenses chargeable thereon have been agreed to or adjusted, and been paid or offered to him, or who is guilty of any fraud, embezzlement or extortion in the discharge of his duties, or violates any provision of this article, shall forfeit treble damages to the party injured, and is guilty of a misdemeanor.

2 R. S., 103, § 24.

§ 304. Every person who takes away any goods from any stranded vessel, or any goods cast by the sea upon the land, or found in any bay or creek, or who knowingly becomes possessed of any such, and does not deliver the same, within forty-eight hours thereafter, to the sheriff or one of the coroners, or wreck-masters of the county where the same were found, shall forfeit treble their value to the owner or consignee thereof, and is guilty of a misdemeanor.

Persons having wrecked property to deliver it to an officer.

Ib., 103, § 25.

§ 305. Every person who defaces or obliterates the marks on wrecked property, or in any manner disguises the appearance thereof, with intent to prevent the owner from discovering its identity, and every person who destroys or suppresses any invoice, bill of lading, or other document tending to show the ownership, is guilty of a misdemeanor.

Defacing marks and destroying invoices.

Ib., 105, § 26.

§ 306. Wrecked property may be kept or reclaimed at the time of the wreck, by the owner, consignee, or other person entitled to possession, but if any person has a just claim for salvage and necessary expenses incurred in saving it, they must be paid before the property is recovered.

Owners of wrecked property may recover it.

3 R. S., 100, § 1.

Duty of sheriffs, coroners and wreck-masters.

§ 307. It is the duty of the sheriff, coroners and wreck-masters of every county in which any wrecked property is found, when no owner or other person entitled to possession appears, severally to take possession of it, in whose hands soever it may be, in the name of the people; to cause its value to be appraised by disinterested persons; and to keep it in some safe place, to answer the owner's claims.

2 R. S., 100, § 2.

Perishable property.

§ 308. If it is in a perishable state, so as to render its sale expedient, such officer shall apply to the county judge of the county, by a verified petition, for an order authorizing him to sell it; which the judge shall grant, if he is satisfied that a sale would be most beneficial to the parties interested; and the property shall then be sold by public auction at the time and in the manner specified in the order, and the proceeds, deducting the expenses thereof, as the same shall be settled and allowed by such judge, must be paid to the treasurer of the county.

Ib., §§ 3, 4.

Order for surrender to claimant.

§ 309. If within a year after the finding, any person claim the property or its proceeds, as owner, consignee, or otherwise, and establishes his claim by evidence satisfactory to the county judge, such judge shall make an order directing the officer in whose possession the property or its proceeds may be, to deliver the same to the claimant, upon his paying a reasonable salvage, and the expenses of preservation.

2 R. S., 100, § 5.

§ 310. Before making the order the judge shall require from the claimant a bond to the people, with one or more sufficient sureties, to be approved by the judge, and filed with the clerk of the county, in a penalty double the value of the property or proceeds, conditioned for the payment of all damages that may be recovered against such claimant or his representatives, within two years after its date, by any person establishing his title to the property or proceeds. Claimant first to give bond

Ib., 101, § 6, and first clause of § 7.

§ 311. If the bond becomes forfeited, the county judge, upon the application, supported by due proof, of the person entitled to the benefit of it, shall make an order for its prosecution for his benefit, and at his risk and expense. Action on the bond.

Ib., § 7.

§ 312. The rejection by the judge of any claim shall not preclude the claimant from maintaining an action for the recovery of such property or its proceeds, against the officer; but if the plaintiff in any such action prevails, there shall be deducted from the damages, in addition to salvage and expenses, all the defendant's costs. Owner may sue, although claim rejected.

Ib., § 8.

Salvage to be stated in writing.

§ 313. It is the duty of every officer to whom an order under section 309 is directed, to present to the claimant exhibiting it a written statement of the claim for salvage and expenses. If the claimant refuse to allow such amount it shall be adjusted as hereinafter provided.

2 R. S., 101, § 9.

Proceedings to fix disputed salvage.

§ 314. If, in any case, the amount of salvage and expenses be not settled by agreement, the county court of the county, on the application of the owner or consignee of the property, or the master or supercargo having charge thereof at the time of the wreck, or of a claimant having an order therefor, or of the person entitled to salvage and expenses, shall determine the same, in a summary way, either by itself hearing the proofs and allegations of the parties, or by referring the questions to three disinterested freeholders of the county, not inhabitants of the town in which the property was saved, who shall proceed as in civil actions, and be entitled to the same compensation, and whose decision as to the whole amount, and as to the sums to be paid to each person interested, shall be made a judgment of the county court.

Ib., 102, §§ 14 to 17.

If no claimant appears, property to be sold.

§ 315. If within a year after saving wrecked property no claimant of the property or its proceeds appears, or within three months after a claim the salvage and expenses have not been paid, or a suit for the recovery of the property or its proceeds has not been commenced, the officer in whose custody it may be shall sell it at public auction, if not already sold, and when sold shall pay the proceeds, deducting salvage and expenses, into the treasury of this state, for the benefit of the parties interested; but in no case shall any deduction of salvage and expenses be made, unless the amount has been determined by the county court of the county, a copy of whose order, and of the evidence in support thereof, shall be transmitted by the judge to the comptroller. If any money paid to a county treasurer, under section 308, remains in his hands more than a year after the finding, the same shall be also paid into the treasury of the state.

2 R. S., 102, § 18.

§ 316. Public notice of every sale of wrecked property, under the provisions of this article, shall be previously published by the officer making the sale, for at least two weeks in succession, in one or more of the newspapers printed in the city of New York. Every such notice must state the time and place of the sale, and contain a particular description of the property to be sold. Notice of sale.

Ib., 103, § 20.

§ 317. Every sheriff, coroner or wreck-master, into whose possession any wrecked property may come, must immediately thereafter publish, for at Notice of wrecked property.

least four weeks in succession, in one or more of the newspapers printed in the city of New York, a notice directed to all parties interested, giving a minute description of the property, and of every bale, bag, box, cask, piece or parcel thereof, and of all the marks on each, and stating where the same then is, and its actual condition, the name, if known, of the vessel from which it came, her master and supercargo, and the place where such vessel then is, and her actual condition.

2 R. S., 103, §§ 21, 22.

Expense of notice.

§ 318. The expenses of publishing every notice under the provisions of this article shall be charged on the property or proceeds to which it relates.

Ib., § 23.

Officers to present all offenses.

§ 319. It is the duty of all judges, sheriffs, justices of the peace, coroners, constables and wreck-masters, to present to the grand jury, at the next court of sessions therein, all offenses and offenders against the provisions of this article, within their respective counties, that come to their knowledge.

Ib., § 27.

ARTICLE V.

SANDY HOOK PILOTS.

The existing laws provide separate systems for the Sandy Hook and Hellgate pilots. Though the necessity of this is not perceived, the commissioners have not attempted to change them. The legislature may, however, think it advisable to establish the same regulations for both.

The provisions of this article are from the following statutes: Laws of 1853, ch. 467; Laws of 1854, ch. 196; Laws of 1857, ch. 243.

§ 320. The pilotage of vessels to and from the port of New York is regulated by law, as provided in this and the next article. Pilotage.

§ 321. Commissioners of pilots, of whom there are five, are elected within thirty days before the expiration of the term of office of their respective predecessors, or upon the happening of a vacancy, in the following manner: Mode of appointment of pilot commissioners.

Three of them, and their successors, are elected at a meeting of the chamber of commerce of the city of New York, to be called for the purpose, which is to be specified in the call.

Two of them, and their successors, are elected by the presidents and vice-presidents of the marine insurance companies of the city of New York, represented in the board of underwriters of that city, at a regular meeting of the board, on notice that such election will take place, given in writing by the secretary of the board, or by a member duly authorized, at least one day before the election, and delivered at the office of each company Each company represented is entitled to one vote

The certificate of the secretary, or other officer acting as such, of such electing body, is presumptive evidence of the result. Each commissioner holds his office two years; but in case of a vacancy, the remaining commissioners have power to perform all the duties of the commissioners for the time being.

Office, meetings, and records.

§ 322. The commissioners shall maintain an office, in a convenient place, in the city of New York, where their secretary shall be in attendance at all reasonable hours; and they shall meet on the first Tuesday of every month, and as much oftener by adjournment, or upon notice given by any one of them, or by the secretary, as circumstances require, and where they shall cause to be kept the following records, which shall be open to the inspection of all persons interested therein:

1. A record of all the regulations made by them, and all their official action, and of such other matters pertaining to their duties or to the pilot service as they deem useful;

2. A register of the names and residences of all pilots licensed by them, with the dates of the licenses.

§ 323. The pilot commissioners have power: Powers of board.

1. To appoint a secretary to hold office during their pleasure, and fix his duties and compensation;

2. To grant licenses for piloting vessels to and from the port of New York, by way of Sandy hook, to such persons as pass a satisfactory examination and give security as hereinafter provided; the number of the pilots and the term of the licenses to be fixed in the discretion of the commissioners; and the licenses to specify all or portions of the different branches of the pilot service, according to the qualifications of applicants; but no license shall be granted to any person holding any license or authority under any other state;

3. To suspend at any time a pilot for any period they may think proper, and also to revoke any license on satisfactory proof of negligence, intoxication or misconduct in duty, on the part of

the person licensed, or in case he is not connected with a boat approved by them; but any pilot suspended may at any time, on due notice, appeal to the commissioners for a rehearing; and the commissioners may confirm or reverse their previous decision;

4. To regulate the stationing of pilot-boats, for the purpose of receiving pilots from outward bound vessels;

5. To amend existing regulations for pilots, and make and duly promulgate and enforce new rules or regulations, not inconsistent with the laws of this state or of the United States, which shall be binding and effectual upon all pilots licensed by them, and upon all parties employing such pilots;

6. To declare and enforce forfeitures of pilotage upon any mismanagement or neglect of duty by the pilots licensed by them; and to declare and collect fines and penalties, not exceeding two hundred and fifty dollars for each offense;

7. To prevent any of the pilots licensed by them from combining injuriously with each other, or with other persons, and to prevent any person licensed by them from acting as a pilot during his suspension or after his license may be revoked;

8. To establish and enforce all other needful rules and regulations for the conduct and government of the pilots licensed by them, and the par-

ties employing them, in respect to such employment;

9. To receive and enforce accounts of all monies collected for pilotage, by the pilots licensed by them;

10. To impose and collect from such pilots a sum not exceeding three per cent on the amount thereof, to defray the necessary expenses of the board;

11. To provide, out of any funds which may be obtained, rewards to encourage the prompt relief of disabled vessels, and the speedy report of the same, and also not only the energetic performance of duty, but benevolent and praiseworthy efforts to relieve vessels and passengers from distress;

12. To perform such further duties as are prescribed by article IX of this chapter, entitled "*Special regulations for the port of New York.*"

§ 324. Before any person can receive a license he must be examined, within one week after his application, by the commissioners and one or more of the licensed Sandy Hook pilots, in respect to his qualifications, and in particular upon the following points: **Examination of candidates.**

1. His experience and skill to act as pilot;

2. His knowledge of the sailing and management of a square-rigged vessel;

3. His knowledge of the tides, soundings, the bearing and distance of the several shoals, rocks, bars, points and night lights in the navigation for which he applies for license;

4. His moral character;

5. His temperate habits.

It is the duty of pilots to attend and assist in the examinations whenever required by the commissioners; but in case of their failure to attend at any time, the examination may proceed in their absence.

Security. § 325. Before granting a license, the commissioners shall require each pilot to enter into recognizance to the people of this state, with two sureties, to be approved by the commissioners, in a penalty not exceeding five hundred dollars, conditioned that the pilot shall diligently and faithfully perform his duties as pilot, and observe the regulations and decisions of the commissioners, which recognizance may be prosecuted in the name of the people of the State of New York, whenever a majority so direct. Any amount collected shall be paid to the commissioners, who may direct the same to be applied to the purposes mentioned in subdivision 11, of section 322.

Tariff of pilotage. § 326. The fees for pilotage, by the Sandy Hook pilots, are as follows:

1. For merchant vessels inward bound, if drawing less than fourteen feet of water, two dollars and forty-four cents per foot;

If drawing fourteen and less than eighteen feet three dollars and six cents per foot;

If drawing eighteen and less than twenty-one feet, three dollars and seventy cents per foot;

If drawing twenty-one feet and upwards, four dollars and thirty cents per foot;

If the masters or owners of any vessel request the pilot to moor the same at any place within Sandy Hook, and not to take it to the wharf or harbor of New York, or the vessel be detained at quarantine, the same pilotage shall be allowed, and the pilot entitled to his discharge;

2. For merchant vessels outward bound, if drawing less than fourteen feet, one dollar and eighty cents per foot;

If drawing fourteen and less than eighteen feet, two dollars and twelve cents per foot;

If drawing eighteen and less than twenty-one feet. two dollars and seventy-five cents per foot;

If drawing twenty-one feet and upwards, three dollars and twenty cents per foot;

3. For national armed vessels of the United States or of other nations, five dollars per foot;

4. For moving vessels within the harbor of New York, as follows:

For moving from the North to the East river, or from the East to the North river, if a seventy-four gun ship, twenty dollars; if a sloop of war, ten dollars; if a merchant vessel, five dollars, except if such merchant vessel arrived from sea, or is ready for and bound to sea on the day such services for moving are rendered, a separate fee shall not be charged for the moving;

For moving any vessel from the quarantine to the city of New York, one-quarter of the sum that would be due for the inward pilotage of such vessel;

For hauling any vessel from the river to a wharf or from a wharf into the river, three dollars, except on the day of arrival or departure of such vessels;

5. When any vessel bound to the port of New York is boarded at such distance to the southward or eastward of Sandy Hook lighthouse as that that lighthouse could not be seen from its deck in the daytime and in fair weather, the addition of one-fourth to the rates of pilotage shall be allowed to the pilot;

6. Between the first day of November, and the first day of April, inclusive, four dollars shall be added to the full pilotage of every vessel coming into or going out of the port of New York;

7. For every day of detention in the harbor of an outward-bound vessel, after the services of a pilot have been required and given, unless such detention is caused by adverse weather; and for every day of detention of an inward-bound vessel, by ice, longer than two days for passage from sea to wharf, three dollars shall be added to the pilotage, and if any pilot is detained at quarantine, or elsewhere, by the health officer, for being or having been on board a sickly vessel as pilot, he shall be paid all necessary expenses of living and three dollars for each day of such detention;

8. A pilot who is carried to sea, when a boat is attending to receive him, shall receive at the rate of one hundred dollars a month during his necessary absence;

9. The board shall prescribe and promulgate in their regulations the rates for any intermediate distances and other services which do not fall within the foregoing provisions.

Fractional and uneven sums in the fees prescribed by subdivisions 1 and 2 we have slightly modified from the statute, to reduce them to even sums. Thus, seventy cents was sixty-nine; thirty cents was thirty-one and a quarter, &c.

§ 327. The master of each vessel shall give an account to the pilot, when boarding, of the draught of the vessel; and in case the draught given is less than the actual draught, he is liable to a penalty of twenty-five dollars. **Masters to state draught of vessel.**

Fees, by whom payable.

§ 328. The master, owner, consignee or agent, entering or clearing a vessel at the port of New York, are jointly and severally liable for all charges of a pilot for services and expenses respecting the vessel, pursuant to this article.

Others than pilots not to act as such.

§ 329. No master of a vessel, under three hundred tons burden, belonging to a citizen of the United States, and licensed and employed in the coasting trade by the way of Sandy hook, shall be required to employ a licensed pilot; but in case the services of a pilot shall have been given, the pilot shall be entitled to the rates established. If the master of any vessel above three hundred tons burden, and owned by a citizen of the United States, and sailing under a coasting license to or from the port of New York by the way of Sandy hook, is desirous of piloting his own vessel, he must first obtain a license for the purpose from the commissioners who must grant it, if upon an examination pursuant to section 323, he is found competent. Such license shall continue in force one year from its date, or until the termination of any voyage during which the year expires. For such license, the master to whom it is granted shall pay to the board four cents per ton. All masters of foreign vessels and vessels from a foreign port, and all vessels sailing under register, bound to or from the port of New York by the way of Sandy hook, shall take a licensed pilot, or, in case of refusal to take such pilot, shall themselves, owners or consignees, pay the pilotage as if one had been employed; which pilotage shall be paid to the pilot first speaking or offering his services as pilot to such vessel.

Any person not holding a license as pilot under this article, or under the laws of the State of New Jersey, who pilots or offers to pilot any vessel to or from the port of New York by the way of Sandy hook, except such as are exempt, or any master or person on board a steam-tug or tow-boat, who tows such vessel without a licensed pilot on board, is guilty of a misdemeanor; and every person employing as pilot a person not holding a license under this article, or under the laws of the State of New Jersey, is liable to a penalty of one hundred dollars. But this section does not apply to vessels propelled wholly or in part by steam, owned or belonging to citizens of the United States, and engaged in the coasting trade.

Complaints against pilots and others.

§ 330. It is the duty of the commissioners to hear and examine all complaints made in writing against any pilot licensed by them, or against any person connected with a boat of such pilot, for misbehavior, neglect of duty or breach of the regulations; and also all complaints made in like manner by any licensed pilot against any master, owner or seaman of a vessel, for misbehavior towards such pilot in the performance of his duty, or any breach of the regulations. Before proceeding on any complaint, and before any suspension for longer than one month, and before any removal, such person or pilot shall be served with a written notice, signed by the secretary, to appear before the commissioners at a specified time and place, stating the nature and substance of the complaint, which notice shall be served, personally, at least five days before the time specified, and the commissioners, for just cause, shall adjourn the hearing from time to time. A certificate of such commissioners, or a majority of them, with proof of such service or notice, shall be presumptive evidence that the party upon whom the notice was served, and a fine or penalty thereupon imposed, is liable to pay the same.

Witnesses. § 331. The secretary, under the supervision of the commissioners, shall, at the instance either of the complaining or defending party, issue subpœnas for compelling the attendance of witnesses to testify before the commissioners in all cases in which the power to hear and determine is conferred by this article; and it is the duty of the commissioners to examine all material witnesses on oath, to be administered by them. Each witness is entitled to the same compensation from the party requiring his attendance, and is subject to the same penalties and punishments for disobedience or for false swearing, as for the same acts in civil actions in courts of record.

Power of of board. § 332. The decision of a majority of the commissioners shall be conclusive upon all questions arising under this article, except when otherwise provided.

§ 333. It is the duty of the secretary and his clerks, if any, when not employed under the provisions of this article, to aid the licensed pilots in keeping their accounts of pilotage and in collecting the same, if desired, and in keeping a register of calls for pilots. Further duty of secretary and clerks.

§ 334. Penalties incurred under this article, and fines and penalties imposed by the commissioners, may be recovered by them in the name of the commissioners. Penalties, how recovered.

ARTICLE VI.

HELLGATE PILOTS.

The provisions of this article are taken from 1 R. S., 1063, 1064, 1065, 1066.

§ 335. Hellgate pilots are appointed by the governor, with the consent of the senate, upon the recommendation of the port-wardens of New York, and hold office during good behavior. Their func- Hellgate pilots, how appointed.

tions are the pilotage of vessels through the channel of the East river, known as Hellgate.

Port-wardens to recommend. § 336. The port-wardens shall recommend from time to time to the governor, for appointment, among those who have served two years as deputy pilots, so many as they may deem necessary, and the governor shall nominate the same

Apprentices and deputy pilots. § 337. Any person may serve an apprenticeship with any Hellgate pilot or deputy pilot. After serving as such three years next before attaining the age of twenty-one at least, and upon passing examination, they may be authorized by certificate of the board to serve as deputy pilots. All apprentices must be examined twice, during the last year of their apprenticeship, by the board and at least two of the Hellgate pilots, whose duty it is to attend and assist in the examinations whenever required by the port-wardens. The indenture of every apprentice under this article must be filed in the office of the port-wardens within ten days after its execution.

Regulations to be made by board of wardens. § 338. The port-wardens have power to make, from time to time, regulations not inconsistent with the Constitution and laws of this state or of the United States, for the better government of the Hellgate pilots, with reasonable fines and penalties for violations thereof. Every such regulation must be entered at length upon their minutes, and they shall furnish a copy to each Hellgate pilot.

§ 339. The port-wardens have cognizance of all charges made against any Hellgate pilot for official misconduct. No charges shall be received unless verified by the complainant's oath. Before proceeding thereon the port-wardens shall furnish the pilot with a copy thereof, which shall contain a full specification of the charges preferred, and with a notice of the time (not less than six days) and the place when they require him to appear before them to answer. **Charges against pilots.**

§ 340. Upon the pilot appearing, it is the duty of the port-wardens to take testimony, and to examine into the facts, and if after a full hearing of the case, and of competent proof tending to establish the charge, a majority of the port-wardens in office deem him guilty of official misconduct, they have power to suspend him. They must thereupon, within ten days transmit to the governor a full account of their proceedings, with a copy of the charges specified and of the testimony taken. The governor shall either remove the pilot from office, or annul or confirm his suspension, as to him seems just. **Proceedings.**

§ 341. It is the duty of the Hellgate pilots to keep two or more good and sufficient deck boats, of not less than twenty tons burden, on the East river, and no more than seven pilots shall be interested in one deck boat, and no apprentice shall be taken by the pilot, but in those deck boats; and no other than a Hellgate pilot shall own any part of a boat engaged **Deck boat.**

in the business under pain of a forfeiture of his title therein. All the deck boats shall be registered in the office of the port-wardens.

Tariff of pilotage.

§ 342. The fees for pilotage by the Hellgate pilots for any vessel of ninety-five tons burden and upwards are as follows:

1. Between Sands point or Execution rocks, or any place eastward thereof, and New York, going either way, one dollar and fifty cents per foot for each foot of water the vessel draws;

2. Between the eastward of Hellgate and New York, going either way, one dollar per foot for each foot the vessel draws;

3 For a square-rigged vessel, in addition to the above rates, twenty-five cents for each foot the vessel draws;

4. For any government vessel piloted through Hellgate, instead of the rates above, five dollars per foot for each foot the vessel draws;

5. For each day during which the pilot is detained on board, beyond the term of twenty-four hours, he is entitled to be paid two dollars in addition to the rates above prescribed;

6. Between the first day of November and the first day of April, inclusive, two dollars shall be added to the full pilotage of every ship, bark or brig, and one dollar to that of every sloop or schooner;

7. A pilot who renders extra service to any vessel in distress is entitled to be paid therefor, in addition, a reasonable compensation to be fixed by the board.

The rate fixed by subdivision 4 is the rate now provided for such service by the Sandy hook pilots. Section 325, subdivision 3, *ante*.

§ 343. The pilot who brings any vessel into the port by way of Hellgate is entitled to a preference in piloting it out on its next outward passage, if the same is by way of Hellgate; and any Hellgate pilot who first tenders his services to any vessel navigating the channel of Hellgate, in either direction, is, if refused, entitled to receive one-half the rates prescribed by the preceding section. But such half pilotage is not chargeable to any vessel under ninety-five tons burden, sailing under a coasting license, unless such vessel makes a signal for a pilot; nor is such half pilotage chargeable to any vessel more than once for the same passage. **Pilots to have preference in certain cases.**

§ 344. The master, owner, consignee or agent entering or clearing a vessel at the port of New York, are jointly and severally liable for all charges of a pilot respecting the vessel, pursuant to this article. **Pilotage, by whom payable.**

From similar provision respecting Sandy hook pilots, § 327, *ante*.

Other than pilots not to act as such.

§ 345. No person other than a Hellgate pilot, or one of the crew of the vessel, shall pilot for any other person any vessel through Hellgate, or board such vessel for that purpose, or offer so to do, under penalty of thirty dollars for each offense. A violation of this section is a misdemeanor.

Penalties, &c.

§ 346. All fines, penalties and forfeitures, imposed by or under authority of this article, are to be recovered by the port-wardens, in the name of the port-wardens of the port of New York.

Steamboats excepted.

§ 347. The provisions of this article do not apply to steamboats.

ARTICLE VIII.

NEW YORK PORT-WARDENS.

The provisions of this article are from Laws of 1857, ch. 405.

The officers of the board.

§ 348. The nine wardens of the port of New York shall annually elect one of their number president and another vice-president. They may also appoint a secretary and fix his compensation, which shall be paid out of the receipts of the office. They shall keep an office in the city of New York, at which office a majority of them and their secretary shall give attendance daily (Sundays and public holidays excepted.)

§ 349. Any warden neglecting to perform the duties of his office, or violating the regulations of the board, after due notice from the board, shall be liable to suspension by a vote of the majority of the whole board, and during such suspension shall not be allowed to participate in the emoluments of the office, unless reinstated by the governor, to whom an appeal may be taken. Suspension of wardens.

§ 350. It is the duty of the secretary to keep a complete record of all their acts, proceedings, surveys and reports, which record shall be kept open to inspection of all persons interested therein. Duty of secretary.

§ 351. The port-wardens have a common seal, and each warden has power to administer oaths, concerning the business of the office; and all willful false swearing, under such oaths, is perjury. The port-wardens also have power to make such reasonable regulations for their own government and the discharge of their duties as they may deem proper, and they have the exclusive right to perform all the duties of port-wardens for the port of New York. General powers of the board.

Their powers in respect to pilots are prescribed

by article VI of this chapter, entitled "*Hellgate Pilots.*" Their other powers and duties are as follows:

1. Upon request of any of the parties in interest, one or more of the port-wardens must proceed in person on board of any vessel for the purpose of examining the condition and stowage of the cargo, and if there be any damaged goods, to ascertain if possible the cause of such damage, and if, after the arrival in port of any vessel, the hatches are first opened by any person not a port-warden, and the cargo or any part thereof comes from on shipboard in a damaged condition, these facts shall be presumptive evidence that the cause of such damage was improper stowage or negligence on the part of the person in charge of the vessel, and the loss shall be chargeable to the owner, consignee, and master, jointly and severally;

2. The board shall be exclusive surveyors of any vessel which may have suffered wreck or damage, or which shall be deemed unfit to proceed to sea, and shall examine the condition of the hull, spars, sails, rigging, and all appurtenances thereof, and decide what repairs are necessary to render the vessel seaworthy, in which examination they may call to their assistance one or more disinterested carpenters, sail-makers, riggers, shipwrights or other such person skilled in his profession, to aid them in their examination and survey, who shall be sworn

and shall each be allowed a fee of two dollars, to be paid by the person requiring the examination;

3. They shall have exclusive cognizance of all matters relating to the surveys of vessels and their cargoes arriving at the port of New York, in distress, or damaged in that port, and shall be the judges of the fitness of any vessel or cargo to proceed to its port of destination, or whether it shall be sold for the benefit of whom it may concern;

4. They shall also, if called upon so to do, estimate the value or measurement of any vessel when the same is in dispute, or libeled, and record the same in the books of the office;

5. Upon the request of any of the parties in interest, one or more of the port-wardens must proceed, in person, to any warehouse, store or dwelling, or any public street, or wharf, and examine any merchandise, vessel's materials or other property alleged to have been damaged on board of any vessel, and ascertain the cause of such damage;

6. One or more of the port-wardens must attend personally all sales of vessels condemned, vessel's materials, and goods in a damaged state, which are sold by public auction in the port of New York, by reason of such damages, for the benefit of the owners or underwriters, or for account of whom it may concern; all which sales shall be made by auctioneers under the direction of the wardens;

7. To keep in their office a full record of all damage inquired into by them, and the cause thereof, if ascertained, and of all other inquiries, examinations, surveys, determinations and reports, and of all sales made by them or under their direction, and the expenses thereof;

8. To furnish a certificate of any record in the books of the office to any party interested, upon request and payment of the fee for the certificate. All the certificates issued shall be under the seal of the office, and signed by the president or vice-president and secretary and shall be evidence of the existence and contents of the record, in all cases of inquiries, examinations, and surveys relating to vessels and cargoes thereof, as specified in this article.

Notice of proceedings. § 352. The board must give notice to all persons interested in or having charge of the subject, of any inquiry, examination or survey, by personal notice, or by advertisement in at least two daily newspapers printed and published in the city of New York, of the pendency of such inquiry, examination or survey, and of the time and place of completing the same, and the expense of such notice shall be added to and paid with the fee for the inquiry, examination or survey.

Auctioneer's duty. § 353. It is the duty of auctioneers making sale of vessels condemned, vessel's materials and goods in a damaged state, immediately to give notice thereof to the port-wardens; and also to make monthly statements to the board, to be filed in their office, specifying the total amount of each day's sale made by them under this article.

§ 354. The board of wardens shall be allowed the following fees: Fees.

For each survey held on board of any vessel, on hatches, stowage of cargo, or damaged goods, or at any warehouse, store or dwelling, or in the public street or on the wharf, within the limits of the port of New York, on goods said to be damaged, the sum of two dollars, and for each certificate given in consequence thereof the sum of one dollar;

For each survey on the hull, sails, spars or rigging of any vessel damaged, or arriving at that port in distress, the sum of five dollars, and for each certificate given in consequence thereof the sum of two dollars and fifty cents. For each valuation or measurement of any vessel the sum of ten dollars. For each sale made under their direction, one-half of one per cent on the gross amount of sales, to be paid by the auctioneer making the sale. The emoluments of the office shall be divided equally between the nine wardens composing the board.

§ 355. No person, except the port-wardens, shall assume to act as such, or undertake to act as such, or undertake the performance of any of the duties prescribed in this article as pertaining to the office of port-warden, or employ any other than the war- None but port-wardens to act.

dens for the performance of such duties, or issue certificates of surveys on vessels, materials or goods damaged, with the intent to avoid the provisions of this article. A violation of any provision of this section is a misdemeanor, and the person violating it is also liable to a penalty of one hundred dollars for each offense, to be recovered by the port-wardens.

Special wardens at quarantine.

§ 356 The two special wardens for the port of New York shall reside at quarantine. It is their duty to act as wardens only in regard to vessels and goods that are actually under and subject to quarantine detention, and their duties do not apply to vessels stopping at quarantine for the purpose only of visitation by a health officer and not détained. They shall make returns in detail of all surveys made by them, and of all other duties by them performed, to the wardens' office in the city of New York, within forty-eight hours after such survey or service performed; and all regulations adopted by the board of wardens shall apply to the special wardens. The special wardens are entitled to receive for each examination or survey made by them the sum of five dollars; and the emoluments of their office shall be divided equally between them.

Receipts and expenses.

§ 257. The port-wardens shall keep a full and accurate account of all their receipts and expenditures, and transmit to the comptroller annually, on the first Monday of January in each year, a true copy thereof, verified by the oaths of the president and secretary; and each warden shall append to such account an affidavit that he has not taken or received, directly or indirectly, any money or other property for or in relation to any act or omission to act as warden, except the legal fees.

ARTICLE VIII.

NEW YORK HARBOR-MASTERS.

The provisions of this article are taken from 1 R. S., 1060, 1062; Laws of 1857, ch. 367.

§ 358. At least five of the eleven harbor-masters for the port of New York must have been either masters of vessels sailing from, or pilots or seamen engaged in navigating, the port of New York. Nine of them must reside in the city of New York and two in Brooklyn. Qualifications of harbor-masters.

§ 359. Each harbor-master, before entering on the duties of his office, must execute a bond to the people in the penalty of two thousand five hundred dollars, with two sufficient sureties, to be approved Official bond.

by the mayor of the city of New York, conditioned for the faithful performance of his duties.

Harbor-masters to share duties and compensation.

§ 360. The harbor-masters may, jointly and severally, perform all the duties and functions, and shall divide equally the emoluments of their offices.

General powers.

§ 361. They or either of them have power:

1. To station and regulate all vessels in the stream of the East or North rivers, within the limits of the city of New York and the wharves thereof, and to remove, from time to time, vessels not employed in the transfer of cargo, to make room for others that require accommodation for that purpose; of which, and of a vessel not being employed in the transfer of cargo, or requiring accommodation, they are the sole judges;

2. To determine how far, and in what instances, it is the duty of masters of vessels to accommodate each other, in their respective situations.

Penalties.

§ 362. Any master who neglects to obey, and any person whatever who resists the direction of any harbor-master, given under the authority of this article, is liable to a penalty of fifty dollars, to be recovered in the name of the treasurer of the New York hospital, for the use of the hospital.

Fees.

§ 363. The harbor-masters are entitled to receive from the commanders, owners and consignees, or either of them, of any vessel which enters the port of New York, and loads or unloads any part of her cargo, or makes fast to any wharf, the following fees:

1. On all vessels of the United States, or of any foreign nation permitted by the laws of the United States, to enter on the same terms as vessels of the United States, one and one-half of one cent per ton of the vessel's tonnage, as expressed in its register or enrollment;

2. On all other foreign vessels, three cents per ton of the vessel's tonnage, to be ascertained by its register or other documents on board.

But this section does not apply to any sloop or schooner employed in the coasting trade within the United States.

§ 364. The master, owner or consignees of every vessel shall, within forty-eight hours after its arrival, pay the fees due thereon at the office of the harbor-masters, or one of them. If after default of payment they are not paid on demand, the master, owner or consignee, on whom the demand was made, shall forfeit double the amount of the fees. Payment and penalty for default.

§ 365. When, upon the application of the master of any sloop or schooner employed in the coasting trade, any harbor-master adjusts any difference happening respecting the situation of such vessel, and it is the duty of any harbor-master, on application, to hear and determine such differences, he is entitled, Fees for adjusting controversy.

upon adjusting the difference, to receive from the party in default the sum of two dollars, except in case of canal barges and canal boats, and then one dollar.

Duty of harbor-master respecting piers.

§ 366. It is the duty of the harbor-masters to enforce the laws of the state and the ordinances of the city for cleaning the wharves and docks, and for preventing and removing all nuisances therefrom; and if any one whose duty it is to remove a nuisance, neglects to remove it within forty-eight hours after notice to do so, from a harbor-master, he is liable to a penalty of two dollars and fifty cents.

Piers for canal boats and barges, railway barges and packets.

§ 367. The water adjacent to the wharves, from the east side of pier number two to the east side of pier number nine, East river, shall, from the twentieth day of March to the twentieth day of December, in each year, be reserved, so far as necessary, for the use of canal boats and barges engaged in transporting property on the River Hudson, or coming to tide-water from the canals of the state or arriving in New York from Albany or any place north or west thereof, and of barges transporting property to and from the ferry stations of the New York and Erie, New York Central and Hudson River railways.

Piers for packets.

§ 368. Piers number ten, eleven, and the west side of pier number twelve, East river, shall during the same period, be reserved for the use of the regular packet lines of sailing vessels, propellers and barges which, on the 13th day of April, 1857, occupied berths on piers nine, ten, eleven, and the west side of pier twelve, and running to and from the following ports: Boston, Massachusetts; Portsmouth, New Hampshire; Philadelphia, by way of the Delaware and Raritan Canal; Wilmington, North Carolina; Savannah, Georgia; Charleston, South Carolina; Appalachicola, Florida; Mobile, Alabama; New Orleans, Louisiana; and Matagorda, Texas.

§ 369. The harbor-masters shall enforce the last two sections by preventing other boats, barges and vessels from entering those piers, and by removing them therefrom so far as necessary for the accommodation of the boats, barges and vessels mentioned. They shall also give a copy of this article to any captain, owner or consignee requesting it, who shall not be liable to any penalty for a violation of its provisions until that has been done. Duty of harbor-masters to enforce this regulation.

§ 370. The last three sections shall not be construed to impair the right of the owner or lessee of any wharf to collect legal wharfage from vessels using the same, nor to prevent the free use of the wharves mentioned when not required for the uses specified: nor to prevent any vessel from hauling alongside of any vessel, barge or canal boat and lying there for the purpose of the transfer of cargo Saving clause.

with all reasonable dispatch; nor to impair any existing rights of occupancy granted by ordinance or resolution of the mayor and common council of the city of New York in favor of any of the lines of river barges or canal boats mentioned.

Fees and penalties; annual report.

§ 371. All penalties under this article, not otherwise provided for, may be recovered by the harbor-masters by action, and they shall report to the governor the whole amount of penalties recovered and of fees received by them, to the 30th of December, inclusive, in each year.

ARTICLE IX.

SPECIAL REGULATIONS FOR THE PORT OF NEW YORK.

The provisions of this article are taken from the Laws of 1852, ch. 266; 1857, ch. 367, ch. 671, ch. 763; 1858, ch. 226, ch. 261, ch. 290.

Ashes and cinders not to be thrown

§ 372 No person shall throw or cause to be thrown from any steamer into the waters of the port of New York, below Spuyten Duyvel creek, on the River Hudson, or below Throg's point on the East river, nor in the bay, inside of Sandy hook, any cinders or ashes, under the penalty of twenty-five dollars for each offense, recoverable against such person or from the steamer from which the cinders or ashes were thrown. Into New York harbor.

§ 373. No person shall in the port of New York throw any ballast, rubbish, ashes or cinders, from any vessel or lighter, or from any pier or bulkhead, into the water, or upon any public pier or bulkhead, unless to discharge the same immediately into carts, under penalty of five dollars for each offense, and the further sum of two dollars for each cubic yard of material so thrown out, recoverable against such person or against the vessel from which such material is discharged. Ballast, rubbish.

§ 374. No person shall throw or put any stones, earth, shavings, night soil, dirt or rubbish into any dock or slip, or upon any public pier or bulkhead in that port, under the penalty of twenty-five dollars for each offense, recoverable of such person or against the horse or cart used in any offense against this section. One-half of any penalty under this section shall be paid to the person lawfully entitled to the occupation of the dock, slip or pier. Ballast, rubbish, &c.

§ 375. It is the duty of every owner, master, mate, or other person having the charge or manage- Protection of piers.

ment of any vessel, from which or into which ballast or any loose matter is conveyed, to fasten canvas, mats or cloth between the pier or bulkhead and vessel, or between vessels lying alongside each other, so as to prevent any part thereof falling into the waters of the port, and if to be landed, to place such material at least two feet from the edge of the pier or bulkhead, under the penalty of ten dollars for each offense against any provision of this section, recoverable against the person or the vessel.

Protection of piers. § 376. No person shall throw any metal, or any package weighing over fifty pounds, from a vessel upon a pier in the port of New York, without adequate protection to the planking of the pier, under the penalty of five dollars for each offense. No person shall draw, or cause to be drawn, over any pier in that port, any anchor or blocks of stone, otherwise than upon carts, rollers, wheel carriages or sleds, under the penalty of five dollars for every offense. These penalties are recoverable from the person or the vessel from which the thing is thrown, or to which it is drawn, and one-half thereof shall be paid to the person lawfully entitled to the occupation of the pier.

Dredging. § 377. It is the duty of any person causing any dredging or excavating in the port of New York to be done, to cause the matter removed to be deposited in some place above high water mark, or deposited within a bulkhead for filling, or in some place to be approved by the commissioners of pilots; under penalty of five dollars for every cubic yard removed.

§ 378. If any pier or bulkhead is incumbered by any obstruction, the commissioners of pilots shall give notice to the person placing or keeping it there to remove it within twenty-four hours; and if such person fails to do so, he is liable to pay to the commissioners twenty-five dollars for each day during which it remains. If the obstruction consists of merchandise deposited there, the commissioners may remove the same, and cause it to be stored, and the expenses of removal and storage shall be paid by the owner of the same to the commissioners, and are a lien on the property till paid. Every six months the commissioners shall advertise unclaimed merchandise, setting forth the marks and numbers of each package, the description of the merchandise, the pier whence it was removed, and the date of its removal: and if any of it remain unclaimed for three months after being advertised, they may sell the same, after further advertisement, by auction, to pay its expenses. Any surplus shall be held in trust by the commissioners for the owner, for twelve months, when, if not claimed, it shall form part of the fund of the commissioners, hereinafter mentioned. Each advertisement required by this section shall be published for at least one week in at least three daily papers in the cities of New York and Brooklyn. Incumbrances removed.

Storage at owner's expense.

§ 379. If the merchandise is not, in the judgment of the commissioners, of sufficient value to pay the expenses of removal and storage, it shall be removed and stored at the expense of the owner, consignee or master of the vessel from which it was discharged.

Cleaning and repairs.

§ 380. It is the duty of the commissioners to require the owners and lessees of the piers and bulkheads of the cities of New York and Brooklyn to keep them clean and in good repair. In giving notice of repairs required, they shall specify the particulars of the repairs to be made. Every person who neglects to comply therewith shall pay a penalty of five dollars for each day's neglect.

Buoys and beacons.

§ 381. No person shall moor a vessel to any of the buoys or beacons placed in the harbor of New York by the United States lighthouse board, or in any manner hang with a boat or vessel to any such buoy or beacon, under a penalty of fifty dollars for every offense. Any person who willfully removes any such buoy or beacon is guilty of a misdemeanor, and, in addition to the punishment therefor, is liable to a penalty of two hundred and fifty dollars for every offense.

Use of nets, &c., at and below New York city.

§ 382. No person shall set, or cause to be set, during the months of March, April or May, in any of the waters of this state at or below the city of New York, any net or weir, by means of any pole, anchor or other fixture, to extend into the channel more than the distance of twenty rods from ordinary low water mark;[1] or at any time set any poles in the harbor at any place where the water is more than six feet deep at mean low tide,[2] under penalty of one hundred and fifty dollars. It is the duty of the commissioners to cause any obstructions placed in the harbor in violation hereof to be removed.

But this section does not affect any special statute respecting the waters adjacent to Staten Island and to the towns of New Utrecht[3] and Gravesend.[4]

[1] 2 R. S., 97, § 38.
[2] Laws of 1857, 671, § 13.
[3] 2 R. S., 97, § 39.
[4] The special act as to Gravesend is Laws of 1836, ch. 127; 2 R. S., 97, § 41.

At present these penalties are recoverable by the district attorney of any adjoining county. As the supervision of the harbor in these respects has been placed under the charge of commissioners, it seems better to make the system uniform by charging them with the duty of enforcing the provisions of this section.

§ 383. It is the duty of the owner of every lighter which is engaged exclusively in the business of lightering in the port of New York to cause the name and place of business of one of the owners thereof to be painted in letters at least three inches long on the sides of his lighter, under the penalty of five dollars for neglect. If after notice he still neglects, he shall pay an additional penalty of ten dollars for every week of the further neglect. **Lighters.**

§ 384. For the purposes of this article all piers and bulkheads shall be taken to extend six feet into **Piers and bulkheads defined.**

the street adjoining in the rear. But it shall not apply to private wharves, piers and bulkheads, occupied by the respective owners for special purposes.

Laws of 1858, ch. 226, §§ 8, 9.

Duty of harbor-masters and pilots.

§ 385. It is the duty of the harbor-masters and pilots to report to the commissioners of pilots all violations of the provisions of this article of which they may have information.

Penalties.

§ 386. All penalties under this article are recoverable by the commissioners of pilots. They have power to remit any penalty. Any penalty which is recoverable against any vessel or other property as in this article provided, shall be a lien on such vessel or property and may be enforced as other liens.

See Laws of 1858, ch. 226, § 8.

Wharfage of lighters.

§ 387. The owners of wharves, piers and bulkheads in the port of New York may charge vessels under fifty tons burden, known as lighters and exclusively used as such, wharfage not exceeding twenty-five cents per day each, when occupying an inside berth, and not exceeding fifteen cents per day each, when occupying an outside berth; but no other charge whatever.

Compensation of commissioners.

§ 388. The commissioners of pilots shall pay into the state treasury all penalties collected by them under this article, not otherwise provided for, and the treasurer shall keep account thereof. The treasurer shall annually pay to the commissioners their expenses incurred under this article, as certified by their president and secretary, but not exceeding five thousand dollars per annum; and also the further sum of five thousand dollars, to be divided as follows: To the president of the board, two thousand dollars; and to each of the other commissioners, seven hundred and fifty dollars per annum.

ARTICLE X.

ALBANY HARBOR-MASTERS.

The provisions of this article are taken from 1 R. S., 1062, 1063.

§ 389. It is the duty of the harbor-master of the port of Albany to station and regulate all vessels in the Hudson river, within the limits of that city, and at its piers and wharves; to remove, from time to time, such vessels as are not employed in the transfer of cargoes, to accommodate others; and also to prevent any vessel from obstructing, for an unreasonable time, the entrance into the basin, of which facts of a vessel not being employed or requiring accommodation, or obstructing the entrance into the basin, he is the sole judge. He may also remove, at the expense of the master or owner

Duty of the harbor-master of Albany.

of the vessel, any vessel lying within the limits of the city having no person in charge of the same

His powers. § 390. He has authority to determine how far, and in what instances, it is the duty of masters to accommodate each other in their respective situations; and any master who neglects to obey his directions in matters within his authority, or any person whatever who resists him in the execution of his duties, is liable to a penalty of twenty-five dollars, to be recovered in the name of the mayor, aldermen and commonalty of the city of Albany, for the poor of the county

Vessels coming to wharves. § 391. All vessels, on coming to the wharves, shall take in their anchors upon deck, so as to prevent injury therefrom to other vessels, and shall rig in their jib-boom.

Compensation. § 392. All collectors of wharfage of the public and private docks within the city of Albany shall collect, in addition to the amount now paid by vessels for wharfage, the further sum of one and a half cent per ton per annum, excepting steamers navigating the canals of this state, which money shall be paid to the harbor-master for his services.

Fees for deciding differences. § 393. In case the harbor-master is called upon to decide any difference between the masters of vessels as to berths, the party in fault, by his decision, shall pay to him the sum of two dollars; but if both parties are in fault, each shall pay him the sum of one dollar.

§ 349. He shall keep an exact account of all monies received by him, and report the same to the legislature on or before the first day of February in each year. Annual report.

§ 395. In case of sickness, inability or absence of the harbor-master, it is the duty of the mayor of Albany to appoint some proper person to attend to the duties of the office in the meantime. Appointment in case of his inability.

CHAPTER II.

HIGHWAYS.

The passage of a number of local acts respecting highways, since the enactment of the Revised Statutes, has caused much diversity in the system in different parts of the state. We present here one uniform system for the highways of the whole state, with a few local provisions. Its preparation has been guided by the following principles:

1. To present, on the basis of the provisions of the Revised Statutes, as modified by subsequent legislation and expounded by judicial decisions, one complete and harmonious system for the whole state;

2. To add thereto those provisions or qualifications, contained in local acts, which are susceptible of convenient and useful general application, and which provide for points not covered by the general law;

3. To retain in force and embody, or refer to as exceptions to the general rules, such local provisions as might be founded in any local necessity.

But there are several local acts which present a variance from the general system not founded on any local want, but on a diversity of view as to the best system of highway labor to be pursued. These we have disregarded. They may be enumerated and briefly characterized as follows:

Laws of 1838, ch. 326. Highway tax in the various towns of Livingston county to be paid in money, if so determined by the electors;

Laws of 1849, ch. 11. Raising and application of moneys for highways in the town of Eastchester;

Laws of 1852, ch. 338. Empowers voluntary associations to construct public roads in the county of Erie;

Laws of 1853, ch. 608. Highways in Montgomery county to be worked and repaired by contract, and payment to be raised by tax;

Laws of 1854, ch. 275. Mode of proceedings to certify to necessity of new road or alteration in the town of Greenburgh. But see Laws of 1859, ch. 497;

Laws of 1857, ch. 287. Bridges may be bought in Richmond county;

Laws of 1859, ch. 147. Requires highway taxes in the town of Haverstraw, in the county of Rockland, to be paid in money;

Laws of 1859, ch. 268. Regulates proceedings to lay out or alter roads in the towns of Northcastle, Bedford and Lewisborough, in the county of Westchester.

ARTICLE I.

ENUMERATION OF HIGHWAYS.

§ 396. Highways are roads or streets and bridges, laid out or erected by the public; or if laid out or erected by others, dedicated or abandoned to the public. What are highways.

§ 397. Roads recorded as highways, according to law, and any roads used as such for a period of twenty years, are highways.[1] Whenever any corporation owning a toll-bridge,[2] or a turnpike,[3] or plankroad is dissolved, or discontinues the road, the bridge or road becomes a highway. Origin of highways.

[1] 1 R. S., 1049, § 115.
[2] Ib., 1054, § 146.
[3] Ib., 1049, § 114.

§ 398. A road not worked or used for the period of six years ceases to be a highway for any purpose whatever. Abandonment.

1 R. S., 1149, § 113. Lyon *v.* Munson, 2 Cow., 426.

ARTICLE II.

RULES AND RESTRICTIONS RESPECTING THE USE OF HIGHWAYS.

The public easement.

§ 399. By taking or accepting land for a highway the public acquires only the right of way[1] and the incidents necessary to enjoying and maintaining it,[2] subject to the regulation of the towns as in this Code provided, and the right of pasturage.[3] All trees within the highway, except only such as are requisite to make or repair the road or bridges, on the same land, are for the use of the owner or occupant of the land.[4]

[1] 16 N. Y. R., 97; 15 Johns., 447; 2 Ib., 357; 14 Barb., 692; 11 Barb., 390.
[2] 7 Barb., 309; 5 Den., 6.
[3] 7 Barb., 297; 25 Ib., 9.
[4] 1 R. S., 1055, § 153.

Restrictions upon the weight of loads upon roads in the county of Dutchess are contained in local statutes. (Laws of 1857, chs. 116, 404, 417.) So of restrictions upon the allowing of animals to run at large in the county of Westchester. (Ib., chs. 447, 582;) and in the town of Flatbush, in the county of Kings. (Ib., ch. 137.)

Adjoining owner may construct sidewalk.

§ 400. Any owner or occupant of land may construct a sidewalk on the highway, along the line of his land, subject, however, to the authority conferred by law on the overseers of highways; and any person who takes a horse or team upon such sidewalk shall forfeit one dollar to the use of such owner or occupant.

1 R. S., 1052, §§ 137, 138, as amended by Laws of 1854, ch. 324.

May plant trees.

§ 401. Any owner or occupant of land adjoining a highway not less than three rods wide, may plant trees on the side contiguous to his land. They shall be set in regular rows at a distance of at least six feet from each other, and not more than six feet from the boundary of the highway. If the highway is more than six rods wide the row shall not be less than six nor more than twelve feet from the boundary of the highway. Whoever injures any of them is liable to the owner and to the occupant for the damages which they may respectively have sustained, and is guilty of a misdemeanor.

1 R. S., 1055, § 154, and Laws of 1857, ch. 181, § 22.

§ 42. Any gas-light company, incorporated under the laws of the state, has power to lay conductors for conducting gas through the public ways and squares in the city, village or town where it is established, with the consent of the municipal authorities thereof, and under such reasonable regulations as they may prescribe. Gas companies may lay conductors.

From 1 R. S., 1269, § 18.

§ 403. The cases and the manner in which railway, toll-bridge, plankroad and turnpike companies may acquire a right of way upon the public highways are provided in subsequent chapters of this Code. Other corporations may acquire right of way.

ARTICLE III.

POWERS AND DUTIES OF HIGHWAY OFFICERS.

Office of commissioners and overseers of highways.

§ 404. The mode of determining the number of commissioners of highways in each town; the conditions of eligibility to office, the manner of their election and qualification, and the security they are required to give; the compensation for serving; the penalty for not serving; the mode of filling vacancies, are prescribed by the general laws relating to the government of towns contained in part IV of this Code.

Duties of commissioners of highways.

§ 405. The commissioners of highways in each town have charge of the highways therein. It is their duty:

1. To cause them to be kept in repair;

2. To regulate highways, public landings and watering places laid out, and to alter such as a majority of them deem inconvenient;

3. To cause to be recorded, opened and worked, such highways as are laid out by them, pursuant to the provisions of article VI of this chapter, or by special commissioners appointed under article I of chapter II, of title II, of part IV, of this Code; and to ascertain, describe, and enter of record in the town clerk's office, such roads used as highways as have been laid out but not sufficiently described, and such as have been used for twenty years but have not been recorded;

> The act for the counties composing Long Island (Suffolk, Kings and Queens) directs them to enter of record such highways "as shall have been laid out but not sufficiently described, and such as were used as highways for twenty years or more next preceding the twenty-first day of March, one thousand seven hundred and ninety-seven, and which shall have been worked and used as such constantly for the last six years."

4. To divide their town into so many road districts as they deem convenient, by writing under their hands, to be lodged with the town clerk and by him entered in the town book; such division to be made annually, if they deem it necessary, and in all cases at least ten days before the annual town meeting;

5. To assign to each district such persons liable to highway labor as they deem proper, having regard to proximity of residence as much as may be; subject, however, to the provisions of article V of this chapter;

6. As often as they deem necessary, to require

the overseers of highways to warn such persons to work, with such cattle, implements, carriages, or sleds as one of the commissioners may direct;[1]

7. To cause to be erected and maintained on the post-roads, and on such other highways as they deem proper, mile-boards or stones with proper inscriptions, and, at the intersections of the like roads, guide-posts with proper inscriptions;[2]

8. To render to the town auditors at their annual meeting a written account for the year, stating: 1. The labor assessed and performed; 2. All sums received by them under this chapter; 3. The manner in which they have been expended; 4. The improvements which have been made on the highways during the preceding year, and their present condition; 5. The further improvements necessary, and the probable expense of making them beyond the assessment in that year;[3]

9. To deliver to the town supervisor a statement of the improvements necessary, together with their probable expense;[4]

[1] 1 R. S., 1020, § 1.
[2] 1 R. S., 1030, § 5; 1039, § 9.
[3] Laws of 1830, ch. 56; 1 R. S., 1030, § 3.
[4] 1 R. S., 1030, § 4, first clause.

Application for additional appropriation. § 406. When the commissioners deem the sum of two hundred and fifty dollars insufficient to pay for such improvements and for arrears due for part improvements, they may apply in the town meeting for a vote authorizing the necessary additional sum, not exceeding seven hundred and fifty dollars, to be raised; and at the time of such application they shall exhibit a statement of their accounts and an estimate of the expenses necessary for improvements during the ensuing year.

1 R. S., 647, §§ 9, 11; Laws of 1857, ch. 615, vol. 2, p. 338, § 1.

§ 407. Before making such application they shall post in a conspicuous manner, in not less than five of the most public places in the town, at least four weeks before the meeting, a notice specifying the amount to be applied for and the purposes to which it is to be appropriated, and the probable amount necessary to be expended at each place if there be more than one. Notice of application.

1 R. S., 647, § 10.

§ 408. If the town meeting, by vote, allow an additional sum, the clerk shall enter their resolution respecting it in his minutes, and shall deliver a copy of the same to the town supervisor Resolution allowing same to be furnished to supervisor.

Ib., § 11; first clause.

§ 409. The supervisor shall lay such statement of the commissioners, together with the resolution of the town, before the next meeting of the board of supervisors, who shall cause the required sum to be raised in the town, in the same manner as other town charges, but the moneys raised upon the statement of the commissioners shall not exceed $250 in any one year. Duty of supervisors.

Ib.

From 1 R. S., 1030, § 4; 647, § 11, last clause. By the Long Island counties' act, the limit of the amount to be raised upon commissioners' estimate was seventy-five dollars. Laws of 1838, ch. 56, § 4.

Repairs in case there is not time for such application.

§ 410. In case of damage to any highway after any town meeting, or when too late to give the notice required by section 407, the commissioners may, with consent of the board of town auditors, cause the damage to be immediately repaired; and the vouchers for the expense thereof they shall present at the next annual meeting of the town auditors, or at a special meeting to be convened by the supervisor, or in his absence by the town clerk, upon the written request of any commissioner. Such bills, after being audited, shall be collected, if audited at an annual meeting, as though the amount had been voted at a town meeting. If audited at a special meeting, the supervisor and town clerk shall issue a certificate setting forth the amount audited, in whose favor, and the nature of the work or materials, and such certificate shall bear interest from date, and shall be levied and collected as other town charges. But no such account shall be allowed by the board unless it be verified by the claimant, and the commissioners certify that at their request the work has been actually, performed and the materials actually furnished; and the board may require such other proof as they deem proper to establish the claim and the value of the work and materials.

Laws of 1858, ch. 103, p. 200, §§ 1, 2, 5.

§ 411. It is the duty of the overseers of highways, in their respective districts: Duties of overseers of highways.

1. To keep in good order and repair the highways and guide-posts thereon;

2. When required by a commissioner, to warn all persons assessed to work;

3. To cause the noxious weeds on the highways to be cut down twice in each year; once before the first of July and again before the first of September;

4. Once in every month from April to November inclusive, to cause all loose stones to be removed from the beaten track of the highways;

5. To cause the boundaries of highways to be publicly marked, and keep up the monuments erected to indicate them;

6. To collect all fines and commutation monies, and to execute all lawful directions of the commissioners;

7. When the labor assessed for a district is, in the opinion of the commissioner for that district, insufficient to keep the roads in order, and break them out when obstructed by snow, he is to make another assessment on the actual residents of the districts, as near as may be in the same proportion as an assessment by the commissioners, and not exceeding one-third the number of days additional, and to be performed or commuted for in like manner.

1 R. S., 1031. The clause of the last subdivision, specifying obstructions by snow, is from the Long Island act, as amended in 1857. Laws of 1857, ch. 181.

Sidewalks and trees.

§ 412. The commissioners have power to expend a part of the highway tax in each district upon the sidewalks therein, and in planting shade trees on the public squares, and places in the town, the highways being kept in good repair.

Laws of 1854, ch. 324, § 2.

Scraper and plough.

§ 413. The commissioners may, in their discretion, direct any overseer in the town to procure an iron or steel-shod scraper or plough, or both, for use on his district, to be paid for from the commutation monies arising therein. If such monies are insufficient, the overseer shall assess the deficiency on the inhabitants in the proportion of their assessments in the assessment roll of the town. If any one neglects to pay such assessment, the overseer may recover it by action.

1 R. S., 1031, §§ 11, 12.

Extra work by overseer.

§ 414. An overseer, whose duties as such employ him a greater number of days than those for which he is assessed, is entitled to be paid at the rate of seventy-five cents per day for the excess, and may retain the amount out of fines received by him under this chapter.

1 R. S., 1031, § 13. By the Long Island act the total compensation of the overseer for extra work is restricted not to exceed ten dollars in any one year.

§ 415. Any overseer who neglects to collect the monies that may arise from fines or commutations, or to perform any of the duties required by this chapter or by the commissioners of highways, is liable to a penalty of ten dollars, except where otherwise provided.

Penalties on overseers for neglect.

1 R. S., 1032, § 16.

§ 416. Whenever any resident of the town makes complaint to a commissioner that an overseer has neglected any duty referred to in the preceding section, and offers sufficient indemnity against costs, it is the duty of such commissioner forthwith to prosecute such overseer for the same, under penalty of ten dollars for every refusal to prosecute, to be recovered by the person who made the complaint.

Duty of commissioner to prosecute.

Ib., §§ 17, 18.

§ 417. All penalties collected by the commissioners are to be expended on the highways of the town.

Application of penalties.

§ 418. If it appear in any order made by commissioners of highways that all the commissioners of the town met and deliberated upon the subject thereof, or received due notice to attend a meeting for that purpose, it shall be no objection to the validity of the order that it was made by only two commissioners.

Order made by two commissioners.

1 R. S., 1054, § 151; Tucker *v.* Rankin, 15 Barb., 471; but see Fitch's case, 22 Wend., 132.

Actions against railway corporations.

§ 419. The commissioners may maintain a civil action against any railway corporation, for the purpose of sustaining the rights of the public in any highway in the town, or of enforcing the performance of any duty enjoined upon any such corporation in relation to any highway in the town; and to maintain an action for damages or expenses sustained by the town in consequence of any act or omission of any such corporation in violation of any law in relation to such highway. But this section shall not impair the right of action of any other person.

Laws of 1855, ch. 255, p 388, §§ 1, 2.

Onondaga Indian reservation.

§ 420. The powers and duties of the commissioners of highways, in respect to highways through the Indian reservation in the county of Onondaga, are the subjects of a special statute.

Laws of 1845, ch. 309, SS; 1 R. S., 1049, §§ 118, 119.

ARTICLE VI.

HIGHWAY TAXES.

Overseers to make lists of inhabitants

§ 421. Each overseer of highways, within sixteen days after his election or appointment, shall deliver to the town clerk a list of all the inhabitants of his district liable to work; which lists the town clerk shall deliver to the commissioners. liable to work.

1 R. S., 1033, § 22, 25.

§ 422. The commissioners shall meet at the place of town meeting within eighteen days after they are chosen, and afterwards in their discretion. They shall make out a statement showing the description of every lot of land owned by non-residents, in the manner that assessors are required to describe them, and opposite thereto the value affixed to each lot in the last assessment roll of the town. If the lot of any owner was not separately valued, the valuation of the commissioners shall be in proportion to the value affixed to the whole tract in which such lot was included. Commissioners duties.

Ib.

§ 423. The commissioners shall ascertain and assess the highway labor of each year as follows: Mode of assessing highway tax.

1. The whole number of days' work to be required in the town shall be at least three times the number of its taxable inhabitants;

2. Every male resident, of full age (except ministers of the gospel and priests of every denomination, paupers, idiots and lunatics), shall be assessed at least one day;

3. The residue of the days' work required shall be apportioned upon the property, real and per-

sonal, of every resident, as the same appears by the last assessment roll of the town, including all monied or stock corporations which appear therein to have been assessed, and upon the non-residents' lands contained in the list made out by the commissioners;

4. If, thereafter, there remains any deficiency, it shall be assessed upon the property, real and personal, of every resident, including such corporations, and upon each tract or parcel of land of which the owners are non-residents, according to the last assessment roll;

5. The commissioners shall affix to the name of each person in the overseers' list of inhabitants, and to the description of each lot in their list of non-residents' lands, the number of days which such person or tract is assessed, and shall subscribe the list and file them with the town clerk.

1 R. S., 1033, §§ 20, 21, 26, 27. In the Long Island act the number of days is required to be at least twice the number of inhabitants assessed to work, with a proviso that no person be required to work more than thirty days in one year. The act of 1855, in reference to the counties of Oneida and Steuben, provides that no greater amount shall be levied on an individual, as mentioned in subdivision 2, than is levied on each $1,000 of property; nor shall it be lawful to refuse such service as the person assessed may be able to perform. Laws of 1855, ch. 517.

§ 424. Whenever the assessors of the town have omitted to assess any inhabitant or property, the commissioner shall assess the same and apportion highway labor thereupon in the same manner as if not originally omitted. Omissions in assessment roll to be supplied.

1 R. S., 1035, § 32.

§ 425. Whenever the overseer's annual return shows that any person failed to perform or commute for the whole number of days' work required of him, the commissioners shall reassess the deficiency, adding it to his assessment for the following year. But this shall not exonerate the overseer from any penalty which he may have incurred. Persons failing to work to be reassessed.

Ib., 1040, § 65.

§ 426. The commissioners shall direct the town clerk to make a copy of the lists, and they shall subscribe the same and cause them to be delivered to the respective overseers of the several districts in which the labor is assessed. Copies of lists to be given to overseers.

Ib., 1035, § 34.

§ 427. The overseers shall add, from time to time, names of persons omitted and of new inhabitants, and rate them to work in proportion to their real and personal estates, subject to an appeal to the commissioners. Overseers to add names omitted and new inhabitants.

Ib., § 35.

§ 428. A non-resident deeming himself aggrieved by his assessment, may within thirty days after the assessment appeal to the county judge of the county, Non-residents' appeal from assessment.

giving to the commissioners eight days' notice of the time of the hearing. The decision of the county judge, which it is his duty to render within twenty days after the hearing, is not the subject of appeal. The fees of the county judge are two dollars for each day employed, to be paid in the first instance by the party appealing; if the decision is reversed or modified in favor of the appellant, the amount is to be levied as a part of the contingent charges of the town.

1 R. S., 1035, §§ 36, 37.

Lands occupied by another than the owner.

§ 429. Lands occupied by one person, but owned by another are not to be assessed to both. When the occupant is assessed for such land, the officers making the assessment shall distinguish in their list the amount charged on account of the land, from the personal tax, if any, of the occupant. Whenever any tenant of lands for a term less than twenty-five years is assessed for such land, and has actually performed or commuted for the same, he is, in absence of agreement to the contrary, entitled to a deduction from the rent due or to become due, equal to the full amount of such assessment, estimating it at the rate of sixty-three cents per day.

Ib., 1036, §§ 39, 40.

Tuscarora nation.

§ 430. The subject of highway labor on the lands of the Tuscarora nation of Indians, in the county of Niagara, is regulated by special statute.

Laws of 1854, ch. 175.

ARTICLE V.

PERFORMANCE OF HIGHWAY LABOR AND COMMUTATION.

§ 431. It is the duty of the overseer to give at least twenty-four hours' oral or written notice to all persons assessed and required to work within his district, of the time and place when and where they are to appear for that purpose, and with what implements; but no individual resident shall be required to work out of the district in which he resides; except that, if he has land in another district, he may, with the approval of the com- **Notice to residents to work** missioners, apply in such district the labor assessed upon his land there.

1 R. S., 1037, § 42.

Notice to corporations.

§ 432. Notice to be given to a corporation may be oral or written, and may be served on any officer, clerk or agent thereof at its principal office or place of business; and its labor is to be performed in such districts as the commissioners direct. Any number of the days' work required of a corporation, not exceeding fifty, may be required to be performed by it in any one day.

Ib., 1034, § 28.

Notice to non-residents.

§ 433. Notice to a non-resident must be in writing, and served at least five days previously on his agent, if he has one residing in the town. If the overseer cannot ascertain that he has such agent, he shall, at least twenty days before the time when performance is required, affix upon the outer door of the town-house a notice containing the name of such non-resident, when known, a description of the land assessed, together with the number of days' labor assessed, and the time and place when and where it is to be performed.

Ib., 1037, § 44.

Formation of private districts.

§ 434. The commissioners of highways may, at their first meeting subsequent to their election, assign to any one or more residentss, with his or their consent, for a period not exceeding ten years, a section of the highways through or adjoining his or their lands, the requisite highway labor on which will, in the opinion of the commissioners, be equivalent to the highway labor which he or they would otherwise be required to perform, to be worked as a private road district.

§ 435. The commissioners shall file in the town clerk's office a statement of the district, and the time for which they have assigned the same subscribed by them, to which shall be added the written consent of the persons to whom it is assigned. Such persons shall keep in order the highways in such private district, and shall at all times work thereon when required by a commissioner; and shall not meanwhile be required to work on the highways in any other district. Record of private district.

§ 436. If any such person neglects to put any part of the highway, in the district, in good repair, within a reasonable time after being required so to do by a commissioner, he shall incur a penalty of ten dollars; and after recovering the penalty, the commissioner shall annex such private district to an adjoining public district; and those to whom it was assigned shall work in the proper public districts. Neglect to work same

The provisions of the three preceding sections are taken from the Long Island counties' act.

Highway labor on plankroads.

§ 437. If any person liable to highway labor, by reason of real property on the line of a plankroad, make application, in writing, to the commissioners of the town, before the issuing of the highway warrants, they shall assess him the labor for such property, to be performed on the plankroad, as a separate road district.[1] They shall thereupon make a separate list of persons and land for every such separate road district, which shall be delivered to one of the directors of the plankroad, who shall proceed to have the highway labor worked on the road in the same manner as overseers of highways.[2] The directors possess the same powers respecting the performance of such highway labor or commutation therefor as overseers of highways, and shall make the like return to the commissioners of highways.[3]

[1] Laws of 1855, ch. 495. 15 How. Pr. R., 76.
[2] Laws of 1853, ch. 626, p. 1206, § 2.
[3] Ib., § 3.

Local provisions.

§ 438. Every person liable to perform highway labor in respect to real property on the line of the Antwerp, Rossie and Hammond plankroad, the Morristown and Hammond plankroad, or the Gouverneur, Richville and Canton plankroad, shall perform or commute for such labor under the orders of the directors of those roads respectively.

Laws of 1858, ch. 193, p. 314.

Work on private roads.

§ 439. The commissioners shall credit persons living on a private road and working the same, so much on account of their assessments as they deem necessary to work such road, or they shall annex it to some highway district.

1 R. S., 1035, § 38.

§ 440. When the commissioners neglect for a year to open or work any part of a road that has been duly laid out and title thereto acquired, any of the residents, who desire to apply the whole or any part of their highway labor to working it, may give the commissioners ten days' notice thereof, and thereupon they shall assign such residents to such road, and direct their labor to be applied thereto, and cause it to be put in good order within a year, under the direction of any one of such residents whom the commissioners may appoint as overseer of the labor so applied. When the labor assessed to such residents is not sufficient for the purpose, they may anticipate, in whole or in part, the labor of three years. But more than one-half the labor of any district shall not be taken and applied to a road not embraced in the district. Residents may apply labor to new road.

Laws of 1853, ch. 63, p. 87, § 1.

§ 441. The residents of any highway district may grade, gravel or plank the highways in their district, by anticipating the labor of the district for one or more years, and applying it to the immediate construction of such plank or gravel highways, and after the completion thereof, shall be Residents may grade, gravel or plank a road.

exempted from the labor so anticipated, except so far as may be necessary to keep the highways in repair.

1 R. S., 1035, § 41.

Commutation.

§ 442. Any resident other than an overseer may commute his labor, or a part of it, at the rate of sixty-three cents per day, to be paid to the overseer of his district within twenty-four hours after he has notice to work. Corporations may commute in like manner by payment to the overseer or to a commissioner of highways of the town.

1 R. S., 1037, §§ 45, 46, 47. Sixty-three cents is here substituted for sixty-two and a half.

Appropriation of commutation moneis.

§ 443. The commutation monies of corporations are to be expended by the commissioners upon any districts in the town; and for this purpose they may require overseers who have received such to pay over to them the whole or any portion thereof. Other commutation monies in the hands of overseers are to be expended by them on their respective districts.

Ib., § 45, last clause; § 47, first clause.

Implements and assistance may be required.

§ 444. The overseer may require a team or a cart, wagon or plough, and a man to manage them, from any person in his district who has been assessed three days or more and does not commute, and such person is entitled to a credit of three days for each day's service therewith.

Ib., § 47.

§ 445. Each person appearing shall actually work eight hours each day, under penalty of thirteen cents for each hour of default, to be paid by the person assessed. If any one, after appearing, does not work faithfully, or hinders others from working, he is liable to the penalty of one dollar for every offense. Any person may work by an able-bodied substitute. Penalties for loss of time; substitutes.

1 R. S., 1038, §§ 48, 49. Thirteen cents is here substituted for twelve and a half.

§ 446. Every person receiving due notice, who does not commute and neglects to appear, is liable to a penalty of one dollar for each day's neglect. If he was required to furnish implements or assistance, he is liable to the following penalties for each day's neglect: Penalties for neglect to appear.

1. For wholly omitting to comply, three dollars;

2. For omitting to furnish a cart, wagon, or plough, one dollar;

3. For omitting to furnish a pair of horses or oxen, one dollar;

4. For omitting to furnish a man to manage the team, one dollar.

1 R. S., 1038, § 50.

§ 447. Within six days after any person incurs a penalty under this article, it is the duty of the overseer, unless a satisfactory excuse is rendered to him, to make complaint on oath to a justice of the peace of the town. Duty of overseer to prosecute.

Ib., § 51.

Mode of collection.

§ 448. The justice to whom complaint is made shall forthwith issue a summons directed to any constable of the town, requiring him to summons the delinquent to appear forthwith before the justice, at a place specified, and show cause why he should not be fined for such neglect. The summons shall be served upon the delinquent personally or by leaving it at his residence.[1] If the delinquents be a corporation, the summons may be for any number of offenses, and shall be served in the manner provided by law for service of summons in the supreme court against corporations.[2] If upon return of the summons no sufficient cause be shown, the justice shall impose the penalty prescribed and issue a warrant under his hand, directed to any constable of the town where the delinquent resides, commanding him to levy it with costs,[3] which he shall forthwith do, and pay the same, deducting his fees, to the justice, who shall pay the same to the overseer making the complaint, to be expended by him on his district.[4] But penalties collected from corporations shall be paid by the constable collecting the same to the commissioners of highways, and may be expended by them in any district of the town.[5]

[1] R. S., 1038, § 52.
[2] Ib., 1034, § 30.
[3] Ib., 1038, § 53.
[4] 1 R. S., 1038, § 54.
[5] Ib., 1034, § 30.

Further remedies against corporations.

§ 449. In case the penalties incurred by a corporation cannot thus be collected, the commissioners of highways may bring an action against it therefor, or the same proceedings may be had as in the collection of county taxes against corporations.

1 R. S., 1835, § 31.

§ 450. Penalties collected for neglect to work are to be set off against the assessments upon which they were founded, estimating one dollar as a satisfaction for one day's work.

Penalties collected to be set off against assessments.

Ib., 1038, § 55.

§ 451. The overseer's acceptance of an excuse for a neglect in no case exempts the person excused from performing or commuting for the whole number of days' work for which he was assessed.

Excuse for neglect does not exempt from labor.

Ib.

§ 452. Every overseer shall, on or before the first day of October in each year, deliver to the supervisors a list of all the lands of non-residents and of persons unknown, and of those in charge of executors or administrators, which were assessed in his lists, on which the labor assessed has not been paid, stating the amount of labor unpaid; with his affidavit, made before a justice of the peace of the town, that he gave the notice required by section 431, and that the labor for which such land is returned has not been performed. For neglect thereof the overseer shall forfeit five dollars, and also the amount of unpaid labor, at the rate of

Overseers to return arrearages to the supervisors.

sixty-three cents for each day thereof, to be recovered by the commissioners and expended on the highways of the town.

1 R. S., 1039, §§ 57, 58. Sixty-three cents is here substituted for sixty-two and a half. The clause including lands under care of executors, &c., is from the Long Island act, as amended 1857, ch. 181, § 8.

Supervisors to assess arrearages by tax.

§ 453. The supervisor shall lay such return before the board of supervisors, who shall, at their next meeting, cause the unpaid labor (estimated at sixty-three cents per day) to be levied on the lands returned, and to be collected like the contingent charges of the county, and shall order the same, when collected, to be paid to the commissioners of the town, to be expended on the district for whose benefit the labor was assessed.

1 R. S., 1039, §§ 59, 60.

Overseers to render account to the commissioners.

§ 454. Every overseer shall, on the second Tuesday next preceding the time for the annual town meeting, within the year for which he is appointed or elected, render to one of the commissioners a written account, verified by his oath, which may be taken before one of the commissioners, containing:

1. The names of all persons assessed to work in his district;

2. The names of all who have actually worked and the number of days they have done so;

3. The names of all who have been fined, and the sums in which they were fined;

4. The names of all who have commuted, and the manner in which he has expended the fines and commutations;

5. A list of all lands returned to the supervisor for non-payment, and the amount of tax on each parcel.

1 R. S., 1029, § 61.

§ 455. At the same time the overseer shall pay to the commissioner all monies remaining in his hands unexpended, to be applied by the commissioners upon the highways of the town. And pay over moneys unexpended.

Ib., 1040, § 62.

§ 456. Every overseer who neglects to make the return to the commissioner, or, making it, neglects to pay over the balance, shall forfeit five dollars, to be recovered, with the balance, by the commissioners; and it is the duty of the commissioners to prosecute for such a penalty in every instance in which no return is made. Penalty for failure to return or pay over

Ib., § 63.

ARTICLE VI.

LAYING OUT, ALTERING AND DISCONTINUING ROADS.

Who may apply for change.

§ 457. Any person liable to be assessed in any town, either as owner or as resident therein, may make application in writing, signed by him and addressed to the commissioners, to alter or discontinue any road, or lay out any new road therein.

1 R. S., 1141, § 66; and see The People *ex rel.* Wait *v.* Eggleston, 13 How. Pr. R., 123.

§ 458. In all cases of laying out, altering or discontinuing a road, the commissioners shall cause a survey of the same to be made, and incorporate it in an order, signed by them and filed and recorded in the office of the town clerk, who shall note thereon the time of recording it, and at the time of receiving it post a copy of such order upon the outer door of the town-house. A survey to be recorded and notice given.

1 R. S., 1041, § 67, and first clause of § 68.

§ 459. No public or private road shall, without the consent of the owner and occupant, be laid out through any orchard of four years' growth, nor through any garden four years cultivated, nor through any buildings, nor through any fixtures or erections for the purposes of trade or manufacture, nor through any yard or inclosure necessary to the use or enjoyment of such buildings, fixtures or erections. But this section does not apply to orchards and gardens in the counties of Westchester and Putnam. Roads through orchards, gardens, buildings and yards.

1 R. S., 1041, § 69; Ex parte Clapper, 3 Hill, 458; Laws of 1834, ch. 300. By the Long Island act, gardens and orchards are not protected thus, unless of the growth or cultivation of ten years, instead of four.

§ 460. No highway shall be laid out through any inclosed or improved land without consent of the owner and occupant, unless certified to be Road through inclosed or improved land.

necessary by twelve reputable residents of the town, in manner following:

From 1 R. S., 1041, § 70, and Laws of 1830, ch. 225.

Applicant to give notice of route, and of meeting of examiners.

§ 461. Every applicant for a highway through any such land must post notices at three of the most public places of the town, specifying, as near as may be, the route proposed, the several tracts of land through which the same is proposed to be laid and the time and place at which the residents will meet to examine the ground. The notice must be posted at least six days before the time specified for the meeting.

1 R. S., 1041, § 71.

Qualification of the examiners.

§ 462. If twelve reputable residents of the town, not interested in the lands through which the highway is to be laid, nor of kin to the owner thereof, appear at the time and place specified, they shall be sworn, by any officer authorized to administer oaths, well and truly to examine and certify as to the propriety and necessity of the highway applied for.

1 R. S. 1042, § 72.

Action of the examiners.

§ 463. They shall then personally examine the route, and hear any reasons that are offered for or against the laying out of the highway. If they are of opinion that such highway is proper or necessary, they shall make a certificate to that effect, and deliver it to the commissioners.

1 R. S., 1042, § 73.

§ 464. Before the commissioners proceed to lay out the highway, they shall cause at least three days' notice, in writing, to be given to the occupant of the land through which it is to run, of the time and place of their meeting to decide on the application. The notice is to be served upon the occupant personally, or in his absence by leaving it at his residence. Commissioners to give owner notice of their meeting.

1 R. S., 1042, § 74.

§ 465. At the meeting the commissioners shall hear any reasons that are offered for or against the application. If they determine for it, they shall make an order accordingly, describing the highway so laid out, particularly, by bounds, courses and distances, and deposit it with the town clerk. Action of commissioners.

Ib., 1042, § 75.

§ 466. The commissioners have power to adjust, by agreement with any owner, the amount of his damages for the land taken, if such amount do not exceed one hundred dollars. The agreement, or the owner's release of all claim to damages, shall be filed in the town clerk's office, and shall be conclusive against any further claim by him for damages. If such agreement or lease is not made the damages shall be ascertained in the mode prescribed by the CODE OF CIVIL PROCEDURE for assessing damages for private property taken for public use. Ascertaining damages.

1 R. S., 1042, § 76, and Laws of 1857, ch, 491, as amended by Laws of 1858, ch. 51.

Roads, &c., across railways.

§ 467. The authorities of any city, village or town who are by law empowered to lay out streets or highways, may lay out any street or highway across the track of the railway of any corporation formed since the 20th day of March, 1853, without compensation to the corporation; but such street or highway shall not be actually opened for use until thirty days after notice of such laying out has been served personally upon the president, vice-president, treasurer or a director of such corporation.

Laws of 1853, ch. 62, p. 86, § 1.

Duty of railway corporation.

§ 468. Immediately after the service of such notice the corporation shall cause the street or highway to be taken across their track, as shall be most convenient and useful for public travel, and shall cause all necessary embankments, excavation and other work to be done on their road, under the penalty of twenty dollars for every day's neglect after the thirty days to be recovered by the officers laying out such street or highway, and to be expended on the same; but the time may be extended, not more than thirty days, by the county judge of the county, if, in his opinion, the work cannot be performed within that time.

Ib., ch. 62, p. 86, § 3.

Collection of damages and expenses.

§ 469. The amount of damages ascertained upon the laying out of any highway, together with the expenses incurred therein, shall be laid by the supervisor of the town before the board of supervisors, who shall cause the same to be levied and collected in the town, and paid to the commissioners of highways, by whom the damages shall be paid and the residue applied to the expenses.

1 R. S., 1045, § 86.

§ 470. In case of roads extending or proposed to be extended from one town into another, whether in the same or different counties, if the commissioners disagree, they shall all meet together, at the request of either, and make their determination thereon. Disagreement between commissioners of different towns.

Ib., § 89.

§ 471. A highway laid out along a town line or a part thereof, shall be laid out by two or more of the commissioners of each town, and either upon the line or as near upon either side as convenient. They shall at the time divide such highway into districts, and allot the same in such manner as to divide equally between the towns the burden of opening and maintaining it; and the like division shall be made of the burdens of highways already laid out along town lines. They shall cause such highway and its division and allotment to be recorded in the town clerk's office of each town, and each district shall be considered to belong wholly to the town to which it is allotted. Highway upon a town line.

Ib., §§ 90 to 93.

Width of roads.

§ 472. All highways hereafter laid out shall be not less than three rods wide.

1 R. S., 1047, § 99.

Discontinuing useless road.

§ 473. Upon application for the discontinuance of an old highway as useless, the commissioners shall summon twelve disinterested residents of the town to meet on a day certain and consider the application. When met, they shall be sworn well and truly to examine and certify as to the propriety of the discontinuance. They shall then proceed to view the road, and if of opinion that it is useless, shall make a certificate to that effect and deliver it to the commissioners, who shall thereupon proceed to decide upon the application.

Ib., §§ 100, 101.

Discontinuing abandoned road.

§ 474. Whenever a highway, or any part thereof, is abandoned by the public, the commissioners shall file in the town clerk's office of the town a description in writing, signed by them, of the highway so abandoned, and the same shall thereupon be discontinued.

Laws of 1853, ch. 174, p. 310, § 15.

Papers to be filed.

§ 475. It is the duty of the commissioners to file in the town clerk's office all papers relating to any proceeding for laying out, altering or discontinuing a highway, as soon as they have decided thereon.

1 R. S., 1047, § 102.

Appeals may be taken from the order of the commissioners.

§ 476. Any person deeming himself aggrieved by the commissioners' decision upon any application under this article, or by any decision made by special commissioners appointed under subdivision 10 of section 82 of this Code, may, within sixty days after the filing of their order, as hereinbefore prescribed, appeal therefrom to the county court of the county in which the highway or proposed route lies. An appeal by one person does not preclude an appeal by any other: but to the end that the decision may embrace the whole subject, the court to which the first appeal is taken has exclusive jurisdiction of all appeals from the same order, and shall take no proceedings upon any appeal till the time to appeal has expired

1 R. S., 1047, § 103, first clause; 1 R. S., 1st ed., 518, § 84, last clause, and § 85. By the Long Island act the town clerk is required to post notice of the commissioners' determination on the town-house door, and the time of appeal is to be computed from the time the notice was so posted. § 45.

§ 477. The notice of appeal must be in writing, addressed to the court and signed by the appellant, and must state the ground of the appeal, and whether it is brought to reverse the whole order or some specified part thereof. Notice of appeal.

1 R. S., 1047, § 104.

§ 478. The county judge, or (if he is a resident in the town, or is interested, or of kin to any person interested, in any lands to be taken, or is under disability for any cause) the special county judge, if there be one, or in case of any like disqualification on his part, then one of the justices of the Appointment and qualification of referees.

sessions shall, after the time to appeal has expired, appoint, in writing, three disinterested residents of the county, but not of the town, and not named by any of the parties interested in the appeals, as referees to hear and determine all the appeals, and shall give them notice thereof, and deliver to them all papers pertaining to the matter, and thereupon the referees shall be sworn, before any officer authorized to take affidavits, faithfully to hear and determine the matters referred.

1 R. S., 1047, § 103, except first clause. By the Long Island act the appeal is heard by the county judge without appointment of referees. The legislature may think it advisable to adopt that course for the state.

Filling vacancies; orders of appointment.

§ 479. If any referee fails to serve, the court or officer who appointed him has power to appoint another to fill his place. All orders for appointment of such referees shall be filed in the clerk's office of the town where the highway or proposed route lies.

1 R. S., 1044, §§ 84, 85.

Powers and compensation of the referees.

§ 480. The referees have the powers conferred by law upon referees in civil actions. Their fees are two dollars each for every day employed, to be paid by the appellant if the commissioners' order is confirmed; if reversed, to be a county charge; if modified, to be paid by either, as directed by the court.

From 1 R. S., 1048, § 107, and first clause of § 108.

§ 481. The referee shall give at least eight days' notice, in writing, of the time and place of the hearing, to be served, in all cases, on the commissioners, and, in case of an appeal from an order in favor of an application, to be served on the applicant. Such notice is to be served personally, or, in case of the absence of the person to be served, by leaving it as his residence. Notice of hearing to be given to commissioners and applicant.

1 R. S., 1048, §§ 105, 106.

§ 482. If the referees reverse an order of the commissioners refusing an application to lay out or alter a highway, they must proceed and lay out the new road or the alteration as they deem the commissioners should have done.[1] In all cases they must file their decision, in writing, signed by them, with the town clerk, who shall record the same;[2] and it shall remain unaltered four years from the time of filing,[3] and shall not be the subject of appeal. Decision of the referees.

[1] The People v. Cherry Valley, 4 Seld., 476.

[2] 1 R. S., 1048, § 107.

[3] Ib., § 108, last clause.

By the Long Island act it cannot be modified so long as the same judge holds office, except on application to him with the approval of the commissioners, and before granting the application he must view the premises.

§ 483. It is the duty of the commissioners to carry into effect any decision in favor of an appli- Duty of the commissioners.

cation in the same manner as if it had been their own and there had been no appeal.

1 R. S., 1048, § 109.

Notice to owner to remove fences.

§ 484. After the time to appeal has expired, or the decision upon the appeal has been filed, the commissioners, before opening a road through inclosed land, must give to the owner sixty days' notice, in writing, to remove his fences. The notice must be served on him personally, or by leaving it at his residence in case of his absence, or, if he has none in the town, by leaving it with his agent in the town. If the commissioners cannot ascertain that he has such, the notice must be affixed upon the outer door of the town-house. If the fences are not removed at the expiration of that time, the court may cause them to be removed and the road opened.

Ib., § 110; 1049, § 111.

Width of certain roads.

§ 485. It is the duty of the commissioners to cause all roads used as highways for twenty years to be opened to the width of at least two rods.

Ib., 1049, § 116.

Reference to local provisions.

§ 486. The width of highways in Stockport in the county of Columbia,[1] and in New Hartford in the county of Oneida,[2] is the subject of special statutes.

[1] Laws of 1853, ch. 106. [2] Laws of 1851, ch. 109.

ARTICLE VII.

ERECTION AND MAINTENANCE OF BRIDGES.

§ 487. In all cases where a highway, laid out by legal authority, lies in such a direction as to cross the line of any canal of this state which was constructed before the highway was laid out, worked and used, the construction and maintenance of any bridge required for the crossing is to be, like other highway bridges, under the charge of the officers and at the expense of the proper town or towns, but the construction is to be subject to the provisions of law relative to the canals of the state. **Bridges across canals.**

1 R. S., 514, §§ 269, 270.

§ 488. All public bridges must be constructed with a sufficient railing on each side. **Bridges to be railed.**

Laws of 1830, ch. 56, § 97.

Bridges to be railed.

§ 489. All persons whose duty it is to make and maintain bridges across their mill-dams shall provide them with sufficient railings, and keep the same in repair; and in case of neglect to erect or to keep in repair such railings, on the order of a commissioner, they shall be liable, for every offense, to a penalty of five dollars, and a further penalty of one dollar for every day such neglect is continued.

Laws of 1830, ch. 56, § 97.

When the expense of a bridge may be levied on the county.

§ 490. All public bridges, except such as are otherwise provided for by statute, are maintained by the town in the same manner as the other highways.[1] But where it appears to the supervisors of any county that a town therein would be unreasonably burdened by the expense, they may, in their discretion, cause a part or the whole thereof —but not exceeding one thousand dollars in any one year, and, in the counties of Kings, Queens and Suffolk, not exceeding five hundred dollars in any one year—to be levied on the county.[2]

[1] Hill *v.* Supervisors of Livingston, 2 Kern., 52.

[2] 1 R. S., 1053, § 140; Laws of 1830, ch. 56, § 96.

Allowance may be reviewed by the sessions.

§ 491. If the commissioners of any town are dissatisfied with such allowance, the court of sessions of the county shall, upon their application, review the same, and their order in the premises shall be binding upon the supervisors.

Ib., 141.

§ 492. Bridges which adjoining towns are liable to maintain are to be maintained at the joint expense of the towns, without reference to town lines. Bridges between towns.

1 R. S., 1054, § 347; as amended, Laws of 1857, ch. 383, § 1.

§ 493. For the purpose of building and maintaining such bridges, the commissioners of such towns, or of either one or more, if the others refuse to act, may enter into joint contracts, and the same may be enforced by action against them or their successors, respectively, jointly or severally; and the commissioners of towns so liable may be proceeded against jointly for neglect of duty in reference to such bridges. Joint contracts for such.

1 R. S., 1054, § 148; as amended, Laws of 1857, ch. 383, § 2.

§ 494. If the commissioners of any such town, after written notice from those of another, do not, in twenty days, give a consent, in writing, to build or repair such a bridge, those who gave the notice may build or repair it, and then maintain an action in their official capacity against the commissioners neglecting to join, and may recover against them respectively, the amount which their town would be liable to contribute, with interest and costs. In such action it shall not be necessary for the plaintiffs to prove any contract, or that the defendants or their predecessors had funds of their town sufficient to build or make the repairs, nor Remedy if commissioners of adjoining town refuse to act.

41

shall the contrary be any defense. And the board of supervisors shall levy the amount of any judgment in such action, with interest and costs, upon the town against whose commissioners it was recovered.

1 R. S., 1054, § 149; as amended, Laws of 1857, ch. 384, § 3.

Commissioners, when personally liable.

§ 495. The commissioners are not personally liable for such judgment, except where the court certifies that their neglect was willful and malicious, in which case it may be collected against them as against individuals.

1 R. S., 1054, § 150, and Laws of 1857, ch. 384, § 3, last clause.

Motion to compel commissioners to build or repair.

§ 496. When the commissioners of one or more of such towns refuse to build or repair, the remaining commissioners — or, if all refuse, any three freeholders of either town, who have petitioned, in writing, the commissioners in each town to do so and have been refused — may move in the supreme court, in a judicial district in which such bridge or any part of it is located, either at special term or before a judge at chambers, for an order requiring the commissioners to build, rebuild, or repair the bridge. The motion shall be made on affidavit, and eight days' notice, with a copy of the affidavit, shall be served on each of the commissioners.

Laws of 1857, ch. 639, § 1, first clause.

§ 497. The court or judge may, in doubtful cases, before making an order upon the motion, refer it to some disinterested person to ascertain the facts and report the evidence. The referee shall appoint a time and place for taking the evidence, and shall give notice thereof to one of the moving parties and one of the commissioners. He has the powers which are conferred by law upon referees in civil actions. His fees are three dollars a day, to be paid, in the first instance, by the moving party. Reference thereon.

Laws of 1857, ch. 639, § 3.

§ 498. The court or judge shall make such order on the motion as is just; if, on its being granted, in whole or in part, funds are needed by the commissioners to carry it into effect, the amount required for the purpose, and the portion of it to be raised in each town, shall be specified in the order. Decision of the motion.

2 Laws of 1857, ch. 639, § 1, last clause.

§ 499. Costs, as upon a motion, including witness' fees, referees' fees and disbursements, may be granted or refused by the court. Costs thereon.

2 Laws of 1857, ch. 639, § 7, first clause.

§ 500. Upon the service of a copy of such order upon the commissioners of the adjoining towns respectively, they shall forthwith meet and fix on the plan of such bridge or the manner of repairing it, and shall cause it to be built, rebuilt or repaired Compliance with the order.

out of any funds, in their hands, or the funds of either of them, applicable thereto. If there are not adequate funds, they shall cause the work to be done on credit, or in part for cash and in part on credit, according to the exigency of the case; and they have authority to pledge the credit of each town for its appropriate share, as far as may be necessary to that end.

2 Laws of 1857, ch. 639, § 4.

Report of commissioners and levying the expenses.

§ 501. The commissioners of each town shall, at the time of their annual report, make a full report of all such proceedings to the town auditors. They shall deliver to the supervisor the copy of the order mentioned in section 498, with an account, under oath, annexed thereto, of what has been done in the premises. The board of supervisors, at their annual meeting, shall levy upon each town, or upon the appropriate town, if they are in different counties, its share of the cost, after deducting the payments actually made by its commissioners; but the amount of such tax and such prior payments shall not exceed the amount specified in the order.

2 Laws of 1857, ch. 639, § 5.

Any person may rebuild or repair on neglect by the commissioners.

§ 502. When any such bridge is destroyed, or becomes impassable or unsafe to pass, and the commissioners of the adjoining towns, after reasonable notice, neglect to rebuild or repair it, whatever funds are reasonably laid out in rebuilding or repairing it, by any person, shall be a charge upon the adjoining towns in their proper proportion. Such person may move in the manner and on the notice provided by section 496, for an order requiring them to reimburse him, and the court or judge may grant the order, specifying the just proportion. The commissioners of each town shall deliver a copy of such order to their supervisor, who shall lay it before his board, and the amount shall be raised as provided in section 501, and paid over to the person entitled.

2 Laws of 1857, ch. 639, § 8.

Appeal from orders made under sections 498 or 501.

§ 503. Either party, deeming himself aggrieved by the decision of any motion made under sections 498 or 501, may appeal therefrom to the general term, which have power to affirm, modify or reverse, with or without costs. The appeal shall conform to the practice of that court in appeals to the general term, from an order made at special term.

2 Laws of 1857, ch. 639, § 6, and last clause of § 7.

Reference to local provisions.

§ 504. The construction of bridges over Newtown creek,[1] and over the creeks between New York and New Rochelle,[2] is the subject of special statutes.

[1] Laws of 1854, ch. 258; 1853, ch. 164; 1852, ch. 276.

[2] Laws of 1852, ch. 382.

ARTICLE VIII.

OBSTRUCTIONS AND INJURIES TO HIGHWAYS.

Removal of encroachments.

§ 505. If a highway, duly laid out or erected, is encroached upon by fences, buildings or otherwise, the commissioners may, in their discretion, make an order in writing, and signed, requiring the encroachment to be removed from the highway.

1 R. S., 1050, § 121, first clause.

This provision is extended to include all obstructions.

Notice to occupant.

§ 506. They shall give to the occupant of the land, or, if it be unoccupied, to the owner, if he reside in the town, written notice, to be served on him personally or by leaving it at his residence in his absence, specifying the breadth of the highway, the place and extent of such encroachment, and requiring him to remove the same within sixty days.

1 R. S., 1050, § 121, second clause, and from § 122.

§ 507. Such person shall forfeit fifty cents for every day after the expiration of the notice that the encroachment continues unremoved, unless the encroachment is denied, as hereinafter provided. Penalty for neglect.

Ib., § 122; Laws of 1858, ch. 260.

§ 508. If the occupant or owner, within five days after the notice, answers, in writing,[1] denying the encroachment, one of the commissioners shall apply to any justice of the peace of the county, who shall issue a precept to any constable of the town, requiring him to summon twelve residents thereof to meet at a time and place specified, which shall be not less than four days from the issuing, to inquire into the premises. The constable shall give at least three days' notice of the time and place to the commissioners and the party denying the encroachment.[2] If the encroachment is denied, a jury to be summoned.

[1] Lane *v.* Cory, 19 Barb., 537; Laws of 1858, ch. 260.

[2] 1 R. S., 1050, § 123.

§ 509. At the time appointed the jury shall be sworn by the justice well and truly to inquire whether any such encroachment has been made, and by whom. Witnesses produced by either party shall be sworn, and the jury shall hear the proofs and allegations submitted. Trial of the encroachment.

1 R. S., 1051, § 124.

Proceedings if an encroachment is found.

§ 510. If the jury find an encroachment they shall make and subscribe a certificate stating the particulars of it and by whom made, which shall be filed in the town clerk's office. Within sixty days of the filing the owner or occupant shall remove the encroachment whether made by him or not, under the penalty provided by section 507. He shall also pay the costs of the inquiry, and if they are not paid in ten days the justice shall issue a warrant therefor, as provided in section 448.

1 R. S., 1051, § 125.

Proceedings if no encroachment is found.

§ 511. If the jury find no encroachment they shall so certify; and ascertain and certify the damages sustained in the proceeding by the occupant or owner, which, together with the costs, the commissioners shall pay, and the same shall be a charge in their favor against the town.

Ib., § 126.

Removal not to be required in the winter.

§ 512. No person shall be required to remove encroachments, except between the first day of April and the first day of December ensuing. unless the same obstruct the free passage of the highway.

Ib., § 127. The last clause is new.

Removal by commissioners.

§ 513. If a person required under these provisions to remove an encroachment, shall not do so in due time, or if the owner is a non-resident of the town, and there is no occupant, the commissioners may cause it to be removed at his expense. Their charges therefor may be recovered as provided in section 448.

1 R. S., 1050, § 122; Laws of 1858, ch. 261, § 7.

Gates across highways, when allowed.

§ 514. No gates shall be allowed on any public highway duly laid out, except on highways running through lands liable to be overflowed in such manner as to remove the fences.

1 R. S., 1052, § 151.

Such gates to be at the occupant's expense,

§ 515. Such gates shall be erected and maintained by the overseers of highways at the expense of the occupant or owner for whose benefit they are erected. If intermediate lands between any two such gates are severally occupied or owned by more than one person benefited, the whole expense shall be borne by all, in proportion to the extent of land each occupies or owns adjoining the highway between the gates.

Ib., §§ 132, 133.

Overseer to file statement of expenses and collect them.

§ 516. The overseer of the district shall annually, on or before the first day of November, make and file with the town clerk a statement, verified by oath, of such expenses, stating the amount to be paid by each person, which amounts, within ten days after filing it, he shall demand of each such person. If any one neglects to pay within six days after demand, the overseer shall proceed to collect the same as provided in section 448.

Ib., § 135.

Account of the gates and penalty for leaving open.

§ 517. The commissioners of highways shall file in the town clerk's office an account of such gates; and if any person passing such a gate leaves it open, or willfully and unnecessarily rides over ground adjoining the road on which such gate is erected he shall forfeit to the party injured treble damages.

1 R. S., 1052, § 136.

Penalties for injuries to highways.

§ 518. Whoever obstructs or injures any highway, or obstructs or diverts any water-course thereon is liable to a penalty of ten dollars. Whoever removes or injures any mile-board or mile-stone or guide-post, or any inscription on such, erected upon any highway, is liable to a penalty of ten dollars for every offense, and is guilty of a misdemeanor.

Modified from Ib., 1055, §§ 155 to 157; 1053, § 141.

Removal of fallen trees.

§ 519. Any person may give notice to the occupant or owner of any inclosed land, from which a tree is fallen upon a highway, to remove such tree within two days; and if it is not removed within that time the occupant or owner is liable to a penalty of fifty cents for every day thereafter till it is removed.

1 R. S., 1051, § 128.

Penalty for unauthorized felling.

§ 520. Whoever cuts down a tree on land not occupied by him, so that it falls into any highway, river or stream, unless by the occupant's consent, shall forfeit to such occupant one dollar for every tree so felled, and the like sum for every day the same remains in such highway, river or stream.

1 R. S., 1051, § 129.

§ 521. The commissioners may put up and maintain at each end of any public bridge, the length of whose cord is not less than twenty-five feet, a notice in these words, in large characters: "One dollar fine for riding or driving on this bridge faster than a walk;" and whoever rides or drives faster than a walk on such bridge is liable to a penalty of one dollar for each offense.

Notice on bridges, and penalty for disregarding.

Ib., 1053, §§ 142, 143.

§ 522. All penalties or forfeitures given in the provisions of this Code respecting highways, and not otherwise specially provided for, shall be recovered of the commissioners of highways of the town where the offense is committed, and be expended on the highways.

Application of penalties.

CHAPTER III.

RAILWAYS.

ARTICLE I.

GENERAL POWERS AND DUTIES OF RAILWAY COMPANIES.

Powers of company.

§ 523. In addition to the general powers of corporations, every railway company has power:

1. To make all surveys necessary for the choice of its route, and for such purpose to enter upon the lands or waters of any person, but subject to responsibility for all damage done;

2. To take and hold by purchase, or by voluntary grants, any property to aid in the purposes of its incorporation; but real estate received by voluntary grant shall be held and used for the purposes of such grant only;

3. To lay out its road, not exceeding six rods in width, and to construct the same, and for purposes of cuttings and embankments to take as much more land as necessary for its secure construction; and to cut down any trees that may be in danger of falling upon it, making compensation therefor in the same way as for lands taken;

4. To construct their road across, along or upon any stream, water-course or public way which its route intersects or touches, restoring the same to its former state, or to such state as not unnecessarily to impair its usefulness: and subject to the powers, with respect to railways, conferred by law upon the canal commissioners.[1] Nothing in this chapter contained shall be construed to authorize the erection of any bridge or other obstruction at

[1] R. S., 474, § 24.

a place on any stream or lake navigated by any steam or sail boats; nor the construction of any railroad in or across any city street without the assent of the corporation of the city; nor upon any land within a public way, without compensation to the owner of the fee thereof;[1]

5. To cross, intersect and unite its road with any railway before constructed, and upon the ground of such other railway company, with the necessary turn-outs, sidings and switches, and other conveniences in furtherance of the objects of its connections. Every company whose road is intersected by a new road shall unite with the company owning such new road in forming such intersections and connections, and grant the necessary facilities; and if they cannot agree upon the compensation therefor, or the points and manner of such crossings and connections, the same shall be ascertained in the manner provided by law for lands taken;

6. To carry persons and property on their railway by the power of steam or of animals, or by any mechanical power;

7. To erect and maintain all necessary and convenient buildings, stations, fixtures and machinery for the accommodation and use of their passengers, freights and business;

8. To regulate the time and manner in which

[1] Williams *v.* The N. Y. Central R. R. Co., and § 57.

passengers and property shall be transported, and the compensation therefor; but the compensation for any passenger and his ordinary baggage shall not exceed three cents per mile. But this subdivision does not apply to corporations formed under special charter before April 2d, 1850;

9. From time to time to borrow such sums as are necessary for completing or operating their railway, and to issue and dispose of their bonds for any amount so borrowed, and to mortgage their corporate property and franchises to secure any debt contracted for such purposes; and the directors may confer, under such regulations as they see fit, on any holder of any such bond, the right to convert the principal thereof into stock of the company, at any time not exceeding ten years from the date of the bond.

1 R. S., 1230, § 28.

Annual report.

§ 524. Every company shall make an annual report to the state engineer and surveyor of the operations of the year ending on the thirtieth day of September; which report shall be verified by the oath of the treasurer or president, and acting superintendent of operations, and be filed in the office of the state engineer and surveyor by the first day of December in each year, and shall state:

1. The amount of capital as by charter;
2. The amount of stock subscribed;

3. The amount paid in as by last report;

4. The amount now of capital stock paid in;

5. The funded debt by last report;

6. The amount now of funded debt;

7. The floating debt as by last report;

8. The amount now of floating debt;

9. The total amount now of funded and floating debt;

10. The average rate per annum of interest on funded debt.

COST OF ROAD AND EQUIPMENT:

11. For graduation and masonry by last report;

12. The amount now expended for the same;

13. The amount for bridges by last report;

14. The amount now expended for the same;

15. The amount for superstructure, including iron, by last report;

16. Amount now expended for the same;

17. For passengers and freight stations, building and fixtures, by last report;

18. Amount now expended for the same;

19. For engine and car-houses, machine shops, and machinery and fixtures, by last report;

20. Amount now expended for the same;

21. For land, land damages and fences, by last report;

22. Amount now expended for the same;

23. For locomotives and fixtures and snow-plows, by last report;

24. Amount now expended for the same;

25. For passenger and baggage cars by last report;

26. Amount now expended for the same;

27. For freight cars as by last report;

28. Amount now expended for the same;

29. For engineering and agencies by last report;

30. Amount now expended for the same;

31. Total cost of road and equipment.

CHARACTERISTICS OF ROAD:

32. Length of road;

33. Length of road laid;

34. Length of double track, including sidings;

35. Length of branches owned by the company laid;

36. Length of double track on the same;

37. Weight of rail by yard on main track;

38. The number of engine houses and shops, of engines and cars, and their character;

39. Each company shall also transmit to him, within three months after any portion of the road is in use, the following maps, profiles and drawings: The map to show the length and direction of each straight line and the length and radius of each curve, the point of crossing of each town and county line, and the length of line in each town and county, accurately determined by measurements to be taken after the completion of the road; the profile to be on the map and to show the grade, line and surface of ground in the usual method; also, the elevation of grades above tides at each change in the inclination thereof; the maps and profile to be made on a scale of five hundred feet to one-tenth of a foot; vertical scale of profile to be one hundred feet to one-tenth of a foot.

DOINGS OF THE YEAR IN TRANSPORTATION, AND TOTAL MILES RUN:

40. Miles run by passenger trains;

41. Miles run by freight trains;

42. The rate of fare for passengers, charged for the respective classes, per mile;

43. Number of passengers carried in cars;

44. Number of miles traveled by passengers;

45. Number of tons, of two thousand pounds, of freight carried in cars;

46. Number of miles carried, or total movement of freight in miles; all to be accurately compiled

from the daily records or evidences of earnings, manifest and way-bills;

47. Average rate of speed adopted by ordinary passenger trains, including stops;

48. Average rate of speed adopted by ordinary passenger trains when in motion;

49. Average rate of speed adopted by express trains, including stops;

50. Average rate of speed adopted by express trains when in motion;

51. Average rate of speed adopted by freight trains, including stops;

52. Average rate of speed adopted by freight trains when in motion;

53. Average weight, in tons of two thousand pounds, of passenger trains, exclusive of passengers and baggage;

54. Average weight, in tons, of freight trains, exclusive of freight;

55. The amount of freight, specifying the quantity in tons, of the products of the forest, of animals, of vegetable food, other agricultural products, manufactures, merchandise and other articles.

EXPENSES OF MAINTAINING THE ROAD OR REAL PROPERTY OF THE CORPORATION:

56. For repairs of road-bed and railway, except-

ing cost of iron, which shall be the cost of labor and materials used during the year; also, use and cost of engines engaged in ballasting; also, the renewal and repairs of gravel and stone cars, and all items of cost connected with keeping the road in order:

57. For depreciation of way;

58. Length, in feet, of iron used in renewals, with weight and cost;

59. Repairs of buildings;

60. Repairs of fences and gates;

61. Taxes on real property;

62. Total expenses of maintaining road or real property for the year;

63. Expenses of machinery or personal property of the corporation;

64. Repairs of engines and tenders;

65. Depreciation of engines and tenders;

66. Repairs of passenger and baggage cars;

67. Depreciation of passenger and baggage cars;

68. Repairs of freight cars;

69. Depreciation of freight cars;

70. Repairs of tools and machinery in shops;

71. Incidental expenses, including fuel, oil, clerks, watchmen about shops;

72. To expenses of repair of machinery;

73. Office expenses, stationery;

74. Agents and clerks;

75. Labor, handling freight, loading and unloading;

76. Porters, watch and switchmen;

77. Wood and water station attendance;

78. Conductors, baggage and brakemen;

79. Enginemen and firemen;

80, Fuel, first cost, and labor preparing for use;

81 Oil and waste for engines and tenders;

82. Oil and waste for freight cars;

83. Oil and waste for baggage and passenger cars;

84. Loss and damage of goods and baggage;

85. Damages for injuries of persons;

86. Damages to property, including damages by fire, cattle killed on road.

87. General superintendence;

88. Contingencies;

89. Total expenses of operating road;

90. The above statements are to be made without reference to the sums actually received or paid during the year. The following statement of the earnings, and cash receipts and payments, are required;

91. From passengers;

92. From freight;

93. From other sources;

94. The above to be stated without reference to the amount actually collected;

95. Receipts during the year from freight;

96. From passengers;

97. From other sources, specifying what, in detail;

98. Payments for transportation expenses;

99. For interest;

100. Dividends on stock, amount and rate per cent;

101. Payments to surplus fund, and the total amount of the fund;

102. The number of persons injured in life and limb, and the cause of the injury, and whether passengers or persons employed; whether any such accidents have arisen from carelessness or negligence of any person in the employment of the corporation, and whether such person is retained in the service of the corporation;

103. The provisions of this section shall apply to all existing railway corporations; and the reports made in pursuance hereof shall be deemed a full compliance with any existing law or resolution requiring annual reports.

1 R. S., 1232, § 30.

Penalty for neglect.

§ 525. Any company which neglects so to report is liable to a penalty of two hundred and fifty dollars.

1 R. S., 1235, § 31.

Legislature may reduce the rates of fare and freight.

§ 526. If on an examination at any time by the state engineer and surveyor, and the comptroller, it is ascertained that the total net income of any company for the year then passed, has exceeded ten per cent upon the capital of the company actually expended, the legislature may alter or reduce the rates of freight, fare or other profits; but not so as to produce less than ten per cent, except by the consent of the company.

Ib., § 32.

ARTICLE II.

CONSTRUCTION OF RAILWAYS.

§ 527. Lands belonging to the state, or to any county or town, and required for the purposes of any railway, may be granted to the company by the commissioners of the land office, or the county or town officers having charge of such lands, as the case may be, upon such compensation as agreed by such respective officers. State and municipal authorities may make grants.

R. S., 1230, § 25.

§ 528. The common council of no city shall permit the construction along any street or avenue therein of a railway for the transportation of passengers, commencing ann ending within the city, except in the following manner: City railways.

They shall give public notice in one or more of the principal newspapers published in the city, of intention to grant authority to establish such a road, and of the terms and conditions upon which the grant will be made, and inviting proposals therefor to be made at a specified time and place. If the majority in interest of the owners of property, estimating the same at the assessed value thereof, upon the whole of the street or avenue, have consented to the construction of the railway therein, the common council may then grant authority to construct such railway to such person proposing for the same as agrees to carry passengers thereon at the lowest rates of fare, and gives adequate security to comply in all respects with the terms and conditions prescribed.

Laws of 1854, ch. 140, §§ 1, 2.

Commissioners of highways may permit certain railways to cross public roads.

§ 529. When any person or association constructs a railway upon land purchased for the purpose on a route crossing any public road, they may be authorized, by the written consent of the commissioners of highways having charge of such road, to construct their railway across or on the same, but they shall restore it to its former state, so as not to impair its usefulness.

1 R. S., 1054, § 152.

Indian chiefs may grant right of way.

§ 530. The chiefs of any nation of Indians may with the approval of the county court of the county, grant to a company the right of way over their lands; but nothing more can be so granted than the right to use, for the purposes of the railway, the lands taken.

Ib., 1243, §§ 62, 63.

Grants by owner not having capacity to convey.

§ 531. The supreme court has power, by a summary proceeding, on petition, to authorize any trustee not otherwise authorized, or the general guardian or committee of any infant, idiot or person of unsound mind, to sell and convey to any railroad corporation, on such terms as shall be just, the title vested in such trustee, or in such infant, idiot or person of unsound mind, to any real property which is required for the purposes of such company's incorporation. In case such infant, idiot or person of unsound mind has no general guardian or committee, the court may appoint a special guardian or committee for the purpose, and may require from him such security as it deems proper. Before the conveyance is executed, the terms thereof shall be reported to the court on oath, and if the court is satisfied they are just to the party interested in the estate, it shall confirm the report and direct the proper conveyance or release to be executed, which shall have the same effect as if executed by an owner having legal power to sell and convey.

1 R. S., 1230, § 26.

§ 532. In case any railway corporation, the line of whose road has been surveyed and designated, and a certificate thereof duly filed, as required by section 533, is unable to agree for the purchase of any real property required for purposes of its incorporation, it has the right to acquire title to the same in the mode provided by the CODE OF CIVIL PROCEDURE for taking private property for public use. **Acquiring title by appraisal.**

From 1 R. S., 1224, § 13, amended by Laws of 1853, ch. 282, § 4. By that act, real property, between certain streets in the city of Buffalo, is excepted.

§ 533. All lands acquired by any railway company by appraisal, for passenger and freight depots shall be held in fee. **Lands acquired to be held in fee.**

Laws of 1854, ch. 282, § 17.

Route to be fixed before construction. § 534. Every railway company formed under the general laws of the state shall in each county, before constructing any part of their road therein, make a map and profile of their route therein, which shall be certified by their president and engineer, or a majority of the directors, and filed in the county clerk's office. The company shall give written notice of such route to all actual occupants of lands over which it lies and not belonging to the company.

1 R. S., 1229, § 22, first part.

Commission to review route. § 535. Any party feeling aggrieved by the location may, within fifteen days after receiving such notice, apply to the county court by a verified petition setting forth his objections, and the court may, if it deems there is sufficient cause, appoint three disinterested persons, one of whom must be a practical engineer, as commissioners to examine the route, and after hearing the parties to confirm or alter the same as may be just to all parties and the public; but no alteration shall be made without concurrence of the commissioner who is a practical engineer. Their determination shall be made, certified and filed in the county clerk's office within thirty days after their appointment. They are entitled to three dollars each per day for services and expenses, to be paid by the petitioner, and if the route is altered by them the company shall refund it.

Ib., last part.

§ 536. Any company may at any time by a two-thirds vote of the directors, alter any part of their route; and when their grade is required to be altered at a canal-crossing in consequence of directions from the canal commissioners, they may with the assent of such commissioners lay out a new line for the purpose of crossing at a more favorable grade, and without being compelled to abandon the existing line. In any alteration of their route or any addition of such new line, they shall file in the proper county clerk's office a survey, map and certificate; but no such alteration of a route or addition of a new line shall be made in any city or village after the road is constructed, unless by the sanction of a two-thirds vote of the common council or trustees. In case of any alteration of route after grading has been commenced, compensation shall be made to all persons for injury so done to lands that were donated to the company. Company may alter their routes.

1 R. S., 1229, § 23; Laws of 1854, ch. 282, § 17.

§ 537. Any railway company may at any time alter the grade in any part of their route; damages arising therefrom to be appraised as upon taking lands. Company may alter their grades.

From Laws of 1855, ch. 478, § 1. The city of Buffalo is excepted in that act.

§ 538. Where the route crosses a highway, turnpike or plankroad already or hereafter laid out, the latter may be carried under or over the track. Where an embankment or cutting makes Construction of crossings and intersections a change in the line of such an intersecting public way desirable for ease of ascent or descent, the company may take for such change such additional lands as are requisite, in the same manner as lands acquired by the corporation for its own roadway; and the same become part of such intersecting way, and are held by the same tenure therewith.

1 R. S., 1229, § 24; Laws of 1853, ch. 62, § 2, last clause.

Weight of rail.

§ 539. No company shall use for their track, except for turnouts, sidings and switches, any iron rail of less than fifty-six pounds to the lineal yard.

1 R. S., 1230, § 27.

Map of completed road to be filed.

§ 540. Every company shall, within a reasonable time after their road is constructed, cause to be made a map and profile thereof, and of the land obtained for the use thereof, and file the same in the office of the state engineer and surveyor; and also like maps of the parts thereof located in different counties and file the same in the offices for recording deeds, in the county in which such parts are. Every such map shall be drawn on a scale, and on paper, to be designated by the state engineer and surveyor, and shall be certified and signed by the president or engineer of such corporation.

Ib., 1238, § 44.

Lines common to two railways.

§ 541. Whenever two companies embrace the same location for a portion of their line, or whenever, by the connection of two or more railways, the same points of termination are reached by railway, any two such railways may, by agreement, provide for the construction by one of the companies of so much of the line as is common to both, and for the manner and terms upon which the business thereon shall be performed. Any company so connecting may alter its articles of association, so as to terminate at the point of intersection, and may reduce its capital to a sum not less than ten thousand dollars for each mile of its road thus shortened. This section does not apply to any part of the line within the bounds of a city.

Laws of 1854, ch. 282, p. 608, § 13.

§ 542. Any company formed under the general laws may, if necessary, under a two-thirds vote of the directors, locate and construct in an adjoining state a part of their road between any two points within this state; and the sections of such road lying within this state shall be deemed a connected line according to the articles of association. The directors may, in such case, reduce the capital to an amount not less than that required by law for the number of miles of the line actually within the state. Lines without the state.

1 R. S., 1240, § 55.

§ 543. Every company whose line is open for use, and before opening a new line for use, shall erect and maintain on the sides of their road, wherever fences are necessary to prevent horses, Company to erect and maintain fences and cattle-guards.

cattle, sheep and hogs from getting on to the railroad from the adjoining lands, a fence of the height and strength of a division fence, as required by law, or a sufficient post and wire fence, with openings, gates or bars at the farm-crossings for the use of the adjoining owners; and also shall erect and maintain cattle guards at all road-crossings (whether of roads already or hereafter laid out), suitable to prevent such animals from getting on to the railway. When such fences or guards are not made or not in good repair, the company and its agents are liable for damages done by the agents or engines of any company to any such animals thereon under any circumstances, except where the willful act of the owner cause the injury: but when such fences and guards are duly made and in good repair they are not liable for any such damages, unless negligently or willfuly done.

Laws of 1854, ch. 282, § 8; Laws of 1853, ch. 62, § 2 last clause.

Agreement of adjoining owner to fence. § 544. It is the duty of every owner of land adjoining any railway, who has received or whose grantor has received a specific sum as compensation to fence, and has agreed to build and maintain a lawful fence on the line of said road, to build and maintain such fence; and if the owner, his heirs or assigns, within thirty days after notice so to do from the company, neglects to build or maintain the same, if built, the company shall build and maintain it, and may maintain an action for the expense thereof against the person so neglecting.

Laws of 1854, ch. 282, p. 608, § 9.

§ 545. No person not connected with or employed upon the railway shall walk along its track, except where the same is laid along a public road or street. Walking on railway track prohibited.

From 1 R. S., 1237, § 43, last clause.

ARTICLE III.

RAILWAY TRAFFIC.

§ 546. Every company shall, when applied to by the postmaster-general, convey the mails of the United States on their road; and in case they do not agree as to the mode and terms of the service, the governor may appoint three commissioners, who, or a majority of them, after fifteen days' notice, to the company, in writing, of the time and place of meeting, shall determine the mode and Duty to carry mails.

terms; but the price shall not be less than the freight on a like weight of merchandise transported in their freight trains, and a fair compensation for the post-office car. And in case the postmaster-general requires the mail to be carried at other hours, or at a higher speed than the passenger trains are run, the company shall furnish an extra train for the mail, and be allowed an extra compensation.

1 R. S., 1235, § 33.

Duty of company towards rival connecting roads.

§ 547. Every company shall grant to other companies whose routes touch its own, equal terms in respect to the transportation of trains, persons and property upon its road, and equal facilities in the interchange of cars and in the furnishing of tickets for the business of each connecting road. The governor shall, upon the petition of the proprietors of any such connecting road who feel aggrieved in respect to such arrangements, presented on fourteen days' notice to the others, appoint three disinterested persons as commissioners, who shall summarily examine the grievances and prescribe such regulations as they deem just to secure to the connecting roads equal accommodations, and shall fix the terms and conditions thereof. Their award, when approved by the county court of the county where such intersection is, shall be binding for two years; and the court may compel performance by appropriate process. The expense of the proceedings shall be paid as determined by the court.

1 R. S., 1239, § 52.

§ 548. Every person employed by a company on a passenger train, or at a passenger station, shall wear upon his hat or cap a badge indicating his office and the initials of the company's name, and without such badge no such person shall exercise any of the powers of his office or employment, or interfere with any passenger, his baggage or property. Employees to wear badges.

Ib., 1232, § 29.

§ 549. Any company which asks and receives a greater rate of fare than that allowed by law shall forfeit fifty dollars, to be recovered, with the excess so received, by the party paying the same. But it is lawful for any company to take the legal rate of fare for one mile for any fractional distance of a mile. Penalty for exacting illegal fares.

Laws of 1857, ch. 185, vol. 1, p. 432.

§ 550. If any passenger refuses to pay his fare, or to exhibit or surrender his ticket when reasonably required so to do, it is lawful for the conductor and the servants of the company to put him and his baggage out of the cars, using no unnecessary force, at any usual stopping-place, or near any dwelling-house on stopping the train. Passenger refusing to pay fare.

1 R. S., 1236 § 34.

§ 551. Every company shall start and run their cars for the transportation of passengers and pro- Accommodations.

perty at regular times to be fixed by public notice, and shall furnish sufficient accommodation for the transportation of all such passengers and property as are, within a reasonable time previous thereto, offered for transportation at the place of starting and the junctions of other railroads, and at usual stopping-places established for receiving and discharging way passengers and freights for that train; and shall transport the same between such places, on payment of the legal freight or fare, and shall be liable to the party aggrieved, in an action for damages, for any neglect or refusal in the premises.

1 R. S., 1236, § 35.

Baggage checks.

§ 552. A check shall be affixed to every parcel of baggage when it is taken for transportation if there is a handle, loop or fixture, so that the same can be attached upon it, and a duplicate thereof given to the passenger or person delivering the same in his behalf; and if such check be refused, on demand, the company shall pay to such passenger ten dollars, to be recovered in a civil action, and shall take no fare or toll from him; and if he has paid his fare it shall be refunded by the conductor.

Ib., § 36.

Sleeping cars.

§ 553. Any patentee of a sleeping car, or his legal representative, may place his car upon any railroad, with the assent of the company, and may charge each passenger occupying it forty cents for the use of a berth for one hundred miles; and at the rate of three mills for every additional mile, but in no case shall the charge exceed eighty cents. All persons using such car shall be furnished with tickets, with the words "Sleeping car" plainly written or printed thereon.

Laws of 1858, ch. 125, p. 234, § 1, and part of § 2.

§ 554. Such company shall not be interested in the sums so charged. They shall maintain sufficient first-class cars of other kinds for the accommodation of all passengers not using the sleeping car, and be liable for damages for injuries to the same extent as if the sleeping cars were owned and provided by them. Duty and liability of companies as to sleeping cars.

Ib., ch. 125, § 3, part of 2 and 4.

§ 555. In forming a passenger train, baggage, freight, merchandise or lumber cars shall not be placed in rear of the passenger cars; and the officer or agent who directs or knowingly suffers such arrangement, and the conductor of the train, are guilty of a misdemeanor. Position of passenger cars in trains.

1 R. S., 1236, § 37.

§ 556. In case any passenger on any railway is injured, while on the platform of a car, or in any baggage, wood or freight car, in violation of the printed regulations of the company posted up at the time in a conspicuous place inside of its passenger cars then in the train, such company shall not be liable for the injury, provided there was, Duty of passengers.

at the time, room inside its passenger cars for the proper accommodation of the passengers.

1 R. S., 1238, § 45.

Crossing signals.

§ 557. A bell shall be placed on each locomotive engine run on any railway, and rung at the distance of at least eighty rods from the place where the tract crosses, on the same level, any traveled public way, and be kept ringing until the engine has crossed the same; or a steam whistle shall be attached, and be sounded, except in cities, at the like distance, and be kept sounding at intervals until it has crossed the same; and every neglect thereof subjects the company to a fine not exceeding twenty dollars, in the discretion of the court; and every engineer having charge of the engine, to a fine not exceeding fifty dollars, or imprisonment in the county jail not exceeding sixty days, in the discretion of the court; and the company shall be liable for all damages sustained by any person by reason of such neglect.

The penalties under this section may be sued for in the name of the people of the state, by the district attorney of the county in which they accrue, within ten days, and in case he omits to sue therefor within that time, then any person aggrieved may sue therefor in the name of the overseers of the poor of the town wherein the same accrued, which, when recovered, shall be paid to the overseers for the benefit of the poor. If such person fails in the action the court shall give judgment against him for costs.

Laws of 1854, ch. 282, p. 608, § 7.

§ 558. If any person, while in charge of a locomotive engine or while acting as conductor, is intoxicated, he is guilty of a misdemeanor. Intoxication of company's servants.

1 R. S., 1237, § 40.

§ 559. The liability of railway companies as common carriers is regulated by the CIVIL CODE. Railway companies as common carriers.

CHAPTER IV.

CANALS.

Boat owner or master to furnish certificate of registry.

§ 560. The owners of every boat navigating the canals shall subscribe and deliver to the collector from whom the first clearance for it is demanded a "certificate of registry," containing the owners' names and places of abode, the name of the boat and of some place as that where it is owned. If the owners reside out of the state, the certificate shall be signed and delivered by the master as owner; and whenever such master is changed, the new master shall sign and deliver a new certificate to the collector of whom he first demands a clearance. The persons thus specified as owners shall be deemed the true owners for all purposes of this chapter.

1 R. S., 507, §§ 205, 206, 212.

§ 561. The collector shall give a receipt for the certificate to the master, and without delay transmit the certificate to the auditor of the canal department. Duty of collector.

1 R. S., 507, § 207.

§ 562. The auditor shall keep with the books and papers relating to the canals, and open to inspection during office hours, a register of all such boats. If any persons residing in the state, claiming to own such a boat by transfer from former owners, produce to him due proof of such transfer, and a new certificate of registry signed by themselves, he shall accordingly change the register of such boat. He shall, from time to time, transmit to the several collectors a certified copy of his register and of changes therein. Duty of auditor.

Ib., §§ 208, 209, 210.

§ 563. The name of no registered boat shall be changed without the auditor's order, under a penalty upon the owner who makes such change, and also upon any master who reports or enters a boat by a changed name, of twenty-five dollars for every offense. Penalty for changing name without order.

Ib., § 208, last clause § 213.

§ 564. No collector shall grant a clearance for any boat unless he has evidence that it is duly registered, or a proper certificate of registry has been delivered to him, or the receipt of some other collector therefor has been exhibited to him Clearances not granted to unregistered boats.

Ib., § 211.

Name to be on each boat.

§ 565. No boat shall receive a clearance or be permitted to pass unless it has its name and the place where it is owned, according to the existing certificate of registry, painted in some conspicuous and permanent part of the outside of the boat, in letters at least four inches in height.

1 R. S., 507, § 214.

The bill of lading and its requisites.

§ 566. Every master of a boat conveying property shall exhibit, as hereinafter required, a bill of lading signed by himself and the consignor, and, if so required by the collector receiving it, verified by his oath to be taken before such collector, and containing:

1. The name of every place on the canal where any portion of such property was shipped, and of the place for which it is intended to be cleared;

2. A statement of the names, description and weight of all the articles thereof on which toll is charged by the ton, of the number of those on which toll is charged by number, and of the feet of each article on which toll is charged by the foot;

3. A specification of the weight or quantity of each article where a different rate of toll is charged on different articles, on which toll is so computed.

1 R. S., 508, § 215; 509, § 220; amended by Laws of 1859, ch. 16, § 1, subdiv. 1, 2, 3.

§ 567. Every such bill shall be exhibited: To whom to be exhibited.

1. To every collector of whom a clearance is required;

2. To every collector whose office is next in order in course of the voyage to the place where a clearance has been given;

3. To the collector wherever any of the cargo is unladen or received, or, if there be none there, to the collector whose office is next on the voyage;

4. To every other collector who demands it.

No clearance shall be granted, except on the production of such a bill.

1 R. S., 508, § 216; Laws of 1859, ch. 16, § 1, subdiv. 4.

§ 568. If there is no collector's office at the place where any articles are laden, nor where they are delivered, nor at any intermediate place, the master shall, within ten days after the delivery of such articles, exhibit the bill of lading thereof to the collector whose office is nearest to such place of delivery, and pay to him the tolls due thereon, under the penalty of twenty-five dollars for every omission. Provision where there is no collector on the route.

Ib., § 217.

§ 569. Every master who omits to deliver a true bill of lading to any collector, when required, or who delivers any articles mentioned in any bill of lading at a place beyond that to which they are cleared, shall forfeit twenty-five dollars. Every Penalties.

person who signs or delivers to any collector a false bill of lading shall pay, on all property omitted in such bill, treble the toll usually charged on such property, to any collector demanding it, for the whole distance the same is conveyed.

Making a false bill knowingly is a misdemeanor.

§ 570. Every person who knowingly signs or delivers a false bill is guilty of a misdemeanor.

1 R. S., 509, § 219

Clearances.

§ 571. Each boat shall have a separate clearance, and no part of any cargo shall be cleared to a place beyond that to which the boat is cleared.

Ib., § 221.

Delivery of clearance.

§ 572. No boat shall go beyond the place to which it is cleared, nor unlade any article before or after its arrival at the place to which such article is cleared, nor proceed beyond such place, until the master has delivered the clearance of the boat or articles to the collector at the place for which they are cleared.

Ib., § 222.

Provision if there is no collector there.

§ 573. If there is no collector at such place, the master shall deliver the clearance to the last collector whose office is passed in the order of the voyage, and receive from him a permit to proceed to such place.

Ib., § 223.

Penalty for omitting to deliver clearance.

§ 574. Every master who omits to deliver a clearance to the collector to whom it ought to be delivered incurs a penalty of twenty-five dollars.

1 R. S., 509, § 224.

§ 575. Every collector issuing a clearance, or in whose office any clearance is on file, shall, on request, give a certified copy of it, with the additional cargo entered thereon and the several indorsements of other collectors, which copy shall have the same validity as the original. The collector shall receive for such copy, if it does not exceed two folios, six cents, and if over two folios, twelve and a half cents; for which he shall account to the canal fund as the auditor directs. Certified copies of clearances.

Ib., §§ 225, 226.

§ 576. All articles charged by the ton shall be charged according to their real weight. Tonnage.

Ib., § 227.

§ 577. When a difference arises as to the amount of tolls to be paid, the collector shall detain the boat, and weigh, count or measure the articles, as the case may require, and if the weight, number or feet exceeds the amount contained in the bill of lading, the collector shall charge for the excess; and also at the rate of twenty-five cents for every ton weight, five mills a piece for articles counted, and five cents a hundred feet for those measured. The boat, the cargo and the master are liable for the tolls and for such expenses; and the collector Weighing, counting and measuring freight.

shall detain the boat and cargo until they are paid. He shall distrain enough of the property to satisfy them; and after eight days, shall sell the same by public auction, at his usual place of receiving tolls. Any surplus, after payment of the charges and costs, shall be paid on demand to the master or to the owner of the property distrained.

1 R. S., 510, §§ 228 to 232.

Fraud in clearance.

§ 578. Whenever any property transported is, to the knowledge of the captain or owner of the boat, cleared as articles paying a lower rate of toll than they ought to pay, or wholly or partially omitted from the clearance, the boat shall be confiscated to the state.

Laws of 1855, ch. 534, § 1.

Fraud in package.

§ 579. Whenever any property transported is, to the knowledge of the owner, contained in packages falsely marked as containing articles of a description chargeable with a lower rate of toll than they ought to pay, and is thus cleared, such property shall be confiscated to the state.

Ib., § 2.

Disposition of confiscated property.

§ 580. Boats and property mentioned in the two preceding sections shall be seized by any collector of tolls, or officer acting under his direction, as the property of the state, and advertised and sold at public auction, and the proceeds paid into the treasury. The auditor shall pay one-third of the proceeds of such sale to the informant, and one-third to the collector or other officer making the seizure.

Laws of 1855, ch. 534, §§ 1, 2, 3.

§ 581. Every master of a boat carrying passengers shall, at least once in every thirty days of the navigable season, and oftener, if required by the canal board, and under such regulations as that board establishes, deliver to some collector of tolls a statement containing the names of all the passengers, and the distance to which each was carried, since the time embraced in the preceding statement. The statement shall be verified by the master before the collector, and he shall pay to the collector, thereupon, the tolls on such passengers. Statement of passengers.

From 1 R. S., 510, §§ 233, 234.

§ 582. When no passenger has been carried, the master shall make affidavit before a collector that no passenger has been conveyed in such boat during the time for which a statement is required. Affidavit that no passengers have been carried.

Ib., § 235.

§ 583. If during the time for which a statement is required different persons have been masters or had charge of one boat, each person shall furnish such statement or affidavit for such portion of the time as the boat was under his charge. Different masters.

Ib., § 236.

§ 584. In case any master neglects to furnish Penalty.

the affidavit or statement, or to pay the tolls, the master and every owner of the boat is liable to a penalty of twenty-five dollars for each offense. The commissioners of the canal fund may, in their discretion, prohibit such boat from receiving a clearance and navigating the canals, until such statement or affidavit be furnished and the tolls paid.

1 R. S., 510, §§ 237, 238.

Collector's duty.

§ 585. Every collector receiving such statement or affidavit shall give to the person furnishing it a written acknowledgment thereof, and transmit such statement and affidavit to the auditor.

Ib., §§ 287, 239.

Evidence of neglect to make statement.

§ 586. The auditor's certificate, under his official seal, made after thirty days from the time when a statement ought to be made, that no statement or affidavit in respect to a boat, for the time specified therein, has been received at his office, is presumptive evidence that none such has been made.

Ib., 511, § 240.

Tolls on passengers in other cases.

§ 587. Masters of boats, other than boats which usually run night and day, or belong to any regular line of packet or freight boats, shall pay tolls on all passengers conveyed in such boat, in the same manner as tolls on property.

From Ib., § 241.

§ 588. The commissioners of the canal fund may, in their discretion, and at such time and manner as they prescribe, receive from the owners of any boat a specified sum, by the year, for a license to carry passengers therein, as a commutation for tolls upon passengers; and no statement or affidavit, relative to conveying passengers, shall be required from the master of any boat so licensed. Commutation.

1 R. S., 511, §§ 242, 243.

§ 589. Any collector may authorize a clerk to perform all his duties and exercise all his powers in his absence, and he shall be responsible for the acts of his clerk. Collector's clerks.

Ib., § 244.

§ 590. Every collector, or, if no collector is present, every superintendent, shall assign berths to all boats when loading or unloading at any landing-place on a canal, whenever disputes arise concerning the same. Collector to assign berths.

Ib., § 245.

§ 591. No float shall move on any canal faster than at the rate of four miles an hour, without a written permit signed by a majority of the canal commissioners; under penalty of ten dollars for each offense, to be imposed upon the master. Speed.

Ib., § 246.

§ 592. Where a boat, used chiefly for the conveyance of persons, overtakes any other float not Boats overtaking.

chiefly so used, the master of the latter shall give the former every practical facility for passing, and whenever necessary shall stop for that purpose.

1 R. S., 511, § 247.

Boats to turn to the right.

§ 593. When floats meet, the master of each shall turn to the right of the centre of the canal.

Ib., § 248.

Boats meeting in narrow places.

§ 594. Where floats approach any place less than thirty feet wide on the surface, or which will not safely permit their passing, the master of the float going from the navigable waters of the Hudson river shall stop at sufficient distance from such narrow place, and their await the passage of the float going towards such navigable waters.

. Ib., 512, § 249.

Penalty.

§ 595. Every master or boatman violating any provision of the three preceding sections is liable to a penalty of ten dollars for each offense.

Ib., § 250.

Passing locks.

§ 596. Every float within one hundred yards of a lock, if on the same level that the waters in the lock then is, shall be permitted to pass the lock before any other float not on the same level.

Ib., § 251.

Lock-keeper to determine disputes.

§ 597. If a question arises between the masters of floats arriving at any lock as to which is entitled to pass first it shall be determined by the lock-keeper.

Ib., § 252.

§ 598. Every master, owner or navigator of any float refusing to conform to such determination, or detaining or unnecessarily hindering the passage of any float through a lock, in violation of any provision of the two preceding sections, is liable to a penalty of twenty-five dollars for each offense. Penalty.

1 R. S., 512, § 253.

§ 599. No person navigating any of the canals shall use therein any setting pole or shaft, pointed with iron or any other metal, under penalty of twenty-five dollars for each offense. Setting poles.

Ib., § 254.

§ 600. No covered or decked boat shall navigate any canal without a sharp metallic instrument, so affixed upon the bow as to cut apart any tow rope which otherwise might pass over such bow, under penalty of twenty-five dollars for each offense, to be imposed on the owner or master. Knife on the bow.

Ib., §§ 255, 256.

§ 601. Every person who obstructs the navigation of any canal by the improper conduct of any boat or floating thing, or by sinking anything to the bottom, or by placing any obstruction on either path, is liable to a penalty of twenty-five dollars for each offense. Obstructions.

Ib., §§ 257, 258.

§ 602. It is the duty of every canal officer or agent employed on any of the canals, to seize sunken or floating boats and other things found Articles found to be sold.

in a canal, or any article found on the tow path, not in charge of any person; and, after giving ten days' written notice of sale at two public places nearest the place of finding, unless the owner claims the same and pays the cost of seizure and removal, to sell the same by public auction

1 R. S., 512, §§ 259, 260.

Application of proceeds. § 603. The officer, if not a collector, shall account for the same to the nearest collector. The collector receiving such account or making such sale shall account for the same to the commissioners of the canal fund. The commissioners may, after they have received the same, upon application of the owners and due proof of ownership, pay the same over, deducting the penalty and all costs and reasonable charges.

Ib., 513, §§ 261, 262.

Penalty for taking rails, &c. § 604. If any person on a boat takes, without right, any rails, boards, planks or staves, fire-wood or fencing-posts, from the banks or vicinity of the canal, the master shall forfeit to the owner treble their value; and the possession of such property on board the boat shall be presumptive evidence of such taking. The person taking such property shall forfeit twenty-five dollars to any person who will prosecute therefor.

Ib., §§ 263, 264.

Boat liable for penalties. § 605. Every penalty and forfeiture which, by this chapter, is recoverable against the owner, master, boatman, navigator or other person in charge of any boat or float, is chargeable on such boat or float, and an action for it may be brought against any person having possession or charge of the same at the time of commencing the suit.

1 R. S., 513, § 265.

§ 606. In any action, for such penalty or forfeiture, the magistrate issuing the process may therein direct the officer executing it to detain the boat or float, its furniture and horses, until the suit is determined or adequate security given for payment of any judgment that may be recovered. **Boat may be detained**

Ib., § 266.

§ 607. If such security is given, or the defendant prevail, the same shall be released. Otherwise, if judgment is recovered and is not immediately paid, with costs, an execution shall be issued, under which the same may be sold as if the judgment had been obtained against the owner. **Releasing or selling same**

Ib. § 267.

§ 608. Other provisions, applicable to actions for such penalties, are contained in the "*Fiscal Laws.*" **Reference to fiscal laws.**

CHAPTER V.

TURNPIKES AND PLANKROADS.

ARTICLE I.

CONSTRUCTION OF TURNPIKES AND PLANKROADS.

Application by corporation for leave to construct.

§ 609. Any turnpike or plankroad company, before constructing a road through any part of any county, if they have not, as provided in section 619, acquired all necessary lands within such county, shall publish a notice in at least three of the public newspapers printed in the county (and if there are not three therein, then in that, and adjoining counties), once in each week for six weeks successively, specifying the character of the road, each town, city and village through which it is proposed to construct it, and the time when the application hereinafter required will be made. After such notice, it shall apply to the board of supervisors of the county, at any meeting specified in the notice, for authority to take the necessary land and construct the road. The application shall specify the route and character of the road.

1 R. S., 1096, § 63.

§ 610. If the applicant desires a special meeting for the purpose any three supervisors may fix the time therefor, and at least twenty days' notice thereof shall be served on each of the others, either personally, or, in his absence, by leaving it at his residence. The expenses of the meeting thus called, and of serving the notices, shall be paid by the applicant. Special meeting of the supervisors.

Ib., § 64.

§ 611. On the hearing of the application, all residents of the county, and all persons interested in the application, may appear and be heard. The board may take testimony or authorize it to be taken by any judicial officer of the county; and it may adjourn the hearing from time to time. The hearing on the application.

Ib., § 65.

Action of the supervisors.

§ 612. If the board are then of opinion that the public interests will be promoted thereby, it may, by the assent of a majority of all the members elected to the board, make an order granting the application and authorizing the company to take the real property necessary, and appointing three commissioners to lay out the road. The commissioners shall be disinterested persons, and not owners of real property in any town in which the road will lie, nor in any town adjoining such towns. The company shall cause a certified copy of the order of the board to be recorded in the county clerk's office, before they proceed under it.

1 R. S., 1096, § 66.

Road extending into several counties.

§ 613. If the route extends into more than one county, the application shall specify the number of commissioners the company desire, not exceeding three for each county, and an equal number of them shall be appointed by the board of supervisors of each county. The whole number shall be not less than three, nor, without the company's consent, more than six; unless the number of counties exceeds six.

Ib., § 67.

Laying out the road.

§ 614. The commissioners, after taking the oath of office, shall proceed to lay out the road as in their opinion will best promote the public interest. They shall hear all persons interested and may take testimony; they may determine the breadth of the way, but it shall not exceed four rods, except where the company acquire a greater breadth by grant. They shall make, sign and acknowledge (as a deed is acknowledged) an accurate survey and description of the route, and the land taken for the road and for necessary buildings and gates in each county, and record the same in the office of the county clerk thereof. Where the breadth of the road is not fixed by the commissioners, it may be fixed by the inspectors of turnpike and plank roads of the county, or a majority of them.

1 R. S., 1096, §§ 67, 68; Ib., 1104, § 99.

§ 615. The company shall pay to each commissioner his expenses, and two dollars a day for his services. **Compensation of the commissioners.**

Ib., § 67, last clause.

§ 616. The directors of any such company may, with the written consent of holders of two-thirds of the stock, proceed in the manner prescribed by the preceding seven sections, to construct branches to the road or to extend it, or alter any part of the route of it or its branches. **Branches and extensions.**

From Laws of 1859, 465, ch. 208. By that act, the construction of branches, &c., was restricted to routes lying through uncultivated land, and it was not made necessary to obtain the consent of the supervisors. It is supposed that, so far as other parties and the public are concerned, the same provisions should govern both cases.

Acquiring lands by grant.

§ 617. Any such company may acquire necessary lands by grant. The supreme court have power to authorize a grant of necessary real property vested in a person not having capacity to convey, in the same cases and manner as provided in respect to railway companies by section 426.[1] Whenever the land within a highway is necessary to be used, the supervisor and commissioners of highways of the town, or a majority of them, may, after obtaining the written consent of at least two-thirds in number of all the residents on the part of the highway proposed to be taken, fix, by written agreement with the company, the damages to be paid therefor. Such agreement shall be filed in the town clerk's office. Except in actions commenced before the 18th of April, 1855, every such agreement shall be conclusively presumed to have been made at a regular meeting of the supervisor aud commissioners.[2]

[1] Modified from Laws of 1859, 465, ch. 208.

[2] 1 R. S., 1096, § 70; Ib., 1102, §§ 90, 91; Laws of 1855, ch. 546, § 3

Appropriation of damages for highway taken.

§ 618. Damages for lands forming part of a highway are to be paid to the commissioners of highways of the town, to be expended on the highways.

1 R. S., 1102, § 90, last clause.

Application when unnecessary.

§ 619. When a company has obtained by grant or agreement all the lands necessary in any county, it may construct the road in such county without making the application therein required by section

609. But before proceeding to do so, it shall cause an accurate survey of such part of the road to be made by a practical surveyor, signed by its president and secretary, and acknowledged by them (as a deed is acknowledged), and recorded in the county clerk's office; and also, if the road extends into another county, it shall first obtain authority to construct the road there.

1 R. S., 1098, §§ 69, 70.

§ 620. The mode of proceeding to acquire the necessary lands, when it is not done by agreement, is prescribed by the CODE OF CIVIL PROCEDURE. Acquiring right of way.

§ 621. After acquiring title to any lands in pursuance of the foregoing provisions, and not before, the company may take possession thereof and hold the same, subject to the provisions of this chapter. Taking possession.

Ib., § 75.

§ 622. No such road shall be laid out through any orchard of four years' growth, to the injury of the fruit trees; or any garden of four years' cultivation, or any dwelling-house, or building connected with a dwelling-house, or any yard, or inclosures necessary thereto, without the consent of the owner. Orchards and gardens.

Ib., § 73.

§ 623. No such company shall bridge any stream, except under the restrictions imposed by § 652 of this Code. Streams.

From Ib., § 73.

Plankroads on turnpike roads.

§ 624. No plankroad company shall construct its road on the road of a turnpike company (except in case of crossings) without consent of the latter. When a plankroad is constructed on or adjoining any portion of a turnpike road, the company owning the latter may abandon such portion.

From 1 R. S., 1098, § 74, amended 1857, ch. 643.

Restriction on contracts for construction.

§ 625. No director shall be concerned, directly or indirectly, in any contract for making or working any part of the road belonging to his company; and no contractor, for making any part of such road, shall make a new contract for the performance of any part, other than by hiring services and implements, to be superintended and paid by himself, unless such new contract is first approved by the board of directors.

1 R. S., 1088, §§ 23, 24.

Quality of road.

§ 626. Every such road shall be laid out at least four rods wide. The track of plankroads shall be constructed of timber, plank or other hard material. The track of turnpikes shall be bedded with stone, gravel, or such other material found on the line thereof, to the width of eighteen feet, and faced with broken stone or gravel, and with ditches on each side wherever practicable.

Both shall be so constructed as to permit vehicles to pass each other conveniently, and to pass off and on the track at all intersections of roads.

Every company that has once laid their road with plank may relay it, or any part of it, with broken stone, gravel, shells or other hard material, whereby they keep a good, substantial road.

1 R. S., 1104, §§ 96, 97; Laws of 1854, ch. 87, § 2, as amended, 1855, ch. 546.

§ 627. A mile-stone or post shall be maintained by the company at every mile, with an inscription showing the distance from the commencement of the road. If the road commences at the end of any other road, having mile-stones or posts on which the distance from any city or town is marked, a continuation of that distance shall also be inscribed. **Mile-stones**

Ib., 1088, § 21.

§ 628. A guide-post shall also be erected at every place where the road is intersected by a public road, with an inscription showing the name of the place to which such intersecting road leads, in the direction to which the name on the guide-post points. **Guide-posts**

Ib., § 22.

§ 629. When the road or three consecutive miles thereof is completed, any two of the inspectors of turnpikes and plankroads in the county shall, on request of the company, inspect the same, and if satisfied that the road conforms to the requirement of the law, they shall make a certificate thereof, which shall be filed in the county clerk's office. The inspectors are entitled to receive from the **Inspection.**

company two dollars per day for their services. When only three consecutive miles of any plank-road are completed, the company shall not collect tolls for more than one year, unless the road or five consecutive miles are completed within the year.

1 R. S., 1104, § 99; 1105, § 105.

Erection of gates.

§ 630. Upon filing such certificate the company may erect one or more toll-gates, and collect tolls upon the road or such portion as is specified in the certificate. No hoist-gate shall hereafter be erected, and no toll-gate, gate-house or other building shall be put up by such a company within ten rods of the front of any dwelling-house, barn or out-house, without written consent of the owner thereof, except that in the county of Kings they may be put up at not less than seven rods therefrom. Any erection contrary to this section the county judge shall, on application, order to be removed.

1 R. S., 1104, § 101, first clause; 1105, § 106, first clause; 1106, §§ 107, 109; Laws of 1857, ch. 636.

Changing location of gates.

§ 631. If the commissioners of highways deem the location of any gate, within their town or an adjoining town, unjust to the public interest, they may, on fifteen days' notice to the company, apply to the county court for a change of the location. After a hearing the court may make such order as it deems just, and enforce the same, if not appealed from, by attachment or otherwise.

1 R. S., 1106, § 112.

§ 632. Either party may appeal to the supreme court on giving such security as the county court requires. The supreme court, on motion of either party, on due notice, shall refer it to three disinterested persons, not residents of any town in respect to which the road is a thoroughfare, to determine the appeal. The referees have the same powers and are entitled to the same compensation (to be paid in the first instance by the prevailing party) as referees in civil actions. They shall view the premises, hear the parties, and report to the court their decision, the grounds thereof and the evidence taken by them. The court shall thereupon render judgment as they deem just, and may award reasonable costs and expenses to the prevailing party, and execution may be issued for the same. Appeal

1 R. S., 1107, § 13.

§ 633. The directors of any company may abandon the whole of their road or any part of it, at either or both ends (whenever two-thirds in amount of the stockholders consent) by a written surrender thereof, to be attested by the seal of the company and acknowledged by the president and secretary as a deed is acknowledged, and recorded in the clerk's office of each county where the surrendered road lies. Thereafter the surrendered road belongs to the several towns in which it lies; but the company may take toll on any part not surrendered if three consecutive miles in length. Abandonment of road.

Laws of 1854, ch. 87, § 1.

ARTICLE II.

USE OF TURNPIKES AND PLANKROADS.

Tariff of tolls on plankroads.

§ 634. The rates of tolls on plankroads, except in the county of Sullivan, shall not exceed the following:[1]

For every vehicle drawn by one animal, one cent a mile; and, except on roads located wholly or in part in the counties of Chenango, Otsego, St. Lawrence and Oneida, one cent a mile for each additional animal;

For every vehicle used chiefly for conveying passengers, drawn by two animals, three cents a mile, and one cent a mile for each additional animal;

For every horse rode, led or driven, three-quarters of a cent a mile;

For every score of sheep or swine, one and a half cents a mile;

For every score of neat cattle, two cents a mile;

The rates in the county of Sullivan shall be fixed by the board of supervisors, and at not less

[1] Laws of 1853, ch. 241, § 1; ch. 481.

than two nor more than four cents a mile for any vehicle drawn by two horses, and in a ratable proportion for others; but the rates for any company shall not be fixed so high as to enable it, after keeping the road in repair, to divide more than ten per cent on its capital stock and reserve ten per cent as a fund for the reconstruction of the road. The rates as fixed shall not be changed by the board oftener than once in five years.[1]

[1] 1 R. S., 1105, §§ 102, 103, 104.

§ 635. The rates of toll on turnpikes shall not exceed the following: Tariff of tolls on turnpikes.

For every vehicle drawn by one animal, three-quarters of a cent a mile;

For every vehicle drawn by two animals, one and one-quarter cents a mile; and one-quarter cent additional a mile for each additional animal;

For neat cattle, at the rate of one cent a mile for a score;

For sheep or swine, at the rate of one-half cent a mile for a score;

For every horse and rider, or led horse, one-half cent a mile;

In no case shall a company charge greater rates than will enable it, after paying expenses and repairs to divide more than twelve per cent on its capital actually paid in cash.

1 R. S., 1105, § 106; as amended, Laws of 1854, ch. 87, § 3.

Persons exempt.

§ 636. The following persons, and no others, are exempt from payment of toll on any plankroad or turnpike:

1. Persons going to or from religious meetings held at the place where they usually attend for worship, in the town where they reside or an adjoining town, or within eight miles of their residence;

2. Persons going to or from any funeral, and all funeral processions, except that on the Williamsburgh and Cypress Hills plankroad the exemption as to funeral processions shall only extend to the hearse and three carriages;

3. Troops in actual service of the state or of the United States, and persons going to or from a militia training which by law they are required to attend;

4. Persons going to any town meeting or general election at which they are entitled to vote, and for the purpose of voting, or returing therefrom;

5. Persons living within a mile of any gate by the most usually traveled road, except those living in a city or village, may pass it at one-half toll, when not engaged in the transportation of others or the property of others;

6. Farmers living on their farms within one mile of any gate, by the most usually traveled road, and persons driving or leading animals to or from the pasture or field where the animals are usually kept, may pass it free when going to or from their work on such farms.

1 R. S., 1106, § 108.
Laws of 1855, ch. 546, § 4.

§ 637. The toll gatherer may prevent from passing his gate any person, vehicle or animal, liable to toll, unless the toll is paid; but if he unreasonably delays any passenger liable to the payment of toll, or demands and receives from any person more toll than by law he is authorized to collect, he is liable to a penalty of five dollars for each offense, to be recovered by the person aggrieved. Collection of tolls.

Ib., 1090, § 35; 1110, § 126; 1093, § 53.

§ 638. Any person who falsely claims to be exempt, or who, being liable to pay toll, passes a gate, either over the road or by turning off over adjacent ground and again entering the road, without payment and with intent to avoid payment, is liable to a penalty of ten dollars for each offense. Any person who, being liable to pay toll, forcibly or fraudulently passes a gate without paying it, is liable to a penalty of twenty-five dollars for each offense, in addition to any damages caused by him. Penalties.

1 R. S., 1106, § 111; 1094, § 58; Ib., § 57, subd. 3; Laws of 1855, ch. 485, § 3. There may be some difference of opinion as to whether the penalty for

falsely claiming exemptions was not repealed by the act of 1850 (1 R. S., 1106, § 108), which provided new qualifications for exemption, but imposed no penalty.

Commutation.

§ 639. Any company may commute, for a term not exceeding one year at a time, with any person, for the toll payable at the nearest gate on each side of his place of residence.

From 1 R. S., 1049, § 55.

Injuries and obstructions.

§ 640. Any person who injures or obstructs, or causes any act which injures or obstructs, the road-bed, ditch, drain or culvert, or diverts any stream of water so as to endanger the same, is liable to a penalty of five dollars in addition to the damages. Any person who designedly leaves, or causes to be left, any material within any turnpike or plankroad in such a way as to obstruct or endanger travelers, and neglects to remove it within forty-eight hours after written notice from a director to do so, is liable to a penalty of ten dollars for every twenty-four hours of neglect after such notice.

Laws of 1855, ch. 485, §§ 1, 2.

Encroachments.

§ 641. On application by an officer of any company, any inspector shall inquire into any alleged encroachment by any fence or other building upon the lands of the company, and, if found to exist, shall order it to be removed within a period to be specified by him, not less than twenty days nor more than ninety; but an encroachment shall not be required to be removed between the first day of December and the first day of April ensuing, unless the same obstruct the free passage of the road. Every person who neglects to remove an encroachment within the time specified, is liable to a penalty of five dollars for every day of such neglect.

Laws of 1855, ch. 485, § 4.

§ 642. The penalties of this article are recoverable, except where otherwise provided, by the company in respect of whose road they are incurred. An action for such penalties and an action for trespass on or injury to such roads, may be maintained in the county where the act was done or in that where the defendant resides. Penalties, how recovered.

From Laws of 1849, ch. 250, § 9.

ARTICLE III.

INSPECTION AND REPAIRS.

§ 643. Every inspector to whom complaint in writing is made that any part of a turnpike or plankroad in his county, or any part of such road the gate nearest to which is in his county, is out of repair, shall examine it without delay, and give notice of each defect, particularly describing the same to the person attending the gate nearest Inspection.

thereto. After three days after the service of such notice the inspector may, in his discretion, order such gate to be thrown open.

1 R. S., 1092, §§ 44, 46.

Closing gates.

§ 644. A gate so ordered to be opened shall not be shut, nor any toll be collected thereat, until one of the inspectors for the county has granted a certificate that the road is in sufficient repair, and that such gate ought to be closed. Any gate-keeper violating this section or the order given pursuant to the preceding section, is liable in a penalty of ten dollars for each offense, to be recovered by the party aggrieved.

Ib., §§ 45, 47.

Inspectors to report defects to company.

§ 645. Every inspector, who, upon due examination, discovers a defect in any such road within his county, or a gate placed in a situation contrary to law, shall give written notice thereof to one or more of the directors of the company, requiring the defective road to be repaired or the gate removed within a specified time; and in his discretion may order that in the meantime the gates, or such as he specifies, be thrown open.

Ib., 1093, §§ 48, 49.

Enforcing obedience.

§ 646. If such notice be not obeyed, the inspector shall make immediate complaint to the attorney-general or the district attorney for the county, who shall prosecute the company, in the name of the people; and if it is convicted of having suffered the road to be out of repair, or having placed any gate in a situation contrary to the law, the company shall be fined in a sum not exceeding two hundred dollars.

1 R. S., 1093, § 50.

§ 647. The inspector to whom complaint is made shall be paid by the complainant, before he acts thereon, the sum of two dollars for each day to be spent by him in the inspection. If he adjudges the road to be out of repair, such fees shall be repaid by the company to the complainant. It is the duty of the toll gatherer nearest the road adjudged out of repair to pay on demand, and out of the tolls, the fees for which the company is liable to the complainant; and the same may be recovered, with costs, of such toll gatherer, if he neglects to pay them. Fees.

Ib., §§ 51, 52.

CHAPTER VI.

TOLL BRIDGES.

§ 648. Any bridge corporation shall, before constructing a bridge, publish a notice in at least one public newspaper in each county in which the Application by corporation for leave to erect.

bridge or any part of it, is to be, or, if no paper is published therein, in an adjoining county, once in each week for six weeks successively, specifying the location, the length and breadth of the bridge, and the time at which the application hereinafter required will be made. After such notice it shall apply to the board of supervisors of the county, or of each county in which any part of such bridge is located, at any meeting specified in the notice, for authority to construct it. The application shall specify the location and the length and breadth of the bridge.

1 R. S., 1272, first part of § 6.

The hearing on the application.

§ 649. On the hearing, any persons residing in the county or interested in the application may appear and be heard. The board may take testimony, or authorize it to be taken by any judicial officer of the county; and it may adjourn the hearing from time to time. A copy of the articles of association of the corporation, certified by the state engineer and surveyor or by the clerk where they are filed, shall be attached to and filed with the application.

From 1 R. S., 1272, § 6; 2 Ib., 1014.

Action of the board of supervisors.

§ 650. If the board are then of opinion that the public interests will be promoted thereby, it may, by the assent of a majority of all the members elected to the board, grant the application by an order entered in its minutes and particularly describing the bridge. The corporation shall cause a certified copy of the order, with a copy of the application, to be recorded in the office of the clerk of the county, before proceeding under it. The board, after finally acting on the application, shall cause it, with all other papers relating to it or to the proceedings, to be filed in such clerk's office, at the expense of the corporation.

§ 651. The corporation may use, in such manner as prescribed by the board, so much of any public road on either side of the stream as may be necessary for constructing and maintaining the bridge and toll-houses. *Use of highways.*

1 R. S., 1273, § 7, last clause.

§ 652. Corporations shall not be authorized under these provisions to construct any bridge within limits prescribed by any existing law for the erection or maintenance of any other bridge, nor to bridge any water where the tide flows, nor any water used for a harbor or which is navigable for sail vessels or steamers of the burden of tons and upwards, nor to bridge any stream navigated by rafts or arks, in a manner to prevent or endanger the passage of any raft forty-five feet in width, or any ark. *Restrictions.*

Ib., 1275, § 20; 1273, § 6, last clause.

§ 653. Any such corporation bridging a stream navigated by rafts shall at all times keep the channel above and below the bridge clear from all *Channel of streams navigable by rafts to be kept clear.*

deposits occasioned by its erection and prejudicial to such navigation; and shall be liable to pay to all persons unreasonably hindered or delayed, in passing such bridge with rafts or arks, all damages sustained thereby.

1 R. S., 1273, §§ 8, 9.

Completion of bridge and rates of toll. § 654. Every bridge erected under these provisions, shall have good and substantial railings or sidings, at least four and a half feet high. When a bridge is completed, and a certificate that it is so, and is safe and convenient for the public use, is signed by the county judge of, and filed in the county clerk's office in, the county or counties in which it is located, the directors may erect a toll-gate at such bridge and require such toll as the supervisors of the county or counties from time to time prescribe.

Ib., 1273, § 10.

Persons exempt. § 665. Any person going to or from public worship, a funeral, school, a town meeting or election at which he is entitled to vote for the purpose of giving such vote, highway labor, or a military parade or court, which, by law, he is required to attend, is exempt from the payment of tolls.

Ib., 1274, § 11.

Penalty. § 656. Any person who, being liable to pay toll, forcibly or fraudulently passes the gate of a toll-bridge without paying the toll is liable to a penalty of twenty-five dollars, in addition to the damages caused, to be recovered by the company.

Laws of 1854, ch. 120.

CHAPTER VII.

FERRIES.

§ 657. The county court of each county shall grant licenses for keeping ferries in the county, or upon waters dividing it from another county, to as many suitable persons as they deem proper, each license to be for a fixed term, not exceeding three years. Every such license is to be entered in the minutes of the court by the clerk, and a copy, attested by him, delivered to the licensee. County court to grant licenses.

1 R. S., 1056, §§ 1, 5, 6.

§ 658. No license shall be granted to a person other than the owner of the land through which the highway adjoining the ferry runs, unless, after at least eight days' written notice to such owner of the application therefor, he neglects to apply for it. Riparian owner has prior right to a license.

Ib., §§ 2, 3.

§ 659. Before a license is granted the applicant shall enter into recognizance to the people of the Applicant to give recognizance.

state, in open court, in the sum of one hundred dollars, faithfully to keep and attend the ferry, with such and so many sufficient and safe boats, so many men to work the same, together with sufficient implements, and during such hours in each day, and at such rates as the court, from time to time, orders, which recognizance shall forthwith be filed with the clerk of the county.

1 R. S., 1056, § 4.

Violation of recognizance.

§ 660. The violation of the condition of any such recognizance is a misdemeanor, punishable with such fine as the court may adjudge, not exceeding twenty-five dollars for each offense. On proof of such conviction the county court shall direct the recognizance to be estreated for the use of the people.

Ib., § 7.

Penalty for unlicensed ferrying.

§ 661. Any person who, except in the counties of Essex, Clinton, Orange, Rockland, Westchester, Suffolk, Richmond and Queens, maintains any ferry for profit or hire on any river, stream or lake, without authority of law, is guilty of a misdemeanor, punishable with the like fine for each offense. For an offense on waters dividing two counties, the offender may be prosecuted in each, but the fine in such case shall not exceed twelve dollars and fifty cents in each county.

Ib., §§ 8, 9.

§ 662. The foregoing provisions respecting ferries do not affect any grants or charters heretofore made by the state, or any rights already vested. Vested rights not affected.

1 R. S., 1057, § 10.

§ 663. The establishment of ferries on the River St. Lawrence from the towns of Morristown[1] and Hammond,[2] and on the River Hudson between the city of Troy and West Troy,[3] are regulated by special statutes. Ferries on the Rivers St. Lawrence and Hudson.

[1] Laws of 1851, ch. 240, S. S.; 1 R. S., 1057, §§ 22, 26.
[2] Laws of 1853, ch. 555.
[3] Laws of 1854, ch. 226.

§ 664. Other provisions applicable to the conduct of ferries are contained in article I of chapter I of this title, entitled "*Navigation*." Other provisions.

CHAPTER VIII.

MISCELLANEOUS PROVISIONS RELATING TO SEVERAL OF THE PUBLIC WAYS.

§ 665. When vehicles meet, it is the duty of the drivers of each to turn seasonably to the right of the center of the highway, so as to pass without interference, under the penalty of five dollars for every neglect, to be recovered by the party injured. Law of the highway.

Where the whole breadth of a roadway is nc worked, the center of the worked part is to be deemed the center of the highway. In time of snow, where there is a beaten track, the center of that is to be deemed the center of the highway. But this section does not apply to vehicles meeting cars running on rails or grooved tracks.

From 2 R. S., 104, § 1; 12 Barb., 613; 7 Wend., 185; 15 N. Y. R., 380.

Driver addicted to intoxication.

§ 666. No person shall employ, to drive any vehicle for the conveyance of passengers upon any public highway, a person addicted to drunkenness, under penalty of five dollars for every day such person shall have been in his employment.

2 R. S., 104, § 2.

Notice to employer of driver's intoxication.

§ 667. If any driver, whilst actually employed in driving any such vehicle, is intoxicated to such a degree as to endanger the safety of his passengers, the owner, on receiving from any such passenger a written notice of the fact, verified by his oath, shall forthwith discharge such driver; and if he has such driver in his service within six months after such notice, he incurs the like penalty.

Ib., § 3.

Horses to be fastened while standing.

§ 668. The driver of any vehicle, used to convey passengers, shall not leave the horses attached thereto, while passengers remain in the same, without first securely fastening the horses or placing the lines in the hands of some other person, so as to prevent their running; under penalty of twenty dollars for each offense.

2 R. S., 105, § 5.

§ 669. Every person driving any vehicle upon any road, with or without passengers, and permitting his horses to run upon any occasion whatever, is guilty of a misdemeanor. Horses not to be run.

Ib., § 4.

§ 670. The penalties provided by the three preceding sections are to be recovered by the district attorney of the county in which the offender resides, for the use of the poor. The court may allow a portion, not exceeding twenty-five dollars, of any recovered under section 666 or 667, to be retained by the district attorney, in addition to his costs. But any action for a penalty incurred under section 668 must be commenced within six months. Penalties, how recovered.

Ib., 104, §§ 2, 3, 5.

§ 671. The owners of every vehicle running or traveling upon any road for the conveyance of passengers, are liable, jointly and severally, for all damages to person or property done by any person in their employment as a driver, while driving such vehicle, whether done willfully or negligently or otherwise, in the same manner as such driver would be liable. Liability of owner for damage done by driver.

Ib., 105, § 6.

§ 672. Nothing contained in the seven preceding sections shall affect any law concerning hackney Saving clause as to city ordinances.

coaches or carriages in any city, nor affect laws or ordinances of any city for the licensing or regulating such coaches or carriages.

2 R. S., 105, § 8.

Telegraph lines may be erected.

§ 673. Incorporated telegraph companies may construct their lines on any of the public ways and across any of the public waters of this state, in such manner as not to incommode the public use of such ways. But this is not to be construed to impair private rights, nor to authorize the construction of any bridge or similar erection.

Ib., 98, § 42; 1278, § 5.

Protection of bridges.

§ 674. The owner of any toll-bridge, and any plankroad company owning a bridge of not less than twenty-five feet span, may put up, conspicuously, at each end of it, notice in these words, in large characters: "One dollar fine for riding or driving on this bridge faster than a walk;" and whoever rides or drives faster than a walk on such bridge shall forfeit to the owner the sum of one dollar.

1 R. S., 1053, § 145; Laws of 1854, ch. 87, § 5.

Canal and railway companies to furnish maps, &c.

§ 675. Every canal company and railway company in this state, which asks the aid of the state, shall, so far as may be in their power without making a new survey, furnish to the state engineer and surveyor copies of all maps, plans, drawings, levels and surveys of every description which may be made in connection with the construction of their canal or railway.

Ib., 401, § 9.

TITLE IV.

GENERAL POLICE OF THE STATE.

The provisions respecting stock-jobbing we have wholly omitted. By the act of 1858 (Laws of 1858, ch. 134, p. 251) the provisions of the Revised Statutes on this subject were repealed. The first section of that act declared that no contract for the transfer of stock, &c., should be voidable for want of consideration. The object of the act seems to be, not to make that which is a nude pact binding as a contract; but rather to place contracts for sale of stocks on the same basis as other contracts in this respect. This object is best answered by omitting all provisions in reference to such contracts; which we have accordingly done.

CHAPTER I.

WEIGHTS AND MEASURES.

The provisions of this chapter, except when otherwise indicated, are from 2 R. S., 2 to 6, as amended by Laws of 1857, ch. 560, and from Laws of 1854, ch. 326, and Laws of 1857, ch. 725.

The standards. § 676. The standard weights and measures now in charge of the secretary of state, being the same that were furnished to this state by the government of the United States in accordance with a joint resolution of congress, approved June 14, 1836, and consisting of one standard yard measure; one set of standard weights, comprising one troy pound and nine avoirdupois weights of one, two, three, four, five, ten, twenty, twenty-five and fifty pounds respectively; one set of standard troy ounce weights, divided decimally from ten ounces to the one ten-thousandth of an ounce; one set of standard liquid capacity measures, consisting of one wine gallon of two hundred and thirty-one cubic inches, one half-gallon, one quart, one pint, and one half-pint measure; and one standard half-bushel, containing one thousand and seventy-five cubic inches and twenty-one hundredths of a cubic inch, according to the inch hereby adopted as standard, are the standards of weights and measures throughout the state.

§ 677. The unit, or standard measure of length and surface, from which all other measures of extension, whether they be lineal, superficial or solid, shall be derived and ascertained, is the standard yard. The unit of extension.

§ 678. The yard is divided into three equal parts called feet, and each foot into twelve equal parts called inches; for measures of cloths and other commodities commonly sold by the yard, it Divisions of the yard.

may be divided into halves, quarters, eighths and sixteenths.

The rod, the mile and the chain.

§ 679. The rod, pole or perch contains five and a half yards, and the mile one thousand seven hundred and sixty yards; the chain for measuring land is twenty-two yards long, and divided into one hundred equal parts called links.

The acre.

§ 680. The acre for land measure shall be measured horizontally, and contains ten square chains, and is equivalent, in area, to a rectangle sixteen rods in length and ten in breadth; six hundred and forty acres being contained in a square mile.

The unit of weight.

§ 681. The units or standards of weight, from which all other weights shall be derived and ascertained, are the standard avoirdupois and troy weights.

Divisions of the pound.

§ 682. The avoirdupois pound, which bears to the troy pound the ratio of seven thousand to five thousand seven hundred and sixty, is divided into sixteen equal parts called ounces; the hundred weight consists of one hundred avoirdupois pounds, and twenty hundred weight constitute a ton. The troy ounce is equal to the twelfth part of the troy pound.

Unit of liquid measures.

§ 683. The units or standards of measure of capacity for liquids, from which all other measures of liquids shall be derived and ascertained, are the standard gallon and its parts.

§ 684. The barrel is equal to thirty-one and a half gallons, and two barrels constitute a hogshead. The barrel and the hogshead.

§ 685. The unit or standard measure of capacity for substances not being liquids, from which all other measures of such substances shall be derived and ascertained, is the standard half bushel. Unit of solid measures.

§ 686. The peck, half-peck, quarter-peck, quart and pint measures, for measuring commodities which are not liquid, are derived from the half-bushel, by successively dividing that measure by two. Divisions of the half bushel.

§ 687. The measures of capacity for coal, ashes, marl, manure, indian corn in the ear, fruit and roots of every kind, and for all other commodities commonly sold by heap measure, shall be the half-bushel and its multiples and subdivisions; and the measures used to measure such commodities shall be made cylindrical, with plane and even bottom, and shall be of the following diameters, from outside to outside: the bushel, nineteen and a half inches; half-bushel, fifteen and a half inches; and the peck, twelve and a third inches; Measures of capacity for commodities sold by heap measure.

§ 688. All commodities sold by heap measure shall be duly heaped up in the form of a cone; the outside of the measure by which the same shall be Heap measure.

measured to be the limit of the base of the cone and such cone to be as high as the article will admit.

Contracts construed accordingly.

§ 689. All contracts, made after the eleventh day of April, 1851, within this state, for work to be done, or for anything to be sold or delivered, by weight or measure, shall be construed according to the foregoing standards.

Weights of bushels of various products.

§ 690. Whenever wheat, rye, indian corn, buckwheat, barley, oats, beans, peas, clover seed, timothy seed, flax seed or potatoes are sold by the bushel, and no special agreement is made by the parties as to the mode of measuring, the bushel shall consist of sixty-two pounds of beans, sixty pounds of wheat, peas, clover seed or potatoes, fifty-eight pounds of indian corn, fifty-six pounds of rye, fifty-five pounds of flax seed, forty-eight pounds of buckwheat or barley, forty-four pounds of timothy seed and thirty-two pounds of oats.

Duty of the state superintendent of weights and measures.

§ 691. The state superintendent of weights and measures is charged with a general supervision of the weights and measures of the state. He shall take charge of the standards and see that they are kept in, and in no case removed from, a fireproof building belonging to the state. He shall correct the standards of the cities and counties, provide them with necessary standards, balances and other means of adjustment, and as often as once in ten years compare the same with those in his possession.

§ 692. For the purpose of providing the same for those counties that are without them, and for any new counties that may be erected, he has power, from time to time, to contract for the construction of the same, of such materials, denominations and fashion as those heretofore constructed, and on his certificate that the same have been delivered to and examined and approved by him, and that he deems the cost thereof just and reasonable, they shall be paid for by the treasurer on the warrant of the comptroller.

State superintendent may contract for construction of standards.

§ 693. The superintendent shall verify each such set of standards, and cause it to conform to the state standard, and then send it to the county clerk or county sealer of the county for the use of which it is prepared. The county treasurer shall defray the cost of transportation, and shall pay to the superintendent, on his order, his fees and expenses for verification and sealing.

Verification and transmission of standards.

§ 694. The prime cost of the set shall be charged by the state treasurer to the county, but such charge shall not bear interest until one year after the delivery of the set. The board of supervisors, at their first annual meeting after the delivery, shall provide the means to meet these expenses, and authorize the county treasurer to pay to the state treasury the prime cost, and interest, if any accrues.

Cost of standards to be borne by the county.

Copies of standards.

§ 695. The superintendent shall maintain a complete set of copies of the original standards, which shall be used for adjusting county standards, and in no case shall the original standards be used for any other purpose than the adjustment of this set of copies, and for scientific purposes; he shall also maintain such apparatus and fixtures as are necessary in the comparison and adjustment of the county standards.

Duty of the county sealer.

§ 696. The county sealer shall take charge of the county standards and standard balances, and provide for their safe keeping; provide the town with such standard weights and measures and standard balances as may be wanting, and compare the town standards with those in his possession as often as once in every five years.

Duty of the town sealer.

§ 697. The town sealer shall take charge and provide for the safe keeping of the town standards, and see that the weights, measures and all apparatus used for determining the quantity of commodities used throughout the town, which are brought to him for that purpose, agree with those standards in his possession.

Supervisors to procure town standards.

§ 698. The supervisors of each county shall provide for procuring the proper standards of weights and measures for each of the towns in their respective counties, and at the expense of such towns respectively.

§ 699. The state superintendent shall see that there are impressed on all the city and county standards the emblem of the United States, the letters N. Y., and such other device as he shall direct for the particular county; and the county sealers shall see that, in addition to the above device, there is impressed on the town standards such other device as the board of supervisors shall direct for the several towns. Marks upon the standards.

§ 700. Whenever the several sealers of the cities, counties and towns compare weights and measures, and find or make them to correspond with the standards in their possession, they shall seal and mark such weights and measures with the appropriate devices. Sealing weights and measures.

§ 701. Each sealer shall be entitled to receive for his services, from the owner of the weights or measures sealed: Sealer's fees.

For sealing and marking every beam, ten cents;

For sealing and marking measures of extension at the rate of ten cents per yard, not to exceed fifty cents for any one measure;

For sealing and marking every weight, five cents;

For sealing and marking liquid and dry measures, ten cents for each measure. He is also entitled to a reasonable compensation for making weights and measures conform to the standards.

Delivery of standards to successor in office. § 702. Whenever the state superintendent resigns, is removed from office, or removes from the city of Albany, or whenever any city, county or town sealer resigns, is removed from office, or removes from the city, county or town in which he was appointed, it is his duty, and in case of the death of such officer it is the duty of his representatives to deliver to his successor in office all the standards in his possession. In case of any neglect to do so the successor may prosecute the person neglecting, and shall recover double the value of such standards as have not been delivered, with double costs, one-half of the damages to be retained by the person so recovering, and the other to be applied to the purchase of such standards as may be required in his office.

False weights and measures. § 703. If any person uses any weights, measures, beams or other apparatus for determining quantity of commodities, not conformable to the standards of this state, whereby any person is injured or defrauded, he shall be subject to a fine not exceeding five dollars for each offense, to be sued for and collected by the city or town sealer; he shall also be subject to an action, in which the defrauded person shall recover treble damages and costs; and every person keeping any place of traffic in commodities usually sold by weight or measure, shall have his weights and measures compared annually with the standard, under penalty of five dollars for every neglect, to be recovered by any one who shall prosecute therefor.

§ 704. When any person in this state puts up for sale any articles in casks or packages, and marks or stamps on such cask or package the weight of its contents, with a view to sell the same, such mark or stamp shall express the true weight thereof, and also the true tare of such cask or package; and if any person knowingly marks or stamps false or short weight, or false tare, on any cask or package, or sells or offers it for sale so marked, he shall forfeit the sum of twenty-five dollars, for every cask or package, to any person aggrieved, and is guilty of a misdemeanor. False marks.

Laws of 1857, ch. 725.

§ 705. No surveyor shall give evidence, in any case depending in any court, or before arbitrators, respecting his surveys or measurements, unless he makes oath, if required, that the chain or measure used by him was conformable to the standards which were at the time the standards of the state. Surveyor's testimony.

CHAPTER II.

TIME.

The provisions of this chapter, except the last two sections, are from 2 R. S., 1; Ib., 182, § 9.

Time computed by new style.

§ 706. Time is computed according to the Gregorian or new style; and the first day of January, in every year, passed since 1752, or to come, shall be reckoned as the first day of the year.

Leap years.

§ 707. The several years 1900, 2100, 2200, 2300, or any other future hundredth year, of which the year 2000 shall be the first, except only every fourth hundredth year, shall not be deemed leap years, but shall be common years of 365 days; and the years 2000, 2400, 2800, and every other fourth hundredth year, from the year 2000 inclusive, and also every fourth year, except as first above mentioned, which, by usage in this state, is considered a leap year, shall be deemed leap years, consisting of 366 days.

The year

§ 708. The term year means a period of three hundred and sixty-five days; a half year, one hundred and eighty-two days; a quarter of a year, ninety-one days; and the added day of a leap year and the day immediately preceding, if they occur in any such period, shall be reckoned together as one day.

§ 709. Except for the purpose of computing interest, the term "month" means a calendar not a lunar month, unless otherwise expressed. For the purpose of calculating interest, a month shall be considered the twelfth part of a year, and as consisting of thirty days; and interest for any number of days less than a month shall be estimated by the proportion which such number bears to thirty. **The month.**

§ 710. A week consists of seven consecutive days. **The week.**

§ 711. A day is the period of time between any midnight and the midnight following. **The day.**

CHAPTER III.

MONEY.

From 1 R. S., 6.

§ 712. All accounts of public offices, judicial proceedings, and all accounts between persons in this state, shall be kept in the decimal currency of the United States. **Accounts to be kept in decimal currency.**

§ 713. All judgments and executions shall be computed in dollars and cents, rejecting lesser fractions. **Judgments and executions.**

CHAPTER IV.

AUCTIONS.

ARTICLE I.

AUCTION DUTIES.

The provisions of this article are from 1 R. S. 1067, §§ 1 to 5.

Tariff of auction duties.

§ 714. All personal property at any time exposed to sale by public auction, with the exceptions hereinafter mentioned, shall be subject, each time it is struck off, to duties, to be paid by the seller, and calculated on the sums at which the same is struck off, at the following rates;

1. All wines and ardent spirits, foreign or domestic, at the rate of one dollar on every one hundred dollars;

2. All property imported from any place beyond the Cape of Good Hope, at the rate of fifty cents on every one hundred dollars;

3. All other things which are the production of any foreign country, at the rate of seventy-five cents on every one hundred dollars.

§ 715. Goods sold by auction shall in all cases be struck off to the highest bidder. They are in all cases subject to the duties, whether actually sold, or bid in. But this section shall not be construed to render valid any sale that would otherwise be deemed fraudulent and void. Mode of sale.

§ 716. All dutiable articles which are sold on commission by an auctioneer, by a copartner or clerk of an auctioneer, or by a person in any way connected in the auction business or in auction sales with an auctioneer, whether sold by auction or private sale, are subject to duties. Articles sold at private sale by auctioneer liable to duty.

§ 717. The following articles are exempt from duties: Articles exempt.

1. Ships and vessels;

2. Utensils of husbandry, horses, neat cattle, hogs and sheep;

3. Articles of the growth, produce and manufacture of the United States, except wines and distilled spirits;

4. Property belonging to the United States or to this state;

5. Property sold under judicial or executive

authority, or in the settlement of estates of deceased persons or insolvents, excepting under assignments with preference.

ARTICLE II.

AUCTIONEERS.

Qualification of auctioneer.

§ 718. Any citizen of this state may become and act as an auctioneer in the county in which he resides, on depositing with the comptroller an approved bond with sureties, in the penalty of ten thousand dollars, conditioned that he will render the semi-annual account hereinafter required; will pay all duties imposed by law in respect to his business, and will, in all respects, comply with the requirements of this chapter. Such bond shall be renewed on or before the first Monday in January in every year.

From 1 R. S., 1070, §§ 15, 19, 20; 1071, § 24.

Approval and delivery of bond.

§ 719. Such bond, if executed by an auctioneer resident in a city, shall be taken and approved by the mayor or recorder thereof, and if otherwise, by the county judge of the county, who shall certify upon it his approbation, and the date thereof. The auctioneer, within ten days thereafter, shall deliver it to the comptroller.

1 R. S., 1070, §§ 16, 17.

§ 720. Such officer shall also, without delay, transmit a notice to the comptroller, stating the name of the auctioneer and his sureties in the bond, and the day on which it was executed and approved

Officer to give notice to comptroller.

Ib., § 18.

§ 721. Every auctioneer in the cities of New York and Buffalo shall, within ten days after the execution and approval of his bond, file a copy of the bond and of the certificate thereon with the clerk of the county, who shall record the same in a book with an alphabetical index, to be kept by him for the purpose; and he shall be paid by the auctioneer fifty cents therefor.

Certain auctioneers to file certified copies.

Ib., 1071, §§ 25, 26.

§ 722. Every auctioneer neglecting to file such certified copy within the time above required, shall forfeit for every such neglect one hundred dollars, to be recovered by the district attorney and paid into the treasury of the state.

Penalty

Ib., § 27.

§ 723. Any person who acts as auctioneer in selling any goods liable to auction duties, or in selling in the cities of New York, Brooklyn, Albany, Troy or Buffalo, any personal property whatsoever, except such as is sold under the authority of the

Penalties for acting as auctioneer without authority.

United States, without having filed the bond hereinbefore required, or being authorized as assistant to one who has filed such bond, as provided by section 725, shall forfeit one hundred and twenty-five dollars for each article so exposed by him to sale; and he is guilty of a misdemeanor.

From 1 R, S., 1069, §§ 7, 8, 9, 10; Laws of 1856, ch. 26; 1 R. S., 1071, §§ 23, 28; 1069, § 11.

What goods may be sold by any one.

§ 724. Except in the cities mentioned in the preceding section, sales where no duties are imposed may be made by any citizen of the state.

From 1 R. S., 1069, § 10.

Assistant.

§ 725. Every auctioneer, in case of his inability to attend an auction, by sickness, by duty as a fireman, by reason of military orders, or necessary attendance in a court of justice, or in case of temporary absence from the city or county within which he is auctioneer, may employ a copartner or clerk to hold such auction in his name and behalf; such copartner or clerk having previously taken an oath, to be filed with the clerk of such county, fully and faithfully to perform the duties incumbent on him by the provisions of this chapter, and which oath shall also contain a true statement of the connection that exists between him and the auctioneer.

1 R. S., 1069, § 12.

Auctioneers only to act in this state.

§ 726. Every auctioneer who accepts an appointment as auctioneer from any other state, or who is concerned as principal or partner in selling any property in any other state by public auction, or who receives any benefit on account of any such sale, is guilty of a misdemeanor, and on conviction shall be incapable, forever thereafter, of acting as an auctioneer within this state.

1 R. S., 1071, § 29.

ARTICLE III.

REGULATIONS RESPECTING SALES.

§ 727. No auctioneer, in any city of this state shall at one time have more than one place for holding auctions; and every such auctioneer, before acting as such, shall file with the clerk of such city a writing, signed by him, designating such place, and naming therein the partners, if any, engaged with him in business. Auctioneers in cities to designate their places of sale.

1 R. S., 1071, § 30.

§ 728. No such auctioneer shall expose to sale, by public auction, any articles liable to auction duties, at any other place than that so designated, except goods sold in original packages as imported household furniture, and such bulky articles as have To sell at no other place.

usually been sold in warehouses, or in the public streets or on the wharves.

1 R. S., 1071, § 31.

Penalty.

§ 729. A violation of any provision of the last two sections is a misdemeanor, and punishable by a fine not exceeding two hundred and fifty dollars for each offense.

Ib., 1072, § 32.

Power of common councils.

§ 730. The common council of each city may designate such place or places therein, for the sale by auction of horses, carriages and household furniture, as they deem expedient.

Ib., § 33.

Advertisements of auctions in New York city.

§ 731. Every auctioneer in the city of New York shall, under his own name, give previous notice, in one or more of the public newspapers printed in that city, of every auction sale made by him; and in case he is connected with any person or firm, his name shall in all cases precede, separately and individually, the name of such person or the title of the firm. Any person carrying on, interested in, or employed about such business in the city of New York, who advertises a sale by auction in any other manner, or is concerned in any sale by auction not so advertised, is guilty of a misdemeanor.

Ib., §§ 34, 35.

Evening sales in New York and Albany.

§ 732. All sales of goods by public auction in the cities of New York and Albany, shall be made in the daytime, between sunrise and sunset, excepting:

1. Book or prints;

2. Goods sold in the original package, as imported, according to a printed catalogue, of which samples shall have been opened and exposed to public inspection at least one day previous to the sale.

Every auctioneer who violates the provisions of this section is guilty of a misdemeanor, and on conviction shall be disqualified to act as such.

1 R. S., 1074, §§ 51, 52.

§ 733. All auctioneers doing business in the city of New York, must, between the first and fifteenth of June, in each year, obtain from the mayor of the city a license therefor, on filing a bond with two good sureties in the penalty of two thousand dollars. The mayor, on the complaint of any person having been defrauded by any auctioneer or his clerk, agent or assignee, doing business in that city, shall take testimony under oath relating thereto; and if the charge is in his opinion sustained, he shall revoke the license and commit the offender for trial, and direct the bonds to be forfeited.

Suppression of mock auctions in New York city.

Laws of 1853, ch. 138, § 210.

§ 734. No auctioneer shall demand or receive a higher compensation for his services than a commission of two and one half per cent on the amount of any sales, public or private, made by him, unless by virtue of a previous agreement in writing, between him and the owner or consignee; and every auctioneer who violates this section shall forfeit two

Commissions.

hundred and fifty dollars, and shall also refund the excess to the party aggrieved.

1 R. S., 1072, §§ 36, 37.

Private sales on same day prohibited.

§ 735. No auctioneer, on the day and at the place of his auction, nor any person whatever, on the same day and at the same place, shall sell at private sale any property liable to auction duties, under penalty of a sum equal to the price for which such goods are sold.

Ib., § 38.

Sale not executed at the time.

§ 736. When goods are struck off and the bargain is not immediately executed by payment or delivery it is the duty of the auctioneer to enter, in a sale book to be kept by him for that purpose, a memo randum of the sale, specifying the nature, quantity and price of the goods, the terms of sale, and the names of the purchaser and of the party on whose account the sale is made.

Ib., § 39.

Goods damaged at sea.

§ 737. Sales of vessels condemned, vessels materials and goods in a damaged state, sold in the port of New York, by reason of such damage, for the benefit of owners and underwriters or for account of whom it may concern, and duties of auctioneers in relation to such sales, are regulated by chapter I of title III of this part. In other cities and counties they are sold under the direction of the inspectors of damaged goods therein

Ib., 1069, § 13.

ARTICLE IV.

ACCOUNTING.

§ 738. Every auctioneer who has given bond shall make a semi-annual account, dated on the first Monday of January and July in each year, stating in detail: Semi-annual account.

1. The sums for which any goods have been sold at every auction held by him, or in his behalf, since his first giving bond or the close of his last account;

2. The days on which sales were so made and the amount of each day's sale, designating the sales made by himself or in his presence, and those made in his absence by a partner or clerk acting in his behalf and specifying the causes of such absence;

3. The amount of all private sales made by himself or any of his partners, on commission, and the days on which such sales were made;

4. A distinct statement of all goods struck off but not actually sold;

5. The amount of the duties chargeable on all the sales, public or private, and on all the goods struck off.

1 R. S., 1072, § 40; Ib.. 1070, § 20.

Exhibition of account and auctioneer's oath.

§ 739. The auctioneer shall, within twenty days after the date of the account, exhibit it, if he resides in a city, to the mayor or recorder thereof, if otherwise, to the county judge of the county, and before him take and subscribe the following oath, to be indorsed on the account:

"I, ——— do solemnly and sincerely swear or [affirm] that the account now exhibited by me, and to which I have subscribed my name, contains a just and true account of all the goods, wares, merchandise and effects sold or struck off or bought in by me at public sale, or sold by me at private sale on commission, whether subject to duty or not, or sold, struck off or bought in as aforesaid, by others in my name or under my direction or for my benefit, within the time mentioned in the within account, and of the days upon which the same were respectively sold; and that I have attended personally such of the said public sales as are not stated in said account to have been made without my attendance, and that the causes therein mentioned of my absence from such sales as I did not attend are truly stated; that I have examined the entries of all the sales mentioned in said account, in the book kept by me for that purpose, and fully believe this account to be in all respects correct; and further that I have, during the time therein mentioned, conformed in all things to the true intent and meaning of the laws regulating sales by auctioneers, according to the best of my knowledge, information and belief."

1 R. S., 1073, §§ 41, 42.

§ 740. Every partner, clerk, or other person in any way connected in business with such auctioneer, who shall have made any sale contained in the account, shall also make and subscribe an oath, to be indorsed on the account, that he believes the account so rendered to be just and true in every particular, and shall also set his name or initials opposite to such sale in the account, and shall make and subscribe an affidavit, to be annexed thereto, stating that the sales so noted are all the sales, public or private, and all the goods struck off, liable to auction duties, by him within the time mentioned in the account; and that the account of such sales, so therein stated, is just and true; that such sales were made by him in the absence of such auctioneer, who was unable to attend from the causes specified in his account; and that in all acts performed by him, in behalf of such auctioneer, during the time specified, he had endeavored to conform to the provisions of this chapter. Partner's and clerk's oath.

1 R. S., 1073, § 43; Ib., 1074, § 44.

§ 741. Every auctioneer, within ten days after exhibiting his account, shall pay the duties thereon, and immediately after such payment shall transmit such account, with the affidavits indorsed and annexed thereto, to the comptroller, to be filed in his office. Duties, when to be paid.

Ib., 1074, § 45.

§ 742. Auctioneers, residing in the city of New Duties, how to be paid.

York, shall pay the duties to such bank in that city as is designated by the comptroller to receive the state deposits, taking its receipts therefor, and shall immediately transmit them to the comptroller, who shall certify the payments to the treasurer and charge him with the same. Other auctioneers shall pay the duties to the state treasurer.

1 R. S., 1074, §§ 46, 47.

Affidavit of no sales.

§ 743. Every auctioneer, except those in the city of New York, who, within the period limited for his accounting, has made no sales, public or private, liable to auction duties; and every auctioneer in the city of New York who has made no sales whatever, shall, instead of rendering an account, make affidavit of those facts before the officer mentioned in section 739, and transmit the same to the comptroller, within the same time that an account is required to be exhibited.

Ib., § 48.

Penalty.

§ 744. Every auctioneer, partner or clerk of an auctioneer, and every person whatever in any way connected in business with an auctioneer, who neglects to perform any act required of him by the last seven sections, is liable to a penalty of seven hundred and fifty dollars for each offense.

Ib., § 49.

Notice of neglect.

§ 745. The comptroller shall certify and publish in the state paper every such neglect of an auctioneer; and from the time of the publication such auctioneer shall be deemed disqualified to act as such.

1 R. S., 1874, § 50.

§ 746. The comptroller shall cause an examination to be made, at least once in each year, of the books and accounts of sales of auctioneers who have given bonds, employing, for that purpose, at reasonable compensation, such agent or agents as he deems necessary. The agents have power to administer oaths to auctioneers, and to require information necessary to ascertain the true amount of goods sold. Auctioneer's book to be examined.

Ib., 1076, § 59, first clause, and § 60.

§ 747. If any auctioneer neglects to make a report in the manner and within the time required or pay the duties thereupon, or if a false report, the comptroller shall cause an action to be brought against him and his sureties upon the bond. Action on the bond.

1 R. S., 1070, § 59, last clause.

§ 748. Every auctioner who willfully neglects to render the report required by section 738 is guilty of a misdemeanor. Punishment of willful neglect.

2 R. S., 878, § 36.

ARTICLE V.

FRAUDS AND PENALTIES.

§ 749. The penalties imposed by the provisions of this chapter, not otherwise appropriated, shall Penalties, how recovered.

be prosecuted for by the district attorney of the county in which the offense is committed. The comptroller shall give immediate notice of every offense to the proper district attorney, or he may, if he deems necessary, give such notice to the attorney-general, who thereupon may prosecute therefor. The moneys recovered, deducting a proper compensation to the prosecuting officer, to be fixed by the comptroller, shall be paid to the treasurer of the county.

1 R. S., 1075, §§ 54, 55.

Fraud. § 750. Every auctioneer, or other person acting as such, who is guilty of any fraudulent practices in business or in executing or eluding the provisions of this chapter, is guilty of a misdemeanor, and is liable in treble damages to any party injured.

1 R. S., 1070, § 21; 1075, § 53.

CHAPTER V.

PEDDLING.

Peddling without license forbidden. § 751. No person shall carry for sale, from place to place, any articles, the growth, produce or manufacture of any foreign county, except pursuant to the terms of, a license first obtained by him in the manner hereinafter provided, under penalty of twenty-five dollars for each offense, for the use of the poor of the town where the offense is committed.

1 R. S., 1080, §§ 1, 6.

§ 752. Every applicant for a license shall first pay into the state treasury the following duties for one year's license, or at a proportionate rate for any shorter time not less than six months: Applicant to pay duties.

1. If he intends to travel on foot, twenty dollars;

2. If with a single horse or other beast, carrying or drawing a burden, or with a boat or boats, thirty dollars; with any vehicle drawn by more than one horse or other animal, fifty dollars.

Ib., § 3.

§ 753. He shall then deliver to the secretary of state the treasurer's receipt for such duties, countersigned by the comptroller, together with an application signed by himself or his authorized agent, specifying in which mode he intends to travel; and the secretary of state shall thereupon, on payment of his fees, issue a license under his seal of office, and signed by himself or his deputy, authorizing such applicant to travel and trade within this state as a hawker or peddler, in the manner stated in the application, for a specified term, not less than six months, nor more than one year, according to the application and duties; and on the expiration of Application how made.

any license it shall be renewed, on the like payment of duties and application therefor, upon the same terms.

1 R. S., 1080, §§ 2, 5.

Peddlers to produce license.

§ 754. Every person found trading, as described in section 751, who refuses to produce a license therefor to any citizen who demands the same, shall, for each offense, forfeit the sum of ten dollars to the overseers of the poor of the town in which the demand is made, for the use of the poor therein; and every such offender, who, after notice, neglects to pay the above penalty, shall be committed, by the justice before whom the conviction is had, to the county jail for the term of one month.

Ib., 1081, § 7.

Citizens may apprehend offenders; duty of overseers of the poor.

§ 755. Any citizen may arrest any person who violates sections 753 or 754, and convey him before any justice of the peace in the county. The overseers of the poor in each town shall enforce these provisions, whenever any violation comes to their knowledge.

Ib., § 8.

Prosecution of offender.

§ 756. Such justice, if a sufficient license is not produced and if the fact of trading is proved or confessed, shall convict the offender accordingly, and issue his warrant, directed to some constable of the county, commanding him to cause twenty-five dollars, with costs not to exceed five dollars, to be forthwith levied of the goods of the offender. The moneys collected, exclusive of costs, shall be paid by the justice to the overseers of the poor of the town in which the offense was committed.

1 R. S., 1081, § 9.

§ 757. No costs of such prosecution shall be allowed to the defendant, if it appears that before the commencement of the prosecution he refused to produce his license or to disclose his name when lawfully required; nor in such case shall he be entitled to maintain any action against the complainant, the constable, or magistrate, for their acts in pursuance of this chapter. Costs.

Ib., § 11.

§ 758. No proceeeding for any penalty imposed by this chapter shall be maintained, unless brought within sixty days after the offense. Limitation.

Ib., 1082, § 12.

CHAPTER VI.

DRUGS.

SECTION 759. Poisonous drugs to be labeled.

§ 759. Any person who sells or delivers any poisonous substance without having the word "Poison" written or printed upon a label attached to the phial, box or parcel in which the same is so sold or delivered, or who sells or delivers any tartar emetic, without having the true name thereof upon such label, is guilty of a misdemeanor.[1] Any person who violates this section, or whose partner, Poisonous drugs to be labeled.

clerk or servant does so, is liable in damages to any party injured in consequence thereof.

[1]2 R. S., 877, § 25.

CHAPTER VII.

FIRES.

Fire companies.

§ 760. Except in an incorporated city or village, fire companies may be formed in any town as follows; The supervisor and the justices of the peace may appoint, in writing, any number of the inhabitants, not exceeding forty, to each fire engine procured for the town, and, in the same manner, may fill vacancies from time to time, in such company. Every such fireman, and all the members of any fire company, or hook and ladder company, appointed pursuant to any statute, are exempt, while they are such, from jury service in courts of record, and, except in war, insurrection or invasion, from military duty.

1 R. S., 666, § 5; 667, § 8.

Powers of companies.

§ 761. Each such fire company shall choose a captain and clerk, and may establish such by-laws and regulations, and impose such penalties, not exceeding five dollars for each offense, as necessary to enforce performance, by the firemen, of their duty.

1 R. S., 667, § 6.

§ 762. Such penalties may be collected by the captains in any court having cognizance thereof, and shall be expended for the repair and preservation of the engines and apparatus. Penalties, how collected and expended.

Ib., 667, § 7.

§ 763. Every person negligently setting fire to his own woods, or negligently suffering any fire to extend beyond his own land, is liable in treble damages to the party injured, and is guilty of a misdemeanor. Firing woods.

2 Ib., 106, § 1.

§ 764. Whenever the woods in any town are on fire, the justice of the peace, the supervisor and the commissioners of highways, and each of them, shall order so many of the inhabitants liable to work on the highways, and residing in the vicinity, as they severally deem necessary, to repair to the place of the fire and assist in extinguishing or stopping it. Extinguishing fires in woods.

Ib., § 2.

§ 765. Any person who neglects to comply is liable to a penalty of fifty dollars, and is guilty of a misdemeanor. The penalty shall be applied as a reward to such person or persons as a majority of the officers mentioned deem best entitled thereto Penalty.

for superior exertions in extinguishing or stopping the fire.

2 R. S. 107, § 3, 4.

Investigation into origin of fires.

§ 766. The coroner, sheriff or any deputy sheriff of any county, on the written request of any officer or agent of any insurance company, or of any two reputable freeholders, accompanied by affidavit of a credible witness, showing ground to believe that any building in such county, excepting the cities of New York, Brooklyn or Buffalo, has been designedly set on fire or attempted to be, shall investigate, without delay, the truth thereof, for which purpose they shall possess the powers conferred by law upon coroners for the purpose of holding inquests, and their compensation and expenses shall be fixed and paid in the same manner.

Laws of 1857, ch. 504, §§ 1, 2, 7, 8.

Inquest.

§ 767. The jury, after inspecting the place of the fire, or of the attempt, and hearing the testimony, shall deliver to such officer their inquisition in writing, and signed, certifying how such fire happened or was attempted, and all the circumstances attending the same, and who were guilty thereof, either as principal or accessory, and in what manner. If unable to ascertain the same, they shall certify accordingly.

Ib., § 3.

Officer holding inquest to hold the

§ 768. If the jury find that any building has been designedly set or attempted to be set on fire, the officer holding the inquest shall bind over the witnesses to appear and testify at the next criminal court of record in the county at which an indictment for such offense can be found; and if the party charged with the offense is not in custody, the officer has the same power to issue process for his arrest, and to examine him when arrested, as is possessed by a justice of the peace, and shall in all respects proceed in like manner. offender and the witnesses.

Laws of 1857, ch. 504, §§ 4, 5.

§ 769. The testimony of all witnesses examined shall be reduced to writing by the officer, and shall be returned by him, together with the inquisition of the jury and all recognizances and examinations taken by him, to the next criminal court of record held in the county. Proceedings to be returned to criminal court.

Ib., § 6.

§ 770. The subject of fires in the cities of New York[1] and Brooklyn,[2] and the burning of coal-kilns in the county of Suffolk,[3] is regulated by special statutes.[4] Local acts respecting fires.

[1] Laws of 1855, ch. 112; 1856, ch. 18.
[2] Laws of 1852, ch. 355; 1857, ch. 76?
[3] Laws of 1859, ch. 282.
[4] Laws of 1852, ch. 382; Ib., ch. 355; Laws of 1853, ch. 542.

CHAPTER VIII.

FISHING AND HUNTING.

Local provisions respecting fisheries in various places are contained in special statutes.

Poisoning fish.

§ 771. No person shall put into any of the waters of this state, for the purpose of taking or destroying any fish, any of the berry commonly called cocculus indicus, or any other poisonous substance, whether it be mixed with any other substance or not.

From 2 R. S., 98, §§ 1, 2.

Preservation of trout.

§ 882. No person shall, on any of the inland public waters of this state, except the Cayuga, Seneca, Crooked and Otsego lakes, take any trout, at any time, by any means except a hook and line, nor any speckled or brook trout at any time between the 15th day of September and the 15th day of February, by any means whatever.

1 Laws of 1857, 585, ch. 290, §§ 1, 2; Laws of 1859, 1185, ch. 511, § 6.

Preservation of deer.

§ 773. No person shall, within this state, kill any wild deer, partridge, quail, woodcock or snipe during the months of February, March, April, May, June or July. The having in possession, in such months any green deer skin or fresh venison, is presumptive evidence of having violated this section.

1 Laws of 1857, 582, ch. 287, §§ 1, 3; 1859, 1185, ch. 511.

§ 774. Whoever offends against any provision of this chapter incurs a penalty of twenty-five dollars for each offense, to be recovered, before any justice of the peace of the state, by any complainant, or by a superintendent of the poor in the county where the offense was committed. If the latter is plaintiff, one-half of the recovery shall be paid to him for the use of the poor, and the other half to the complainant. Penalty.

2 R. S., 98, § 2; Laws of 1857, ch. 287, §§ 4, 5; Ib., ch. 290, §§ 3, 4; 1859, 1185, ch. 511, § 5.

CHAPTER IX.

RACING.

§ 775. All racing or trial of speed between horses or other animals, for any bet, stake or reward, except such as are allowed by special laws, is a common nuisance, and parties acting or aiding therein, or interested in any such bet, stake or reward, are guilty of a misdemeanor. Racing forbidden.

2 R. S., 80, § 49.

Duty of officers of justice.

§ 776. All officers concerned in the administration of justice shall attend at the place where they are informed that any such race is to be, and there give notice of its illegality, and endeavor to prevent it by dispersing the persons collected, and by all other means in their power. Upon their own view of any offense, as well as upon the testimony of others, such judges and justices shall issue warrants for the immediate apprehension of the offenders, and shall require recognizances with sufficient sureties for their good behavior, and for their appearance for trial.

2 R. S., 80, § 50.

Penalty on bettors.

§ 777. Every person who contributes or collects or solicits any money, goods or things in action, for the purpose of making up a bet, stake or reward to be raced for by any animal, contrary to law, is liable to a penalty of twenty-five dollars.

Ib., § 51.

Penalty on owners.

§ 778. The owner or part owner of any animal used by his privity, in racing contrary to law, shall forfeit the value of the animal. Every person concerned in any bet upon any illegal race, or in contributing to a stake for such race, shall forfeit the amount of such bet or such contribution.

Ib., § 52.

Racing in New Utrecht.

§ 779. All such racing and trials of speed within the town of New Utrecht, in the county of Kings, whether for any bet or stakes, or not, is a misdemeanor, and the owner or part owner of any animal used by his privity, in a violation of this section, shall forfeit the value of the animal.

2 R. S., 81, §§ 53, 54.

§ 780. The forfeitures and penalties imposed by this chapter shall be recovered by the overseers of the poor of the town where the offense is committed. Penalties, how recovered.

Ib., §§ 51, 52, 53.

§ 781. Every person who is concerned in any racing or trial of speed between any horses or other animals, within one mile of a place where any court is actually sitting, is guilty of a misdemeanor. Racing in vicinity of a court.

Ib., 875, § 13.

CHAPTER X.

PRIZE AND GAME FIGHTING, AND GAMING.

From Laws of 1856, ch. 98; 1859, ch. 37; 2 R. S., 71, §§ 6, 7.

§ 782. Every person who engages in any premeditated fight or contention, or who, within this state, instigates or promotes such a fight, either as witness or umpire, or by going out of the state to be present thereat, or by sending, in writing, or publishing, a challenge or acceptance of a challenge thereto, or by assisting in training a combatant Fights prohibited.

therefor, whether such fight is between persons or animals, and whether it is to take place within or without the state, is guilty of a misdemeanor.

Laws of 1856, ch. 98; 1859, ch. 37.

Complaint

§ 783. Upon complaint under oath, specifying the grounds or reason to believe that a violation of the preceding section is about to be committed, any magistrate having power to take complaints of a criminal nature may, in his discretion, issue a warrant stating the complainant's name and residence, and requiring the officer to arrest the person about to offend, and any person whom he may find offending.

Execution of warrant.

§ 784. The officer may call to his aid the civil power of the county, and shall take any person arrested before the magistrate, who shall require such person to give bond to the people in the penalty of not more than one thousand dollars, with or without sureties, conditioned that he will not, for one year from its date, violate section 782. Such bond is to be transmitted to the district attorney of the county, and, when broken, to be prosecuted by him in any court of the state. If he fails to give the bond, the magistrate shall commit him to the county jail; but he may be discharged therefrom upon habeas corpus, upon executing the required bond; if such bond was required to be with surety the officer taking it shall approve the surety,

§ 785. No cock-fighting, playing with cards or dice, nor any kind of gaming by lot or chance, nor any billiard table, shall be allowed within any house kept as an inn, or in any grocery or other place where the sale of spirituous liquors is licensed, or any out-house or garden belonging thereto; nor shall there be any playing with cards or dice for gain or money, or any kind of gaming by lot or chance, or any billiard table on board any vessel or canal boat used for the transportation of passengers, under penalty of ten dollars for each offense, to be recovered from the keeper of the inn or other place, or the master of the vessel or boat, as the case may be, by the overseer of the poor of the town where the offense is committed. Gaming.

CHAPTER XI.

LICENSES.

Time of meeting of commissioners of excise.

§ 786. The commissioners of excise shall meet in their respective counties, at the place where the county courts are required to be held, on the third Tuesday of May in each year, and on such other days as a majority of the commissioners appoint, not exceeding ten days in any one year, and in the county of Onondaga not exceeding thirty days, and in the city of New York not exceeding fifty days, for the purpose of granting licenses.

Laws of 1857, ch. 139, § 2; 1858, ch. 143; 1859, ch. 494.

Powers of commissioners.

§ 787. They have power to grant licenses to inn-keepers, residents of the town or city where the inn is to be kept, to sell strong and spirituous liquors and wines, to be drank in their houses respectively; and to store-keepers, being such residents, a license to sell such liquors and wines in quantities less than five gallons, but not to be drank in their shops, houses, out-houses, yards or gardens. No license shall be granted to any person or firm to sell in more than one place.

§ 788. The commissioners have power to determine the sum to be paid for each license within the following limits: In towns and incorporated villages, not less than thirty nor more than one hundred dollars; and in cities, not less than thirty nor more than two hundred and fifty dollars. No other fees shall be taken by the board, by any commissioner or clerk. The whole amount of all fees shall be paid over by the commissioners to the county treasurer for the use of the poor, except where otherwise specially provided by statute. Amount of license fees.

Laws of 1857, ch. 139, §§ 2, 5.

The payment of excise moneys in the town of Newburgh was otherwise directed by the act of 1859, ch. 362.

§ 789. All licenses shall be signed by the commissioners granting the same. They shall not be issued until the requirements fixed by the board shall have been complied with; when issued they shall be in force, unless revoked, until ten days after the third Tuesday in May next succeeding the granting thereof, and in the city of New York until fifty days thereafter. Conditions and term of license.

§ 790. Each board may appoint a clerk for the time they may be actually in session, in accordance with section 787, and shall keep a book of minutes of proceedings, in which shall be entered the names of all applicants for license; and also a list of all licenses granted, with the names of the parties to To appoint a clerk and keep books of minutes.

whom granted, and the names of the securities to the bond required in each case; which book shall be deposited in the office of the county clerk. A book of minutes for each town or city for which they grant a license shall be made by them, in which shall be entered every resolution passed by them granting a license to any person for such city or town, with the sum required to be paid, which minutes, verified by their signatures, shall be filed with the clerk of the town or city within eight days.

Salaries and expenses.

§ 791. Each commissioner of excise and the clerk of each board is entitled to three dollars per day for services actually performed. No other compensation shall be allowed. The expense of necessary books for minutes and necessary blanks, when actually incurred, together with the salaries, shall be audited and paid in like manner as other county charges.

License for drinking places.

§ 792. License shall not be granted to any person to sell strong and spirituous liquors and wines to be drank on the premises of the person licensed, unless such person proposes to keep an inn, nor unless the commissioners are satisfied that the applicant is of good moral character, that he has sufficient ability to keep an inn, and the necessary accommodations to entertain travelers, and that an inn is required for the actual accommodation of travelers at the place where such applicant resides or proposes to keep the same, all which shall be expressly stated in the license; and no such license shall be granted except on the petition of not less than twenty respectable freeholders of this state residing in the election district where such inn is proposed to be kept, by them duly signed, and verified by the oath of a subscribing witness, and not then unless in the opinion of the commissioners such inn is necessary or proper: and not more than one license shall be granted on the memorial of the same petitioners or any of them. All petitions upon which such licenses are granted shall be filed with the county clerk within eight days. Commissioners granting any license contrary to the provisions of this chapter are guilty of a misdemeanor.

§ 793. No such license to keep an inn shall be granted until the applicant has executed and delivered to the board a bond to the people of the state, in the penalty of two hundred and fifty dollars, with sufficient sureties, who shall duly justify in the sum of five hundred dollars, to be approved by the board of commissioners, with a condition that the applicant, during the time he shall keep any inn, will not suffer it to be disorderly, or suffer any gambling, or keep a gambling table of any description, within the inn so kept by him, or in any outhouse, yard or garden belonging thereto. **Bond to be executed.**

§ 794. In all licenses granted (excepting to inn- **In other.**

cases liquors not to be drank on premises where sold.

keepers) to sell strong or spirituous liquors or wines, in quantities less than five gallons, there shall be inserted an express declaration that the license does not authorize the sale of any strong or spirituous liquor or wine to be drank in the house or shop of the person receiving such license, or in any out-house, yard or garden appertaining thereto or connected therewith.

Moral character to be proved and bond given.

§ 795. Such licenses shall not be granted, unless the commissioners are satisfied that the applicant is of good moral character, nor until the applicant has executed a bond to the people of the state in the penalty of five hundred dollars, with sufficient sureties, who shall duly justify in the sum of one thousand dollars, to be approved by and delivered to the commissioners, conditioned that during the term for which his license is granted he will not suffer his place of business to become disorderly, nor sell, nor suffer to be sold, any strong or spirituous liquors or wines to be drank in his shop or house, or in any out-house, yard or garden appertaining thereto, nor suffer any such liquor, sold by virtue of such license, to be drank in his shop or house, or in any out-house, yard or garden, belonging thereto; and whenever any person is seen to drink in such shop or house, out-house, yard or garden, belonging thereto, any spirituous liquors or wines, forbidden to be drank therein, it shall be presumptive evidence that such spirituous liquors or wines were sold by the occupant of such premises, or his agent, with the intent that the same should be drank therein. On any trial for the offense last mentioned, the occupant or agent may be allowed to testify respecting the sale.

§ 796. Whoever sells any strong or spirituous liquors or wines in quantities less than five gallons at a time, without having a license therefor, and whoever sells any strong or spirituous liquors or wines to be drank in his house or shop, or any out-house, yard or garden appertaining thereto, or permits any such liquors or wines sold by him or under his direction or authority, to be drank in his house or shop, or in any out-house, yard or garden thereto belonging, without having obtained a license therefor as an inn, tavern or hotel keeper, incurs a penalty of fifty dollars for each offense. Penalty for selling without license.

§ 797. No inn keeper or any other person licensed to sell any strong or spirituous liquors or wines, shall sell or give away any such liquors or wines to any Indian or apprentice, knowing or having reason to believe him to be such, without the consent of his master or mistress, nor to any minor under the age of eighteen years, without the consent of his father or mother or guardian. Whoever offends against either of these provisions, incurs a penalty of ten dollars, to be recovered by the master or parent or guardian, as the case may be; and any person who No liquor to be sold to Indians, apprentices or minors.

sells or gives away any strong or spirituous liquor to any Indian in this state is guilty of a misdemeanor.

Proceedings in case of violation of this chapter.

§ 798. Every sheriff, undersheriff, deputy sheriff, constable, marshal, policeman or officer of police, shall arrest all persons found actually engaged in the commission of any offense in violation of this chapter, and forthwith carry such person before any magistrate of the same city or town, to be dealt with according to law; and the magistrate shall, on sufficient proof that such offense has been committed, unless the person elects to be tried before such magistrate, require a bond to be executed by such offender in the penalty of one hundred dollars, with sureties who shall justify in double the amount severally, conditioned that such offender will appear and answer the charge at the next term of the court of oyer and terminer or sessions to be held in said county, and abide the order and judgment of the court thereon, or he shall commit the offender to the county jail until such judgment of said court, or until he be discharged according to law. And the magistrate shall entertain any complaint of a violation of this chapter, made by any person under oath, and forthwith issue a warrant and cause such offender to be brought before him, to comply with the provisions of this section; and such magistrate shall, within ten days cause such bond, together with all papers and affidavits, with a list of the names and residences of the complainants and witnesses examined before him, to be delivered to the district attorney of the county, who shall forthwith prosecute the same.

Intoxicated persons to be arrested, tried and punished.

§ 799. Every such officer, whenever he shall find any person intoxicated in any public place, shall apprehend such person and take him before some magistrate of the same city or town; and if such magistrate shall, after due examination, deem him too much intoxicated to be examined or to answer an oath correctly, he shall direct the officer to keep him in some jail, lock-up or other safe and convenient place, until he becomes sober, and thereupon forthwith bring him before the same magistrate; and whenever any person is brought before any magistrate, as provided in this section, such magistrate shall administer to such person an oath or affirmation, and examine him as to the cause of such intoxication, and ascertain the person or persons who sold or gave the liquor to such person; such intoxication being hereby declared to be an offense against the provisions of this chapter, punishable, upon conviction, by a fine of ten dollars, and costs at the same rate as in courts of special sessions, and imprisonment in the county jail, workhouse or penitentiary until paid; not, however, to exceed ten days. Such officers shall arrest or cause to be arrested all such persons, when so intoxicated, and the magistrate shall entertain such complaints and make such examination, under the penalty of fifty dollars, with costs, for any neglect to comply with the provisions of this section.

No liquor to be given to intoxicated persons.

§ 800. Whoever sells or gives away, or suffers to be sold or given away, under his direction or authority, any strong or spirituous liquors or wines, to any intoxicated person, shall forfeit not less than ten nor more than twenty-five dollars for each offense.

Intemperate husbands, wives and children.

§ 801. Magistrates and overseers of the poor in any town or city, on complaint and satisfactory proof by a wife that her husband is an habitual drinker of intoxicating liquors, shall issue written notices to all dealers in intoxicating liquors against whom such complaint is made, forbidding the sale or giving of such liquor to such husband for the term of six months from the date of the notice, under a penalty of fifty dollars, with costs, for each offense after such notice; to be sued for in her own name and for her own use. Such magistrates and overseers of the poor shall forbid the sale, in like manner, in all cases when a husband makes like satisfactory proof concerning the wife, or a parent concerning a child who is a minor under the age of twenty-one years, or a child concerning a parent; and all the provisions of this section shall apply as in the first cases named.

§ 802. It is not lawful to sell intoxicating liquors to any person guilty of habitual drunkenness, nor to any person to whom the seller has been requested by parent, guardian, husband or wife not to sell intoxicating liquors; and every party so selling intoxicating liquors shall, on proof thereof before any court of competent jurisdiction, be deprived of his license and shall not be allowed a renewal of it; and, in addition, on conviction, shall be punished by a fine of not less than twenty dollars nor more than fifty dollars for each offense. If any inn-keeper, or any other person, knowingly (outside of any poor-house), shall sell or give to any pauper or inmate of any poor-house or alms-house strong or spirituous liquors or wines, such person shall be fined twenty-five dollars and is guilty of a misdemeanor. Habitual drunkards and paupers.

§ 803. No inn-keeper or person licensed to sell liquors shall sell or give away any intoxicating liquors or wines on Sunday, or upon any day on which a general or special election or town meeting is held, and within one-quarter of a mile from the place where it is held, in any of the cities, villages or towns of this state, to any person whatever. In case the election or town meeting is not general throughout the state, the provisions of this section in such case, shall only apply to the city, county, village or towns in which such election or town meeting is held. Whoever offends No traffic on Sunday.

against the provisions of this section is guilty of a misdemeanor.

Penalties, how recovered.

§ 804. The penalties imposed by this chapter, except where otherwise provided, shall be recovered in the name of the board of commissioners of excise, and paid over to the treasurer of the county for the support of the poor of the county.

Bonds to be filed.

§ 805. Every bond, taken pursuant to the provisions of this act, shall, within ten days after its execution, be filed in the office of the clerk of the town, city or village in which the license is granted.

Forfeited bonds.

§ 806. Whenever a breach of the condition of such bond happens, the commissioners of excise, the supervisor of the town, or mayor of the city or trustees of the village in which the person who incurs the penalty resides, shall prosecute the same.

When judgments are obtained.

§ 807. Whenever any conviction or judgment is obtained against any person licensed, for any violation of the provisions of this chapter, either in an action for a penalty or upon a bond, the justice or court before whom the same is had shall transmit to the next court of sessions of the county a statement of such conviction or judgment, and of the offense for which it was obtained.

How licenses may be revoked.

§ 808. The court of sessions shall give notice to such persons to appear on a day specified, to show cause why his license should not be revoked. At the day appointed, and on such other days as the court shall appoint, it shall proceed to inquire into the circumstances, and shall revoke the licenses of persons violating the provisions of this chapter. A person whose license is revoked shall be incapable of receiving any license for the space of three years from the time of such revocation.

§ 809. Any person who sells any strong or spirituous liquors or wines to any of the individuals to whom it is declared by this chapter to be unlawful to make such sale, shall be liable for all damages which may be sustained in consequence of such sale, and may be sued in any of the courts of this state by any individual sustaining such injuries, or by the overseers of poor of the town where the injured party may reside, and the sum recovered may be for the benefit of the party injured. Damages for unlawful sale.

§ 810. Any person who adulterates intoxicating liquors or wines with poisonous or deleterious drugs or mixtures, or knowingly imports or sells intoxicating liquors or wines so adulterated, is guilty of a misdemeanor. Adulterated liquors

§ 811. In case any person whose duty it is to prosecute, neglects to prosecute for any penalty provided by this chapter, for the period of ten days after complaint to them, accompanied with When any person may prosecute.

reasonable proof of the violation, any other person may prosecute therefor in the name of the board of commissioners of excise.

Employees of incorporated companies.

§ 812. All persons in this state engaged in conveying passengers, and all railroad, steamboat and ferry companies, and all corporations conveying, for hire, persons or property, shall refuse employment to all persons who, on good and sufficient proof, are shown to indulge in the intemperate use of intoxicating drinks; and any such person or company who retains in employ any person who, on competent proof, is shown to be intoxicated at any period whilst in active service of the company or person, either as engineer, conductor, fireman, switch-tender, commander, pilot, mate or foreman, or in any way connected with the moving power or management, or whose duty, if neglected, would diminish the safety and security of life, limb or property entrusted thereto, is liable to pay not less than fifty dollars nor more than one hundred dollars to the county treasurer, in the county where the offense is committed, and proved before any court of competent jurisdiction.

Judgments rendered.

§ 813. A person against whom a judgment is rendered on any bond given or for any penalty imposed under this chapter shall not be entitled, under any execution issued on such judgment, to the liberties of the jail.

§ 814. The words "inn" and "inn-keeper," in this chapter, include any tavern or hotel and the keeper of any tavern or hotel. Meaning of inn and inn-keeper.

CHAPTER XII.

INNS.

§ 815. Every inn-keeper shall keep at least three spare beds for his guests, with good and sufficient bedding, and every inn-keeper in any town or village shall also keep, for four horses more than his own stock, good and sufficient stabling and grain, and in the winter provender of hay, and in the summer hay or pasturage, for the same, under penalty of ten dollars for every neglect to have either of such articles, to be recovered by the overseers of the poor, for the use of the poor Inn-keeper's accommodations.

Laws of 1857, vol. 2, ch. 628, p. 409, § 8.

§ 816. Every inn-keeper licensed under the provisions of chapter XI of this title, entitled "*Licenses*," shall maintain, so long as he keeps an inn, a proper sign, on or adjacent to the front of his house, with his name, and indicating that he keeps an inn, tavern or hotel, under penalty of ten dollars for Sign.

every month's neglect so to do after thirty days after obtaining his license.

Laws of 1857, ch. 628, § 9.

Giving credit for intoxicating drinks.

§ 817. No debts incurred to any inn-keeper by other than his lodgers for any sort of strong or spirituous liquors or wines can be recovered in any action. All securities for such debts are void, and any inn-keeper taking such with intent to evade this section shall forfeit double the sum intended to be secured.

Laws of 1857, vol. 2, ch. 628, p. 409, § 10.

Penalties, how recovered.

§ 818. Penalties under the two preceding sections shall be recovered by the board of commissioners of excise and paid to the county treasurer for the use of the poor.

Laws of 1857, vol. 2, ch. 628, p. 414, § 22.

Inn-keeper's liability.

§ 819. Whenever an inn-keeper provides in his inn a convenient place for the safe keeping of the money, jewels and ornaments of his guests, and notifies them by posting, conspicuously, a notice thereof in the room or rooms occupied by such guest, he shall not be liable for any loss of money, jewels or ornaments which such guest neglected to deposit in such place.

Laws of 1855, ch. 421.

Meaning of inn and inn-keeper.

§ 820. The words "inn" and "inn-keeper," in this chapter, include a tavern or hotel and the keeper thereof.

CHAPTER XIII.

UNCLAIMED PROPERTY.

§ 821. Any person engaged in the transportation of persons or property, and any inn-keeper, who has any unclaimed property in his custody, shall immediately enter in a book, to be kept by him for the purpose, a description of each article or package, and the time when it was left. He is entitled to be paid, by the owner, thirteen cents for each package so entered. If the name of the owner is ascertained, he shall immediately send to him, by mail, notice to claim the same. Registry of unclaimed property, and notice to owner.

2 R. S., 105, § 9; thirteen cents substituted for twelve and a half.

§ 882. Every person or company engaged in the express business, and every railway company, in whose possession any such property, not perishable, has remained for a year, may sell it by public auction, after giving notice, containing a description of the articles or packages, the place and time when left, and, if the same be known, the name of Express and railway companies may sell on notice.

the owner or consignee, by advertisement once a week for four weeks successively in the state paper, in a paper published at the place of sale, in a paper published in the city of New York, and, in case of property directed to be left at a specified place, in a paper published at or nearest such place. Perishable articles unclaimed may be sold as soon as they can be, at the best terms that can be obtained.

Laws of 1857, ch. 444; Laws of 1856, ch. 523, § 1.

Application of proceeds.

§ 823. The proceeds, after deducting charges and expenses for transportation, storage, advertising, commissions for selling, and the amount previously paid for non-delivery of freight or baggage, shall be deposited by the company, with a report thereof and proof of advertisement, with the comptroller, for the benefit of the general fund of the state, to be held by him in trust for the persons entitled to the same. No such sale shall be valid, unless, at least two weeks before it, a copy of the notice required by the preceding section is served on the comptroller.

Laws of 1857, vol. 1, ch. 444, p. 871, § 3.

By the two preceding sections a uniform system is prescribed for railway companies and for express companies. The act of 1854 respecting railway freight, &c., and the act of 1855 respecting express freight, each left the proceeds in the hands of the company making the sale, to be refunded to the owner, on claim, within five years. In case of the express companies it was further provided that, if not claimed at that time, they should be paid over for the benefit of the county poor.

The amendment of 1857, relating to railway companies, provides for a regular accounting by them to the comptroller. We have so far modified the provisions as to put express companies under the same rule in this respect.

§ 824. Persons other than those mentioned in section 822 shall proceed as follows: When any property remains unclaimed for thirty days, they shall send a correct description thereof to the proprietor of the state paper, whose duty it is, on the first Monday of January, April, July and October in each year, to publish the same once a week for three weeks successively. **Persons other than railway and express companies.**

§ 825. If for sixty days after the publication the property remains unclaimed, the person having custody of it shall apply to a magistrate of the town or city, under whose sight and direction it shall be opened and examined, and by whom an inventory shall be taken. The magistrate shall send immediate notice to the owner, by mail, if his name is ascertained. **Examination of articles.**

§ 826. If for three months after the examination it remains unclaimed, such person shall apply to a magistrate of the city or town, who shall, if the property is of sufficient value, order it to be sold by **Sale.**

58

public auction, on six days' previous notice of the time and place.

Proceeds. § 827. After payment of expenses, the magistrate shall pay the proceeds to the overseers of the poor, for the use of the poor, and they shall make an entry of the amount, and the time of receiving it, upon their official records, and at any time within seven years it shall be refunded, on claim and proof of title, to whoever is entitled thereto.

Lien for advertising. § 828. Any person proceeding under the provisions of this chapter has a lien on the articles, until the sale, for the amount of fees for entering the same, and the expenses of the advertising or a ratable proportion thereof.

Penalty. § 829. Any person who neglects to comply with the provisions of this chapter is liable to a penalty of five dollars, to be recovered by any person who will bring action therefor.

CHAPTER XIV.

REGISTRY OF BIRTHS, MARRIAGES AND DEATHS.

The provisions of this chapter are from 2 R. S., 323, 324, and Laws of 1853, ch. 75.

§ 830. All persons who perform the marriage ceremony shall keep a registry of the time of each marriage so celebrated, the residence, the names in full, the place of birth, the age and condition, whether married or single, of each party. Registry of marriages.

§ 831. All physicians and professional midwives shall keep a registry of the time of each birth at which they assist professionally, the sex and color of the child and the names and residences of the parents. Registry of births.

§ 832. Physicians who have attended deceased persons in their last sickness, clergymen who have officiated at a funeral, and sextons who have buried deceased persons shall each keep a registry of the name, age, residence and time of death of such persons. Registry of deaths.

§ 833. In the city of New York, all such persons shall report the same, on or before the first Monday of each month, to the city inspector. A physician's certificate of death and a coroner's certificate where an inquest has been held, shall specify, as near as can be ascertained, the name in full, age, occupation, term of residence in that city, birthplace, condition, whether single, married, widow or widower, color, last place of residence, and the direct and indirect cause of death of the deceased. Reports in the city of New York to the city inspector.

If at any birth in that city no physician or midwife attends, the parents shall report it to the city inspector.

City inspector's record.

§ 834. The city inspector shall record all births, marriages and deaths so reported, numbering them in the order in which they are reported, and stating the date of the record and the several points of information, in several columns, and also the name, residence and official station of the persons making such report.

City inspector's report.

§ 835. He shall, on the third Monday of each month, transmit to the secretary of state a certified abstract of his records, prepared in accordance with the secretary's instructions, and in blanks to be furnished for the purpose by the secretary.

Duty of clerks of school districts.

§ 836. In each school district in the state, except in the city of New York, the clerk of the district, or, if there is none capable of acting, the trustees or one of them shall, on or before the fifteenth day of January in each year, ascertain for the year passed, and report to the town clerk or to one of the aldermen of the ward in which the school-house of the district is, the information which it is the duty of the persons mentioned in sections 832, 833 and 834 to record, and such persons shall for this purpose afford an inspection of their registers and all other information in their power.

837. Each town clerk and alderman shall, within fifteen days, record such report in a book to be kept by him for the purpose, and transmit a copy or abstract, in such form as the secretary of state prescribes, to the county clerk; who shall within fifteen days, transmit a certified abstract in the like form to the secretary of state. Duty of town clerk alderman and county clerk.

§ 838. The district, town, city and county officers shall receive, from their respective counties, such compensation for these services as the boards of supervisors may determine; except that in the city of New York the fee for recording a birth or a marriage shall not exceed ten cents, and the fee for the latter shall be paid by the person reporting it. Every person solemnizing a marriage in that city may require a fee of one dollar from the parties, out of which he shall pay for recording it. Fees of officers.

§ 839. Any person who neglects compliance with or violates any provision of this chapter relating to the city of New York, is liable to a penalty of fifty dollars, to be recovered by the mayor, aldermen and commonalty, and one-half thereof to be paid to the person making complaint. Penalty.

CHAPTER XV.

SEPULTURE.

Title to cemetery grounds.

§ 840. The title to any land, which was used by the inhabitants of any town as a cemetery for fourteen years immediately before the first day of January, eighteen hundred and thirty, shall be deemed to be vested in the town in which it lies, and is subject as other town property to the government and direction of the electors in town meeting. But the same shall never be used for any other purpose than a public cemetery.

1 R. S., 669, § 1; 2 Ib., 974, § 8.

Cemeteries in towns divided.

§ 841. Any cemetery the property of a town which is to be divided or altered, shall not be included among the property to be apportioned, or otherwise disposed of, but the same shall belong to the town in which it is situated after the division or alteration.

1 R. S., 644, § 9.

Protection of birds.

§ 842. Any person who kills, wounds or catches any bird, or destroys or removes any bird's nest, or eggs or young birds therein, within any cemetery, or in any place within two miles of the inclosure of

Greenwood cemetery in the county of Kings, and any person who knowingly buys or sells or has on sale any bird so killed or caught, is guilty of a misdemeanor, and is punishable by a fine of five dollars for every bird, nest, eggs or young so meddled with, to be recovered in any justice's court of the county where the offense is committed, by the person making complaint, and for the use of the poor of the county.

Laws of 1853, ch. 629; as amended by Laws of 1855, ch. 564.

§ 843. No public way shall be laid out through any part of a cemetery, during the time it is in use as such, without the consent of the trustees of the cemetery. Public ways through cemeteries.

1 R. S., 1198, § 10, last clause.

§ 844. Further provisions respecting cemeteries in villages are contained in chapter V of title V of part IV of this Code. Village cemeteries.

CHAPTER XVI.

DISSECTION.

From Laws of 1854, ch. 123.

§ 845. In cities of over thirty thousand population the remains of deceased persons which have not been buried, and have not, within twenty-four hours after death, been requested by any relative What remains may be delivered for dissection.

or friend for burial, may be delivered to professors and teachers of medical schools in this state for the use of medical and surgical study; but no remains of a person detained for debt or as a witness, or on suspicion of crime, or of any traveler, or of any person who expressed a desire, in his last sickness, that his remains be buried, shall be so delivered, but shall be buried in the usual manner; and no remains of a person known to have any relative or friend shall be so delivered, without their consent.

Remains may be reclaimed.

§ 846. Any remains that have been so delivered shall be given up at any time to any relative or friend claiming them.

Restrictions on use.

§ 847. Such remains shall be used for no other purpose than medical and surgical study, and shall not be in any manner trafficked in nor removed out of the state. Any person who violates any provision of this or the two preceding sections, or who knowingly receives any remains delivered up in violation of any such provision, is guilty of a misdemeanor.

Final burial.

§ 848. Those to whom such remains are so delivered shall after such uses bury the same decently in a public cemetery, under penalty of not less than twenty-five nor more than fifty dollars for each neglect, to be recovered by the health officer of the place for the benefit of his department.

CHAPTER XVII.

OBSERVANCE OF SUNDAY.

§ 849. No papers shall be served, and no process, judgment or order, of any court or officer of justice shall be served or executed on Sunday, except in cases of breach or apprehended breach of the peace, or for the apprehension of persons charged with crimes, misdemeanors, and except in cases specially authorized by law. A person violating this section is liable in damages therefor to the injured party. Service of process, &c

2 R. S., 83, § 65.

§ 850. There shall be no shooting, hunting, fishing, sporting, playing, horse-racing, gaming, frequenting of tippling-houses, or any unlawful exercise or pastime on Sunday; nor shall any person travel on that day, unless in cases of charity or necessity, or in going to or returning from some place of worship within twenty miles, or in going for medical aid or for medicines and returning, or in visiting the sick and returning, or Recreations and traveling.

in carrying the mail of the United States, or in going express by order of some public officer, or in removing his family or household furniture, when such removal was commenced on some other day; nor shall there be any servile laboring or working on that day, excepting works of necessity and charity, unless done by some person who uniformly keeps Saturday as holy time, and does not labor or work on that day, and whose labor shall not disturb other persons in the observance of Sunday. Any person fourteen years of age or upwards, who violates any provision of this section, is liable to a penalty of one dollar for each offense.

2 R. S., 83, § 66.

Selling on Sunday.

§ 851. No person shall expose to sale any articles on Sunday; except meats, milk and fish, which may be sold before nine o'clock in the morning; and except medicines, which may be sold at any time; and the articles so exposed for sale shall be forfeited. Upon conviction of the offender by any justice of the peace of the county, or mayor, recorder or alderman of the city, such officers shall issue a warrant for the seizure of the forfeited articles, which, when seized, shall be sold on one day's notice, and the proceeds shall be paid to the overseers of the poor for the use of the poor of the town or city.

Ib., § 67.

§ 852. Every person who keeps Saturday as holy time and does not labor on that day is exempt, on that day, from performance of military duty, except in case of war, invasion or insurrection, and from performance of jury duty. Observance of Saturday.

2 R. S., 84, § 69.

§ 853. Whoever maliciously procures any process in a civil action to be served on that day upon any such person, or serves any such process returnable on that day, or maliciously procures any civil action, to which such person is a party, to be adjourned to that day for trial, is guilty of a misdemeanor. Service of process on persons who observe Saturday.

Ib., §§ 70, 71.

§ 854. On complaint made to any justice of the peace, mayor, recorder or alderman, of a violation of any provision of this chapter, or when such magistrate witnesses any such violation, he shall cause the offender to be brought before him; and if upon summary inquiry he is found guilty, the magistrate shall make a record of his conviction. Such conviction is not the subject of review upon the merits. No process to enforce it shall issue before the record is signed. Prosecution of offenders.

Ib., § 72.

§ 855. No prosecution shall be had for any of the violations specified in the preceding section, unless by issuing process to apprehend the offender, Limitation.

or by his actual appearance to answer the complaint, within twenty days after the offense.

2 R. S., 84, § 73.

Collection of penalties.

§ 856. Upon a conviction for any such offense, the magistrate shall, except where it is otherwise provided, issue an execution to any constable of the county, commanding him to levy the penalties and costs, of the personal property of the offender, and in case sufficient cannot be found, then to commit him to the county jail for a specified time, not less than one nor more than three days.

Ib., § 74.

Certificate of convictions, &c., to be filed.

§ 857. Within thirty days after any such conviction, the magistrate shall cause to be filed, in the office of the clerk of the county, a certificate thereof, briefly stating the offense charged, the conviction and judgment thereon, and, if any fine has been collected, the amount thereof and to whom paid.

Ib., 85, § 75.

Costs.

§ 858. The same fees shall be paid by the convict as in civil suits before justices of the peace, but in no case to exceed five dollars; but no fees shall be allowed in case of his imprisonment.

Ib., § 76.

CHAPTER XVIII.

WILLFUL MISCHIEF.

§ 859. Willfully injuring or defacing the property of another, whether real or personal, or any public way, or willfully obstructing any railway property or work, is a misdemeanor. Willful mischief is a misdemeanor.

§ 860. Whoever commits any act embraced in the preceding section is liable in treble damages to the owner of the property or public way, or to the public officer having charge thereof. Damages.

The existing provisions respecting liability for the commission of willful mischief are very diverse (1 R. S., 1094, § 57; Laws of 1854, ch. 120; 1 R. S., 1238, § 40; Laws of 1854, ch. 573; 1 R. S., 1197, § 8; Laws of 1854, ch. 112), some authorizing a recovery of damages merely, some treble, some quintuple damages, some a fixed penalty.

PART IV.

GENERAL LAWS FOR THE GOVERNMENT OF COUNTIES, CITIES, TOWNS AND VILLAGES.

TITLE I.

GENERAL PROVISIONS.

§ 861. A county is the largest civil division of the state having corporate powers. Its chief officer is the sheriff. County defined.

Town defined. § 862. Towns are smaller civil divisions with corporate powers, into which the county is divided. Their chief officer is the supervisor.

City defined. § 863. A city is a civil division, with corporate powers, for the government of a crowded population, and having a mayor as its head. It may include towns or counties, or part or parts thereof.

Village defined. § 864. A village is a civil division within a town, with corporate powers, and having a board of trustees, with a president as its head.

Municipal corporation defined. § 865. A municipal corporation is the corporation of a city or village.

Insurance. § 866. Officers having custody of any public buildings of any county, city, town or village, may insure them at public expense and for public benefit.

1 R. S., 683, § 40.

Officers may administer oaths. § 867. The officers mentioned in Part IV of this Code, including the chairman of committees and the clerks of all boards or bodies of officers, charged with any inquiry or action requiring the administering of oaths, have power to administer oaths and affirmations to witnesses and jurors brought before them.

From 1 R. S., 667, § 17; 646, § 7; 1244, § 36.

Officers not to be interested in contracts. § 868. No member of a common council, trustee of a village, or supervisor shall become a contractor under any contract authorized by the common council, board of trustees, or board of supervisors of which he is a member, or be in any manner interested, directly or indirectly, either as principal or surety, in such contract.

1 R. S., 667, § 14.

§ 869. No town, county, city or state officer shall be interested in any contract made by him, or be a purchaser, or interested in any purchase, at any sale made by him, or a seller at any purchase made by him as such officer. Officers not to be interested in contracts.

Ib., § 15.

§ 870. Contracts in violation of any provisions of the two preceding sections may be declared void at the instance of the city, county, village or town interested, or of any other party interested in such contract, except the officer violating the provision. Contracts voidable.

Ib., § 16.

§ 871. No municipal corporation shall, in any manner, loan or give its credit to or in aid of any person. Loaning credit forbidden.

This and the four following sections are from Laws of 1853, ch. 603.

§ 872. No municipal corporation shall contract any debt, the amount of which, exclusive of the debt owing by such corporation on the 21st day of July, 1853, shall exceed, at any time, a sum equal to five per cent, nor inclusive of such debt, shall exceed eight per cent of the value of Contracting debts restricted.

all the real property within its bounds, to be ascertained by the last corrected valuations of the assessors thereof, as established by the board of trustees, common council or board of supervisors, as the case may be.

Temporary loans. § 873. No money shall be borrowed on temporary loan by any municipal corporation, except in anticipation of the taxes of the current fiscal year, and the same shall always be made payable and shall be paid within eight months from the time of making the loan.

Funded debt. § 874. No funded debt shall be contracted by any municipal corporation, except for a specific object expressly stated in the ordinance proposing it, nor unless such ordinance was passed by two-thirds of all the members elected to the common council or board of trustees, and submitted to and approved by a majority of the tax-payers of the corporation, at a special election to be appointed for that purpose by the common council or board of trustees, nor unless the legislature shall by law have ratified the ordinance and have provided for raising annually, by tax, a sum sufficient to pay the interest and to provide a sinking fund of at least five per cent, upon the amount of the debt, per annum. Such tax shall be annually collected and the sinking fund remain inviolate until sufficient is realized to pay and extinguish both principal and interest. All the laws relating to the election of municipal officers of any such corporation shall apply, so far as applicable, to every election pursuant to this section.

§ 875. No municipal corporation shall borrow any money or incur any debt, except in the mode provided in the preceding four sections; and any evidences of debt not issued in conformity therewith are void. But nothing in this or the four preceding sections affects any law existing on the 21st day of July, 1853, authorizing any corporation to do so. Borrowing or incurring debt in other modes forbidden.

The provisions of the Revised Statutes (1 R. S., 665, 711) relating to the cases in which justices, jurors and witnesses are disqualified, by reason of being inhabitants of a county or town interested, and relating to costs and judgments in actions against counties, towns or officers, are properly within the scope of the CODE OF CIVIL PROCEDURE.

TITLE II.

THE GOVERNMENT OF COUNTIES.

CHAPTER I.

COUNTIES AS BODIES CORPORATE.

From 1 R. S., 676.

Every county is a body corporate.

§ 876. Every county is a body politic and corporate, and as such has the powers specified or necessarily implied in this title, or in special statutes, and no others.

Power vested in board of supervisors.

§ 877. Its powers can only be exercised by the board of supervisors, or in pursuance of a resolution adopted by them; but a conveyance authorized by subdivision 2 of the following section, made in any manner, for the use of the inhabitants, shall have the same effect as if made to the board of supervisors.

Enumeration of powers.

§ 878. It has power:

1. To sue and be sued in the name of the board of supervisors;

2. To purchase and hold lands within its limits and for the use of its inhabitants, subject to the power of the legislature;

3. To make such contracts and purchase and hold such personal property as necessary to the exercise of its powers;

4. To make such orders for the disposition or use of its property as the interests of its inhabitants require.

CHAPTER II.

COUNTY OFFICERS.

ARTICLE I.

THE BOARD OF SUPERVISORS.

Meetings of the board of supervisors.

§ 879. The board of supervisors in each county shall hold an annual meeting at such time and place as they may fix. They may hold special meetings at the call of their clerk, on the written request of a majority of the board, and in such other cases as are specially provided by law. They may adjourn from time to time. Every meeting shall be open to all persons.

Quorum.

§ 880. A majority of the board constitute a quorum.

Chairman.

§ 881. They shall at each annual meeting choose one of their number as chairman for the ensuing year. In his absence at any meeting, the members present shall choose a temporary chairman.

Powers of the board.

§ 882. The board have power:

1. To make such orders respecting the corporate property of the county as they deem expedient;

2. To liquidate and audit accounts against the county, and direct the raising of the sums necessary to defray them;

3. To purchase real property necessary for any public county building, and for the support of the poor, and to determine the site thereof when it has not been already located;

4. To remove or designate a new site for any county building under the restrictions provided in section 885;

5. To erect necessary county buildings, and to raise, by tax upon the county, the moneys necessary for their erection, not exceeding five thousand dollars in any one year;

6. To borrow money for the purposes of the three preceding subdivisions, and provide for its payment, with interest, in yearly installments or otherwise, within ten years, by tax;

7. To repair the county buildings and raise the expense thereof by tax; but the sums expended in repairs of the court-house and jail in any one year shall not exceed five hundred dollars;

8. To construct and repair bridges in the county and raise by tax the moneys necessary therefor, apportioning the tax among the several towns as they deem just;

9. To raise by tax the necessary highway moneys

in pursuance of chapter II of title III of Part III of this Code;

10. To appoint special commissioners to lay out a highway, if they deem the highway important and are satisfied that the authority of the town commissioners will not be exercised to lay it out; but such appointment shall not be made unless the applicant presents proof of service on the commissioners of highways of each town through which the route lies, of written notice of the application six days previous to its presentation, and specifying its object and the names of the proposed commissioners;

11. To provide for the payment of the services and expenses of such special commissioners;

12. To erect and alter towns as prescribed in subsequent sections of this article;

13. To authorize a town to borrow, by its vote, money to build or repair highways, not exceeding four thousand dollars in one year, and provide for its payment, with interest, within ten years, by tax upon the town;

14. To sell or lease any real property of the county, and prescribe the mode of conveyance;

15. To abolish or revive the distinction between town and county poor;

16. To fix at any annual meeting the time when

each collector shall make return to the county treasurer before the first of March then next ensuing;

17. To make regulations for destruction of wild beasts and noxious weeds, and for the protection of game, fish and shell fish, and for the prevention of the injury of sheep by dogs, and to tax dogs, and direct the application of the tax;

18. To require from any county officer, or officer whose salary is paid by the county, a report under oath on any matter connected with their duties. A neglect to comply with such a requirement is a misdemeanor;

19. To adopt a seal for their board; a description and impression whereof shall be filed by their clerk in the offices of the county clerk and the secretary of state;

20. To perform such other acts as they are authorized to do by the provisions of this Code or by special statutes.

1 R. S., 677, &c.; Laws of 1855, ch. 249.

§ 883. For the exercise of the powers mentioned in subdivisions 3, 5, 6, 13, 14, 16 and 18 of the preceding section, a vote of the majority of all the members elected is necessary; for those mentioned in subdivisions 4, 12, 15 and 17 a vote of two-thirds of all the members elected is necessary. All other questions are determined by a vote of a majority of the members present. Votes.

Notice of certain applications.

§ 884. All persons intending to apply to any board of supervisors for the imposing of any tax, pursuant to subdivisions 7, 8, 10, 11 of section 882, shall first publish a notice of such application once in each week for four successive weeks immediately preceding the meeting of the board, in a newspaper printed in the county; or, if no newspaper is printed in the county, then in one printed nearest thereto.

Removal of county buildings.

§ 885. The site of any county building already located shall not be changed, unless notice of the proposed change, specifying the new site, and signed by at least twelve freeholders, has been published, for six successive weeks immediately preceding the meeting of the board, in a newspaper printed in the county. The site shall not be changed to a distance exceeding one mile, unless such notice is given immediately before, and the resolution passed at two successive annual meetings.

Record of change.

§ 886. The resolution authorizing a change of any such site shall be signed by the chairman and clerk of the board, and recorded in the book of miscellaneous records of the county.

Application to alter towns.

§ 887. In any county, except that of New York, any twelve freeholders of each town to be affected may, after giving the notice required by the next section, apply to the board of supervisors, at any annual meeting, to erect a new town, or divide an existing town, or alter the boundaries thereof. But no alteration shall be made that would place parts of the same town in more than one assembly district.

§ 888. Notice of the application, signed by not less than twelve freeholders of the towns to be affected, shall be posted for four weeks previous in each of such towns, and published in all the newspapers published in the county, not exceeding three, for at least six weeks successively immediately preceding the meeting of the board. Mode of notice.

§ 889. A map and survey of all the towns affected, showing the proposed alterations, shall be furnished to the board, a copy of which, if the application is granted, shall be filed with a certified statement of the action of the board, in the office of the secretary of state. Map to be furnished.

§ 890. Whenever the board erect a new town, they shall designate its name, the time and place of holding the first annual town meeting, and three electors of the town to preside thereat, to appoint a clerk, open and keep the polls, and exercise the same powers as justices of the peace when presiding at town meetings. Certain provisions for new towns.

§ 891. The secretary of state shall cause the statement mentioned in section 889 to be printed in the Duty of secretary of state.

next volume of statutes, and to be published in the same manner as statutes are to be published.

Power to require attendance of witnesses.

§ 892. The board have power by their chairman, or by the chairman of any committee authorized to send for persons and papers to issue subpœnas to compel the attendance of any person, and the production of any books or papers relating to the affairs of the county, for the purpose of examination upon any matter within their jurisdiction.

Laws of 1858, ch. 190, §§ 1, 3; Laws of 1856, ch. 108.

Service of subpœna.

§ 893. The subpœna shall be served by the sheriff, or any deputy sheriff or constable to whom it is delivered, by reading it to the person named and delivering to him a copy. The officer's return thereon of the time and place of service is presumptive evidence thereof.

Ib., § 2.

Neglect to comply.

§ 894. Whoever neglects to comply with the subpœna, or refuses to answer any question that a majority of the board or committee deem proper, is guilty of contempt. It is the duty of the chairman of the board or committee, or any county judge or judge of the supreme court, or any judge of the superior court or court of common pleas of any city within the state, thereupon to issue to the sheriff of the county where the witness was required to attend, an attachment against him, returnable before the judge granting it; upon the return of which the same proceedings may be had in all respects as in the case of witnesses in civil actions. The action of the judge, if out of court, shall be in writing, signed by him and filed in the office of the clerk of the county where the proceedings are had; and orders entered thereupon by the clerk shall have the same force as if made by the court.

Laws of 1858, ch. 190, §§ 4, 5, 8.

§ 895. The board or committee at whose instance the attachment is issued, shall, if it be not returned at the time of their adjournment, adjourn to a specified time and place, of which their chairman shall give notice to the judge. If the offender is arrested he shall not be discharged until he has given a bond to the board, in the penalty of two hundred and fifty dollars, with two sufficient sureties, approved by the judge, conditioned for his appearing and submitting to examination before the board or committee at the time and place to which they are adjourned. Adjournment; bond to appear.

Ib., § 6.

§ 896. The bond shall be filed in the county clerk's office, and if broken it is the duty of the district attorney to prosecute it for the benefit of the poor of the county. Proceedings on the bond.

Ib., § 7.

§ 897. A witness is bound to answer all questions which he would be bound to answer in the same case in a court of justice; but testimony Examination of witnesses.

given under the five preceding sections shall not be used against the witness, on the trial of any criminal prosecution other than for perjury committed on the examination.

Laws of 1858, ch. 190, § 9.

Form and verification of accounts to be audited.

§ 898. No account shall be audited by the super visors for any services or disbursements unless it is made out in items, and has attached to, and filed with it, the affidavit of the claimant, that the items are correct, and that the disbursements and services charged therein have been in fact made or rendered or are necessary to be made or rendered at that session of the board, and that no part thereof has been paid or satisfied. Each account shall state the nature of the services; and where no specific compensation is provided by law therefor, the time necessarily devoted to its performance. The board may disallow, or require further evidence of the account notwithstanding the verification.

1 R. S., 680, §§ 26, 27; 711, §§ 1, 2.

Fees, &c., of officers for criminal proceedings.

§ 899. All fees and accounts of magistrates and other officers for criminal proceedings, including cases of vagrancy, shall be paid by the town or cities where the offense was committed. Such accounts shall specify the place, and the board shall assess the same upon the town or city specified. But when any person is bound over or committed to await trial at the oyer and terminer, or court of sessions, the cost of the proceedings after he was so bound over or committed, shall be charged to the county. This section does not apply to felonies, nor where the proceedings or trial for the offense are had before any court of oyer and terminer, or court of sessions of the county; nor in any case in the county of Kings. The fines collected in any such cases shall be credited to the town or city respectively.

1 R. S., 680, § 28.

§ 900. No fees shall be allowed for traveling to subpœna a witness, except such as the board are satisfied were indispensably necessary. Fees for subpœnaing witnesses.

Ib., § 30.

§ 901. All accounts presented in any year shall be numbered, from one upwards, in the order in which they are presented; and the time of presentation, the names of the persons in whose favor they are made out, and by whom presented, shall be entered in the minutes of the board; and no such account shall be withdrawn from the custody of the board or its clerk, except to be used as evidence in a judicial proceeding and forthwith returned. Accounts to be numbered and preserved.

Ib.

§ 902. The board shall annually cause to be raised in each town the amount of town charges in the mode prescribed by the "*Fiscal Laws.*" Town charges.

Ib., 663, § 49.

The clerk; his compensation.

§ 903. Each board shall appoint a clerk at a compensation to be fixed by the board. In the county of Albany the compensation of the clerk or clerks shall not exceed five hundred dollars. In the county of Rensselaer it shall not exceed four hundred dollars.

1 R, S., 682, § 37; Laws of 1857, ch. 348, § 2; ch. 331, § 2.

Duty of the clerk.

§ 904. It is the clerk's duty:

1. To record, in a book to be provided for the purpose, all the proceedings of the board;

2. To enter every resolution or decision concerning the raising or payment of moneys;

3. To record the vote of each supervisor on any question submitted to the board, if required by any member present;

4. To preserve and file all accounts presented to or acted on by the board, and to designate, upon every account audited, the amount allowed and the charges for which it was allowed;

5. To keep the books and papers of the board free to the examination of all persons.

1 R. S., 682, §§ 37, 38, 39, 43.

The provision of the acts of 1855 (ch. 249, § 2), that certified copies of the records of the board are evidence, is properly within the scope of the CODE OF CIVIL PROCEDURE.

§ 905. The clerk shall annually, on or within ten days before the thirty-first day of December, make out and certify, and within two weeks cause to be published in a newspaper printed in the county, a statement for the preceding year, showing: Clerk to make annual statement.

1. The amount, items and nature of all compensation audited by the board to the members thereof, severally;

2. The number of days the board was in session, and the distance traveled by the members, respectively, in attending the same;

3. Whether any unverified accounts were audited, and if any, how much and for what.

A clerk who intentionally neglects to publish such statement is guilty of a misdemeanor. Together with such statement the clerk shall publish the abstracts of accounts audited by town auditors furnished to him under article VII of chapter III of title IV of this part.

1 R. S., 682, § 41.

§ 906. The board shall cause to be published annually, in one or more public newspapers in the county, the name of every individual whose account has been audited by them, the amount claimed and the amount allowed, and also their proceedings upon the equalization of the assessment roll Board to publish annual statement of accounts audited.

Ib., § 43.

Solitary cells for convicts.

§ 907. They shall cause to be prepared in the county jail, or elsewhere, so many solitary cells for the reception of convicts as the county court directs.

1 R. S., 682, § 46.

Compensation of the supervisors.

§ 908. Except where otherwise specially provided by law, each supervisor shall receive for his services and expenses in attending the meetings of the board two dollars per day, and eight cents per mile for all necessary travel on official duty; and also for making a copy of the assessment roll for his town, and making out the tax bill to be delivered to the collector, three cents per name for the first hundred names, two cents per name for the second hundred, and one cent per name for each name over two hundred. He is not entitled to a per diem allowance while making out the copy or tax bill.

1 R. S., 677, § 19; 682, § 48.

Supervisors to render accounts.

§ 909. The accounts of supervisors shall be rendered in accordance with section 898.

Ib., 678, § 25.

Penalty for neglect of duty.

§ 910. Any supervisor who neglects to perform any duty required of him by law, as a member of the board, is liable to a penalty of two hundred and fifty dollars for each offense.

Ib., 684, § 48.

ARTICLE II.

THE COUNTY TREASURER.

From 1 R. S., 684, §§ 50 to 70; Laws of 1859, 411, ch. 165.

§ 911. The county treasurer shall, within ten days after his election or appointment, and before entering office, give a bond to the board of supervisors, with three or more sufficient sureties, to be approved by the board, and in such sums as they direct, conditioned that he shall faithfully execute the duties of his office, and shall pay, according to law, all moneys which shall come to his hands as treasurer, and render a just and true account thereof to the board of supervisors or to the comptroller of this state, when required. The board may at any time require him to renew the bond, and his failure to do so within twenty days vacates his office. County treasurer to give bond.

§ 912. The bond, with the approbation of the board indorsed thereon by their clerk, shall be filed in the office of the county clerk. Bond to be filed.

When to file bond in certain counties.

§ 913. In those counties where the annual meeting of the board is before the election the supervisors shall fix the penalty of the bond at their next meeting after the election, and the treasurer may take the oath of office and file the bond at any time before the fifteenth of December after his election, and the sureties may be approved by the county clerk and chairman of the board in the recess of the board.

Treasurer's duties.

§ 914. It is the duty of the treasurer:

1. To receive all moneys belonging to the county, and all other moneys by law directed to be paid to him, and to apply them and render account of them as required by law;

2. To keep a true account of the receipt and expenditure of all such moneys in books provided for the purpose at the expense of the county;

3. On or before the first day of March, in each year, to transmit to the comptroller a statement of all moneys received by him during the preceding year, for penalties, belonging to the people of the state; and, at the same time, to pay to the treasurer of the state the amount of such penalties, after deducting his compensation, in the same manner as state taxes are directed to be paid;

4. To exhibit to the board of supervisors, at their annual meeting, or whenever they direct, all his

books and accounts, and all vouchers relating to the same, to be audited and allowed.

§ 915. Whenever the right of any county treasurer to his office expires, the books and papers belonging to the office, and all moneys in his hands by virtue of his office, shall, upon his oath, or, in case of his death, upon the oath of his executors or administrators, be delivered to his successor. Any person violating this section is liable to the county in a penalty of twelve hundred and fifty dollars. Delivery of books, papers and funds to successor.

§ 916. The delivery of such moneys, as well as the books and papers, may be enforced by proceeding under article VII of chapter VI of title I of part III of this Code, entitled, "*Proceedings to compel the delivery of books and papers by public officers.*" Proceedings to enforce delivery.

§ 917. Except in the counties for which special provision is made by law, the compensation of the treasurer shall be fixed by the board of supervisors, not exceeding one-half of one per cent on moneys received and one-half of one per cent on moneys paid. Compensation.

§ 918. The board of supervisors shall bring action on the treasurer's bond whenever required to do so by the comptroller, or whenever they have knowledge of any breach of the bond. Prosecution of bond.

Application of recovery.

§ 919. The moneys recovered shall be applied by the board to the use of the county, except that any moneys so recovered which were received by the treasurer for the use of the state or other party shall be paid by the supervisors to the treasurer of the state or other party.

Chamberlain of the city of New York.

§ 920. The chamberlain of the city and county of New York is the treasurer thereof; and all the provisions of this article apply to him, except such as are inconsistent with the provisions of law specially relating to him.

Reference to Code of Civil Procedure.

§ 921. Other provisions respecting the county treasurer are contained in the CODE OF CIVIL PROCEDURE.

ARTICLE III.

THE COUNTY CLERK.

From 1 R. S., 685.

Duties of county clerk.

§ 922. It is the duty of the county clerk in each county:

1. To take custody of all the books, records, deeds, parchments, maps and papers now deposited or hereafter to be deposited in his office; and to keep the same in good arrangement and preservation;

2. To provide proper books for recording all matters and documents required or authorized to be recorded in his office;

3. Whenever any commission or supersedeas is received at his office, to give immediate notice, at the expense of the state, to every person named therein;

4. To give immediate notice to the governor whenever an office becomes vacant, by the happening within his county of the event mentioned in subdivisions 1 or 4 of section 232; and on or before the fifteenth day of January in each year, to report to the governor the names of all persons appointed to office in the county who, during the preceding year, have taken the oath or given the bond required, and of all persons required to do so who have neglected it; and of all vacancies in the county in any civil offices;

5. To report to the district attorney of the county all omissions by any town officers to transmit to such clerk any returns or other documents they are by law required to do;

6. On or before the first day of January in each year, to report to the comptroller the names of all religious societies incorporated in the county during the preceding year;

7. To keep in his office a book, free at all times

to public inspection, in which he shall enter all fees charged or received by him for any official service, the time of rendering it, the nature of it, and the person, if known, for whom it was rendered;

8. To transmit annually, free of expense, to the secretary of state, a statement verified by his oath, and showing for the year preceding the first day of January: 1. The amount of all fees charged or received for recording any documents and for certificates thereof; 2. The amount of all fees charged or received for searching and for certificates thereof; 3. The amount of all sums charged or received for services rendered the county; 4. The amount of all sums charged or received for other official services; 5. An account by items, showing all sums paid for assistance, and the persons to whom they were paid, and for fuel, lights, stationery and other incidental expenses;

9. To perform such other duties as are imposed on him by other provisions of the Codes or by special laws.

Compensation from the state.

§ 923. The compensation of the county clerk for services and expenses in performing any duty prescribed in subdivisions 3, 4 and 6 of the preceding section, and the fees for recording any mortgage to the people of this state, shall be audited by the comptroller and paid out of the treasury.

§ 924. The seal of the county is the official seal of the county clerk. Seal.

§ 925. Where the county clerk is authorized to judge of the competency of the sureties in an official bond, and he is absent from the county, or incapable of performing the duties of office, or the office is vacant, the county judge may decide upon the competency of such sureties; and for that purpose administer any oath and make any examination necessary. In what case county judge may decide on sufficiency of sureties.

§ 926. No county clerk shall make any charge against the county for fuel or lights for his office, or for stationery, except record books and stationery furnished by him for courts held in the county. No charge against the county for certain expenses.

ARTICLE IV.

THE SHERIFF.

From 1 R. S., 687, §§ 124 to 134.

§ 927. Every sheriff shall, within twenty days after he receives notice of his election or appointment, and before he enters upon office, execute, with at least two sureties who are freeholders and approved by the county clerk, as sufficient, a joint Sheriff to give bond.

and several bond to the people of the state, conditioned that he shall well and faithfully, in all things, perform and execute the office of sheriff of the county, during his continuance therein, without fraud, deceit or oppression.

The bond of the sheriff of the city and county of New York shall be in the penalty of twenty thousand dollars; that of every other sheriff, ten thousand dollars.

Filing of bond; justification of sureties. § 928. Such bonds shall be filed in the county clerk's office, and the clerk shall, at the time of filing, administer an oath to each surety that he is a freeholder within this state, and worth, over and above all debts whatsoever, if in the city and county of New York the sum of twenty thousand dollars, and if in any other county such sum as is proportionate to the number of sureties and to the amount of the bond: which oath shall be indorsed on the bond and subscribed by each of the sureties in the presence of the clerk, who shall, notwithstanding, determine upon the competency of each surety.

Bond to be renewed annually. § 929. In the same manner the security shall be renewed within twenty days after the first Monday of January in each year.

Notice of sheriff's arrest to be given to the governor. § 930. Whenever a sheriff becomes, and for thirty days remains committed to the custody of another sheriff or of a coroner, under any execution or attachment founded on the non-payment of moneys received by him by virtue of his office, the officer in whose custody he is shall report the fact to the governor, to the end that he may be removed from office.

§ 931. A vacancy in the office is filled as prescribed by section 237. Vacancies.

The Revised Statutes (1 R. S., 696, §§ 135 to 142) contain provisions for designating one of the coroners to serve as sheriff in case of a vacancy in the offices of both sheriff and undersheriff. But by the act of 1848 (ch. 4), the power of appointment to fill a vacancy was vested in the governor. See § 237, *ante*, p. 208.

§ 932. Services on behalf of the people of the state, required by law from a sheriff, and not otherwise provided for, shall be audited by the comptroller and paid for out of the treasury. Fees for service of state.

§ 933. Other provisions respecting sheriffs and coroners are contained in the CODE OF CIVIL PROCEDURE and the CODE OF CRIMINAL PROCEDURE. Reference to Codes of Procedure.

ARTICLE V.

THE SURROGATE.

From R. S., 699, §§ 144, 145.

Surrogate to give bond.

§ 934. Every surrogate, and every other officer authorized to act as surrogate, shall, within twenty days after receiving notice of his election or appointment, and before entering on office, execute to the people of this state, with two or more sureties, being freeholders, a joint and several bond, conditioned for the faithful performance of his duty, and for the application and payment of all moneys and effects that may come into the hands of such surrogate in the execution of his office. The bond of the surrogate of the city and county of New York, and of the county of Erie, shall be in the penalty of ten thousand dollars; of every other surrogate five thousand dollars.

Justification of sureties; filing of bond.

§ 935. The county clerk of the county is the judge of the sufficiency of the sureties; and if he is satisfied, by the oath of the sureties or otherwise, that they are sufficient, he shall indorse on the bond a certificate of his approval, and file the same in his office.

Reference to Code of Civil Procedure.

§ 936. Other provisions respecting the surrogate are contained in the CODE OF CIVIL PROCEDURE.

CHAPTER III.

COUNTY CHARGES.

From 1 R. S., 712, §§ 10, 3, 4, 5, 6, 7, 8, 9, 11. Ib., 682, § 86.

§ 937. Accounts for county charges, of every description, must be presented to the board of supervisors for audit in the mode prescribed by section 898. County charges to be audited.

§ 938. The following are county charges: Examination of county charges.

1. Charges incurred against the county by virtue of any provision of this title;

2. The compensation of the district attorney, and all expenses necessarily incurred by him in criminal cases arising within the county;

3. The accounts of the criers of the courts within the county for attendance in criminal cases;

4. The compensation of the sheriff for commitment and discharge of his prisoners on criminal process within the county; for summoning constables to attend courts; for attending the drawing

of grand juries, and the sums paid by the sheriff to the county clerk for drawing grand juries;

5. Reasonable compensation to the sheriff and county clerk, and to clerks of criminal courts, for making the returns required by law for statistics respecting convictions and convicts;

6. The compensation allowed by law to constables for attending courts of record, and reasonable compensation to constables and other officers for executing process on persons charged with criminal offenses; for services and expenses in conveying criminals to jail; for the service of subpœnas issued by district attorneys, and for other services in relation to criminal proceedings for which no specific compensation is prescribed by law;

7. The expenses necessarily incurred in the support of persons charged with or convicted of crimes and committed therefor to the several jails of the county;

8. The sums required by laws to be paid to prosecutors and witnesses in criminal cases;

9. The accounts of the coroners of the county for such services as are not chargeable to the persons employing them;

10. The moneys necessarily expended by any county officer in executing the duties of his office,

in cases in which no specific compensation for such services is provided by law;

11. The accounts of the county clerks for services and expenses incurred under article III of this chapter;

12. The accounts and expenses of the commissioners of excise allowed by chapter XI of title IV of part III of this Code;

13. All charges and accounts for services rendered by any justice of the peace under the laws for the relief and settlement of the poor of such county, and for their services in the examination of felons, not otherwise provided for by law;

14. The sums necessarily expended in each county in the support of county poor-houses and of indigent persons whose support is chargeable to the county;

15. The contingent expenses necessarily incurred for the use and benefit of a county;

16. Every other sum directed by law to be raised for any county purpose under the direction of a board of supervisors, or declared to be a county charge;

§ 939. The salary of the county judge and of the surrogate shall be paid by the county, and at the close of each quarter. Salary of county judge.

Surrogate's salary, how fixed.

§ 940. Except where otherwise specially provided, the salary of the surrogate is to be fixed by the board of supervisors, and shall not be increased or diminished during his continuance in office.

Compensation of special county judge and special surrogate.

§ 941. The compensation of the special county judge and of the special surrogate, for their respective services, shall be fixed by the board of supervisors.

Fees of office.

§ 942. The officers mentioned in the preceding section shall in no case perform any official services unless upon prepayment of the fees required for such services by the law in force on the thirty-first day of December, 1846, and upon such payment it is the duty of such officer to perform the services required. They shall pay over all sums so received, after deducting their salaries, to the treasurer of the county, on the first Monday of May and November of each year; and also render an annual account, giving each item of fees received, verified by their affidavit, to the board of supervisors at their annual meeting.

Fees of office.

§ 943. The fees of office which any public officer is required to keep an account of, or pay over to the county or state treasurer, include all fees which such officer is entitled to receive for any act or duty done by him in his official capacity, whether such act or duty pertains to his office or the business thereof or not.

§ 944. The moneys necessary to defray the county charges of each county shall be levied on the taxable property in the several towns in such county, in the manner prescribed in the "*Fiscal Laws.*" And in order to enable the county treasurer to pay such contingent expenses as may become payable from time to time, the board of supervisors shall annually cause such sum to be raised in advance in their county, as they deem necessary for the purpose. **County charges; how raised; contingent fund.**

CHAPTER V.

DIVISION OR ALTERATION OF BOUNDS OF COUNTIES.

From 1 R. S., 674, §§ 5 to 7.

§ 945. When a county is divided, or the boundary is altered, real property belonging to it becomes the property of the county within whose limits it lies after the change. **Effect on its real property.**

§ 946. The personal property and debts of such county shall be apportioned between the counties interested, by the supervisors and county treasurers thereof, as to a majority of them seems just; and the debts shall be charged on each county according to the apportionment. **Personal property and debts.**

TITLE III.

THE GOVERNMENT OF CITIES.

CHAPTER I.

CITIES AS BODIES CORPORATE.

General powers. § 947. Every city is a body politic and corporate, with the general powers of corporations, and the powers specified or necessarily implied in this title or in special laws, and no others.

Distribution of powers. § 948. A city has no judicial power; its only political power is legislative and executive. Its legislative power is vested in a common council; its executive power in a mayor and his subordinate officers

CHAPTER II.

CITY OFFICERS.

§ 949. Every city shall be divided into wards, the number and boundaries of which shall be fixed by the common council thereof within the year next after each census of this state, taken under the authority of the state or of the United States. They shall consist of contiguous territory, and shall be as nearly equal in population as in the judgment of the common council may be practicable. But the ordinance which establishes or alters the wards shall not take effect till the close of the next session of the legislature thereafter. Wards.

§ 950. The legislative power of each city shall be vested in a board of aldermen and a board of councilmen, who, together, shall form the common council thereof. Common council.

§ 951. The term of office of the mayor shall be three years; of the aldermen, two years; of the councilmen, one year. But the aldermen first Terms of office.

elected, after a new arrangement of the boards, shall, at their first meeting, divide themselves by lot into two classes, equal in number if the whole number can be equally divided; and if not, then the second class shall have one more than the first. The first class shall go out of office at the end of the first year.

Election of aldermen.

§ 952. One alderman shall be elected for the first and second wards; another for the third and fourth, and so on, one for every two wards, if the whole number of wards can be equally divided; and if not, then for the last ward there shall be one alderman. One councilman shall be elected for each ward.

Time of city election.

§ 953. The elections for such municipal officers as may be elective shall take place on the first Tuesday of December in each year.

Powers of common council.

§ 954. The common council shall have power:

1. To establish executive departments, and other offices subordinate to the mayor, and prescribe their respective duties:

2. To manage the finances and property of the city;

3. To regulate the streets, wharves, piers and slips in the city, and the use thereof;

4. To establish or authorize slaughter-houses and markets, and regulate the same;

5. To provide for lighting, watering and cleaning the city, and protecting it against fire;

6. To license and regulate hacks, cabs and carts, omnibuses, railway cars and all other vehicles; butchers, porters, pawnbrokers, peddlers, showmen, and junk shop keepers, theaters, and all other places of public amusement;

7. To regulate the keeping and use of animals, and the keeping and use of gunpowder and other dangerous substances;

8. To suppress gaming, gambling-houses and other disorderly houses, nuisances of every description, and all kinds of vice and immorality;

9. To prohibit the burial of the dead within the city, except at such places and in such manner as the common council may determine;

10. To establish and regulate a police department, except within the limits of the Metropolitan police district;

11. To establish and regulate a fire department;

12. To impose penalties for the violation of the city ordinances; but no single penalty can exceed a fine of fifty dollars or imprisonment for thirty days, or both. The common council may, however, require any land or building to be cleansed, at the expense of the owner or occupant, and upon his default may do the work and assess the expense upon the land or building;

13. To pass all ordinances which may be necessary or proper for carrying into effect the foregoing powers.

Annual report.

§ 955. The common council shall, once a year, and at least twenty but not more than thirty days before the annual city election, publish, in at least one newspaper printed and distributed in the city, a detailed statement of the receipts and expenditures of the city for the year ending on the first day of November last preceding.

Powers of mayor.

§ 956. The mayor shall have power:

1. To nominate, and, with the consent of the board of aldermen, appoint all officers of the city; but the common council may, by ordinance, vest the appointment of inferior officers in the heads of the executive departments, or any of them;

2. To suspend, and, with the consent of the board of aldermen, remove any of the officers of the city, stating in the suspension or removal the cause thereof;

3. To cause the ordinances of the city to be executed, and to supervise the discharge of official duty by all subordinate officers;

4. To communicate to the common council at the beginning of every session, and oftener if he deems it expedient, a statement of the affairs of

the city, with such recommendations as he may think proper

§ 957. Whenever there shall be a vacancy in the office of mayor, the presiding officer of the board of aldermen shall perform the duties of the office until the commencement of the year next after the first city election which shall take place subsequent to the vacancy. Vacancy in office of mayor.

§ 958. Nothing contained in the preceding provisions of this title shall affect any city heretofore incorporated. Existing cities not affected.

CHAPTER III.

ACTIONS AGAINST CITIES.

§ 959. An action to restrain the common council or any executive officer of the city from a violation of official duty to the injury of the property or finances of the city or the increase of pecuniary burdens upon the citizens, to call such body or officer to account for misbehavior in office to the prejudice of the city property or finances, or the increase of pecuniary burdens upon the citizens, may be maintained by any citizen who during the year preceding the commencement of the action shall have paid taxes to the amount of one hundred dollars into the city treasury, or upon real or personal property in the city. Actions to restrain city authorities.

TITLE IV.

GOVERNMENT OF TOWNS.

CHAPTER I.

THE TOWN AS A CORPORATE BODY.

From 1 R. S., 643.

Every town is a body corporate.

§ 960. Every town is a body politic and corporate, and as such has the powers specified or necessarily implied in this title or in special statutes, and no others.

Enumeration of powers.

§ 961. It has power:

1. To sue and be sued in the town name;

2. To purchase and hold lands within its limits and for the use of its inhabitants, subject to the power of the legislature;

3. To make such contracts, and purchase and hold such personal property as necessary to the exercise of its powers;

4. To make such orders for the disposition or use of its property as the interests of its inhabitants require.

§ 962. All acts or proceedings by or against a town, in its corporate capacity, shall be in the name of the town; but a conveyance authorized by subdivision two of the preceding section, made in any manner, for the use of its inhabitants, shall have the same effect as if made to the town by name. Conveyances.

CHAPTER II.

TOWN MEETINGS.

ARTICLE I.

ANNUAL AND SPECIAL TOWN MEETINGS.

§ 963. The board of supervisors of each county shall fix a day, after the thirty-first day of January and before the second day of May, for the annual town meetings of all the towns in the county, and shall not change the day oftener than once in three Time and place of annual town meeting.

years; and the board shall advertise notice of such day and of any such change. The meetings shall be held at a place, within each town, to be fixed from time to time by the electors at such meetings.

1 R. S., 644, §§ 1, 2; Laws of 1859, 290, ch. 107.

General powers of town meeting.

§ 964. The electors of each town have power at their annual town meeting:

1. To direct any action or special proceeding in any controversy in which the town has an interest, and to raise money therefor;

2. To raise money to establish a town-house, under the restrictions prescribed by section 965, and for keeping it in repair and insured;

3. To establish or discontinue pounds;

4. To determine whether there shall be one or two overseers of the poor, one or three commissioners of highways, and how many constables there shall be, not exceeding five, and whether there shall be any pound-masters, and if so, how many; and in the towns in the counties of Suffolk, Kings, Queens and Richmond, how many overseers of highways there shall be;

5. To take measures and give directions for the exercise of their corporate powers;

6. To make such provisions and allow such rewards for the destruction of noxious weeds as

they deem necessary, and to raise money therefor;

7. To establish the compensation of the fence viewers;

8. To make, from time to time, such regulations as they may think proper for the better improving of all lands owned by the town in its corporate capacity, whether commons or otherwise; for maintaining and amending partition or other fences around the same, or any part thereof, and fences for their lands, gardens, orchards, and meadows; for protecting such lands from any trespass, and for directing the time and manner of using the same;

9. To make the like regulations for ascertaining the sufficiency of all fences in the town; for determining the times and manner in which animals shall be permitted to go at large on highways; and for impounding animals;

10. To impose such penalties on persons offending against any regulation established by such town, excepting such as relate to the keeping and maintaining of fences, as they may think proper, not exceeding twelve dollars and fifty cents for each offense;

11. To apply such penalties, when recovered, in such manner as they may think most conducive to the interests of such town;

12. To direct such sum as they deem necessary to be raised for the support of the poor for the ensuing year; and any money necessary to defray any charges that may exist against the overseers of the poor of the town;

13. To do such other acts as are specially authorized by the provisions of this title or any other provisions of law.

1 R. S., 644, §§ 3, 4, 8, 14, 15, 17, 18; 666, § 1.

Erection of a town-house.

§ 965. The money to purchase a site and erect a town-house in the first instance, shall not be voted except after previous notice, posted in at least five of the most public places in the town for at least ten days immediately preceding the meeting; and the amount thereof shall not exceed, in number of dollars, twice the number of the electors of the town; and the board of supervisors may, in their discretion, instead of levying the amount with the other expenses of the town, require the question to be submitted again at the next annual town meeting.

Ib., §§ 13, 14, 16.

Conveyance of site, and erection and control of town-house.

§ 966. Conveyances for sites shall be made to the towns; sites shall be purchased and houses erected by the supervisor, town clerk and the justices of the town, and the houses shall be controlled by the supervisor, town clerk and the justice of the peace residing nearest the same.

Ib., § 15.

§ 967. The electors designated by the supervisors to preside at the first meeting in a new town shall cause to be posted, in four of the most public places in the town, at least fourteen days' previous notice of the meeting. They shall also fix the place for holding the first town meeting in the town or towns from which the new town is taken. If any of them fail to serve as presiding officer, the place of such may be filled by the electors from their own number. First meeting in new towns

1 R. S., 677, § 11.

§ 968. Special town meetings shall be held to supply vacancies in the several cases hereinafter provided. They shall also be held whenever twelve or more persons, eligible to the office of supervisor of the town, by written application signed by them and addressed to the town clerk, require a special town meeting to be called for the purpose of raising moneys for the support of common schools or of the poor when a proposition to that effect was not acted upon at the annual town meeting, or for the purpose of deliberating in regard to the institution or defense of legal proceedings or the raising of monies therefor. No special meeting has power to act on any subject, other than such as are specified in this section. Special town meetings.

Ib., § 18.

§ 969. No previous notice need be given of the annual town meetings; but the town clerk shall, Notice of meetings.

at least eight days before any special town meeting, cause notice, specifying the time, place and purposes thereof, under his hand, to be posted at four or more of the most public places in the town.

1 R. S., 677, § 19.

Directions and regulations to remain in force till repealed.

§ 970. Every direction given or regulation made by any town meeting shall remain in force until altered or repealed at a subsequent meeting.

Ib., § 20.

Service of process.

§ 971. No civil process shall be served in the town on any elector entitled to vote at any town meeting, on any day during which such meeting is held.

Ib., § 2.

ARTICLE II.

THE CONDUCT OF TOWN MEETING.

From 1 R. S., 649, §§ 22 to 30.

Presiding officer and clerk.

§ 972. It is the duty of the justices of the peace of the town to attend every town meeting and preside, except in the case provided for by section 967. In their absence the electors shall choose a presiding officer from their own number.

§ 973. The presiding officers have the same power to preserve order, to enforce obedience and commit for disorderly conduct, as is possessed by the board of inspectors at a general election. Powers of presiding officers.

§ 974. The town clerk is clerk of the meeting. In his absence the electors shall choose a clerk. Clerk.

§ 975. The clerk shall keep full minutes of all proceedings, entering at length all directions and regulations made by the meeting. The minutes shall be subscribed by the clerk and presiding officers, and filed in the town clerk's office within two days after the meeting. Minutes.

§ 976. Town meetings shall be kept open in the daytime only, between sunrise and sunset, and, if necessary, may be held two days successively, but no longer. Time of meetings.

977. All questions upon motions made at town meetings shall be determined by the majority of the electors voting; and the presiding officers shall ascertain and declare the result of each vote. Vote of majority governs.

§ 978. If any person offering to vote on any question in town meeting is challenged as unqualified, the presiding officers shall proceed thereupon in the manner prescribed by the "*Election Laws.*" Challenged votes.

§ 979. No person whose vote has been received after challenge, shall be again challenged at the same meeting. Voter not to be twice challenged.

ARTICLE III.

ELECTION OF TOWN OFFICERS.

Officers to be chosen.

§ 980. There shall be chosen at the annual town meeting in each town, except where otherwise provided by special laws, a supervisor, one justice of the peace, a town clerk, and assessor, a collector, and as many overseers of highways as there are road districts in the town, and also such of the officers mentioned in subdivision 4 of section 964 as are required by the determination of the town pursuant thereto.

1 R. S., 644, §§ 3, 4.

Fence viewers.

§ 981. The assessors and commissioners of highways are by virtue of their offices the fence viewers of their town.

Ib., § 8.

§ 982. Before the electors proceed to elect any town officer, proclamation shall be made of the opening of the poll, and proclamation shall be made of each adjournment, and of the opening and closing of the poll, until the election is ended. Proclamation.

1 R. S., 650, § 1.

§ 983. The supervisor, justices of the peace, town clerk, assessors, collector, overseers of the poor, commissioners of highways and constables shall be chosen by ballot. Certain officers to be chosen by ballot.

Ib., §§ 2, 22.

§ 984. All other town officers shall be chosen either: Other officers, how chosen.

1. By ballot;

2. By ayes and noes; or

3. By the rising or dividing of the electors, as the meeting may determine.

§ 985. When the vote is by ballot the following rules shall be observed: Vote by ballot.

1. All the officers voted for shall be named in one ballot, which shall contain their names and the offices to which they are intended to be chosen;

2. The ballots shall be delivered to the presiding officers, so folded as to conceal the contents;

3. The clerk shall keep a poll list and enter thereon the name of each person whose vote is received;

4. The presiding officers shall deposit the ballots in a box, to be constructed, kept and disposed of in the manner prescribed in the "*Election Laws;*"

5. The presiding officers are the inspectors to canvass the result of the election;

6. The canvass being completed, a statement of the result shall be entered at length by the clerk in the minutes, which shall be publicly read by him to the meeting.

1 R. S., 650, §§ 4, 5, 6, 20.

Illegal voting.

§ 986. Any person who votes in a town in which he does not reside, or offers to vote in more than one town at any annual town meeting, in the same year, is guilty of a misdemeanor.

Ib., § 16.

Reference to "election laws."

§ 987. Other provisions respecting the conduct of elections are contained in the "*Election Laws.*"

Canvass may be adjourned or continued after sunset.

§ 988. At the close of the polls the canvassers may determine whether the canvass of the votes shall then be had or postponed until the next day; if they determine that it be had then, it may be continued after sunset; but it shall be had publicly at the place where the meeting was held.

Ib., § 18.

Notice of the result.

§ 989. The clerk of the meeting, within ten days thereafter, shall transmit to each person elected to any town office, whose name was not entered on the poll list as a voter, a notice of his election. The reading of the result, as required by section 985, shall be deemed notice to those whose names were so entered. Within ten days after any election for justice of the peace, the town clerk shall transmit to the county clerk his certificate of the result thereof.

1 R. S., 650, §§ 21, 28; Ib., 322, § 70.

§ 990. When any one of several persons elected justices of the peace, at an annual meeting, is then already an incumbent of the office, for a term then unexpired, he shall be deemed elected for four years following the first day of January after the election Classification.

1 R. S., 650, § 25.

§ 991. When at any such town meeting, except the first election in a new town, two or more justices are to be elected, any elector not voting for a person already an incumbent may designate on his ballot the person intended for the term of four years following the first day of January thereafter, by the words, or words and figures, "longest term," "four years," or "4 years." In such case the persons having the greatest number of votes, without reference to such designation, are elected; and the person elected and having the greatest number of such designations, is elected for the regular term of four years. Ballots may designate terms.

Ib., §§ 26, 27.

Determination of result.

§ 992. The presiding officers shall determine who has been elected for the regular term of four years, under the two preceding sections, which determination shall be made, entered on the minutes, and announced as a part of the result of the canvass.

1 R. S., 651, § 28.

Justices in new and altered towns.

§ 993. If by the erection or alteration of boundaries of a town there be more than four justices therein, they shall, notwithstanding, hold their offices in such town according to their classes respectively. But on the expiration of the term of office of two or more in the same class, only one shall be elected to fill the vacancy in such class. If by such a change the number of justices in a town is reduced, the vacancy shall be supplied by election.

Ib., 323, §§ 81, 82.

Classification of justices.

§ 994. Whenever two or more justices are elected at the same time, and the assignment of their respective terms of office is not fixed pursuant to the foregoing provisions, it shall be ascertained as follows: The supervisor shall, within six days after the election, give notice in writing, to the justices elected and to the town clerk, of the time and place where he will meet them, to determine, by lot, their classes; which notice shall be served at least six days, and not more than twelve, before the time. The determination shall be in the following manner: The supervisor and town clerk shall deposit in a box ballots numbered respectively one, two, three and four, or otherwise, according to the number of years in the respective classes of the offices to be filled. Each justice elected shall draw a ballot, and shall hold his office for the term designated thereon. If any justice is absent, the supervisor shall draw for him. In case of inability of the supervisor or a vacancy in his office, the town clerk shall give the notice and conduct the drawing. Duplicate certificates of the drawing and its result shall be made by the officers conducting the same, one of which shall be filed with the town clerk and the other with the county clerk, who shall record them in the books in which the canvasses of votes are recorded; and the same shall be conclusive evidence of the respective classes to which the justices belong.

1 R. S., 323, §§ 77 to 80.

§ 995. When only one commissioner of highways is chosen, he possesses all the powers and shall discharge all the duties of commissioners of highways as prescribed by law, and shall hold his office for one year. Whenever three commissioners are chosen they shall be divided by lot by the canvassers, upon the result of the canvass, into three classes, to be numbered one, two and three: the term of office of the first class shall be one year; of the second, two, and of the third, three; Commissioners of highways.

and thereafter one commissioner shall be elected annually, who shall hold his office for three years. A commissioner elected to fill a vacancy shall hold office only for the unexpired term; and if two vacancies are to be filled, the canvassers shall determine their respective terms as above provided. When a town resolves to reduce the number of commissioners, those then in office shall, notwithstanding, continue till the expiration of their respective terms, but no new election or appointment shall be made until after the number has been reduced to the required number by the expiration of terms of office or the happening of vacancies.

1 R. S., 650, § 5.

CHAPTER III.

TOWN OFFICERS.

ARTICLE I.

QUALIFICATIONS, TERMS OF OFFICE AND COMPENSATION.

§ 996. Within ten days after any collector receives notice of the amount of the taxes to be collected by him, and before entering on the duties of office, he shall execute to the town a bond, with one or more sureties, in double that amount, conditioned for the faithful execution of his duties as collector. Collector to give bond.

1 R. S., 654, § 41.

§ 997. Every commissioner of highways shall execute to the town a bond, with two sureties, in the penalty of one thousand dollars, conditioned that he will faithfully discharge his duties as such commissioner, and, within ten days after the expiration of his term of office, render to his successor a true account of all moneys received and paid out by him as such commissioner, and pay the amount justly due to such successor. Commissioner of highways to give bond.

Ib., § 47.

§ 998. Every overseer of the poor shall execute to the town a bond, with one or more sureties, conditioned that he will faithfully discharge the Overseers of poor to give bond.

duties of his office, and will pay, according to law, all moneys that come into his hands as overseer.

Laws of 1855, ch. 269.

Constable to give undertaking. § 999. Every constable shall execute to the town an undertaking, with one or more sureties, jointly and severally agreeing to pay to every person who may be entitled thereto, any sums the constable may become liable to pay on account of any execution which may be delivered to him.

1 R. S., 654, § 43.

Oath of office. § 1000. Every supervisor, town clerk, assessor, overseer of the poor, commissioner of highways, constable, town sealer and collector, shall take the oath of office as required by section 210 of this Code, before a justice of the peace, commissioner of deeds or the town clerk.

Notice of acceptance. § 1001. Every overseer of highways, or pound-master, shall give written notice to the town clerk of his acceptance of the office.

Ib., § 39.

Filing bonds. § 1002. The sureties in any such bond or undertaking of any town officer shall be approved by the supervisor or town clerk by indorsement upon the instrument. Every such instrument, with the approval thereof, except the collector's bond, and every oath and notice required by the foregoing provisions, shall be filed in the office of the town clerk within ten days after the officer giving it has notice of his being chosen, and before he enters on the duties of his office.

From 1 R. S., §§ 34, 37, 39, 41, 43, 47, 48.

Proof of execution of constable's undertaking.

§ 1003. The constable's undertaking shall be executed by the several obligors in the presence of the officer to whom it is presented for approval; and a copy, certified by the town clerk, is presumptive evidence of its execution by them.

Ib., § 44.

Filing and effects of the collector's bond

§ 1004. The collector's bond shall, within the time required for its execution, be delivered to the supervisor, who shall, within six days thereafter, file such bond, with his approbation indorsed thereon, in the office of the county clerk, who shall make an entry thereof, in a book to be provided for the purpose, in the same manner in which judgments are entered of record; and every such bond shall be a lien on all the real property held jointly or severally by the collector or his sureties within the county, at the time of the filing, and shall continue to be such lien till its condition, together with all costs and charges which may accrue by the prosecution thereof, are fully satisfied.

Ib., § 42.

What neglect is deemed a refusal to serve.

§ 1005. The neglect to take and file the oath, or give the notice, bond or undertaking required from any person by the provisions of this article, within the specified time, shall be deemed a refusal to serve.

1 R. S., 654, §§ 38, 40, 46. By making this provision general, it becomes applicable to the offices of commissioners of highways and overseers of the poor.

Penalties for refusal to serve.

§ 1006. If any person elected or appointed supervisor, town clerk, assessor, commissioner of highways, or overseer of the poor, refuses to serve, he is liable to the town in a penalty of fifty dollars.

1 R. S., 654, § 48.

Penalties for refusal to serve.

§ 1007. If any person elected or appointed to the office of overseer of highways, pound-master or town sealer, refuses to serve, he is liable to the town in the penalty of ten dollars.

Ib., § 49.

Quakers excused from serving as assessors.

§ 1008. No Quaker or reputed Quaker shall be liable to a penalty for refusing to serve as assessor, if he makes affirmation before a justice of the peace, within three days after notice of his being chosen, that he has conscientious scruples about executing the duties of the office; and within eight days after making it files it with the town clerk.

Ib., §§ 50, 51.

No fee for taking oath of office, &c.

§ 1009. The officer before whom any oath or affirmation is by this article required to be taken, shall take and certify the same, specifying the date thereof, and without any fee.

Ib., §§ 35, 36, 51.

§ 1010. If any town officer, required by law to take the oath of office, enters upon the duties of his office before having taken it, he is liable to the town in the penalty of fifty dollars. Penalty for serving without having taken oath.

1 R. S., 654, § 52.

§ 1011. Town officers (excepting justices of the peace, commissioners of highways, where there are more than one, and assessors) shall hold their offices for one year, and until their successors are chosen and have qualified. Assessors each hold office three years. Justices of the peace four years. Terms of office

Ib., § 53; Ib., 321, § 68.

§ 1012. The following officers are entitled to compensation at the rate of one dollar and fifty cents a day for each day actually and necessarily devoted by them to the service of the town in the duties of their offices: The supervisor, except when attending the board of supervisors, town clerks, commissioners of highways, assessors, inspectors of elections, clerks of the polls and overseers of the poor. No town officer shall be allowed any per diem compensation for his services unless expressly provided by law. Certain officers paid by the day.

Laws of 1857, ch. 615; 1 R. S., 663, § 50.

§ 1013. When a town has but one commissioner of highways he is entitled to two dollars a day. Commissioner of highways.

Laws of 1857, ch. 615.

Pound-masters' fees.

§ 1014. The pound-masters shall be allowed the following fees for their services: For taking into the pound and discharging therefrom every horse, ass or mule, and all neat cattle, twelve and a half cents each; for every sheep or lamb, three cents; and for every hog, six cents.

1 R. S., 664, § 55.

ARTICLE II.

VACANCIES.

Resignations.

§ 1015. Any three justices of the peace may, for sufficient cause shown to them accept the resignation of any officer of their town. In such case they shall forthwith give notice thereof to the town clerk.

1 R. S., 657, § 56.

Vacancy in office of supervisor or overseer of poor.

§ 1016. Whenever the office of supervisor or of overseer of the poor becomes vacant, the town clerk shall, within eight days after the happening of such vacancy, call a special town meeting to supply it, unless the next annual meeting will occur within sixty days.

Modified from Ib., § 57.

Vacancies in other offices.

§ 1017. Vacancies in other offices shall be filled as follows, by warrant in writing filed in the office of the town clerk, who shall give notice to the person appointed:

1. A vacancy in the office of justice of the peace shall be filled by the supervisor, town clerk and remaining justices of the peace, or by a majority of them. Before the person appointed enters upon office, a certified copy of the warrant of his appointment must be filed in the office of the county clerk.[1]

2. Vacancies in the offices of commissioner of highways and of assessors shall be filled until the next annual meeting by any three justices of the peace, or any two justices and the supervisor;[2]

3. A vacancy in the office of overseer of highways shall be filled by the commissioners of highways of the town;[3]

4. Vacancies in the office of collector shall be filled in the mode prescribed in the "*Fiscal Laws;*"

5. In case of a failure at any annual town meeting to elect any town officer, and in case of a failure to fill, pursuant to section 1016, any vacancy in an office mentioned in that section, within fifteen days after such vacancy happens, and in case of all other vacancies in town offices except those in this section provided for, such vacancy shall be filled by any three justices of the peace; and if there are less than three justices residing in the town, one or two justices from any adjoining town may be associated with the justice or justices of such town to make up the number.[4]

[1] From Laws of 1859, 1092.
[2] From 1 R. S., 643, § 6.
[3] 1 R. S., 1032, §§ 14, 15.
[4] 1 R. S., 657, §§ 54, 58, 59, 60.

ARTICLE III.

THE SUPERVISOR.

Duties of supervisor.

§ 1018. It is the duty of the supervisor:

1. To receive and pay all monies raised for defraying the town charges, except those raised for highways, common schools and the poor;

2. To prosecute for all penalties, not exceeding fifty dollars, given by law to the town or for its use, and for which no other officer is specially directed to prosecute;

3. To keep a true account of the receipt and expenditure of all monies which come into his hands by virtue of his office, in a book to be provided for that purpose at the expense of the town, and to be delivered to his successor;

4. On the Tuesday preceding the annual town meeting, to account, with the justices of the peace and the town clerk, for the disbursement of all moneys received by him;

5. To attend the annual meeting of the board of supervisors of the county, and every adjourned or special meeting thereof of which he has notice;

6. To lay before the board of supervisors, at their next meeting, all accounts against the town which are presented to him;

7. To lay before the board of supervisors such copies of entries, concerning monies voted to be raised in his town, as are delivered to him by the town clerk;

8. Within sixty days after being required so to do by the state engineer and surveyor, to cause a survey to be made of the bounds of his town and to transmit to him by mail, or otherwise, a map and description thereof, under penalty of fifty dollars (to be recovered as provided in section 129) for a neglect so to do.

1 R. S., 658, §§ 1, 4, 6, 10.

§ 1019. At every accounting mentioned in subdivision 4 of the preceding section, the justices and town clerk shall enter a certificate in the supervisor's book of accounts, showing the state of his accounts at that date. **Auditing supervisor's accounts**

Ib., § 5.

§ 1020. The expense of the surveys and maps mentioned in subdivision 8 of section 1018, shall be apportioned by the board of supervisors upon, and defrayed by, the several towns whose bounds either wholly or in part are described thereby. **Expense of surveys.**

Ib., § 9.

ARTICLE IV.

THE TOWN CLERK.

Duties of town clerk.

§ 1021. It is the duty of the town clerk:

1. To take charge of all the records, books and papers of the town, and file all papers required to be filed in his office;

2. To transcribe at length, in the records of the town, the minutes of every town meeting;

3. To deliver to the supervisor, before each annual meeting of the board of supervisors, certified copies of all entries in the town records of votes for raising money, made since the last meeting of the board;

4. Immediately after the qualifying of any constable, to return his name to the county clerk;

5. To perform such other duties as are imposed upon him by any provision of law.

1 R. S., 659, §§ 11, 14.

Neglect to make return.

§ 1022. Any town clerk who willfully neglects to make any return required by subdivision 4 of the preceding section, is guilty of a misdemeanor, punishable by fine not exceeding ten dollars.

Ib., § 15.

ARTICLE V.

THE FENCE VIEWERS.

In this article we have embraced only those provisions which relate to the duties and powers of fence viewers. The rules respecting the rights and liabilities of coterminous owners are reserved for that part of the CIVIL CODE which regulates real property.

§ 1023. If dispute arises between the owners of adjoining lands, concerning the portion of fence to be maintained or made by either of them, or the amount which one who fences his open land shall pay to an adjoining owner who had previously fenced his land, such dispute shall be settled by any two of the fence viewers of the town. **Disputes to be settled by fence viewers.**

1 R. S., 661, § 33.

§ 1024. Each party to the dispute shall choose one of the two fence viewers, and if either neglect to choose after eight days' notice, the other party may select both. **Fence viewers, how chosen.**

Ib., § 34.

§ 1025. The two fence viewers shall examine the premises and hear the allegations of the parties. If they disagree they shall select a third to act **Proceedings.**

with them. The decision of any two shall be final upon the parties, and all holding under them.

1 R. S., 661, § 35.

Decision to be filed.

§ 1026. Their decision shall be in writing, describing the fence, and the proportion to be maintained by each, and be forthwith filed in the town clerk's office.

Ib., § 36.

Subpœnas.

§ 1027. Either of the fence viewers has power to issue subpœnas to compel the attendance of witnesses in any such proceedings.

Ib., § 43.

ARTICLE VII.

THE BOARD OF AUDITORS.

The board.

§ 1028. The supervisor, town clerk and justices of the peace, or any two of the justices of the peace, constitute a board of town auditors for the purpose of auditing and allowing the accounts of all charges and claims payable by their town.

1 R. S., 663, § 46.

Time and place of meeting.

§ 1029. They shall meet annually, at the place of holding the last town meeting, on the Thursday next preceding the annual meeting of the board of supervisors of the county.

Ib., § 47.

§ 1030. No accounts shall be audited, unless made out and verified in the mode prescribed by section 898, for accounts presented to the board of supervisors. Form and verification of account.

1 R. S., 680, § 26.

§ 1031. The board of town auditors shall make duplicate certificates, to be signed by a majority of them, specifying the name of the claimant, the nature of the demand and the amount allowed; one of the certificates shall be filed in the town clerk's office, for the inspection of any inhabitants of the town, and the other shall be delivered to the supervisor to be by him laid before the board of supervisors at their annual meeting. Certificates of allowance.

Ib., § 48.

§ 1032. The board of town auditors shall annually deliver to the clerk of the board of supervisors a brief abstract of the names of all persons who have presented to them accounts to be audited, the amounts claimed by each and the amounts finally audited by them respectively. Annual statement.

Ib., 683, § 42.

ARTICLE VII.

PROVISIONS RELATING TO SEVERAL TOWN OFFICERS.

§ 1033. Whenever the right of any town officer to his office expires, the books and papers belong- Delivery of books and papers to successor.

ing to the office shall, upon his oath, or, in case of his death, upon the oath of his executors or administrators, be delivered on demand to his successor. The oath may be administered by the successor. Any person violating this section is liable to the town in a penalty of two hundred and fifty dollars.

1 R. S., 667, §§ 9 to 11.

Demand. § 1034. It is the duty of each officer to make such demand on his predecessor or his executors or administrators, and to enforce the same by proceedings under article VII of chapter VI of title I of part III of this Code, entitled "*Proceedings to compel the delivery of books and papers by public officers.*"

Ib.

Funds. § 1035. It is the duty of every supervisor, commissioner of highways and overseer of the poor, going out of office, to pay over to his successor the balance of monies remaining in his hands, as ascertained by the board of town auditors.

Ib.

Posting notice. § 1036. If in any town there is no town-house at a time when any notice is by law required to be posted on the town-house door, it shall be posted on the outer door of the building in which the town meetings then are usually held; or in which the last previous town meeting was held.

CHAPTER IV.

STRAYS.

From 1 R. S., 660, §§ 17 to 29.

§ 1037. Whenever any person has upon his inclosed land any strayed horse at any time, or between the first day of November and the first day of April thereafter, any strayed neat cattle or sheep, he shall, within ten days after the coming of such stray thereon, give written notice of his name and place of abode, and the age, color and marks, natural and artificial, of each stray, as near as may be, to the clerk of the town where the lands lie. If he neglects to do so within the time required, he shall be precluded from all the benefits of this chapter and from all claim to compensation for keeping such strays. Notice of strays.

§ 1038. The town clerk shall immediately enter each notice at large in a book to be provided by him for that purpose; for which entry he shall Entry of notice.

receive six cents each for all neat cattle and horses, and three cents for each sheep, to be paid by the person delivering the notice.

Book to be open to inspection and search.

§ 1039. The book for such entries shall always be kept open to inspection, and no fee shall be taken by the clerk for any search therein.

Charges for keeping strays.

§ 1040. The person delivering the notice shall be entitled to receive therefor, from the owner, nine cents each for all neat cattle and horses, and three cents for each sheep described, together with fees paid or due to the clerk, and all reasonable charges for keeping the strays; such charges being first ascertained by two of the fence viewers of the town, to be selected by him in case he and the owner of the strays cannot otherwise agree. He has a lien on the strays therefor.

Fence viewer's fees.

§ 1041. Each fence viewer is entitled to receive from the owner of the strays six cents for every mile he is obliged to travel from his house to the place where such strays are kept, and twenty-five cents for a certificate of the charges as ascertained by him.

Proceedings if strays are not redeemed.

§ 1042. Every person who gives such notice and keeps any stray described, shall, if it be not sooner redeemed, between the first and twentieth days of May, give notice to one of the fence viewers, who shall fix and certify the reasonable charges of keeping. The fence viewer shall be paid, by the person applying for the certificate, the fees prescribed by the preceding section.

§ 1043. If no owner claims such stray, and pays the sums charged, on or before the first day of May next after the making of the entry, the stray may be sold by public auction to the highest bidder. Sale.

§ 1044. The person selling shall give at least twenty days' previous notice of the time and place of sale, by posting notice thereof at three of the most public places in the town where the strays have been kept. Notice of sale.

§ 1045. Out of the proceeds of sale he shall retain the sums charged by him under this article, and the same charges for sale as are allowed on sales under executions issued out of justices' courts. He shall pay the residue on demand, to the owner of the strays. Proceeds.

§ 1046. If the owner does not appear and demand the same within one year, he shall be forever precluded from recovering the same, and it shall be paid to the supervisor for the use of the town; and his receipt is evidence thereof. Proceeds.

§ 1047. If the person who sold such strays shall not, within thirty days after the expiration of the year, pay such balance to the supervisor of the town, he is liable to the town in a penalty of double Penalty.

the sum so remaining in his hands, together with the amount of such sum.

Cities.

§ 1048. This chapter applies to cities as well as to towns.

CHAPTER V.

LEGAL PROCEEDINGS BY AND AGAINST TOWNS.

From 1 R. S., 665, §§ 3, 6, 7.

Process to be served on supervisor; his duty.

§ 1049. In all legal proceedings against towns by name, the first process and all other proceedings requiring to be served, shall be served on the supervisor of the town; and whenever any such proceeding is commenced it is the duty of the supervisor to attend to the defense thereof, and to lay before the first town meeting a full statement thereof, for their direction in regard to its defense.

Recoveries in actions for penalties for trespass.

§ 1050. If on the trial of any action for a penalty imposed for any trespass committed on the lands of a town it appears that the actual amount of injury to such lands exceeded the sum of twelve dollars and fifty cents, then the amount of the actual damage, with costs, shall be recovered, instead of the penalty for the same trespass imposed by the town meeting; and such recovery shall be a bar to every other suit for the same trespass.

§ 1051. Whenever, by the judicial determination of any controversy in relation to lands the common property of a town, or of any proceeding for the partition thereof, the rights of any town are settled, the court in which such proceedings are had may partition such lands according to the rights so settled. Partition in certain cases.

CHAPTER VI.

TOWN CHARGES.

From 1 R. S., 666.

§ 1052. The following are town charges: Town charges enumerated

1. The compensation of town officers for services rendered for their respective towns;

2. The contingent expenses necessarily incurred for the use of the town;

3. Monies duly authorized to be raised by the vote of the town meeting;

4. Monies directed by law to be raised for any town purpose.

§ 1053. Accounts for the compensation of town officers and the contingent expenses of towns (except for monies received and disbursed, which are to be settled by the board of town auditors) shall Auditing accounts.

be presented to the board of supervisors of the county.

Collection of town charges.

§ 1054. The monies necessary to defray the town charges shall be levied on the taxable property in the town in the manner prescribed in the "*Fiscal Laws.*"

CHAPTER VII.

DIVISION OR ALTERATION OF BOUNDS OF TOWNS.

From 1 R. S., 643, §§ 4 to 10.

Meeting of officers to dispose of real property.

§ 1055. When a town owning real property is divided, or its boundaries altered, the supervisors and overseers of the poor of the several towns shall meet, as soon as may be after the first town meetings subsequently held in such towns, and make such agreement concerning the disposition of such property (excepting all cemeteries and all gospel and school lots) and the apportionment of the proceeds, as they think equitable, and take all measures and execute all conveyances which may be necessary to carry such agreement into effect.

Meeting of officers to dispose of real property.

§ 1056. If no such agreement is made within six months after the change, the supervisor and overseers of the poor of each town in which any portion of the real property lies after the change shall, as soon as may be, sell and convey such portion; and the proceeds shall be apportioned between the several towns interested, by the supervisors and overseers of the poor of all the towns, according to the amount of taxable property in the town divided or altered, as the same existed immediately before the change, to be ascertained by the last assessment list thereof.

§ 1057. When a town is divided or its boundaries altered, the debts and all personal property belonging to the town, including monies in the hands of the town officers, shall be apportioned by the officers, and in the mode, prescribed by section 1056; and the debts shall be charged on such town according to such apportionment. Personal property and debts to be apportioned.

§ 1058. The meetings of the supervisors and overseers of two or more towns, required by this chapter, may be called by either supervisor, by at least three days' written notice of the time and place thereof to all the officers. Meeting of officers to apportion.

TITLE V.

THE GOVERNMENT OF VILLAGES.

CHAPTER I.

INCORPORATION OF VILLAGES.

Requisite population to form a village.

§ 1059. Any part of a town or towns, not included within a city or village and containing a resident population of not less than three hundred, or if more than one square mile in extent, at the rate of three hundred for every square mile, may be incorporated as a village on the application of the residents thereof.

1 R. S., 1244, § 1. All references to the Revised Statutes are to the 4th edition except where otherwise specially indicated.

§ 1060. The applicants for incorporation shall cause a survey and map of the territory to be made by a practical surveyor, showing the course and distances of its bounds and the quantity of land embraced, and verified by the surveyor's oath. Survey and map.

1 R. S., 1244, § 2.

§ 1061. They shall also cause an accurate census of the residents to be taken on a day not more than ten weeks previous to the time of presenting the application, which shall exhibit the name of every head of a family residing within the territory on that day, and the number of persons belonging to such family, and shall be verified by the oath of the person taking it. Census.

Ib., § 3.

§ 1062. The survey, map and census, duly verified, shall be kept within the territory, at the residence or place of business of some resident, open to public examination for five weeks from the first giving of the following notice. Public inspection of survey and census.

Ib., § 4.

§ 1063. The applicants shall give notice that they will, on a day specified, apply to the court of sessions of the county (or if the territory lies in more than one county, to that court in one of the counties to be named in the notice) for an order incorporating the territory as a village. The notice shall state the proposed name, the bounds of the territory by course and distance, and by speci- Notice of application.

fying the town where it lies, and shall state the place where the map, survey and census may be seen.

1 R. S., 1244, § 5.

Mode of notice.

§ 1064. For six successive weeks previous to the day specified in the application, the notice shall be published at least once a week in a newspaper printed in such territory, or if there is no such paper, posted in at least ten of the most public places therein.

Ib., § 6.

Requisites of application.

§ 1065. At the time specified in the notice, or as soon thereafter as the applicants can be heard, they shall present their petition. It shall be subscribed by them, and state the bounds by course and distance, the quantity of land embraced and the population of the territory. The survey, map and census, verified, and an affidavit that they were kept open to public inspection, and a copy of the notice, with an affidavit of publishing or posting the same, as hereinbefore respectively prescribed, shall be annexed to the petition.

Ib., § 7.

The hearing.

§ 1066. The court shall hear all the parties interested, and may adjourn the hearing from time to time. It may direct a resurvey or a new census, or both, and may appoint persons to conduct the same. It may refer any question in respect to the application to three disinterested commissioners to examine and report. The commissioners shall take the oath of office before proceeding.

1 R. S., 1244, § 8.

§ 1067. If the court is satisfied that a correct survey and census have been taken, and the foregoing requirements of this chapter have been complied with, and the census shows the requisite population; and that the interests of the inhabitants will be promoted by the incorporation, and that the lands to be embraced ought justly to be included, it shall make an order setting forth the bounds by course and distance, as in the petition, or modified therefrom, as justice may require, and declaring that if the electors assent, as hereinafter provided, the territory embraced shall be a village by the name specified, or such other name as to the court seems proper. The order shall name three inspectors of elections of the towns in which the village lies to perform the duties hereinafter required. The order.

Ib., § 9.

§ 1068. The inspectors shall forthwith call a meeting of the electors of the territory, to be held therein, to determine whether it shall become a village. The notice shall specify the time, place and purpose of the meeting, and that the polls will be open from ten o'clock in the forenoon till four o'clock in the afternoon; and shall for three weeks previous to the meeting be published or Notice of submission of question to vote.

posted in the same manner as prescribed by section 1064.

1 R. S., 1244, §§ 10, 11.

Conduct of meeting.

§ 1069. The inspectors shall preside at the meeting, and open and close the polls at the hours mentioned in the preceding section. Electors qualified as electors of their town, and residing within the bounds specified in the order are entitled to vote. The ballots shall have thereon the word "*Yes*," or the word "*No*." The provisions of law regulating the election of town officers apply to such meeting so far as they are applicable.

Ib., §§ 12, 13.

Certificate of result.

§ 1070. Within fourteen days after the meeting, the inspectors shall cause to be submitted to the county judge of the county in which the application was made, a certificate of having held the meeting, and of the canvass, showing the number of ballots having "*Yes*" and the number having "*No*," together with a copy of the notice of the meeting and affidavit of publishing or posting it as required.

Ib., § 14.

Order of certificate of county judge.

§ 1071. If the proceedings in the calling, or the conduct, of the meeting, or in making the certificate of result are illegal, the county judge shall order another meeting, which shall be notified, conducted, and the result certified, as hereinbefore prescribed. His order shall be filed in the county clerk's office. If the proceedings are legal he shall certify thereto; and the papers and certificate shall be filed and recorded in the county clerk's office, and are presumptive evidence of the matters therein contained.

1 R. S., 1244, §§ 14, 16.

§ 1072. If a majority of ballots have the word "*Yes*," the inhabitants of the territory shall, from the time of such filing, be a body politic and corporate by the name specified in the order; and a meeting for the election of officers shall forthwith be called by the inspectors, as provided in the next chapter. If otherwise, no further proceedings shall be had in respect to the application Incorporation.

Ib., § 17.

§ 1073. When a written application, signed by at least one-fourth as many electors of the village as voted for village officers at the preceding election, is made to the trustees to call a meeting of the electors to determine whether the village shall remain a corporate body, the trustees shall call such meeting, and conduct it and certify the result as near as may be, in the mode provided in the next chapter for meetings for election of officers. The polls shall be kept open from ten o'clock in the forenoon till four o'clock in the afternoon. Every elector may vote by a ballot having thereon the word "*Yes*" or the word "*No.*" If a majority have the word "*No,*" the village Dissolving incorporation.

shall, at the expiration of six months from the time of the meeting, cease as a corporate body, and within that period the trustees shall call a meeting at which the electors may direct the disposition of the property, if any remain after discharging the village liabilities, or, if there is a deficiency, may raise by tax any sum necessary to discharge such liabilities. At the expiration of that period all books and papers of the village shall be deposited with the clerk of a town in which the village or a part of it was; and the supervisor of the town or supervisors of the towns in which the village was, become trustees of its remaining property.

1 R. S., 1244, §§ 95, 96.

Certain villages may adopt provisions of this title.

§ 1074. The electors of any village incorporated before the 7th day of December, 1847, may, at any annual meeting for election of officers, declare by resolution that any specified sections of this title shall apply to such village, and twenty days after the passage of such resolution the sections specified shall take effect respecting such village, and operate to repeal, as to such village, all laws inconsistent with such sections. Every such resolution shall, within ten days, be published by the trustees in a newspaper printed in the village, or, if there is none, then in the one printed nearest thereto.

Ib., §§ 97, 98.

CHAPTER II.

VILLAGE OFFICERS.

ARTICLE I.

ELECTION AND QUALIFICATION OF OFFICERS.

§ 1075. The officers of a village are five trustees, one of whom is president, three assessors, a collector, a treasurer, a clerk, three street commissioners when the village is not a separate road district, such number of fire-wardens, not exceeding five, as the trustees from time to time fix by ordinance, and a pound-master. Each holds office for one year, beginning on the third Tuesday of March after the election; except that the officers first elected on the formation of a village hold office only till the third Tuesday of March following their election. Officers enumerated

1 R. S., 1244, §§ 23, 25.

§ 1076. The election of officers shall be held on the first Tuesday of March in each year, unless a town meeting of the town is held on that day, in Time of elections.

which case the village meeting shall be upon the Wednesday following the first Tuesday.

1 R. S., 1244, Ib. § 42.

Conduct of elections.

§ 1077. The trustees shall give three weeks' previous notice of every election, specifying the time of opening and closing the polls. The notice shall, for three successive weeks, be published at least once in each week in a newspaper printed in the village, or if there is none, then posted in at least ten of the most public places therein. The polls shall be open at least three hours, between ten o'clock in the forenoon and four o'clock in the afternoon. The trustees shall preside at the meeting and certify the result of the election, which certificate shall be recorded in the village records. The provisions of law relative to the conduct of elections of town officers, the announcement of the result, and the notice to the officers chosen, apply to the election of village officers so far as the same are applicable.

Ib., §§ 17 to 22.

Tie vote to be determined by lot.

§ 1078. If two or more have the greatest and an equal number of votes for one office, the trustees shall determine by lot which shall be deemed elected, and set forth that fact in their certificate.

Ib., § 21.

Provisions peculiar to the first election.

§ 1079. At the first election for officers in a new village, the inspectors, mentioned in the preceding chapter, shall perform the duties which, by the two preceding sections, are thereafter devolved upon the trustees and clerk.

1 R. S., 1244, §§ 17 to 20.

§ 1080. Whenever the offices of more than two of the trustees are vacated, the remaining trustee or trustees shall call a village meeting to fill, for the unexpired term, such vacancies and any other existing vacancies specified in the notice of the meeting. If there is only one trustee, one or more of the assessors shall be associated with him to preside. Vacancies.

Ib., § 27.

§ 1081. Resignations shall not take effect until filed, in writing, with the clerk of the village. Resignations.

Ib., § 25; last clause.

§ 1082. Every officer shall take, before any justice of the peace of the county, and file with the clerk of the village, the oath of office, as required in section 210 of this Code, within ten days after notice of his being chosen; and a neglect to do so vacates the office. Oath of office.

Ib., § 26; Laws of 1857, ch. 552.

§ 1083. The collector, before he receives any warrant to collect, and the treasurer, before he enters on office, shall respectively execute to the village a bond, in an amount to be fixed by the trustees, with sufficient sureties, approved by the trustees by an indorsement thereon, conditioned Certain officers to give security.

for the faithful performance of his official duties. A neglect so to do, within three days after notice from the president to do so, vacates the office.

1 R. S., 1244, §§ 66, 69.

ARTICLE II.

THE BOARD OF TRUSTEES.

Duties of the board.

§ 1084. It is the duty of the trustees:

1. To hold all their meetings open to the public;

2. To appoint, from time to time, one of their number president of the village, who shall preside at the meetings of the trustees; and to appoint also, one to preside at any meeting when he shall be absent;

3. To appoint a person to keep a poll list at any meeting of the village, when a poll list is required and the clerk shall not attend;

4. To fill a vacancy in any village office, except that of trustee, by appointment for the unexpired term;

5. To provide for the custody and preservation of the property and records of the village;

6. To see that the village officers perform their duties faithfully, and to take measures to punish their neglect of duty;

7. To call special meetings of the electors whenever they judge the interests of the village require it;

8. To give notice, in the manner prescribed in this title, of every annual and special meeting, and to preside thereat;

9. To present to every annual meeting a detailed statement for the preceding year, signed by them, showing when and from what sources all monies paid into the treasury were derived, and when, to whom and for what purpose all monies paid from the treasury were paid; how much of each sum raised for, or directed at the last annual or any subsequent special meeting to be applied to, any specific purpose, has been so applied, and how much remains on hand; what sidewalks have been made or repaired at the expense of the owners, what at expense of the village, and the names of owners, and amounts due from each therefor; which statement shall be filed with the clerk;

10. To present at the same time a statement of the estimated expenses for the ensuing year, specifying each item; which statement shall be filed with the clerk;

11. To carry into effect every resolution of a vil-

lage meeting legally convened, and within the authority of the meeting;

12. To number all claims presented against the village in any year, from one upwards, in the order in which they are presented, and to enter in their proceedings a memorandum of the name of the claimant, the person by whom and the time when it is presented, and the amount;

13. To audit such claims against the village, allowing none which the village are not legally bound to pay, or for which a tax could not be voted; and to certify on each one audited the allowance or disallowance thereof, and the amount, if any, allowed and the charges for which it is allowed; and to draw a warrant on the treasurer for each one allowed. Every warrant shall be indorsed on or annexed to the claim, and contain a reference to the claim by its number, and the name of the claimant and the time when presented, and shall specify the fund out of which it is payable; and no such warrant shall be delivered until a memorandum of such reference and the amount of the warrant is entered in the record of the trustees;

14. Within ten days before the annual meeting to publish, in a newspaper printed in the village, or, if there is none there, to post in two of the most public places in the town, a statement showing the name of every person who, since the last annual meeting (or the incorporation of the village), has

had any claim allowed by them, the amount claimed, the amount allowed, and a brief statement of the nature of the demand;

15. To fix the compensation of the assessors, the collector and the clerk, but not exceeding the compensation allowed to the like town officers; and the compensation of the street commissioner, but not exceeding the compensation of overseers of highways; and the compensation of the treasurer, but not exceeding the compensation of county treasurers, respectively, for the same services;

16. To prescribe the method, subject to the provisions of this title, in which the treasurer and clerk shall keep their accounts, vouchers and records, and to examine the same from time to time to detect errors;

17. To enter or authorize others to enter, in the daytime, any building in which there is a fire-place, stove or stove-pipe, to examine and regulate the same, whenever necessary for security against fire; and to compel all persons to keep their ashes safely;

18. To compel every male resident, of the age of sixteen or upwards, attending a fire, to assist in extinguishing it, when required by any fire-warden, trustee, or any officer of a fire or hook and ladder company;

19. To act as commissioners of highways when their village is a separate road district, except in laying out, altering and discontinuing roads;

20. To make such ordinances, not inconsistent with the laws of this state and the United States, as they deem proper to carry into effect the laws relating to villages; and to regulate fire companies and the management and use of village cemeteries and conveyances of lots therein, and prescribe penalties, not exceeding twenty-five dollars, for each offense against such ordinances. But no penalty shall be prescribed for any act prohibited by statute. No ordinance shall take effect until two days after it has been published in a newspaper printed in the village, or, if there is none, until four days after a printed copy has been posted in two of the most public places in the village, of which publication or posting an affidavit shall be made, and filed with the clerk within six days after it takes place. The clerk's certificate of the publication or posting of any ordinance is evidence thereof;

21. To audit and allow the necessary expenses of incorporating the village, and raise the same by tax in the same manner as if it had been directed to be raised by the village meeting;

22. To perform all other duties required of them by any provisions of law.

1 R. S., 1244, §§ 40, 41, 55, 57, 66, 69, 76, 80, 110.

The amendment of 1852 (ch. 184), respecting the payment of judgments, is properly within the scope of the CODE OF CIVIL PROCEDURE.

§ 1085. The trustees have power: Powers of the board.

1. To prohibit the going at large of animals, under penalty upon the owners, not exceeding five dollars for each animal, and impounding of the animals;

2. To protect the sidewalks, highways and shade trees from injury and incumbrance, and to compel adjoining owners or occupants to keep their sidewalks cleared from snow;

3. To prohibit flying kites, rolling hoops and playing ball in any street;

4. To provide by ordinance for the election of fire-wardens, not exceeding five;

5. To compel occupants of buildings in which fires are kept to keep fire-buckets;

6. To license and regulate hacks, cabs, carts, omnibuses and all other vehicles; butchers, porters, pawnbrokers, showmen and junk-shop keepers and guides; theaters and other places of amusement;

7. To prevent or regulate the discharge of fire-arms and fireworks, and other dangerous substances, and the burning of any material in the streets;

8. To suppress gaming, gambling houses, and other disorderly houses, noises, nuisances of every description and all kinds of vice and immorality;

9. To prohibit or regulate bathing and swimming within the village;

10. To prohibit or regulate hawking and peddling;

11. To make ordinances to enforce any of these powers in the mode and under the restrictions prescribed by subdivision 20 of the preceding section.

1 R. S., 1244, §§ 58 to 60.

Form and verification of accounts to be audited. § 1086. No claim shall be paid, unless allowed by the trustees; and none shall be audited by them unless it is made out in items, and has attached to, and filed with it, the affidavit of the person claiming to have done the services or made the disbursements charged, that the several items are correct, that the services charged have been rendered, the disbursements made, and that no part has been paid.

Ib., §§ 35, 36.

Certain proceedings to be recorded. § 1087. Every allowance or disallowance of any claim, every determination to draw a warrant, and every appointment by the trustees, shall be made by a resolution and vote of the trustees, and recorded at length in their proceedings.

From § 77.

Duties of president. § 1088. It is the duty of the president of the village to preside at all meetings of the village and of the trustees; to call special meetings of the trustees whenever the interests of the village require it, or whenever he is requested to do so by two of the trustees; to see that the ordinances are executed; to cause actions to be brought for all penalties incurred by violation thereof; and to perform such other duties as are required by provisions of law or by ordinances of the village.

1 R. S., 1244, § 56.

ARTICLE III.

OTHER OFFICERS.

§ 1089. The assessors shall assess any tax directed, pursuant to section 1096, in the mode prescribed by the "*Fiscal Laws*" for making town assessments, and deliver their assessment to the trustees within sixty days after the meeting. The assessors.

Ib., § 64.

§ 1090. The collecter, within the time prescribed in any warrant for the return thereof, shall collect the same and pay over all sums collected to the treasurer, and return the warrant to the trustees, with his return thereon written and subscribed by him, and specifying any sums not collected by reason of inability to find property out of which to collect them, and if any sums are returned not The collector.

collected, his return shall be accompanied by his affidavit that the facts therein stated are true.

1 R. S., 1244, § 67.

The treasurer. § 1091. It is the duty of the treasurer:

1. To receive and pay all monies of the village;

2. To keep accounts thereof, showing when and from what sources all monies paid to him were received, and when, and to whom, and for what purpose all monies paid out were paid

3. To keep a separate account, in the same manner, of each fund raised for or appropriated to any specific purpose;

4. To make no payment except upon the delivery to him of the warrant of the trustees and accompanying papers, drawn as required by subdivision 13 of section 1084;

5. To file every such warrant and papers, when paid;

6. To exhibit his accounts and vouchers at every annual meeting of the electors, and at any special meeting, when required by any trustee. To keep them always open to the inspection of each of the trustees, and to furnish to them abstracts or statements therefrom, whenever requested.

Ib., §§ 70 to 74.

§ 1092. It is the duty of the clerk: The clerk.

1. To take custody of all the books and papers of the village, except those belonging to the treasurer's office;

2. To attend all meetings of the trustees and record all their proceedings;

3. To attend all meetings of the electors and record all their proceedings, and to keep a poll list when required by the trustees to do so;

4. To record a copy, certified by the county clerk, of the order and proceedings to incorporate the village, which, when so recorded, are presumptive evidence thereof;

5. To file every claim disallowed by the trustees;

6. Within three days after any village meeting, to furnish to the assessors a certified copy of every resolution raising a tax, and to the treasurer a certified copy of every resolution appropriating any fund, passed at such meeting;

7, To perform such other duties as are imposed on him by law, or by the ordinances of the village.

1 R. S., 1224, §§ 76 to 79.

§ 1093. It is the duty of the fire-wardens to inspect, from time to time, the apparatus for extinguishing fires, and report to the trustees The fire-wardens.

thereon; to attend fires and give directions respecting and extinguishing them, and it is the duty of all persons required to assist therein to obey; and they have power to enter, in the daytime, any premises to ascertain if ashes are safely kept therein; and they shall report to the trustees any unsafe fire-place, stove, stove-pipe, or place of keeping ashes.

1 R. S., 1244, § 81.

The street commissioners.

§ 1094. The street commissioners shall, under the direction of the trustees, superintend the making and repairing of sidewalks, and the expenditure on the streets of monies raised for that purpose; and perform the duties of overseers of highways, within the village so far as required.

Ib., § 82.

Delivery of books, papers and funds to successor.

§ 1095. Whenever the right of any treasurer or clerk to his office expires, the books and papers belonging to the office, and all monies and other property in his hands by virtue of his office, shall, upon his oath, or, in case of his death, upon the oath of his executors or administrators, be delivered to his successor. The delivery of such monies and property, as well as of the books and papers, may be enforced by proceedings under article VII of chapter VI of title I of part III of this Code, entitled "*Proceedings to compel the delivery of books and papers by public officers.*"

Ib., §§ 70, 80.

CHAPTER III.

TAXES.

§ 1096. At any meeting of the electors of the village, notified as required by section 1097, such of the electors of the village as own property liable to assessment for taxes therein may, by resolution, direct the trustees to lay a general tax on the taxable property therein, for the following purposes and no other: Power of village to tax.

1. For procuring fire engines and necessary apparatus therefor, and implements for hook and ladder companies, but not exceeding one engine to each thousand of population, and implements for one such company for each two thousand of population;

2. For hiring, purchasing or erecting the necessary engine-houses, and ground therefor, for such engines and implements;

3. For making and maintaining public wells, reservoirs and fixtures therefor, necessary for the extinguishment of fires;

4. For procuring the necessary ground and erecting and maintaining a pound;

5. For providing a cemetery, under the restrictions prescribed by chapter V of this title;

6. For improving any cemetery belonging to the village, but not exceeding one hundred and fifty dollars therefor in any one year;

7. For making and repairing crosswalks, and, in the mode provided in chapter IV, for making and repairing sidewalks;

8. For insuring the public property of the village;

9. For prosecuting and defending legal proceedings to which the village is a party;

10. For procuring the necessary blank books and blanks for village purposes;

11. For publishing the village ordinances, and notices and statements required by law to be published by the village officers;

12. For paying such compensation to its officers as is expressly authorized by law to be paid by the village;

13. For highway purposes, when the village is a separate road district and no other mode of raising money for such purposes is prescribed by law;

14. For the necessary expenses of any specific act for the village which its officers are by law expressly authorized to do;

15. For any other specific purpose for which the village is expressly authorized by law to raise a tax in such manner.

1 R. S., 1244, § 28.

§ 1097. No such tax shall be voted unless three weeks' previous notice of the meeting is given by publication once in each week in a newspaper printed in the village, or, if there is none, then by posting the same in ten of the most public places therein, specifying the amount and objects of the tax, and the specific sum to be raised for each object, and stating that the meeting will be called on to vote in respect to raising the sums so specified. At the meeting, and before the final vote, any such sum may be reduced by the meeting, but cannot be increased. Requisites of notice of meeting.

Ib., §§ 29, 30, 31.

§ 1098. Every resolution directing a tax shall distinctly specify the objects of the tax and the sum to be applied to each object. The final vote in respect to each sum shall be separately taken as a separate resolution, and, if any person entitled to vote so requires, shall be in form a separate resolution and so entered on the proceedings. Every resolution directing a tax, which is not taken as prescribed in this and the preceding section, is void. Requisites of resolution.

Ib., § 31.

§ 1099. No monies belonging to a village shall be appropriated to any object (except that monies Appropriating monies.

raised by tax may be appropriated to the specific object for which they were raised) without such a vote as required by the two preceding sections.

1 R. S., 1244. § 34.

Reference to "Fiscal Laws." § 1100. The mode of assessing and collecting village taxes is regulated by the "*Fiscal Laws.*"

Ib., §§ 33, 50 to 54.

Debts. § 1101. Except where otherwise specially provided, the village is not liable to any debt, except debts incurred for a purpose for which a tax has previously been voted, nor then for an amount beyond the amount voted.

Ib., § 43.

Liability of officers. § 1102. The officers of the village assenting to any such unauthorized indebtedness, are jointly and severally liable to pay the same in their individual capacities.

Ib., § 44.

CHAPTER IV.

SIDEWALKS.

Directions to make or repair a sidewalk. § 1103. At any meeting of the electors, the persons qualified to vote in respect to raising taxes may direct the trustees to cause any sidewalk, on any public road, to be made or repaired, by resolution specifying the sidewalk intended and the road on which it lies, and the materials to be used. But this cannot be done unless the notice of the meeting state that such resolution will be proposed.

1 R. S., 1244, § 45.

§ 1104. If the owner of the lot adjoining any such sidewalk is a resident of the village, the trustees shall give him notice to make or repair the portion in front of his lot, under the superintendence of the town or the street commissioner, in the mode required, within a specified time, not less than sixty days. Owner to make or repair sidewalk.

Ib., § 46.

§ 1105. If the owner is not a resident, or neglects to comply, the trustees shall cause the work to be done, and the expenses shall be a tax against him and a lien on the lot, to be collected by warrant in the same form and by the same mode as taxes. The warrant, in such case, shall also state the time of the adoption of the resolution directing the work to be done and the street and side thereof where the work was done. When trustees shall make or repair sidewalk.

Ib., §§ 46 to 48.

CHAPTER V.

CEMETERIES.

Purchase. § 1106. Village cemeteries shall be purchased in the name of the village, and be inalienable, except as herein provided.

1 R. S., 1244, § 103.

Restrictions on expense. § 1107. The whole expense of purchasing, fencing and preparing a cemetery shall not exceed fifteen hundred dollars, unless the population of the village exceeds four thousand; nor more than two thousand dollars in any case.

Ib.

Restrictions respecting voting the tax. § 1108. No resolution for a tax for such purpose shall be valid, unless notice of an intention to move it is given, by publishing the notice once in each week, for four successive weeks before the meeting, in a newspaper printed in the village, or if there is none, then by posting it in ten public places therein, thirty days before the meeting, nor unless an affidavit of such notice given is filed with the trustees before adoption of the resolution, nor unless the resolution provides for collecting within one year, or in equal portions within three years, a general tax sufficient to pay the whole of such expense. The time fixed for collecting the tax shall not be altered.

1 R. S., 1244, §§ 104, 105.

§ 1109. The trustees may, at such prices and on such conditions as they shall fix, convey lots in the cemetery to individuals, for the sole purpose of making interment therein. Such conveyances shall be recorded as deeds, and also recorded by the clerk of the village; but no such conveyance shall be executed until the price is paid. Lots.

Ib., § 107.

§ 1110. The trustees shall reserve a portion of the ground for the interment of strangers and other persons who may die in the village under circumstances making it unreasonable to require payment for interment. Public grounds.

Ib., § 108.

§ 1111. They shall also keep record of every interment, and the date thereof, the name, age and place of birth of the deceased, so far as they can be ascertained, and showing the spot in which each interment is made. Record of interments.

Ib., § 109.

CHAPTER VI.

FIRE COMPANIES.

Formation of companies.

§ 1112. The trustees of any village that has voted monies for fire apparatus may appoint, in writing, not exceeding thirty inhabitants, members of each hook and ladder company, and any number not exceeding fifty, members of each engine company to be formed; and in the same manner, from time to time, fill vacancies that occur in such companies.

1 R. S., 1244, § 100.

Foreman and assistant foreman

§ 1113. Each company shall annually elect, at such time as the trustees prescribe, a foreman and assistant foreman, who may be removed by the trustees for sufficient cause.

Ib., § 101.

Exemption of members from militia duty.

§ 1114. Every member of such company who, after he is eighteen years of age, serves faithfully, and conforms to all regulations for ten years, shall thereafter be exempt from militia duty, except in case of war, insurrection or invasion; but the time when a company is unprovided with proper implements shall not be estimated as a part of such ten years. The certificate of the president of the village specifying the time of the service and the company, is presumptive evidence thereof.

1 R. S., 1244, § 102.

CHAPTER VII.

POUNDS.

§ 1115. It is the duty of the pound-master, and the right of any person, to distrain and impound any animals going at large in violation of an ordinance of the village. Impounding.

Ib., § 83.

§ 1116. Within twenty-four hours after any animals come into his custody, the pound-master shall give notice thereof to the president, or, in his absence, to one of the trustees, and also to the owner (if he is a resident of the village) within twenty-four hours after he is known. Notice to officers and owner.

Ib., § 84.

§ 1117. If not reclaimed within twenty-four hours after coming into his custody, he shall give Notice of sale.

at least six days' previous notice of their sale, by posting the same in six of the most public places of the village.

1 R. S., 1244, § 85.

Notice when to be published.

§ 1118. If the value of the animal exceeds ten dollars, the notice shall be published once in each week, for two successive weeks, in a newspaper printed in the village, or if there is none, then in the newspaper printed nearest thereto; if it exceeds twenty-five dollars, the notice shall be published in the same way for four successive weeks. In either case, if the residence of the owner is known and is within fifteen miles of the village, such notice shall be served on him personally, or by leaving it at his residence, at least ten days before the sale; but if his residence is more than fifteen miles from the village, it shall be put in the post-office, directed to him at his residence, within two days after its first publication.

Ib., § 86.

Trustee to attend sale.

§ 1119. One of the trustees shall attend and direct the manner of every such sale, and may in his discretion postpone it, of which notice shall be given as in cases of postponement of the sale of personal property by the sheriff.

Ib., § 87.

Reclaiming.

§ 1120. At any time before the sale, the owner is entitled to the strays on paying the pound-master his fees, as audited, on paying to the treasurer the penalty incurred by the going at large of the animals, and on satisfying the trustees of his ownership. The trustees may remit such penalty before or after sale, if they are satisfied by affidavit, to be filed with the clerk, that such going at large was without fault of the owner or his agents.

1 R. S., 1244, § 88.

§ 1121. Out of the proceeds of such sale the pound-master may receive his fees, when audited, and shall, within forty-eight hours after the sale, pay the balance to the treasurer. Proceeds of sale.

Ib., § 89.

§ 1122. If the owner, within a year from the payment to the treasurer of the balance, presents his claim against the village therefor, as required by section 1086, accompanied by affidavit that the claim is well founded, and showing the grounds thereof, the trustees may audit the same. Any such monies, not claimed within two years, may be appropriated by vote of the electors to any purpose specified in section 1096. Disposal of balance.

Ib., §§ 90, 91.

§ 1123. The pound-master is entitled to the following fees, and no other compensation whatever: For impounding and discharging animals, the same as those allowed to pound-masters in towns; for personal service of notice to owners, the same as allowed to constables for serving summons issued Fees.

by a justice (but no travel fee shall be allowed where the owner resides in the village), and reasonable compensation for feeding. The printer's fees are at the same rate as allowed for legal advertisements. All such fees and compensation shall be audited by the trustees before they are received by the pound-master.

1 R. S., 1244, §§ 92, 93.

GENERAL PROVISIONS.

Construction of the Code.

§ 1124. The rule that statutes in derogation of the common law are to be strictly construed has no application to this Code.

Repeal of former statutes.

§ 1125. All statutes, laws, and rules heretofore in force in this state, inconsistent with the provisions of this Code are hereby repealed and abrogated; but such repeal or abrogation does not revive any former law heretofore repealed, nor does it affect any right already existing or accrued, or any proceeding already taken, except as in this Code provided, nor does it affect any private or local statute.

Time when Code takes effect.

§ 1126. This Code shall take effect on the day of , 186 .

REPEALING ACT.[1]

AN ACT

To repeal certain statutes and parts of statutes, revised and consolidated in the Political Code.

The People of the State of New York, represented in Senate and Assembly, do enact as follows:

The following statutes and parts of statutes are hereby repealed, but such repeal does not revive any former law heretofore repealed, nor does it affect any right existing or accrued, or any proceeding already taken, except as in the Political Code provided.

Title I, of chapter I, of part I, of the Revised Statutes, entitled "Of the boundaries of the state."

Political Code, 57, § 20.

Title II, of chapter I, of part I, of the Revised Statutes, entitled "Of the sovereignty and jurisdiction of the state."

Political Code, § 20, first clause, § 223, § 83, subd. 2, § 259.

Title II, of chapter II, of part I, of the Revised Statutes, entitled "Of the senate districts."

Constitution of 1846.

[1] In the foregoing report, statutes passed since the enactment of the Revised Statutes, are for the convenience of reference cited from the fourth edition of the Revised Statutes (1852), so far as that edition contains them. The references in the repealing act are to the original Revised Statutes, and to all subsequent statutes by their titles and dates of enactment. To the title of each statute, or part of a statute. to be repealed, is appended a reference to the provisions of the Political Code, which embody or may supersede it.

Title III, of chapter II, of part I, of the Revised Statutes, entitled "Of the congress districts."

Political Code, § 25.

Title VI, of chapter II, of part I, of the Revised Statutes, entitled "General provisions concerning the erection and alteration of counties, cities, villages and towns."

Political Code, § 47.

Title I, of chapter V, of part I, of the Revised Statutes, entitled "Of the number, location and classification of the public officers of this state."

Political Code, title I, of part III.

Title II, of chapter V, of part I, of the Revised Statutes, entitled "Of legislative officers."

Constitution of 1846; Political Code, title I, of part III.

Title III, of chapter V, of part I, of the Revised Statutes, entitled "Of executive officers."

Constitution of 1846.

Title IV, of chapter V, of part I, of the Revised Statutes, entitled "Of judicial officers."

Political Code, chapter IV, of part III.

Title V, of chapter V, of part I, of the Revised Statutes, entitled "Of administrative officers," excepting sections 6, 7 and 8.[1]

Political Code, articles I and II, of chapter III, of part III.

Title VI, of chapter V, of part I, of the Revised Statutes, entitled "General provisions applicable to all the civil officers of this state, or to certain classes of them."

Political Code, chapter IV, of part III.

Chapter VII, of part I, of the Revised Statutes, entitled "Of the legislature."

Constitution of 1846; Political Code, chapter II, of title I, of part III.

Title I, of chapter VIII, of part I, of the Revised Statutes, entitled "Of the governor, lieutenant-governor, or other person admin-

[1] The sections excepted relate to appointment of subordinate officers of the canal department, and will be embodied in the FISCAL LAWS.

istering the government of the state;" and the act amending the same, passed April 1, 1858, except section 24 [1] of said act. (*Laws of* 1858, 129, *ch.* 64.)

Political Code, §§ 83–89.

Title II, of chapter VIII, of part I, of the Revised Statutes, entitled "Of the secretary of state," excepting section 4.[2]

Constitution of 1846; Political Code, §§ 90–100.

Title III, of chapter VIII, of part I, of the Revised Statutes, entitled "Of the comptroller," excepting sections 11 and 12, and article III, of that title.[3]

Political Code, §§ 110–116.

Title IV, of chapter VIII, of part I, of the Revised Statutes, entitled "Of the treasurer."

Political Code, §§ 117–126.

Title VI, of chapter VIII, of part I, of the Revised Statutes, entitled "Of the surveyor-general."

Political Code, §§ 127–131, 101.

Title VIII, of chapter VIII, of part I, of the Revised Statutes, entitled "Provisions relating to two or more of the executive officers," except sections 13,[4] 16 and 17.[5]

Political Code, §§ 143–146, 103–106, 140, 141, 139.

Article VII, of title IX, of chapter IX, of part I, of the Revised Statutes, entitled "Regulations and penalties concerning the navigation of the canals, and the collection of tolls," and an act amending the same, passed April 7, 1830. (*Laws of* 1830, 122, *ch.* 117.)

Political Code, §§ 560–607.

[1] The excepted section is a special provision relating to the compensation of subordinate officers, and will be embodied in the FISCAL LAWS.

[2] Section 4 is provided for by the CODE OF CIVIL PROCEDURE, as reported complete, § 1741.

[3] These will be embodied in the FISCAL LAWS.

[4] Section 13 will be embodied in the FISCAL LAWS.

[5] Sections 16 and 17, relate to public seals, and to certified copies of documents as evidence, and are embraced in the CODE OF CIVIL PROCEDURE, as reported complete §§ 1750, 1741.

Title XI, of chapter IX, of part I, of the Revised Statutes, entitled "Of the interest of the state in mines."

Political Code, §§ 249–258.

Chapter XI, of part I, of the Revised Statutes, entitled "Of the powers, duties and privileges of towns," except section 18,[1] of title 11; sections 6, 8,[1] and 36,[2] of title III; sections 30, 31, 38, 39, 40, 41, 42 and 45,[3] of title IV; sections 1, 2, 4, 5 and 8, of title V;[4] and section 4, of title VI;[2] and sections 2 to 20 inclusive, of title VII.[5]

Political Code, §§ 960–1058, 13, 1033–1035, 840.

Chapter XII, of part I, of the Revised Statutes, entitled "Of the powers, duties and privileges of counties and of certain county officers;" except[6] article IV, of title II; sections 71, 72, 73, 74, 75, of article V, of title II; article VII, of title II; title III; and sections 6, 7 and 8, of title IV.

Political Code, §§ 876–946.

Chapter XVI, of part I, of the Revised Statutes, entitled "Of highways, bridges and ferries;" except such provisions of said chapter as apply to private roads, and in so far as they do so apply they are not repealed.[7]

Political Code, §§ 396–504, 665–675, 859, 860.

Title I, of chapter XVII, of part I, of the Revised Statutes, entitled "Of sales by auctioneers."

Political Code, §§ 714–750.

Title IV, of chapter XVII, of part I, of the Revised Statutes, entitled "Of hawkers and pedlers," and the act amending the same, passed March 23, 1840. (*Laws of* 1840, 47, *ch.* 70.)

Political Code, §§ 751–758.

[1] This will be embraced in the ELECTION LAWS.

[2] This will be embraced in the FISCAL LAWS.

[3] These provisions will be embodied in the CIVIL CODE.

[4] These are covered by the provisions of the CIVIL CODE OF PROCEDURE, as reported complete.

[5] These are local provisions, not necessary to repeal.

[6] The provisions excepted are in part local, and in part within the provisions of the CODE OF CIVIL PROCEDURE, as reported complete.

[7] Proceedings for laying out private roads are contained in the CODE OF CIVIL PROCEDURE, as reported complete, p. 630.

Chapter XIX, of part I, of the Revised Statutes, entitled "Of the computation of time, of weights and measures and the money of account," and an act amending the same, passed April 15, 1857. (2 *Laws of* 1857, 190, *ch.* 560.)

Political Code, §§ 676–713, 65, 70, 81.

Sections 6 and 7, of title VIII, of chapter XX, of part I, of the Revised Statutes, entitled "Of the prevention and punishment of immorality and disorderly practices."

Political Code, § 785.

Article V, of title VIII, of chapter XX, of part I, of the Revised Statutes, entitled "Of the racing of animals," and article VIII, of that title, entitled "Of the observance of Sunday."

Political Code, §§ 775–781; Ib., §§ 849–858, 803.

Title X, of chapter XX, of part I, of the Revised Statutes, entitled "Of the navigation of rivers and lakes, and the obstruction of certain waters."

Political Code, §§ 262–288.

Title XI, of chapter XX, of part I, of the Revised Statutes, entitled "Of fisheries generally, and particularly in the Hudson river and at and below the city of New York."

Political Code, §§ 771, 265, 266.

Title XII, of chapter XX, of part I, of the Revised Statutes, entitled "Of wrecks."

Political Code, §§ 301–819.

Title XIII, of chapter XX, of part I, of the Revised Statutes, entitled "Of the law of the road, and the regulation of public stages."

Political Code, §§ 665–672.

Title XV, of chapter XX, of part I, of the Revised Statutes, entitled "Of the embezzlement of timber floating."

Political Code, §§ 289–300.

Section 23, of title VI, of chapter I, of part IV, of the Revised Statutes, entitled "Of offenses punishable by imprisonment in a county jail and by fine."

Political Code, § 759.

ALSO

An act relative to applications to the legislature for grants of escheated lands, passed April 25, 1829. (*Laws of* 1828–9, 394, *ch.* 259.)

Political Code, § 147.

An act requiring the publication of notices in certain cases, passed April 27, 1827. (*Laws of* 1828–9, 404, *ch.* 275.)

Political Code, § 147.

An act concerning the election of justices of the peace, passed May 4, 1829. (*Laws of* 1828–9, 545, *ch.* 356.) And an act to amend the same, passed May 4th, 1829, passed April 20, 1830. (*Laws of* 1830, 349, *ch.* 290.)

Political Code, §§ 989, 199, 990, 960, 1017.

Section 3[1] of An act in relation to certain proceedings in criminal cases, in the city of New York, and concerning certain courts therein, passed February 20, 1830. (*Laws of* 1830, 29, *ch.* 42.)

Political Code, § 176, p. 187, §§ 184, 208, 210.

An act regulating highways and bridges in the counties of Suffolk, Queens and Kings, passed February 23, 1830. (*Laws of* 1830, 42, *ch.* 56.) And the act to amend the same, passed March 26, 1857 (1 *Laws of* 1857, 417, *ch.* 181), excepting such provisions of said acts as apply to private roads; and in so far as such provisions do so apply they are not repealed.[2]

Political Code, §§ 396–522.

Sections 2 and 3 of an act requiring the register of the city and county of New York to appoint a deputy, and concerning vacancies in said office and in the offices of sheriffs and clerks of counties, passed February 26, 1830. (*Laws of* 1830, 64, *ch.* 58.)

Political Code, § 237.

Sections 1, 2 and 3, of "An act to amend certain provisions of the Revised Statutes, and in addition thereto," passed April 20, 1830. (*Laws of* 1830, 384, *ch.* 320).

Political Code, 960–1058.

[1] The subject of the remainder of this statute is covered by the CODES OF CIVIL and of CRIMINAL PROCEDURE, as reported complete.

[2] Proceedings for laying out private roads are provided by the CODE OF CIVIL PROCEDURE, as reported complete, p. 630.

Section 22 of an act relative to the finances of this state, and the duties of the comptroller and the commissioners of the canal fund, passed April 26, 1831. (*Laws of* 1831, 423, *ch.* 320.)

Political Code, §§ 123, 938.

An act to amend article second, title first, of the sixteenth chapter, part first, of the Revised Statutes, entitled "Of the persons liable to work on highways, and the making assessments therefor," passed April 10, 1832. (*Laws of* 1832, 170, *ch.* 107.)

Political Code, §§ 423–429.

Sections 1 and 2 of an act relative to the oath of justices of the peace, passed April 11, 1832. (*Laws of* 1832, 171, *ch.* 109.)

Political Code, §§ 212, 214, 992, subd. 5.

An act to authorize the formation of fire companies, passed April 23, 1832. (*Laws of* 1832, 401, *ch.* 222.) And an act amending the same, passed May 13, 1845. (*Laws of* 1845, 264, *ch.* 244.)

Political Code, §§ 760–762.

An act for the more effectual improvement of roads and bridges, passed April 25, 1832. (*Laws of* 1832, 480, *ch.* 274.)

Political Code, §§ 406–409.

An act to authorize commissioners of highways to administer oaths in certain cases, passed April 12, 1833. (*Laws of* 1833, 169, *ch.* 149.)

Political Code, § 867.

An act relative to the election and classification of justices of the peace, passed April 29, 1833. (*Laws of* 1833, 392, *ch.* 270.)

Political Code, §§ 990, 994.

An act to amend the fourth article, of the first part of the Revised Statutes, entitled "Of the laying out of public and private roads, and of the alteration or discontinuance thereof," passed May 3, 1834 (*Laws of* 1834, 470, *ch.* 267); except that in so far as it applies to private roads it is not repealed.

Political Code, § 462.

An act to amend part first, title first, of chapter seventeenth of the Revised Statutes, entitled "Of the regulation of trade in certain cases," passed April 11, 1835. (*Laws of* 1835, 52, *ch.* 62.)

Political Code, §§ 714–750.

An act in relation to the assessment of highway labor, passed April 24, 1835. (*Laws of* 1835, 163, *ch.* 154.)

Political Code, §§ 421–429.

An act to enlarge the powers of commissioners of highways, passed May 11, 1835. (*Laws of* 1835, 340, *ch.* 300.)

Political Code, § 529.

An act to amend article fourth, of title first, of chapter sixteenth, of part first, of the Revised Statutes, entitled "Of the laying out of public and private roads, and of the alteration or discontinuance thereof," passed April 11, 1836. (*Laws of* 1836, 163, *ch.* 122.)

Political Code, § 457.

An act to protect sidewalks along highways, passed May 10, 1836. (*Laws of* 1836, 397, *ch.* 281.) And the act amending the same, passed April 15, 1854. (*Laws of* 1854, 682, *ch.* 324.)

Political Code, §§ 400, 401, 412.

An act authorizing the construction of railroads upon Indian lands, passed May 12, 1836. (*Laws of* 1836, 113, *ch.* 316.)

Political Code, § 530.

An act for the preservation of legislative petitions and papers, passed April 3, 1837, except so much thereof as declares certified copies to be evidence.[1] (*Laws of* 1837, 113, *ch.* 140.)

Political Code, § 43.

An act concerning vessels navigating the Niagara river, Lake Ontario, and the River St. Lawrence, passed April 4, 1837. (*Laws of* 1837, 141, *ch.* 153.)

Political Code, §§ 274–279.

An act relative to unclaimed trunks and baggage, passed May 2, 1837. (*Laws of* 1837, 311, *ch.* 300.)

Political Code, §§ 821–829.

An act for the appointment of a harbor master for the port of Albany, passed May 8, 1837. (*Laws of* 1837, 388, *ch.* 356.)

Political Code, §§ 63, 71, 72, 389–395.

[1] The subject of the provision excepted is covered by provisions of the CODE OF PROCEDURE, as reported complete, §§ 1741, 1742.

An act to subject monied or stock corporations to assessment for highway labor, passed May 15, 1837. (*Laws of* 1837, 488, *ch.* 431.)

Political Code, §§ 432, 443, 448, 449, 424.

An act authorizing any citizen of the State of New York to become an auctioneer, passed February 28, 1838. (*Laws of* 1838, 27, *ch.* 52.)

Political Code, §§ 718–750.

An act respecting the oath of town officers, passed April 6, 1838. (*Laws of* 1833, *ch.* 172.)

Political Code, §§ 1000, 1009.

An act in relation to turnpike roads and toll bridges, passed April 18, 1838. (*Laws of* 1838, 254, *ch.* 262.)

Political Code, §§ 397, 674.

An act to enlarge the powers of boards of supervisors, passed April 18, 1838. (*Laws of* 1838, 314, *ch.* 314.) And an act to amend the same, passed April 3, 1848. (*Laws of* 1848, 278, *ch.* 164.)

Political Code, §§ 879–882.

An act in relation to highway labor in the county of Livingston, passed April 18, 1838. (*Laws of* 1838, 323, *ch.* 327.)

Political Code, p. 280.

An act providing for the settlement of the accounts of the treasurer of this state, passed February 14, 1839. (*Laws of* 1839, 17, *ch.* 23.)

Political Code, § 126.

An act directing the secretary of state to furnish literary colleges with copies of the Laws of the State of New York and of the documents of the senate and assembly, passed April 29, 1839, (*Laws of* 1839, 249, *ch.* 263.)

Political Code, § 93.

Section 1 of an act relative to boards of supervisors and to the town of Vernon, in the county of Oneida, passed May 7, 1839. (*Laws of* 1839, 336, *ch.* 369.)

Political Code, § 906.

Section 15 of an act to preserve the purity of elections, passed May 7, 1839. (*Laws of* 1839, 363, *ch.* 389.)

Political Code, § 963.

An act imposing certain duties on the surveyor-general, passed May 11, 1840. (*Laws of* 1840, 205, *ch.* 259.) And the act to amend the same, passed April 11, 1842. (*Laws of* 1842, 272, *ch.* 220.)

Political Code, §§ 127, 675.

An act to amend the Revised Statutes in relation to highways, passed 14 May, 1840. (*Laws of* 1840, 546, *ch.* 309.)

Political Code, § 505, &c.

An act more effectually to protect the free citizens of this state from being kidnapped or reduced to slavery, passed May 14, 1840. (*Laws of* 1840, 319, *ch.* 375.)

Political Code, §§ 85, 86.

Sections 1, 2 and 3 of an act in relation to the accounts of town officers, passed May 14, 1840. (*Laws of* 1840, 251, *ch.* 305.)[1] And the act amending the same, passed April 29, 1844. (*Laws of* 1844, 354, *ch.* 228.)

Political Code, §§ 1028–1030, 902.

An act to regulate the floating of rafts on the Hudson river, passed March 29, 1841. (*Laws of* 1841, 39, *ch.* 65.)

Political Code, § 278.

An act relating to the examination of the treasurer's accounts and the canal and banking departments, except section 1 thereof,[2] passed May 25, 1841. (*Laws of* 1841, 201, *ch.* 218.)

Political Code, §§ 124, 125.

An act relating to the joint liability of commissioners of highways, passed May 25, 1841. (*Laws of* 1841, 207, *ch.* 225.) And an act amending the same, passed April 13, 1857. (1 *Laws of* 1857, 788, *ch.* 383.)

Political Code, §§ 492–503.

[1] The remaining section will be embodied in the FISCAL LAWS.

[2] Section 1 relates to the rooms occupied by and clerks employed by the canal department.

An act to furnish certain literary and scientific institutions with copies of the laws and of the journals and documents of the senate and assembly of this state, passed May 26, 1841. (*Laws of* 1841, 289, *ch.* 300.)

Political Code, § 93.

An act in relation to the publication of the statutes of this state, passed April 12, 1842. (*Laws of* 1842, 397, *ch.* 306.)

Political Code, §§ 51, 52.

An act to regulate purchases for the state, and the taking of vouchers, passed April 12, 1842. (*Laws of* 1842, 400, *ch.* 310.)

Political Code, §§ 107, 40, 41.

Sections 1 and 2 of an act entitled "An act to divide the state into congressional districts," passed September 6th, 1842. (*Laws of* 1842, 410, *ch.* 325.)

Political Code, § 25.

An act to prohibit members of common councils of cities, trustees of villages, and supervisors of towns, to be interested in certain contracts, passed March 20, 1843. (*Laws of* 1843, 36, *ch.* 57.)

Political Code, §§ 867–870.

Section 1 of an act relative to the publication of the Laws, passed April 12, 1843. (*Laws of* 1843, *ch.* 98.)

Political Code, § 51.

An act to furnish copies of the statutes of this state to the several towns, passed April 22, 1844. (*Laws of* 1844, 270, *ch.* 176.)

Political Code, § 93.

An act to regulate the speed of steamboats navigating the Hudson river, passed May 2, 1844. (*Laws of* 1844, 381, *ch.* 248.)

Political Code, §§ 284–288.

Sections 2, 3, 4, 13, 22, 23, 27, and 28, of an act to reduce the number of town officers, and town and county expenses, and to prevent abuses in auditing town and county accounts, except so much thereof as relates to private roads; passed May 10, 1845. (*Laws of* 1845, 183, *ch.* 180.) And sections 1, 8, 9, 13, 14, 15, 22,

23 and 24 of an act to amend the same, passed December 14, 1847. (2 *Laws of* 1847, 580, *ch.* 455.)

Political Code, §§ 964, 1019, 867, 980, 997, 909, 898-901, 995, 476, &c.; 899, 905, 491, 466, 469, 1032, 905.

An act in relation to the contracts of railroad companies, passed May 13, 1845. (*Laws of* 1845, 251, *ch.* 230.)

See Political Code, § 253.

An action in relation to the members of fire companies and hook and ladder companies, passed May 13, 1845. (*Laws of* 1845, 264, *ch.* 244.)

Political Code, §§ 760–762.

An act for the publication of the Session Laws in two newspapers in each county of this state, passed May 14, 1845. *Laws of* 1845, 305, *ch.* 280.) And the act amending the same, passed April 17, 1858. (*Laws of* 1858, 557, *ch.* 331.)

Political Code, §§ 55–57.

An act to provide for the public printing, passed March 5, 1846, (*Laws of* 1846, 20, *ch.* 24.)

Political Code, §§ 147–155.

An act in relation to duties on goods sold at public auction, and to the bonds of auctioneers, passed April 11, 1846. (*Laws of* 1846, 65, *ch.* 62.)

Political Code, §§ 714–750.

An act concerning the pilots of the channel of the East river, commonly called Hellgate, passed April 15, 1847. (1 *Laws of* 1847, 75, *ch.* 69.)

Political Code, §§ 335–347.

Section 8 of an act authorizing the formation of rural cemetery associations, passed April 27, 1847. (1 *Laws of* 1847, 125, *ch.* 133.)

Political Code, §§ 842, 859.

An act in relation to firemen in incorporated villages, passed April 28, 1847. (1 *Laws of* 1847, 146, *ch.* 151.)

Political Code, §§ 1096, 1112–1114.

An act providing for the registry of births, marriages and deaths, passed April 28, 1847. (*Laws of* 1847, 147, *ch.* 152.) And the act to amend the same, passed April 2, 1853. (*Laws of* 1853, 107, *ch.* 75.)

Political Code, §§ 830–839.

An act authorizing the erection of town houses, passed May 5, 1847. (1 *Laws of* 1847, 190, *ch.* 197.)

Political Code, §§ 964, 965, 966.

An act in relation to cemeteries in incorporated villages, passed May 7, 1847. (1 *Laws of* 1847, 214, *ch.* 209.)

Political Code, §§ 1096, 1106–1111.

Sections 4, 5, 6, 7, 8, 9, 11, 31, 32, 33, 34, 35, 36 and 37 of an act to provide for the incorporation of companies to construct plankroads, and of companies to construct turnpike roads, passed May 7, 1847. (*Laws of* 1847, 216, *ch.* 210.)[1] And an act to amend the same, passed April 12, 1848. (*Laws of* 1848, 480, *ch.* 360.) And an act further to amend the same, passed July 10, 1851. (*Laws of* 1851, 919, *ch.* 487.) And an act to further amend the same, passed July 21, 1853. (*Laws of* 1853, 1206, *ch.* 626.) And an act further to amend the same, passed April 14, 1858. (*Laws of* 1858, 314, *ch.* 193.)

Political Code, §§ 609–647, 65, 80, 437, 438.

An act in relation to railroad corporations, passed May 7, 1847. (1 *Laws of* 1847, 240, *ch.* 222.)

Political Code, § 547.

An act to divide the state into judicial districts, passed May 8, 1847. (1 *Laws of* 1847, 268, *ch.* 241.)

Political Code, § 23.

An act to separate the offices of county judge and surrogate in the county of St. Lawrence, passed May 10, 1847. (1 *Laws of* 1847, 270, *ch.* 244.)

Political Code, § 156.

The excepted sections, relate, will be embodied in the Civil Code, and the Code of Civil Procedure.

An act concerning the enactment and promulgation of the statutes, passed May 12, 1847. (1 *Laws of* 1847, 276, *ch.* 253.)

Political Code, §§ 51, 52, 93.

An act concerning the laws, journals and documents of the legislature, passed May 12, 1847. (1 *Laws of* 1847, 276, *ch.* 254.)

Political Code, §§ 147–152.

Sections 1, 2, 3, 8, 9, 10, 11, 12, 13 and 14 of an act to provide for the election of certain judicial and other officers, and to fix their term of office, passed May 12, 1847. (1 *Laws of* 1847, 306, *ch.* 276.) And sections 1 and 2 of the act amending the same, passed April 15, 1851 (*Laws of* 1851, 331, *ch.* 175), excepting so much of those acts as relate to the powers and duties of the officers mentioned.[1]

Political Code, article II of chapter IV of part III, p. 180, §§ 164, 165, 170.

Sections 4 and 5 of an act to provide for the payment of certain expenses of government, to fix the salaries of certain judicial and other officers, and for other purposes, passed May 12, 1847. (1 *Laws of* 1847, 309, *ch.* 277.)

Political Code, §§ 939–941.

An act in relation to the insurance of public buildings, passed September 8, 1847. (2 *Laws of* 1847, 415, *ch.* 294.)

Political Code, § 866.

An act in relation to proceedings against persons observing as the Sabbath day the day commonly called Saturday, passed November 10, 1847, 451, *ch.* 349.)

Political Code, §§ 852–858.

An act to provide for filling vacancies in the office of canal commissioners, passed Nov. 13, 1847, excepting section 3 thereof.[2] (*Laws of* 1847, 458, *ch.* 360.)

Political Code, § 239.

[1] The provisions here excepted relate to these officers' powers to take acknowledgments, &c., which will be embodied in their proper place in the CIVIL CODE.

[2] The 3d section will be embodied in the ELECTION LAWS.

An act in relation to plankroad and turnpike road companies, passed November 24, 1847. (2 *Laws of* 1847, 496, *ch.* 398.)

Political Code, §§ 609–617.

An act to provide for the incorporation of villages, excepting sections 33, 50, 51, 52, 53 and 54;[1] and passed December 7, 1847. (2 *Laws of* 1847, 532, *ch.* 426.) And the act to amend the same, passed April 6, 1850. (*Laws of* 1850, 338, *ch.* 176.) And sections 1, 2, 3, 4, 6 and 7 of an act further to amend the same, passed July 11, 1851. (*Laws of* 1851, 964, *ch.* 519.) And an act further to amend the same, passed April 1, 1854. (1 *Laws of* 1854, 279, *ch.* 120.)

Political Code, §§ 1059–1123.

An act in relation to the publication and distribution of the Session Laws of this state, passed December 14, 1847. (2 *Laws of* 1847, 592, *ch.* 458.)

Political Code, §§ 53–58.

Sections 2 and 3 of "An act to provide for the election of recorder and surrogate for the city and county of New York," passed December 15, 1847, and so much of the other sections of said act as fixes the term of office of the recorder at three years. (2 *Laws of* 1847, 727, *ch.* 488.)

Political Code, §§ 170, 243.

An act to provide for the filling of vacancies in the office of sheriff, passed January 22, 1848. (*Laws of* 1848, 6, *ch.* 4.)

Political Code, § 237.

Section 19 of an act to authorize the formation of gas light companies, passed February 16, 1848. (*Laws of* 1848, 48, *ch.* 37.)

Political Code, §§ 859, 860.

An act to provide for the appointment of commissioners of deeds in the cities of this state, passed March 7, 1848. (*Laws of* 1848, 84, *ch.* 75.) And the act amending the same, passed March 31, 1848. (*Ib.*, 267, *ch.* 158.)

Political Code, § 176, p. 188.

[1] The provisions excepted will be embodied in the FISCAL LAWS.

An act to provide for the election of county treasurers, and fix their term of office, passed March 27, 1848. (*Laws of* 1848, 214, *ch.* 136.) And the act amending the same, passed April 11, 1849. (*Laws of* 1849, 519, *ch.* 360.)

Political Code, §§ 67, 243, note.

An act in relation to the appointment of commissioners of deeds in and for the cities of this state, except the city of New York, passed March 31, 1848. (*Laws of* 1848, 271, *ch.* 161.)

Political Code, § 176, p. 188.

So much of an act relating to the salary and term of office of the county treasurer of the county of Kings, passed April 5, 1848, as prescribes the time when the clerk enters on office. (*Laws of* 1848, 292, *ch.* 180.)

Political Code, § 67.

Sections 6, 7, 8, 9, 10, 11 and 20[1] of an act to provide for the incorporation of bridge companies, passed April 11, 1848. (*Laws of* 1848, 375, *ch.* 259.) And an act amending the same, passed April 16, 1852. (*Laws of* 1852, 590, *ch.* 372.)

Political Code, §§ 648–656.

An act in relation to the navigation of the East river by steamboats, passed April 12, 1848. (*Laws of* 1848, 450, *ch.* 321.)

Political Code, § 284.

An act for the appointment of wreck masters in Suffolk, Queens, Kings, Richmond and Westchester counties, passed April 12, 1848. (*Laws of* 1848, 464, *ch.* 343.)

Political Code, §§ 65, 76, 77, 301–319.

An act relating to highways in the town of Eastchester and White Plains, passed January 24, 1849. (*Laws of* 1849, 12, *ch.* 11.)

Political Code, p. 280.

An act to provide for filling vacancies in office, passed February 3, 1849; and the act amending the same, passed February 17, 1849. (*Laws of* 1849, 26, *ch.* 28; 36, *ch.* 46.)

Political Code, § 238.

[1] The omitted sections will be embodied in the Civil Code and the Fiscal Laws.

Sections 9 and 10 of an act in relation to the marine court of the city of New York, passed March 27, 1849. (*Laws of* 1849, 199, *ch.* 144.)

Political Code, §§ 173–183.

An act to vest in the board of supervisors certain legislative powers, and to prescribe their fees for certain services, except sections 8 and 9[1] thereof, passed April 3, 1849. (*Laws of* 1849, 293, *ch.* 194.)

Political Code, §§ 879–908.

Sections 2, 3, 4, 6, 7, 9, 10, 11 and 12 of an act in relation to plankroads and turnpike roads, passed April 6, 1849. (*Laws of* 1849, 374, *ch.* 250.)[2]

Political Code, §§ 636, 638, 629, 630, 614, 634, 405, 441.

Sections 1 and 3 of an act to authorize the election of local officers to discharge the duties of county judge and surrogate in the counties of Orange, Chautauqua, Cayuga, St. Lawrence, Tioga, Oneida, Jefferson and Oswego, passed April 10, 1849. (*Laws of* 1849, 437, *ch.* 306.)

Political Code, ch. IV of part III.

An act to prevent fraud in the returns made to the comptroller of sales at auction, passed April 11, 1849. (*Laws of* 1849, 551, *ch.* 399.)

Political Code, §§ 746, 747.

An act requiring steamboats or vessels propelled or driven by steam to carry small boats for the protection of life in case of accident, passed April 11, 1849. (*Laws of* 1849, 568, *ch.* 411.)

Political Code, §§ 280–288.

An act relating to the harbor masters of the port of New York, passed March 16, 1850. (*Laws of* 1850, 81, *ch.* 72.)

Political Code, §§ 63, 71, 72, 265–371.

Sections 22, 23, 24, 25, 26, 27, 28, 30, 31, 32, 33, 34, 35, 36, 37, 38, 41, 42, 44, 45 and 46 of an act to authorize the formation of

[1] These will be embraced in the FISCAL LAWS.

[2] The omitted sections will be embodied in the CIVIL CODE.

railroad corporations, and to regulate the same, passed April 2, 1850. (*Laws of* 1850, 211, *ch.* 140.)[1]

Political Code, §§ 523–559, 859, 860.

An act to extend the time for county treasurers to take the oath of office and file their official bond, passed April 10, 1850. (*Laws of* 1850, 750, *ch.* 346.)

Political Code, § 913.

Sections 1 and 2 of an act in relation to railroad corporations, passed February 13, 1851. (*Laws of* 1851, 20, *ch.* 19.)

Political Code, §§ 541, 542.

An act in relation to plankroads and turnpike roads, passed April 9, 1851. (*Laws of* 1851, 191, *ch.* 107.)

Political Code, §§ 636, 630.

An act in relation to weights and measures, passed April 11, 1851. (*Laws of* 1851, 251, *ch.* 134.) And the act to amend the same, passed April 15, 1854. (*Laws of* 1854, 685, *ch.* 326.)

Political Code, §§ 70, 81.

Section 1 of an act to provide for the election of recorders in cities, passed June 18, 1851.[2] (*Laws of* 1851, 433, *ch.* 217.)

Political Code, § 170.

An act dividing the state into congressional districts, passed July 10, 1851. (*Laws of* 1851, 937, *ch.* 499.)

Political Code, § 25.

Sections 1 and 2 of an act to provide for the election of a special county judge in the county of Chenango, passed July 11, 1851. (*Laws of* 1861, 997, *ch.* 538.) And section 1 of the act amending the same, passed March 19, 1852. (*Laws of* 1852, *ch.* 73.)

Political Code, §§ 156–165.

An act for the more effectual building and repairing of roads in the county of Erie, passed April 16, 1852. (*Laws of* 1852, 506, *ch.* 338.)

Political Code, p. 280.

[1] The remainder of this act will be embraced in the CIVIL CODE and CODE OF CIVIL PROCEDURE.

[2] The remainder of this act relates to the mode of election and will be embraced in the ELECTION LAWS.

Sections 1, 2, 3 and 4, of an act in relation to the marine court of the city of New York, passed April 17, 1852. (*Laws of* 1852, 647, *ch.* 389.)

Political Code, §§ 172, 182.

An act to regulate the construction of roads and streets across railroad tracks, passed March 29, 1853. (*Laws of* 1853, 86, *ch.* 62.)

Political Code, §§ 467, 468.

An act to amend the sixteenth chapter of the first part of the Revised Statutes, passed March 29, 1853. (*Laws of* 1853, 87, *ch.* 63.)

Political Code, § 405.

Section 15 of an act in relation to laying out private roads and discontinuing public highways, passed April 12, 1853, and section 16 of said act, so far as it relates to public highways. (*Laws of* 1853, 308, *ch.* 174.)

Political Code, §§ 474, 471.

Section 1 of an act in relation to plankroads, passed April 15, 1853. (*Laws of* 1853, 535, *ch.* 245.)[1] And an act amending the same, passed June 30, 1853. (*Id.* 945, *ch.* 481.)

Political Code, § 635.

An act providing for the appointment of an additional number of notaries public in the city and county of New York, passed June 8, 1853. (*Laws of* 1853, 718, *ch.* 340.)

Political Code, § 176, p. 187.

An act to provide for the licensing and government of the pilots, and regulating the pilotage of the port of New York, passed June 28, 1853. (*Laws of* 1853, 921, *ch.* 467.) And an act amending the same, passed April 11, 1854. (*Laws of* 1854, 459, *ch.* 196.) And an act further amending the same, passed April 3, 1857. (1 *Laws of* 1857, 500, *ch.* 243.)

Political Code, §§ 320–334.

An act to amend title VI, of chapter VII, of part I, of the Revised Statutes, passed July 18, 1853. (*Laws of* 1853, 993, *ch.*

[1] The remaining section will be embraced in the FISCAL LAWS.

530.) And the act amending the same, passed March, 8, 1854. (*Laws of* 1854, 126, *ch.* 51.)

Political Code, §§ 37, 44.

An act to restrict and regulate the power of municipal corporations to borrow money, contract debts and loan their credit, passed July 21, 1853. (*Laws of* 1853, 1135, *ch.* 603.)

Political Code, § 871, &c.

An act in relation to highways and bridges in the county of Montgomery, passed July 21, 1853. (*Laws of* 1853, 1140, *ch.* 609.)

Political Code, p. 280.

An act for the protection of birds in public cemeteries, passed July 21, 1853. (*Laws of* 1853, 1208, *ch.* 629.) And the act to amend the same, passed April 19, 1855. (*Laws of* 1855, 1071, *ch.* 564.)

Political Code, § 842.

Sections 1, 2, 3 and 5 of an act in relation to plankroads and turnpike roads, passed March 28, 1854. (*Laws of* 1854, 167, *ch.* 87.)

Political Code, §§ 633, 626, 674.

Sections 1 and 3 of an act to authorize the election of a local officer to discharge the duties of county judge and surrogate in the county of Sullivan, passed March 28, 1854. (*Laws of* 1854, 169, *ch.* 88.)

Political Code, § 156.

An act providing for the appointment of an additional number of notaries public and commissioners of deeds in the city of New York, passed March 28, 1854. (*Laws of* 1854, 219, *ch.* 92.)

Political Code, § 176, p. 187.

Section 4 of an act to amend an act entitled "An act to organize and establish a recorder's court in the city of Buffalo, and for other purposes, passed April 20, 1839," passed March 28, 1854. (*Laws of* 1854, 222, *ch.* 96.)

Political Code, §§ 169, 243, note.

Section 5 of an act for the incorporation of private and family cemeteries, passed April 1, 1854. (*Laws of* 1854, 265, *ch.* 112.)

Political Code, §§ 842, 859.

An act to promote medical science, passed April 1, 1854. (*Laws of* 1854, 281, *ch.* 123.)

Political Code, §§ 845–884.

An act relative to the construction of railroads in cities, passed April 4, 1854. (*Laws of* 1854, 323, *ch.* 140.)

Political Code, § 528.

An act to designate a state paper, passed April 11, 1854. (*Laws of* 1855, 462, *ch.* 197.)

Political Code, §§ 153–155.

An act to amend the Revised Statutes in relation to laying out of public roads, and of public roads, and of the alteration thereof in the town of Greenburgh, passed April 15, 1854. (*Laws of* 1854, 583, *ch.* 265.)

Political Code, p. 280.

Sections 7, 8, 9, 10, 11, 12 and 13 of an act to amend the act entitled "An act to authorize the formation of railroad corporations, and to regulate the same," passed April 2, 1850; passed April 15, 1854. (*Laws of* 1854, 608, *ch.* 282.)

Political Code, §§ 557, 543, 544, 821–829, 541.

An act in relation to the census or enumeration of the inhabitants of this state, passed March 12, 1855. (*Laws of* 1855, 90, *ch.* 64.) And the act amending the same, passed April 6, 1855. (*Laws of* 1855, *ch.* 181.)

Political Code, §§ 94–100.

Sections 1 and 3 of an act to authorize the election of local officers to discharge the duties of county judge and surrogate in the county of Washington, and to do chamber business, passed April 3, 1855. (*Laws of* 1855, 228, *ch.* 148.) And the act amending the same, passed April 16, 1858. (*Laws of* 1868, 439, *ch.* 280.)

Political Code, §§ 156, 165.

Section 1 of an act to authorize boards of supervisors to adopt seals, and to make certified copies of their records and proceedings evidence, passed April 10, 1855. (*Laws of* 1855, 383, *ch.* 249.)[1]

Political Code, § 882.

[1] Section 2 is embraced in the provisions on the subject of evidence in the CODE OF CIVIL PROCEDURE, as reported complete, § 1741.

An act to enlarge the powers and duties of commissioners of highways, passed April 10, 1855. (*Laws of* 1855, 388, *ch.* 255.)

Political Code, § 419.

An act requiring overseers of the poor of the several towns of this state to give bonds, passed April 10, 1855. (*Laws of* 1855, 452, *ch.* 269.)

Political Code, §§ 998, 1002.

An act to regulate the liability of hotel-keepers, passed April 13, 1855. (*Laws of* 1855, 774, *ch.* 421.)

Political Code, §§ 819, 820.

An act authorizing a change of the grade of railroads in certain cases, passed April 14, 1855. (*Laws of* 1855, 865, *ch.* 478.)

Political Code, § 536.

An act in relation to turnpikes and plankroads, and to prevent encroachments thereon, passed April 14, 1855. (*Laws of* 1855, 874, *ch.* 485.)

Political Code, §§ 640, 638, 641.

An act to allow the several towns in Oneida and Steuben counties to raise an increased amount of money for the support of roads and bridges, and to provide for the compensation of commissioners of highways, passed April 14, 1855. (*Laws of* 1855, 953, *ch.* 517.)

Political Code, § 423.

An act in regard to unclaimed express freight, passed April 14, 1855. (*Laws of* 1855, 958, *ch.* 523.)

Political Code, §§ 821–829.

An act to authorize the county judges of the several counties in this state to appoint a crier of the courts of record to be held in and for said county, passed April 14, 1855. (*Laws of* 1855, 973, *ch.* 530.)

Political Code, § 181.

Sections 1, 2 and 3, of an act for the prevention of frauds upon the canal revenues, passed April 14, 1855. (*Laws of* 1855, 977, *ch.* 534.)

Political Code, § 580.

Section 3 of an act amendatory of the laws in relation to the appraisal and payment of canal damages, and of chapter 310, of the Laws of 1842, passed April 14, 1855. (*Laws of* 1855, 978, *ch.* 535.)

Political Code, § 142, and see errata.

Sections 3, 4 and 7,[1] of an act in relation to plankroads and turnpike roads, passed April 18, 1855. (*Laws of* 1855, 1043, *ch.* 546.)

Political Code, §§ 617, 636, (and see errata,) 626.

An act to prevent prize fights and fights among game animals, passed April 4, 1856. (*Laws of* 1856, 131, *ch.* 98.)

Political Code, §§ 782–784.

An act to authorize clerks of boards of supervisors to administer oaths in certain cases, passed April 7, 1856. (*Laws of* 1856, 162, *ch.* 108.)

Political Code, § 867.

An act to prevent extortion by railroad companies, passed March 27, 1857. (*Laws of* 1857, 432, *ch.* 185.)

Political Code, § 549.

Section 1 of "An act for the apportionment of the members of assembly of this state," passed April 13, 1857. (1 *Laws of* 1857, 700, *ch.* 337.)

Political Code, § 33.

An act to organize the senate districts of the state, passed April 13, 1857. (1 *Laws of* 1857, 702, *ch.* 339.)

Political Code, § 24.

An act to regulate the use of slips and wharves of the city of New York, between piers numbers 2 and 10, East river, passed April 13, 1857. (1 *Laws of* 1857, 762, *ch.* 367.)

Political Code, §§ 361–388.

An act to reorganize the warden's office of the port of New York, passed April 14, 1857. (1 *Laws of* 1857, 817, *ch.* 405.)

Political Code, §§ 65, 71, 72, 348–357.

Sections 3 and 4 of an act, further to amend the act, entitled "An act to authorize the formation of railroad corporations, and

[1] The other sections will be embodied in the CIVIL CODE and the FISCAL LAWS.

to regulate the same, passed April 2, 1850," passed April 14, 1857. (1 *Laws of* 1857, 871, *ch.* 444.)

Political Code, §§ 821–829.

Sections 1, 2 and 5 of an act to authorize the election of a special county judge and surrogate in the county of Essex, passed April 15, 1857. (2 *Laws of* 1857, 47, *ch.* 461.)

Political Code, §§ 156, 165, 166.

An act to provide for an investigation into the origin of fires in certain cases, passed April 15, 1857. (2 *Laws of* 1857, 47, *ch.* 504.)

Political Code, §§ 766–769.

An act for the preservation of fish in the waters of Crooked lake, passed April 15, 1857. (2 *Laws of* 1857, 94, *ch.* 514.) And an act to amend the same, passed April 12, 1858. (*Laws of* 1858, 285, *ch.* 163.)

Political Code, §§ 772–774.

Section 2 of an act to legalize and confirm the official acts and proceedings of the officers of incorporated villages, passed April 15, 1857. (2 *Laws of* 1857, 178, *ch.* 552.)

Political Code, § 1082.

An act to allow the several towns in this state to raise an increased amount of money for the support of roads and bridges, and to provide for increased compensation of commissioners of highways and other town officers, passed April 15, 1857. (2 *Laws of* 1857, 338, *ch.* 615.)

Political Code, §§ 406–409, 1012, 1013.

An act to suppress intemperance and to regulate the sale of intoxicating liquors, passed April 15, 1857. (2 *Laws of* 1857, 405, *ch.* 628.) And the act to amend the same, passed April 12, 1858. (*Laws of* 1858, 260, *ch.* 143.)

Political Code, §§ 65, 79, 786–820.

An act in relation to plankroads and turnpike roads in the county of Kings, passed April 16, 1857. (2 *Laws of* 1857, 430, *ch.* 636.)

Political Code, § 630.

An act to provide for the raising of funds by tax to pay for the building or repair of bridges across streams dividing towns or counties, passed April 26, 1857. (*Laws of* 1857, 435, *ch.* 639.)

Political Code, §§ 493–503.

An act to establish regulations for the port of New York, passed April 16, 1857. (2 *Laws of* 1857, 487, *ch.* 671.) And an act amending the same, passed April 15, 1858. (*Laws of* 1858, 363, *ch.* 226.)

Political Code, §§ 372, 388.

An act for the election of an additional coroner in the county of Rensselaer, passed April 17, 1857. (2 *Laws of* 1857, 543, *ch.* 715.)

Political Code, §§ 176.

An act to provide for the preservation of fish in the waters of Oneida lake and its tributaries, passed April 17, 1857. (2 *Laws of* 1857, 567, *ch.* 732.)

Political Code, §§ 872–774.

Sections 2 and 3 of an act relative to notaries public in the city and county of New York, passed March 25, 1858. (*Laws of* 1858, 73, *ch.* 44.)

Political Code, § 176, p. 187.

An act to increase the number of notaries public in the city of Troy, passed March 29, 1858. (*Laws of* 1858, 91, *ch.* 57.)

Political Code, § 176.

An act to amend the Revised Statutes concerning the powers and duties of the governor, and to fix the compensation of officers in the executive department, except section 24,[1] passed April 1, 1858. (*Laws of* 1858, 129, *ch.* 64.)

Political Code, § 83.

An act to provide for the speedy construction and repair of roads and bridges, where the same shall have been damaged or destroyed, passed April 6, 1858. (*Laws of* 1858, 200, *ch.* 103.)

Political Code, §§ 493–503.

[1] Section 24 relates to the compensation of subordinate officers.

An act in relation to sleeping cars on railroads, passed April 7, 1858. (*Laws of* 1858, 234, *ch.* 125.)

Political Code, §§ 553, 554.

An act to legalize the sales of stocks on time, passed April 10, 1858. (*Laws of* 1848, 251, *ch.* 134.)

Political Code, p. 399, note.

An act to enlarge the powers of the boards of supervisors, passed April 14, 1858. (*Laws of* 1858, 309, *ch.* 190.)

Political Code, §§ 892–897, 867.

Sections 1 and 3 of "An act relative to the election of a special judge for the county of Tompkins," passed April 16, 1858. (*Laws of* 1858, 438, *ch.* 279.)

Political Code, §§ 156, 165.

An act to regulate the supply of stationery to members and officers of the legislature, passed January 12, 1859. (*Laws of* 1859, 7, *ch.* 1.)

Political Code, §§ 39, 40.

An act relating to the term of office of the county treasurer of the county of Monroe, passed March 4, 1859. (*Laws of* 1859, 48, *ch.* 26.)

Political Code, §§ 67, 243.

An act to prevent and punish prize fighting, passed March 7, 1859, (*Laws of* 1859, 63, *ch.* 37.)

Political Code, §§ 782–784.

Sections 1, 2 and 3 of an act to increase the number of coroners in Queens county, passed April 5, 1859. (*Laws of* 1859, 338, *ch.* 127.)

Political Code, § 176.

An act for the better improvement of highways in the town of Haverstraw, in the county of Rockland, passed April 6, 1859. (*Laws of* 1859, 370, *ch.* 147.)

Political Code, p. 280.

Sections 1, 2 and 3 of an act in relation to plankroads and turnpike roads, passed April 9, 1859. (*Laws of* 1859, 465, *ch.* 209.)

Political Code, § 616.

An act to amend the Revised Statutes in relation to laying out public roads and alterations thereof, in the towns of North Castle, Bedford, and Lewisborough, in the county of Westchester, passed April 12, 1859. (*Laws of* 1859, 576, *ch.* 268.)

Political Code, p. 280.

An act in relation to reports of state officers, passed April 18, 1859. (*Laws of* 1859, 1024, *ch.* 437.)

Political Code, §§ 138, 151, subdivision 3.

An act to supply vacancies in the office of justices of the peace in the several towns of this state, passed April 18, 1859. (*Laws of* 1859, 1092, *ch.* 476.)

Political Code, § 1017.

An act providing for the appointment of an additional number of notaries public in the city and county of New York, passed April 19, 1859. (*Laws of* 1859, 1115, *ch.* 485.)

Political Code, § 176, p. 187.

An act for the preservation of deer and other game, passed April 19, 1859. (*Laws of* 1859, 1185, *ch.* 511.)

Political Code, §§ 772–774.

www.ingramcontent.com/pod-product-compliance
Lightning Source LLC
LaVergne TN
LVHW102006210926
848483LV00009B/103